KYOTO AREA STUDIES ON ASIA
CENTER FOR SOUTHEAST ASIAN STUDIES, KYOTO UNIVERSITY
VOLUME 19

Re-thinking Economic Development

KYOTO AREA STUDIES ON ASIA

CENTER FOR SOUTHEAST ASIAN STUDIES, KYOTO UNIVERSITY

The Nation and Economic Growth: Korea and Thailand
YOSHIHARA Kunio

One Malay Village: A Thirty-Year Community Study
TSUBOUCHI Yoshihiro

Commodifying Marxism:
The Formation of Modern Thai Radical Culture, 1927–1958
Kasian TEJAPIRA

Gender and Modernity: Perspectives from Asia and the Pacific
HAYAMI Yoko, TANABE Akio, TOKITA-TANABE Yumiko

Practical Buddhism among the Thai-Lao:
Religion in the Making of a Region
HAYASHI Yukio

The Political Ecology of Tropical Forests in Southeast Asia:
Historical Perspectives
LYE Tuck-Po, Wil DE JONG, ABE Ken-ichi

Between Hills and Plains:
Power and Practice in Socio-Religious Dynamics among Karen
HAYAMI Yoko

Ecological Destruction, Health and Development:
Advancing Asian Paradigms
FURUKAWA Hisao, NISHIBUCHI Mitsuaki, KONO Yasuyuki, KAIDA Yoshihiro

Searching for Vietnam:
Selected Writings on Vietnamese Culture and Society
A. Terry RAMBO

Laying the Tracks: The Thai Economy and its Railways 1885–1935
KAKIZAKI Ichiro

After the Crisis:
Hegemony, Technocracy and Governance in Southeast Asia
SHIRAISHI Takashi, Patricio N. ABINALES

Dislocating Nation-States: Globalization in Asia and Africa
Patricio N. ABINALES, ISHIKAWA Noboru and TANABE Akio

People on the Move: Rural–Urban Interactions in Sarawak
SODA Ryoji

Living on the Periphery: Development and Islamization among the Orang Asli
NOBUTA Toshihiro

Myths and Realities: The Democratization of Thai Politics
TAMADA Yoshifumi

East Asian Economies and New Regionalism
ABE Shigeyuki and Bhanupong NIDHIPRABA

The Rise of Middle Classes in Southeast Asia
SHIRAISHI Takashi and Pasuk PHONGPAICHIT

KYOTO AREA STUDIES ON ASIA

Center for Southeast Asian Studies, Kyoto University

Farming with Fire and Water: The human ecology of a composite swiddening community in Vietnam's northern mountains
Trần Đức Viên, A. Terry Rambo and Nguyễn Thanh Lâm

Re-thinking Economic Development: The Green Revolution, Agrarian Structure and Transformation in Bangladesh
Fujita Koichi

The Limits of Tradition: Peasants and Land Conflicts in Indonesia
Urano Mariko

KYOTO AREA STUDIES ON ASIA
CENTER FOR SOUTHEAST ASIAN STUDIES, KYOTO UNIVERSITY
VOLUME 19

Re-thinking Economic Development

The Green Revolution, Agrarian Structure and Transformation in Bangladesh

FUJITA Koichi

Translated by
Minako Sato

Kyoto University Press

TRANS PACIFIC PRESS

First published in 2010 jointly by:

Kyoto University Press
Kyodai Kaikan
15-9 Yoshida Kawara-cho
Sakyo-ku, Kyoto 606-8305, Japan
Telephone: +81-75-761-6182
Fax: +81-75-761-6190
Email: sales@kyoto-up.or.jp
Web: http://www.kyoto-up.or.jp

Trans Pacific Press
PO Box 164, Balwyn North, Melbourne
Victoria 3104, Australia
Telephone: +61-3-9859-1112
Fax: +61-3-9859-4110
Email: tpp.mail@gmail.com
Web: http://www.transpacificpress.com

Set by Digital Environs, Melbourne.

Printed in Melbourne by BPA Print Group.

Distributors

Australia and New Zealand
DA Information Services/Central Book Services
648 Whitehorse Road
Mitcham, Victoria 3132
Australia
Telephone: +61-3-9210-7777
Fax: + 61-3-9210-7788
Email: books@dadirect.com
Web: www.dadirect.com

USA and Canada
International Specialized Book Services (ISBS)
920 NE 58th Avenue, Suite 300
Portland, Oregon 97213-3786
USA
Telephone: (800) 944-6190
Fax: (503) 280-8832
Email: orders@isbs.com
Web: http://www.isbs.com

Asia and the Pacific
Kinokuniya Company Ltd.

Head office:
38-1 Sakuragaoka 5-chome
Setagaya-ku, Tokyo 156-8691
Japan
Telephone: +81-3-3439-0161
Fax: +81-3-3439-0839
Email: bkimp@kinokuniya.co.jp
Web: www.kinokuniya.co.jp

Asia-Pacific office:
Kinokuniya Book Stores of Singapore Pte., Ltd.
391B Orchard Road #13-06/07/08
Ngee Ann City Tower B
Singapore 238874
Telephone: +65-6276-5558
Fax: +65-6276-5570
Email: SSO@kinokuniya.co.jp

ISSN 1445–9663 (Kyoto Area Studies on Asia)
ISBN 978–1–920901–16–5

Contents

List of Figures viii
List of Tables ix
Preface xiii

Introduction—Re-thinking Economic Development in Bangladesh: Issues and Approaches 1

1 Economic Development and Rural Transformation in Bangladesh 13

Part I: The Green Revolution and Rural Class Structure

2 The Formation of the Groundwater Market and Rural Income Distribution: The Emergence of Waterlords 39
3 The Transformation of the Groundwater Market during the 1990s 61
4 Irrigation and Agricultural Development in West Bengal, India 89

Part II: The Changing Agrarian Structure and Finance

5 Credit Flow from the Wealthy to the Poor 113
Addendum to Chapter 5: The Fallacy and Reality of Microcredit 155
6 Transformation of the Potato-marketing System and Finance 166

Part III: Infrastructure, Government, and Rural Society

7 Local Administration of Infrastructure Development, Village Society, and Rural Classes 195

Conclusion 231

Notes 242
References 278
Subject Index 290
Name Index 301
Location Index 302

List of Figures

0.1:	The Bengal region and locations of villages under study	7
1.1:	Movement of agricultural labor wage rate in Bangladesh	22
1.2:	Production trend of rice and wheat in Bangladesh	34
1.3:	Real rice price in Bangladesh (1997)	35
2.1:	Water charge rate determination and net irrigation surplus	44
2.2:	Cost composition for irrigated *boro* cropping in Aira village	55
3.1:	Nominal price indices for rice, urea and kerosene in Bangladesh	65
3.2:	Changes in the irrigated area in Bangladesh	66
3.3:	Bogra city and survey villages in the outskirts	67
3.4:	Titkle village's cropping calendar (1999)	71
3.5:	Diesel STW irrigation area and investment profitability in Titkle village	79
3.6:	Map of Titkle village and tubewell installation sites	80
4.1:	The state of West Bengal and the village of Gontra	93
4.2:	Tubewell irrigated area and profitability in Gontra village	101
6.1:	Seasonal fluctuations in the urban wholesale price of potato	167
6.2:	Potato marketing channel	175
7.1:	Illustrated map of Aira village	208

List of Tables

1.1: Changes in Bangladesh's industry structure (GDP shares by sector) (%) 14
1.2: Bangladesh's economic growth rate (real rate) (%) 15
1.3: Changes in Bangladesh's employment structure ('000 persons) 21
1.4: Changes in Bangladesh's macroeconomic indicators (% of GDP) 24
1.5: Bangladesh's annual development expenditure (actual) and sector shares 26
1.6: Bangladesh's manufacturing growth in the 1990s 28
2.1: Introduction of STWs in Aira village 45
2.2: Agricultural use of land in Aira village 45
2.3: Class composition, employment structure and asset holdings in Aira village 46
2.4: STW-irrigation coverage and breakdown by transaction mode 48
2.5: STW operating cost and water charge rate (*taka*/acre) 50
2.6: Examples of groundwater market analyses in Bangladesh 51
2.7: Distribution of net irrigation surplus (*taka*) 52
2.8: Rate of return on STW investment 54
2.9: STW owner's working capital requirement and dependency on borrowings (*taka*) 56
2.10: Cost of rice production in Aira village (*taka*/acre) 58
3.1: STW irrigation in two villages in Bogra district 69
3.2: Changes in the water charge in three villages in Bogra district 69
3.3: Class profile of Titkle village residents 72
3.4: The process of tubewell introduction in Titkle village 73
3.5: List of tubewells and their owners 74
3.6: Profitability of tubewell irrigation investment and operation (*taka*) 76
3.7: Production cost and income for major crops 83
4.1: Changes in *boro* cropping in West Bengal by district 94
4.2: The process of STW diffusion in Gontra village 97
4.3: The size of farmland owned by tubewell owners 99
4.4: Income and expenditure for tubewell operation in Gontra village 100
4.5: Rice crop production cost and income in Gontra village 103
5.1: Composition of rural finance lenders in Bangladesh 116
5.2: Process of STW diffusion in the study villages 119
5.3: Farmland uses in the study villages 120

5.4: Area and population of study villages and local administrative units 121
5.5: Class composition and farmland distribution in the study villages 121
5.6: Employment structure in Daskin Chamuria village—main occupation of the household head 123
5.7: Finance by landholding class in Daskin Chamuria village 125
5.8: Finance by landholding class in Aira village 126
5.9: Inter-class finance flow matrix in Daskin Chamuria village (long-term finance) 128
5.10: Inter-class finance flow matrix in Daskin Chamuria village (short-term finance) 129
5.11: Production costs in Daskin Chamuria village (*taka* per acre) 131
5.12: Long-term and short-term informal finance—Daskin Chamuria village (*taka*) 132
5.13: Long-term and short-term informal finance—Aira village (*taka*) 133
5.14: Correspondence between landholding and wealth in Daskin Chamuria I 135
5.15: Correspondence between landholdings and wealth in Daskin Chamuria II (%) 137
5.16: Borrowers of formal finance in Daskin Chamuria village 138
5.17: Lending–borrowing balance for nonmembers of the Grameen Bank—Daskin Chamuria village 140
5.18: Borrowers of formal finance in Aira village 141
5.19: Lending–borrowing balance for nonmembers of the Grameen Bank—Aira village 141
5.20: Finances of small business operators in Daskin Chamuria village (*taka*) 144
5.21: Distribution of small business operators by landholding size in Daskin Chamuria village 146
5.22: Borrowings and fund sources in the case of one tubewell owner—Daskin Chamuria village (*taka*) 147
5.23: Finances of small business operators in Aira village (*taka*) 148
5.24: Distribution of small business operators by landholding size in Aira village 149
5.25: Informal finance of target households in the Shapla Neer survey villages 151
5A.1: Purposes of Grameen Bank loans in Daskin Chamuria village 158
5A.2: An example of investment profitability in IG projects 160

5A.3: Main occupations of household heads and Grameen Bank participation rates in Daskin Chamuria village 163
6.1: Farmland distribution and employment structure by the farmland holding class in Ashora village 170
6.2: Farmland holding class and informal finance in Ashora village 172
6.3: Informal finance balance by the farmland holding class in Ashora village 173
6.4: Cost of potato production in Ashora village 178
6.5: Potato sale by sample households in 2000/01 179
6.6: Income of sample households derived from potato production and marketing for 2000/01 181
6.7: Estimated profit for the cold storage for 2000/01 182
6.8: Estimated profit for local potato traders for 2000/01 184
6.9: Working capital required by traders for potato storage 185
6.10: Seasonal variations in the potato price and trader's remunerations 186
6.11: Short-term borrowings and their uses by the farmland holding class in Ashora village 189
6.12: Interest rates on short-term loans 190
7.1: Infrastructure programs in Sherpur *Thana* 199
7.2: The road system in Bangladesh 200
7.3: FFW projects allocated to Mirzapur *Union* 203
7.4: TR projects allocated to Mirzapur *Union* in 1993 204
7.5: Fiscal balance of Mirzapur *Union* in 1992 205
7.6: *Union* tax by farmland holding class in Aira village (1991) 206
7.7: Hamlets (*para*) in Aira village and their basic data 209
7.8: *Gusti* of Muslim residents of Aira village and basic data 212
7.9: Length of residency in Aira village by household head's age group 213
7.10: Relationships between Muslim *gusti* and *para* 213
7.11: Composition of committee members by *para* 215
7.12: Composition of committee members (Muslim only) by *gusti* 215
7.13: Profiles of 'leaders' in Aira village 216
7.14: Land donations to the mosque 218
7.15: Revenue and expenditure of the mosque fund (*taka*) 218
7.16: Land donations to the *madrasa* 219
7.17: Revenue and expenditure of the *madrasa* fund (*taka*) 219
7.18: Resource mobilization for the provision of local public goods in Aira village I 221

7.19: Resource mobilization for the provision of local public goods in Aira village II 223
7.20: Progression of works in the 'experiment' in Aira village 226
7.21: Labor input to the 'experiment' in Aira village I 227
7.22: Labor input to the 'experiment' in Aira village II 227

Preface

This book is the English version of my study on rural development in Bangladesh first published in 2005 in Japanese by Kyoto University Press. I am very pleased that I have finally been able to publish the book in a form that English-speakers, especially Bangladeshi and Indian people, can access.

Most of the chapters of this book are based on research conducted between 1992–94 when I was working as a JICA (Japan International Cooperation Agency) expert in an action research project titled 'Japan-Bangladesh Joint Study on Rural Development Experiment' (JERDE). Although I published the results of the research in the form of several academic articles and papers soon after I left Bangladesh in March 1994, more than a decade passed before the findings were published as a book. Because five more years have gone by since the Japanese edition, I am a somewhat concerned that the research presented here is outdated, particularly in light of the drastic changes and development experienced by the Bangladesh economy, including its rural sector, during the first decade of the 2000s. However, I strongly believe that what I wanted to convey to readers of this book about the structure and transformation of the Bangladesh rural economy until the 1990s still has profound implications in terms of understanding the present stage of its development. In addition, I believe this English edition can provide both academics and policy-makers with insights when considering economic development and policy, not only in Bangladesh but also in developing countries in general.

In April 2009 I began another research project that focuses on changes to the Bangladesh village economy between 1992–94 and the present. I have selected only two villages from all the villages studied in this publication and have already finished the basic survey in Daskin Chamuria village in Tangail district including all 754 current households (the figure was 538 in 1992). At present I am initiating the same type of survey in Aira village in Bogra district, now home to 400 households (208 in 1992). This research is now jointly conducted with Dr. W.H.M. Jaim, Professor, Department of Agricultural Economics, Bangladesh Agricultural University (BAU). We are expecting that many interesting and significant findings will eventuate before the project finishes in March 2012.

I am very grateful to the many people who helped bring this volume into existence. First and foremost, I wish to appreciate the villagers and project staff of the study villages as well as the local government staff in each locality who patiently cooperated with the research process. I am deeply indebted to Dr Yoshihiro Kaida (Professor Emeritus, Kyoto University) and Dr Kazuo Ando

(Associate Professor, Center for Southeast Asian Studies, Kyoto University) for inviting me to participate in the JICA project (JSRDE) through which I was enabled to conduct fieldwork and reside in Bangladesh for the first time for the duration of two years, from 1992–94. Special thanks are also extended to the other project members; Ms Saleha Begum (Project Director), Mr Mazahrul Islam, Mr Shiro Akamatsu (General Manager), Ms Keiko Itagaki (co-author of Chapter Seven; original Japanese version), Dr Haruo Uchida, Dr Keiko Yoshino, Dr Altaf Hossain, Dr Habibur Rahman, Dr Ratan Chakravarty, Mr Akkel Ali, Dr W.H.M. Jaim (one of the co-authors of Chapter Four; original version), Mr Feroz Hossain (co-author of Chapter Two; original version), Dr Koichi Usami, Dr Akinobu Kawai, Dr Haruo Noma, Dr Keshav Maharajan, Dr Kichiji Yajima, Dr Shiro Mukai, and many others. For conducting research in Gontra village, West Bengal, India, I deeply appreciate the cooperation of Dr Toshihiko Suda, Dr S.K. Mukhopadhyay, Dr Ashok Kundu (one of the co-authors of Chapter Four; original version) and Dr W.H.M. Jaim (mentioned above). Ashora village in Comilla district was surveyed by Dr K.G. Moazzem (Senior Research Fellow, Center for Policy Dialogue, Bangladesh), a former student under my supervision at the Graduate School of Asian and African Area Studies, Kyoto University, to whom I would like to give special thanks (co-author of Chapter Six; original version). Finally, the publication of this book was facilitated by a Grant-in-Aid for Publication of Scientific Research Results bestowed by the Japan Society for the Promotion of Science (JSPS).

I would like to dedicate this book to my wife, Mieko Fujita, for her patient and whole-hearted support.

Koichi Fujita
December 2009
Rural Development Academy,
Bogra, Bangladesh

Introduction
Re-thinking Economic Development in Bangladesh: Issues and Approaches

Issues: Refocusing on Agricultural Growth and Infrastructure Development

At some time in the future, the present age is likely to be recognized as the time when poverty alleviation became the most important issue in the history of economic development in developing countries, especially in the history of international cooperation and aid led by the World Bank and the International Monetary Fund. Following the age of structural adjustment in the 1980s, the focus of the endeavor to alleviate poverty in developing countries shifted during the 1990s to a more direct approach by way of quantitative target setting. In September 1999, the Development and Interim Committees, consisting of the major member countries of the World Bank and the International Monetary Fund, resolved to effectively make the preparation of Poverty Reduction Strategy Papers a condition for the provision of International Development Association assistance for poverty alleviation to heavily indebted poor countries and all countries eligible for such assistance. Accordingly, many developing countries have begun preparations for the strategy paper and some have completed it.

If the ultimate purpose of economic development (and international cooperation and aid for such development) is the eradication of so-called poverty among the peoples of developing countries, it may be quite natural, or even desirable, for donors to demand such detailed quantitative information about the state and the nature of poverty, and about the establishment of a systematic policy regime for its alleviation. It should also be a welcome move in the sense that the concept of poverty has come to have a much broader meaning than simply low income in recent years. At the same time, however, what is the significance of this renewed focus on poverty alleviation, since it has always been the ultimate purpose of donors' endeavors?

It is common knowledge, so to speak, in the social sciences that the cause of poverty among the peoples of developing countries is so structural, deep-rooted, and complicated by various factors that its eradication will require considerable time (or that multiple steps must be followed in a proper order), and therefore a 'slow and steady approach' is thought to be needed in some cases. In light of this, it is unlikely that I am the only person who senses something rather myopic and shallow about this recent trend and feels somewhat apprehensive. Under such conditions, people are inevitably drawn to (what is generally regarded to be) a quick recipe for poverty alleviation.

Here is one example. In Bangladesh, the poorest country in South Asia and the subject of this study, a microcredit program pioneered by the Grameen Bank began to attract attention from the mid-1980s onwards as a powerful means of poverty alleviation. The microcredit program has been established as the main pillar of the country's development strategy to date. Major donors have injected large amounts of funds into this program, mainly through nongovernmental organizations (NGOs).

I will not go into details here due to limitations of space, but I do very much appreciate the effectiveness of microcredit. However, I am rather skeptical about the way microcredit is treated as if it were a panacea for poverty alleviation. To put it rather unkindly, it has spawned the situation in which thriving aid businesses search high and low to the ends of the earth for impoverished people to which they can lend money.

In the midst of this trend, for example, infrastructure investment, which used to be considered important in the history of economic development and assistance, is now regarded as a relic of heavy and unwieldy investment programs of the past. Such programs now run counter to more *desirable* poverty reduction initiatives involving popular participation, to put it slightly strongly. This new trend also leads easily to the climate in which the Green Revolution is unilaterally criticized, despite its achievements of extreme historical importance, especially in Asia.[1]

One basic premise of this study is the view that the growth of the agricultural sector plays a crucial role in the economic development process of developing countries, especially in its early stages (Mellor 1966).

Agriculture usually cannot become the driving force behind economic development. This role is usually played by the manufacturing sector. However, in quite a number of cases, a development strategy that neglected the agricultural and rural sector (which accounted for a very large share of the economy) in the early stages of economic development paid a heavy price and, eventually, the overall economic development was crippled and frustrated. In particular, the Green Revolution was a very important historical achievement that entailed a dramatic improvement in productivity of grain production, which is the very heart of agriculture.

To put it in a slightly textbook manner, the strategic importance of growth in the agricultural sector can be summarized as follows. First, agricultural growth contributes to a reduction in foreign currency requirements through a reduction in food imports. More of the precious foreign capital can be used to promote industrialization. Second, agricultural growth helps industrialization indirectly by preventing increases in food prices and keeping wage rates (in food price terms) for workers in check. Third, agricultural growth contributes to the development of the non-agricultural sector through the forward and backward linkages effect. Fourth, agricultural growth increases productivity and makes productive resources (land, labor, and capital), which are otherwise tied up in farming, available to the non-agricultural sector. Fifth, agricultural growth increases farm earnings and creates a market for manufactured goods and services. In the process of meeting the needs of domestic consumers, it provides the domestic industrial sector with an opportunity to improve and eventually to grow into an export industry. Sixth, agricultural growth stimulates the growth of the non-agricultural sector within the rural area, increases rural employment, and raises the incomes of non-agricultural rural residents (miscellaneous rural laborers without land). As in the case of the fifth point above, this also creates a domestic market for manufactured goods and services.

Especially important among these points are the so-called final demand effects referred to in the fifth and sixth points. The agricultural sector accounts more than 70% of the total workforce in developing countries in the early stages of development. If the sector continues to grow at an annual rate of 3% to 4%, it will have a far greater impact on the country's economy than a tiny manufacturing sector growing at 10% to 15%. And its impact will mainly be passed on through the formation and strengthening of linkages between the agricultural and non-agricultural sectors in the form of market creation for consumer goods and services in the rural areas.

In this sense, it is almost impossible to overstress the enormous significance of the Green Revolution that took place in Asian countries from the mid-1960s. It becomes very clear when they are compared with sub-Saharan Africa, which is still suffering for its inability to benefit from the Green Revolution.

As for the subject of this study, Bangladesh, the Green Revolution made rapid advances from the 1980s. It was more than ten years behind the Southeast Asian islands of the Philippines and Indonesia. In South Asia, where Bangladesh is located, the Green Revolution began in the Punjab and other northwestern regions of India and Pakistan in the mid-1960s, at around the same time as it started in insular Southeast Asia. India successfully achieved food self-sufficiency by the end of the 1970s.

However, India's Green Revolution through to the end of the 1970s was a wheat revolution, which was highly dependent on a single crop and limited to certain regions. Consequently, India did not achieve the type of agricultural growth that would precede full-scale economic development led by industrialization, even though it attained food self-sufficiency at the national level. Broad-based agricultural growth in this sense was only achieved in the 1980s when the Green Revolution spread throughout the country to most of its non-wheat crops, especially rice.[2] It is perhaps possible to consider Bangladesh as part of a large-scale shift that occurred in its much larger neighbor.

Broadly speaking, the object of this study is to focus on the role of agricultural growth from the 1980s in Bangladesh's economic development process and, based on data collected at the village level, to examine in detail its dynamics and how it spread throughout the rural economy. I would particularly like to look at the driving forces and supporters of agricultural growth and discuss what impacts they had on changes in rural class structure, especially on the economy of the rural lower classes.

There is a need for a specific focus on the changing rural class structure in Bangladesh, and not just because poverty reduction is the biggest challenge. This requires further explanation.

The most notable difference between the Green Revolution of the Southeast Asian islands and that of India and Bangladesh is irrigation technology. As is commonly known, the diffusion of the Green Revolution, which fundamentally consists of plant breeding and fertilizer technologies, is critically dependent on water control. Irrigation is a leading input for agricultural growth (Ishikawa 1966). In short, the gravity-flow canal irrigation system was the main type of irrigation in insular Southeast Asia, whereas groundwater extraction by tubewell installation underpinned the Green Revolution in South Asia, especially in Bangladesh. While irrigation canals are generally constructed with public investment, tubewells are built by private farmers. This is a critical difference that has enormous implications.

The drilling of a tubewell is a considerable investment for individual farmers. That is the case not only with deep tubewells (DTWs) but also with relatively small-scale shallow tubewells (STWs). As a result, only a very small number of wealthy farmers can invest in tubewells. This provides the setting for the following complicated questions about the relationship between the propagation of agricultural technologies and the rural class structure—questions that essentially do not arise with the canal system.

To begin with, did the majority of small- to medium-size farmers without tubewells miss out on the benefits of the Green Revolution? To jump ahead, the answer to this question is that they did not miss out. Wealthy farmers with tubewells began to sell their water for irrigation. When the irrigation water market (the groundwater market) was created, the condition for the introduction of Green Revolution technologies to the majority of small- to medium-size farmers without tubewells was met.

However, there is another question. Were the benefits of the Green Revolution distributed unevenly because the prices of irrigation water were set at unreasonably high levels? If the profits from development were monopolized by a handful of wealthy farmers, the creation of a new rural market for non-agricultural consumer goods and services would be limited. Based on the aforementioned logic, it is highly likely that the impact of agricultural growth on overall economic growth would not be so great in that case.

In other words, the crux of the issue is the functionality of the groundwater market that has developed with the spread of tubewell irrigation.

To sum up, the main purpose of this study is to analyze the dynamics of the Green Revolution in rice production triggered by the diffusion of tubewells, mostly in Bangladesh. There is a special focus on the changing conditions of the irrigation water transaction relationship between those who own tubewells and those who do not, and on the resulting rural income distribution. The analysis of rural income distribution mainly deals with factor shares in rice production and their changes, but it also covers the activities of lenders and borrowers in the rural informal financial market and the larger phenomenon of changing rural class structure.

Accordingly, Part I discusses the structure of the groundwater market and its transformation, and Part II analyzes the changing state of the rural economy brought about by the advancement of agriculture, especially from the perspective of changes in inter-class relationships. They are followed by Part III, which analyzes rural development in Bangladesh from a slightly different point of view. It is concerned with the systematic and organizational issues of local governments and village communities surrounding rural infrastructure development (roads in particular). I would like to refer readers to the final chapter, which explains in a little more detail why I have included discussions on these issues in the study of changing class structure.

At this stage, I will limit my explanation to the following three points. First, the issue of rural class structure and its transformation is closely involved in the issues facing the whole rural community, where people of different classes coexist. Second, microcredit (discussed in Part II) and infrastructure development are treated as the two pillars of rural development policy in Bangladesh and therefore compete for a larger share of limited funds. Third, the issues to be discussed in Part III are fundamental not only to rural infrastructure development but also to almost all initiatives of rural development policy, such as elementary education, health, public hygiene, and rural electrification, and have extremely important implications for the future of rural development in Bangladesh.

As stated earlier, this study adopts the standpoint of re-emphasizing the strategic importance of infrastructure development in achieving the policy target of poverty alleviation. The second point, above, is clearly a specific reflection of this perspective.

Methodology: Economic Analysis by Fieldwork

Except for the introductory discussion in Chapter 1, this study is based on fieldwork conducted in a small number of villages. One reason for this is that I became aware of the limits of studies that relied on secondary data and information such as government statistics. A more positive reason is that I have been blessed with many opportunities to survey these rural communities over the past ten years or so. I am fully aware of the methodological limits of fieldwork, but it also offers many advantages. I have compiled this study in an attempt to present to the world the results of this research in a way that makes the maximum use of these advantages instead of arguing about its merits and demerits. Regarding the issue of general applicability or universality of a small number of cases, which I regard as the most serious limitation of fieldwork-based studies, I have decided not to elaborate in this book, except for some supplementary comments in Chapter 1 and elsewhere, as I have already discussed it in detail in an earlier study, *Banguradeshu nōgyō hatten-ron josetsu* (An introduction to the study of agricultural development in Bangladesh) (Fujita 1993a). I hope readers will treat this study as a sister edition to complement this earlier publication.

I would like to provide a brief explanation of each of the villages studied, including research projects I was involved in. The first village is Daskin Chamuria village in Tangail district (Figure 0.1). This village is discussed in Chapter 5 and in the Addendum to that chapter. At the end of March 1992, I was assigned by the Japan International Cooperation Agency (JICA) as a long-term JICA expert mainly to this village, where I took part in the Joint Study on Rural Development Experiment in Bangladesh.[3] After about two hours of driving from Bangladesh's capital city of Dhaka, past the town of

Figure 0.1: The Bengal region and locations of villages under study

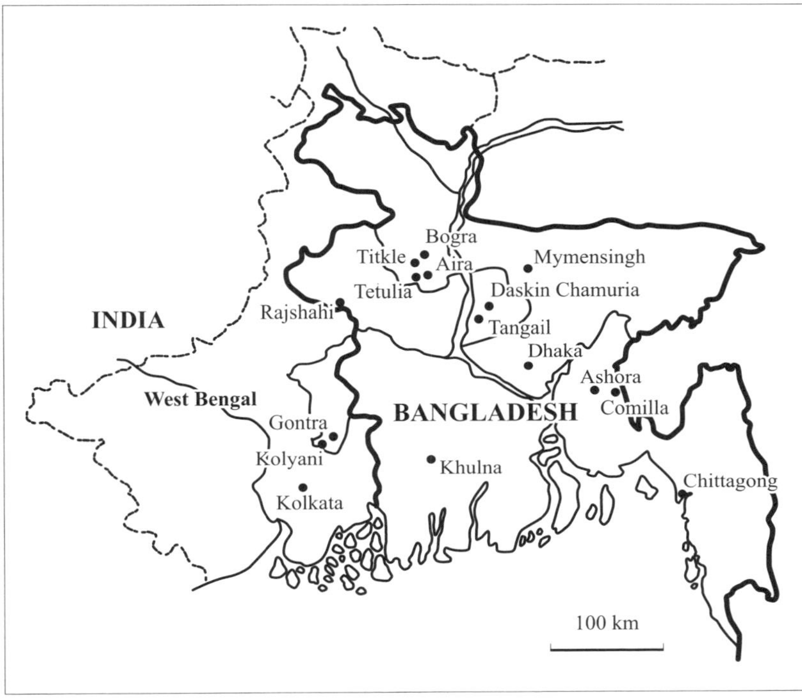

Tangail and across a bridge over the Rohajan River, and getting out of the car and walking on a narrow country road along a natural embankment for about thirty minutes, I reached this village. During the rainy season, floodwaters slowly encroach on the village and give its several hamlets the appearance of small islands in a large lake. The village originally cultivated broadcast *aman* rice, a deepwater variety, but transplanted *aman* rice and dry-season *boro* rice have become its main varieties in recent years.[4] The place was very densely populated and gave the false impression, when I first visited its settlements (especially the south *para*), that I was stepping into urban slums. In addition to agricultural products such as rice, jute, mustard, and wheat, it had a thriving rural industry in handloom weaving, and the pleasant sound of looms was heard throughout the village.

The second village is Aira village in Bogra district. It is the most frequently featured village in this study, and is discussed in Chapters 2, 3 (in part), 5, and 7. This was the other village to which I was assigned in the aforementioned JICA project. Access to Aira from Dhaka has now improved considerably thanks to the completion of the Jamuna Bridge in 1997. When I stayed there from 1992 to 1994, it used to take a total of six to seven hours from Dhaka to the city of Sherpur in Bogra, which was the gateway to Aira, including two-and-a-half hours on a ferry along the Jamuna River. The village was another seven or eight kilometers down a narrow country road off the city's arterial road. It is still clear in my memory that in the wet season I had to get out of my car and walk in a sea of mud (which was typical in the Barind Tract), while, in the dry season, I had to cover my mouth with a handkerchief as I drove through clouds of fine dust. In contrast to Daskin Chamuria village, there were very few employment opportunities apart from farming in Aira, which was purely a rice-producing area cultivating the highly productive transplanted *aman* and *boro* rice varieties.

The third village is Tetulia village in Bogra district, which features in Chapter 3. This village is relatively close to Aira village, but it has much better access as it is located only ten kilometers from Bogra city and is on an arterial road from Bogra city to Rajshahi city via Natore city. It was one of the villages selected in 1996 for *The Study on the Impact of the Grameen Bank* by the Overseas Economic Cooperation Fund (presently Japan Bank for International Cooperation). However, irrigation research in this village was conducted in 1999 and 2000 separately from the Grameen Bank study with a grant-in-aid for scientific research from the Ministry of Education and Science led by Professor Fumio Osanami, Graduate School of Agriculture, Hokkaido University. Like Aira village, Tetulia is on the Barind Tract and is spared regular flooding. It mainly cultivated rice, which was highly productive. Non-agricultural employment opportunities were emerging, but not as many as in Daskin Chamuria, perhaps due to its remoteness from the capital city.

The fourth village is Ashora village in Comilla district, which is a potato-producing village that features in Chapter 6. It was mainly studied by Dr. K. G. Moazzem, an overseas student under my supervision at the Graduate School of Asian and African Area Studies, Kyoto University, now a senior research fellow at the Centre for Policy Dialogue in Bangladesh. The scale of farmland ownership and operation was generally very small in Comilla district, and there were many non-agricultural employment opportunities. Many villagers also traveled overseas to work in places such as the Middle East.

These are the main study villages in Bangladesh and, in terms of the degree of urbanization, Ashora in Comilla was the most advanced, followed by Daskin Chamuria in Tangail, Tetulia in Bogra, and Aira in Bogra.

One village in West Bengal, India, has been included in this study—Gontra village in Nadia district is discussed in Chapter 4. This village was surveyed concurrently with Tetulia in Bogra from 1999 to 2000 using the aforementioned grant-in-aid for scientific research. This village was chosen based on a referral from Dr. Toshihiko Suda of Norinchukin Research Institute (he is now an Associate Professor of Daito Bunka University), who had conducted a study on agricultural cooperatives in 1998. It is located about an hour's drive northeast of Kalyani town, which is two to three hours drive from the state capital of Kolkata and home to many education facilities, including Kalyani University. Its main crops have been transplanted *aman* and *boro* rice, with the emergence of the high-profit farming of bananas and vegetables in recent years. Non-agricultural employment has also increased considerably. This village is also notable for the existence of an excellent agricultural cooperative. In relative terms, villages in West Bengal generally appear to be one step ahead of those in Bangladesh in various aspects of institutional development and the agricultural cooperative is one such example.

Composition of the Study

Here I briefly explain the composition of this book to provide an overview of this study. Chapter 1 outlines the development process of the Bangladeshi economy after the separation and independence of India and Pakistan in 1947, and summarizes the transformation of rural economies in order to provide readers with the preliminary knowledge required to understand technicalities in this study. In particular, it discusses the historical significance of the period from the 1980s onwards when the diffusion of tubewell irrigation and the development of the rural non-agricultural sector took place.

Part I (Chapters 2 to 4), entitled 'The Green Revolution and Rural Class Structure,' discusses the emergence and transformation of the groundwater market and its economic significance, centering on tubewell irrigation, that became the driving force for the Green Revolution.

First, Chapter 2 examines the structure of the groundwater market and income distribution under this system, and is based on the 1992 survey of Aira village in Bogra district. It points to the fact that the rate of water charge was high in the groundwater market and that income distribution under this system greatly favored tubewell owners. It describes and examines the realities surrounding the appearance of the so-called 'waterlords.' In economic terms, it attributes the high water prices to high interest rates in rural informal financial markets.

Chapter 3 points to the major transformation of the groundwater market during the 1990s based on the 1999 survey of some villages in Bogra district

(Tetulia and other villages, in addition to Aira), and discusses various factors and implications of this transformation. Although the diffusion of tubewells had reached a saturation point by the end of the 1980s or the early 1990s, the construction of new tubewells continued, intensifying competition in the groundwater market and substantially reducing the real water charge. This quickly destroyed the exploitative market structure that might have spawned any waterlords, but the reduction in water charges was taken up by a renewed surge in land rent and therefore did not result in an improvement in labor share. It is also argued that the introduction of new tubewells was economically rational for the individuals who introduced them, but was an overinvestment from a social point of view as it reduced irrigation efficiency.

Chapter 4 examines the case of Gontra village in Nadia district in West Bengal, India. After demonstrating that agricultural development in this village was also substantially dictated by the introduction of tubewells, it analyses its groundwater market. It reveals that the diffusion of tubewells in this village also reached a saturation point and initially established high water charges during the 1980s, but that the construction of new tubewells continued into the 1990s, bringing down real water charges and dramatically changing (factor) income distribution in the same way that occurred in rural Bangladesh. Unlike Bangladesh, however, water table levels continued to fall and the problem of groundwater shortage, especially groundwater depletion from April to May at the end of the irrigation period, began to surface from the mid-1990s, prompting some farmers to introduce a new type of STW by drilling deeper to reach the falling water tables. The new type of tubewell has a greater area coverage per well, which will inevitably spark reorganization of the village's groundwater market.

Part II, 'Changing Agrarian Structure and Finance,' includes Chapter 5, the Addendum to Chapter 5, and Chapter 6. In preparation for discussion on the effects of microcredit, Chapter 5 sheds light on the realities of rural informal finance based on the cases of Daskin Chamuria village in Tangail district and Aira village in Bogra district. The survey was conducted from 1992 to 1993. It reveals the fact that credit was flowing in the reverse direction from the poor to the rich in informal financial markets and presents the argument that this phenomenon was occurring independently of the effects of microcredit programs (that is, as a result of equal penetration of the overall rural economic development to the poor).

A type of informal finance called *bhograhani* locally (or *bondak* more generally) secured against land deserves special attention here. A majority of borrowers used to be marginal and small farmers, and this was the main route to the eventual loss of land for those who were unable to repay their loans. By the time of the survey, it had transformed into a means (system) by which landless laborers and marginal farmers provided funds for lending and acquired land as collateral to conduct subsistence rice production. Also, in short-term financial markets, lenders were often the rural poor and many of the borrowers were small business owners in the rural area requiring working capital.

This is followed by a supplementary discussion, the Addendum, which explains the false image and reality of microcredit as revealed by a survey on how funds borrowed from the Grameen Bank were used in Daskin Chamuria village. The 'false image' refers to the scenario that money borrowed from the Grameen Bank is invested in small businesses that create self-employment opportunities and that their success will bring about poverty reduction. In reality, microcredit functions as a means to obtain an *advance for (future) savings* for borrowers rather than for investment in small businesses. In other words, a borrower often makes repayments from the existing permanent income (of a husband or a son). In this sense, borrowers can use their microloans for any purposes without the fear of defaulting, and tend to choose to invest in relatively safe assets (such as *bondak*) that generate stable returns, which in turn contributes to poverty reduction. This situation suggests that microcredit is not suitable for the poorest of the poor without any source of permanent income, and that microcredit in itself creates few businesses and cannot become the driving force for economic development.

Based on the 1999–2003 survey of Ashora village in Comilla district, Chapter 6 demonstrates the fact that a *reverse flow* of credit from the poor to the rich was also occurring in informal financial markets for *bondak* in rural villages with highly developed intensive farming and off-farm employment, and analyzes the structure and transformation of the potato-marketing system through cold storage in refrigerated warehouses. The construction of cold storages is a large-scale investment that may require funds from urban entrepreneurs, and they stood out when they were built in rural areas during the 1980s. About twenty years on, a rise in the overall rural income has boosted the relative financial power of farmers and rural traders and lowered that of urban entrepreneurs. This shift has led to the demise of a credit relationship involving an advance payment called *dadan*, which used to be prevalent in rural areas.

Finally, Chapter 7 in Part III examines and analyzes the true state of local administration and village communities, taking Aira village in Bogra as an example. It is argued that rural infrastructure development programs using wheat food aid as wage payments in kind were very inadequate for the existing needs, and that the problem was caused by a lack of resource mobilization from rural residents, including taxes, and marked a weakness in local administration. It is concluded that the absence of a system for rural residents to build, maintain, and manage infrastructure by themselves is attributable to a low level of accumulation of social capital in rural communities.

I will not mention here the contents of the final chapter, which is a summary of the study.

1
Economic Development and Rural Transformation in Bangladesh

In this chapter I examine the 1980s and the 1990s in the history of economic development in Bangladesh in order to provide the groundwork for detailed discussion about the structure and transformation of the Bangladeshi rural economy. First, the period between the Partition of India and Pakistan and today is divided into four eras: the East Pakistan era (1947–71), the era of post-independence turmoil and recovery (1972–81), the Ershad era (1982–90), and the civilian government era (1991–2001). The characteristics of each era are outlined and the place or significance of the 1980s (and to a lesser extent the 1990s) is discussed.

Post-Partition Economic Policy and Development

The East Pakistan Era (1947–71)

In 1947 British India was split into two independent countries, India and Pakistan, and Bangladesh became part of Pakistan. Pre-Partition Bangladesh was purely a rural region within Kolkata's economic sphere, supplying food, labor, and raw materials (such as jute) and purchasing manufactured goods in return. In 1950, shortly after the Partition, agriculture accounted for 65% of its industrial structure as a percentage of gross domestic product (GDP), the non-agriculture and non-manufacturing sector accounted for 31%, and manufacturing (which was mainly a rural cottage industry; Table 1.1) for just 4%. There was no jute-processing mill in Bangladesh, which was a major jute-producing region. By the way, the situation was no different in West Pakistan, where the manufacturing sector represented only 8% of GDP in 1950.

Unlike India, Pakistan emphasized private capital-led industrialization in its economic development. Private investors, supported by the government's generous development policy, began to invest in import substitution industries (such as the cotton industry) in West Pakistan. However, West Pakistani capital ran into the walls of its small domestic market as early as the end of the 1950s and began to flow to East Pakistan during the 1960s. Investors initially went

Table 1.1: Changes in Bangladesh's industry structure (GDP shares by sector) (%)

YEAR	AGRICULTURE	MANUFACTURING			OTHER SECTORS
		LARGE-SCALE	SMALL-SCALE	TOTAL	
1950	65.2	0.6	3.3	3.9	30.9
1955	63.0	1.4	3.3	4.7	32.3
1961	62.6	3.0	3.4	6.4	31.0
1970	55.3	6.0	2.9	8.9	35.8
1975	54.6	5.8	4.7	10.5	34.9
1980	49.5	6.2	4.6	10.8	39.7
1985	41.7	5.3	4.6	9.9	48.4
1990	38.3	5.8	4.1	9.9	51.8
1995	32.8	7.3	4.0	11.3	55.9
2000	31.9	n.a.	n.a.	11.1	57.0

Notes: year 1950 means Financial Year 1950 (July 1949–June 1950). Likewise for all subsequent years.
Sources: 1950–90: Hossain (1996: 34). 1995–2000: BBS, Statistical Pocket Book of Bangladesh, various issues.

into the textile industry (jute and cotton) jointly with the Pakistan Industrial Development Corporation, then bought the businesses cheaply from the government once the industry got on track and began to grow. By 1970, shortly before the independence of Bangladesh, the textile industry had grown into a key industry of East Pakistan and employed 57% of the total manufacturing workforce, even though it represented only 5% of the total number of factories. Other major industries included tobacco, sugar, tea processing, paper and paper products, pharmaceuticals, and steel.

Thus, industrialization in East Pakistan progressed rapidly during the 1960s. However, the growth rate for the manufacturing sector over a period of twenty years from 1950 to 1970 was only 8.3% per annum and the rate of economic growth stagnated at 3.3% (only 0.5% per capita) (Table 1.2). The annual growth rate of 8.3% was far from satisfactory at the early stage of development when the manufacturing sector's share of GDP was very small. The industrial structure did not change or advance favorably, either, although the share of agriculture in GDP decreased to 55% and that of manufacturing grew to 9% by 1970.

The above economic development process left two major problems.[1] First, the economic disparity between East and West Pakistan widened considerably. The ratio of disparity between East and West was 1:1.32 in 1960 in terms of per capita GDP, and increased to 1:1.61 in 1970. Second, a majority of East Pakistan's key industries were controlled by West Pakistani capital. In terms

Table 1.2: Bangladesh's economic growth rate (real rate) (%)

	GDP growth rate	Per capita GDP growth rate	Growth rate by sector				
				Manufacturing			
			Agriculture	Large-scale	Small-scale	Total	Other sectors
1950–60	2.8	–0.7	1.5	19.4	5.1	9.6	2.0
1960–70	4.3	1.6	3.0	6.8	7.2	7.0	5.8
1970–71	–5.5	–8.4	–4.5	–9.8	–24.0	–15.2	n.a.
1971–72	–14.0	–16.6	–0 .7	–46.1	–43.4	–45.2	n.a.
1972–73	7.5	4.1	–0.3	63.6	72.1	65.7	n.a.
1973–80	3.9	1.3	2.1	20.2	2.9	10.3	4.8
1980–85	3.8	1.4	2.9	2.8	2.9	2.8	5.1
1985–90	4.0	2.1	2.4	6.2	2.9	4.8	5.3
1990–95	4.1	2.3	1.0	9.4	3.4	7.0	5.7
1995–00	5.2	3.6	3.9	n.a.	n.a.	5.4	5.5
2000–01	5.4	4.0	3.1	6.5	7.0	6.7	6.0
2001–02	4.4	3.0	0.0	4.6	7.7	5.5	6.0
2002–03	5.3	3.9	3.3	6.0	8.0	6.6	5.8

Sources: 1950–70: Alamgir and Berlage (1974: 167–8). 1971–73: Osada (1980: 15). 1973–90: BBS (1993a: 108–09). 1990–95: BBS (1997: 274). 1995–: Bangladesh Bank (2003).

of fixed capital value, 34% of its manufacturing industry was owned by the state-controlled East Pakistan Industrial Development Corporation, 48% by non-Bengalis, and only 18% by Bengalis. West Pakistani capital controlled not only the industrial sector but also all other core economic sectors such as finance, insurance, trade, and commerce.

Regarding agricultural and rural development, the following two points are worth noting.

First, the Bangladesh Academy for Rural Development (BARD) was established on the outskirts of Comilla city, about 100 kilometers east of the capital Dhaka, in 1959 to advocate and promote what was called the Comilla Model of rural development. It was designed to promote integrated rural development centering on small-scale farmers by organically combining the following four main initiatives: the formation of a two-tiered agricultural cooperative system (cooperatives at the village level and a federation of cooperatives at the *thana* (subdistrict) level), the establishment of the *Thana* Training and Development Center, the *Thana* Irrigation Program for the introduction of low lift pumps, and the Rural Works Program. This approach was implemented nationally as the Integrated Rural Development Program after the independence of Bangladesh in 1971 and reorganized into the Bangladesh

Rural Development Board (BRDB) in 1982. It continues to date to oversee the implementation of rural development programs through cooperatives (including farmers' cooperatives, women's cooperatives, and landless cooperatives).[2]

Second, the annual agricultural growth rate of 2.3% achieved during the East Pakistan era was considerably lower than the rate of population growth, but it was still a significant achievement by contrast with its total stagnation during the British colonial era. One major factor was the development of dry-season irrigated cropping of *boro* rice under the aforementioned *Thana* Irrigation Program; another important factor was wet-season double rice cropping of non-irrigated *aus* rice and *aman* rice. The advancement of wet-season double rice cropping was mainly the product of the first rice variety improvement project in the Indian subcontinent, which was initiated in Dhaka in 1911.[3]

Post-Independence Economic Turmoil and Recovery (1972–81)

Bangladesh won its independence in December 1971 after a fierce nine-month war. The Awami League, which had led the independence movement, installed Mujibur Rahman as the party leader when he was released from a West Pakistani jail, and set out to rebuild Bangladesh's war-ravaged economy. Liberated from many years of colonial rule (including during the East Pakistan era), the people had high expectations for nation building.

However, Bangladesh's road to economic recovery was fraught with difficulty. Its infrastructure, underdeveloped in the first place, had been devastated by war. Many bridges had been destroyed and its power generation and transmission capacity had been dramatically curtailed. In addition, West Pakistani business owners, engineers, and bureaucrats in the key positions of the Bangladesh economy were repatriated. The economy was forced to endure severe negative growth. The economic downturn at this time was spurred by some unfortunate events such as the first oil shock in 1973, a slump in agriculture due to drought and flooding, and, especially, the famine that was triggered by widespread flooding in August 1974 (tens of thousands of people died from starvation), as well as by the political factors mentioned below.

The Awami League government adopted socialist economic policy modeled on India. It nationalized major manufacturing industries and the banking and insurance sector, implemented a monopoly over international trade by a state-run corporation, and imposed tight foreign currency restrictions. By March 1972 there were 392 state enterprises controlled by ten state-run corporations that owned 92% of the value of fixed assets. Although agriculture, small and cottage industries, and small-scale distribution businesses were left to the private sector, the Bangladesh Agricultural Development Corporation (BADC) had a monopoly in the distribution of agricultural inputs and owned minor irrigation facilities, including low lift pumps, which were rented to farmers' groups.

The Awami League government pursued expansionist fiscal and monetary policies without regard to national finance and foreign currency constraints. The government was faced with a serious fiscal deficit as public sector employment expanded rapidly and tax revenue dropped due to a rise in the land tax exemption point. The fiscal deficit reached 16% of GDP in 1973 and a massive loss was generated from the falling capacity utilization rate and operational efficiency of state enterprises. The deficits had to be covered by the issuance of more paper money in the end, leading to rampant inflation. The annual inflation rate was almost 40% from 1972 to 1975, which directly hit poor families in the urban and rural areas. Real wages of agricultural laborers declined by about 20% from the pre-independence level, especially in the famine year of 1974 when real wages fell by more than 50% from the 1970 level. The endeavor to lift wages for workers of government departments and state enterprises could not keep up with the pace of inflation, and a 44% decline in real wages depressed their morale. The real interest rate on bank deposits was negative 38%, which discouraged people from saving and popularized investment in real assets. The domestic savings rate (as a percentage of GDP) decreased dramatically from 8% before independence to zero. The country's trade deficit was relatively small, simply because it had no foreign currency to import necessities such as food and it had to depend on aid supplies from all over the world. Many NGOs working in Bangladesh today started their operations with their involvement in the distribution of aid supplies during this period. The nation's standard of living dropped considerably from the pre-independence level, and the absolute poverty ratio in the rural areas based on household expenditure survey data (the ratio of households below the absolute poverty line, which was calculated by adding the food expenditure required to achieve 2,112 calories and 30% of it for non-food expenditure) increased sharply from 44% in 1964 (prior to independence) to 71% in 1974.

Having had high expectations, the nation was deeply disappointed by economic exhaustion and chaos during the Mujibur Rahman era. Revelations of corruption in the Awami League in relation to aid supplies led to a rapid decline in popular support. The assassination of Mujibur Rahman in August 1975 under these conditions was coolly received by the people and the League's reign quickly came to an end.

It was Ziaur Rahman who emerged from this political vacuum and headed what was effectively a military junta that was formed in November 1975. His ascendancy was welcomed by the people because of his personality and the heroic role he played in the war of independence. He completed a transition to civilian control and assumed the presidency.

Ziaur Rahman's administration gradually turned the socialist economic policies of the previous Awami League government in the direction of the free-market economy by easing and abolishing private investment caps and selling some small and medium-sized state enterprises. It raised wages substantially for the employees of government departments and state enterprises in an attempt to increase real wages, which had lost much ground to inflation. Despite the continuation of expansionist fiscal and monetary policies, the inflation rate fell to 9.5% and the economic growth rate increased to about 6% as the government was blessed with a steady recovery in agricultural production under good weather conditions, favorable and abundant foreign aid from the West, and ample foreign currency holdings that were built up by remittances from workers in the Middle East.

The period from the independence of Bangladesh to the end of the 1970s can be described as the process of recovery from the post-independence economic exhaustion and turmoil. Rice production and production levels of the major manufacturing industries returned to pre-independence standards in 1977. The real wage rate for agricultural laborers did not show a sign of recovery for several more years and did not return to the highest pre-independence level until the mid-1980s.

The Ershad Era (1982–90)

Ziaur Rahman was assassinated in May 1981 and a military junta led by H. M. Ershad seized power following the bloodless coup of March 1982. Ershad became President in December 1983. He was reappointed in October 1986 as a result of the general election following a transition to civilian control and held power for a long period of almost nine years to December 1990, which was somewhat unusual in Bangladesh.

The Ershad administration inherited Ziaur Rahman's political line but with a clearer emphasis on liberalization of the economy. The following policy changes were pursued under its New Industrial Policy of 1982 and Revised Industrial Policy of 1986. First, a bold plan for disposal of state enterprises was implemented. Many large-scale factories, including those in the jute and cotton industries that had been exempted from a sell-off, were sold to the private sector. Second, private sector investment was encouraged. The number of industries with a private investment ban was reduced, preferential tax treatment was introduced, and the procedures for approval and financing were simplified. Third, foreign capital was introduced. Fourth, export-oriented industries were fostered. Various incentives for export industries were introduced, including lower interest rates for export finance, lower import tariffs and other preferential tax measures, and favorable exchange rates for foreign currency earnings. An export processing zone was established in Chittagong and began operating in 1984.

Despite these investment incentives for private capital, the industrial sector generally failed to achieve strong growth during the 1980s. While the economy as a whole grew at a rate of about 4% per annum, the growth rate for the industrial sector stagnated at 3.8% over the decade. The share of manufacturing industry in GDP fell by almost a percentage point from 10.8% in 1980 to 9.9% in 1990. The only large-scale industry that was newly set up during the 1980s was the chemical fertilizer industry. It is clear that the industrial sector failed to play the role of a powerful driving force behind economic growth during this period.

One major reason for the sluggish industrial sector in spite of numerous government incentives was capital constraint. This is clear from the fact that investment performance increased when access to credit was expanded by development financial institutions such as the Industrial Bank and Industry Financial Corporation. However, development financial institutions were plagued from the start by the nonperformance of their borrowers. They were faced with a rapid increase in unpaid debts in the first half of the 1980s, and foreign donors declared in 1985 that they would freeze the supply of funds unless repayment rates improved. In fact, many of the purchasers of former state-owned factories were slow in making payments. The problem was not a simple matter of capital constraint but rather the behavioral pattern of mercantile capitalist-like industrial capitalists, which hindered the establishment of a sound financial system.

Let us look next at trends in the agricultural sector and agricultural policy in the 1980s. During this period the agricultural sector experienced a major change, which was prompted by a turnaround in agricultural policy. The major shift in agricultural policy was, in fact, initiated at the end of the 1970s and advanced in stages until the end of the 1980s. It entailed a series of deregulation and liberalization measures such as the reduction and abolishment of subsidies for fertilizers and other inputs, the deregulation and privatization of fertilizer distribution, the privatization of irrigation facilities, and import liberalization of diesel engines for irrigation. This process was indirectly supported by the rapid development of rural finances.

The agricultural sector achieved an annual growth rate of 2.7% during the 1980s, which substantially exceeded the population growth rate of 2.2%.

Production of rice, the country's main crop, grew at a high rate of more than 3% per annum. Agricultural growth was mainly reliant on the development of small-scale pump irrigation systems for the dry season. Surface water irrigation using low lift pumps began in the mid-1960s and continued until the mid-1970s. From then on, the development of groundwater irrigation by tubewells accelerated and, in particular, the rapid diffusion of STWs throughout the 1980s boosted the cropped area and yield of dry-season irrigated *boro* rice dramatically.[4] It meant that the Green Revolution had finally arrived in Bangladesh, and the long-held desire for self-sufficiency in rice was fulfilled in the early 1990s.

However, agricultural growth through the diffusion of STWs gave rise to a new problem in income distribution. The irrigation privatization policy prompted wealthy farmers to acquire irrigation facilities. When the availability of rural finance was rapidly expanded from the end of the 1970s to the early 1980s, it was mainly wealthy farmers who took out loans and invested in tubewell construction. The problem was that they fell into serious delinquency on their debts, even though they made massive profits by selling irrigation water to small and medium-sized farmers. Like the development financial institutions for the industrial sector, the supply of funds to agricultural finance was frozen by donors in 1985.

Despite this credit tightening, the pace of agricultural growth did not slow down. A record-breaking heavy flood in 1987 and again in 1988 caused a considerable decrease in production of wet-season *aman* rice in two consecutive seasons. In order to cover the loss by increasing production of dry-season irrigated *boro* rice, the government decided to liberalize the importation of diesel engines for STWs. As a result, Chinese-made engines, which were far cheaper than the previously available Japanese engines, flooded the market and increased the profitability of *boro* rice production and further accelerated its expansion. With a sudden drop in the cost of STWs, wealthy farmers were now able to purchase them with their own money without relying on loans.

The 1980s also witnessed a rapid growth in non-agricultural, non-manufacturing sectors such as the commerce and service sector. According to Table 1.1, which shows trends in GDP shares by sector, during the 1980–90 period agriculture lost its share by about eleven points, which was taken up by the commerce and service sector. It is also clear from a comparison of sector shares in the employment structure between 1961, 1974, 1985–86, and 1995–96 (Table 1.3) that the tertiary sector (such as commerce/hospitality, public/private services, transport/storage/communication, and finance/real estate industries) played a very significant role in absorbing labor compared with the agricultural and manufacturing industries. In the case of Bangladesh, one characteristic of these changes in the industrial and employment structures was that, in relative terms,

Table 1.3: Changes in Bangladesh's employment structure ('000 persons)

	1961		1974		1985–86		1995–96	
Agriculture, forestry and fishery	14,240	(84.6%)	16,840	(78.7%)	17,460	(57.1%)	20,600	(51.1%)
Mining	0		0		0		0	
Manufacturing	810	(4.8%)	1,030	(4.8%)	3,020	(9.9%)	4,000	(9.9%)
Electricity, gas and water	10	(0.1%)	10	(0.0%)	40	(0.1%)	100	(0.3%)
Construction	90	(0.5%)	40	(0.2%)	650	(2.1%)	1,000	(2.5%)
Trade, hotels and restaurants	620	(3.7%)	840	(3.9%)	3,830	(12.5%)	6,000	(14.8%)
Transport, communication and storage	200	(1.2%)	350	(1.6%)	1,320	(4.3%)	2,300	(5.7%)
Finance and real estate	10	(0.1%)	60	(0.3%)	370	(1.2%)	200	(0.5%)
Public and personal services	770	(4.6%)	2,240	(10.5%)	2,560	(8.4%)	5,000	(12.5%)
Servants and others	70	(0.4%)	-		1,210	(4.0%)	1,100	(2.7%)
Total	16830	(100.0%)	21410	(100.0%)	30,560	(100.0%)	40,300	(100.0%)
Growth rate of labor forces (per annum)	–		1.87%		3.01%		2.81%	

Sources: 1961 & 1974: Fujita (1993b: 222). 1985/86 & 1995/96: BBS (1996: 57, 77).

Figure 1.1: Movement of agricultural labor wage rate in Bangladesh

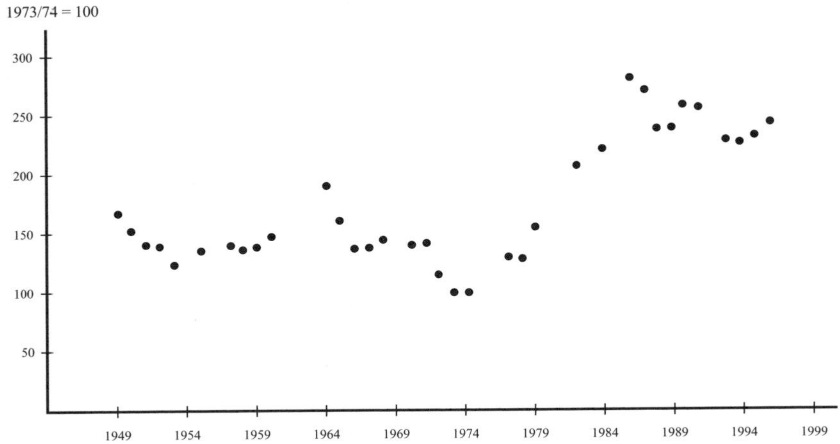

Sources:
1950–1979/80: Khan, A.R., (1984: 190)
1973/74–1995: Sen, (1997: 152)
1994/95–1996/97: *BBS, Monthly Statistical Bulletin of Bangladesh*, various issues

they were not accompanied by a large-scale population influx into major cities. A *rural surplus labor* created by a population explosion was mostly absorbed by medium to small regional cities or the informal sector in the rural area.

The economic growth at an annual rate of about 4% during the 1980s, combined with a fall in population growth, brought about an increase in per capita income of 1.8% per annum. The development of the rural economy driven by the full-scale diffusion of the Green Revolution led to an increase in the real wage rate of agricultural laborers (Figure 1.1). The percentage of absolutely poor households in the rural area decreased from 71% in 1974 to 65% in 1982, 50% in 1984, 41% in 1986, 44% in 1989, and 38% in 1990. In other words, it recovered to the lowest pre-independence level of 44% in 1964.

Rapid Growth in the Civilian Government Era (1991–2001)

Unable to resist the rising tide of the anti-government democratization movement, Ershad finally stepped down from office in December 1990 and the Bangladesh Nationalist Party (BNP) led by Khaleda Zia (the wife of the late President Ziaur Rahman) came to power after the February 1991 general election. Bangladesh's civilian government era from then on can be broadly divided into the BNP administration period to 1995 and the Awami League administration period from 1996 until 2001. Although the BNP returned to power after its landslide victory in a general election at the end of the full term of the government in October 2001, the most recent period from that point to date has to be omitted from this study.

The BNP Administration Period (1991–95)

It appears that the Bangladeshi economy underwent a certain kind of structural change in the 1990s (or possibly slightly earlier, in the second half of the 1980s). This was expressed in the form of an improvement in macroeconomic indicators and a slightly stronger growth of the manufacturing sector.

The improvement in macroeconomic conditions can be seen in changes in various indicators summarized in Table 1.4. (In one aspect, the macroeconomic improvement was a result of the International Monetary Fund/World Bank-led structural adjustment policy pursued from the early 1980s.)

First, the gross domestic saving rate increased. The rate was about 8% when Bangladesh was still called East Pakistan, dropped to 0% in the post-independence turmoil, remained low at 1.2% until the end of the 1980s, then rapidly improved after 1991 to 9% in 1994.

Second, the gross investment rate increased. It remained sluggish at just below 13% until the end of the 1980s, began to rise quickly in 1993, and reached 17% in 1997. The increase was underpinned by a rapid increase in private investment. After staying low at around 7%, the private investment rate rapidly increased from 1993 and reached almost 11% in 1996. The public sector investment rate also rose from 1994. This is clear from Table 1.5, which shows a jump in government development expenditure. In relation to this, it is even more noteworthy that this jump in expenditure was accompanied by a marked decrease in the level of dependency on foreign aid for development expenditure.

Third, the scale of government finances expanded. The government's annual revenue remained low at 8% to 9% of GDP until the end of the 1980s, then increased to over 12% in 1993–96 following the introduction of value-added tax in 1991. Government expenditure (general government expenditure plus development expenditure) also increased from the previous 15% to 16% level to 18% to 19% in the mid-1990s.

Fourth, exports increased rapidly. Exports represented just over 6% of GDP in the mid-1980s but continued to rise during the 1990s, reaching 12.2% in 1996. The variety of exported goods also increased as the country's exports continued to expand. In 1973, shortly after independence, the two traditional export items of raw material jute and jute products accounted for more than 90% of the total export value. From the mid-1980s, the volume of new export items (such as frozen shrimps and other frozen foods, leather products, and garments) increased

Table 1.4: Changes in Bangladesh's macroeconomic indicators (% of GDP)

	1973–75 (MUJIBLE RAHMAN)	1976–81 (ZIAUR RAHMAN)	1982–90 (ERSHAD)	1991–95 (KHALEDA ZIA)	1996	1997	1998	1999
Gross domestic saving	–0.1	1.1	2.4	6.5	7.5	7.5	8.6	8.4
Gross investment	5.5	12.7	12.9	14.0	17.0	17.3	17.8	18.5
Public investment	2.0	6.1	6.2	6.5	6.3	6.5	6.6	7.0
Private investment	3.5	6.6	6.7	7.5	10.7	10.8	11.2	11.5
Savings–investment gap	–5.6	–11.6	–10.5	–7.5	–9.5	–9.8	–9.2	–10.0
Government revenue	5.1	8.3	8.5	11.4	11.9	11.2	12.1	11.9
Government expenditure	13.5	15.8	15.2	17.7	17.2	17.3	17.5	17.2
Fiscal balance	–8.4	–7.5	–6.7	–6.3	–6.3	–5.1	–5.4	–5.3
ADP foreign aid dependency rate	n.a.	n.a.	n.a.	74.1	48.2	47.4	43.3	n.a.
Export	4.3	4.9	6.3	9.5	12.2	13.5	15.2	15.9
Import	11.2	16.6	16.8	16.6	21.6	21.8	22.1	n.a.
Trade balance	–6.9	–10.6	–10.6	–7.1	–9.4	–8.3	–6.9	n.a.
Current account balance	–2.6	–3 .9	–3.9	–2.9	–5.0	–1.6	–1.5	n.a.
Foreign currency reserve (billion dollars)	n.a.	n.a.	n.a.	2.1	2.0	1.7	1.7	1.7
Growth rate of CPI	41.9	9.5	10.1	4.5	4.1	3.9	6.4	n.a.
Real wage of industrial laborers (1970=100)	56	74	102	110	114	120	122	n.a.

Real interest rate of deposit	–38.4	–4.7	–1.7	n.a.	n.a.	n.a.	n.a.	n.a.
Real interest rate of borrowing	–30.6	2.0	4.3	n.a.	n.a.	n.a.	n.a.	n.a.
Financial deepening (M2/GNP)	15.8	15.2	24.2	33.2	35.1	36.1	36.1	34.2
Population growth rate	2.5	2.4	2.0	1.9	N.A.	N.A.	N.A.	N.A.

Note: Government expenditure is a total of general account expenditure and annual development program (ADP).

Sources: To 1990: Hossain, (1996: 90–1, 94–5) From 1991: Ministry of Finance (1999).

Table 1.5: Bangladesh's annual development expenditure (actual) and sector shares

	Nominal expenditure (billion *taka*)	Real expenditure (billion *taka*)	Agriculture, rural development and water resources	Industry	Electricity and natural resources	Transport and communication	Regional planning and housing	Education	Health, family planning and social welfare	Local government	Others
1984	30.1	32.0	31.1	7.8	23.2	9.8	5.5	4.3	5.7	10.6	2.0
1985	31.7	31.7	24.4	4.5	27.3	10.7	3.6	3.9	6.7	12.8	6.1
1986	34.3	31.2	20.9	15.7	27.7	8.7	3.3	3.7	4.9	5.0	10.1
1987	44.4	36.4	17.1	15.7	26.0	10.8	3.1	4.5	4.5	7.7	10.6
1988	41.5	31.6	19.3	10.4	23.6	13.6	4.0	5.1	5.8	9.9	8.3
1989	46.2	32.6	22.0	10.4	21.3	18.4	3.5	4.5	6.3	4.4	9.2
1990	57.2	38.6	25.9	7.5	17.8	16.2	5.0	4.0	6.0	5.8	11.8
1991	52.7	32.5	22.9	1.8	14.2	14.1	4.4	3.3	8.7	2.8	27.8
1992	60.2	35.6	21.2	2.0	17.8	16.6	5.2	5.0	6.8	5.2	20.2
1993	65.5	38.7	20.7	1.1	22.7	17.0	3.6	8.1	7.4	8.2	11.2
1994	89.8	50.9	17.4	1.7	21.1	23.2	3.5	10.2	7.6	7.6	7.7
1995	103.0	53.7	18.1	1.3	17.1	23.3	4.7	14.2	8.2	4.0	9.1
1996	100.2	49.3	16.9	1.5	17.8	23.0	4.3	13.0	6.8	n.a.	16.7
1997	110.4	53.4	21.6	1.4	17.9	24.2	5.4	13.2	7.9	n.a.	8.9
1998	110.4	51.4	23.3	1.0	25.2	21.0	5.0	12.2	9.6	n.a.	2.7

Note: Real expenditures were calculated using the GDP deflator based on the 1985 price.

Sources: World Bank (1990: 194). World Bank (1996: 75). Ministry of Finance (1999).

rapidly. The growth of exported garment (and knit) products was particularly marked, with its share in the total export value jumping from 12% in 1985 to 50% in 1991 and to 63% in 1996. However, imports accounted for just below 17% from the mid-1970s to 1990 before falling to below 15% in 1991–92, and rising again to reach 21.6% in 1996 and to contribute to a widening trade deficit.

Fifth, Bangladesh's foreign currency position improved. A marked improvement in its current account balance from 1992 to 1994, in particular, resulted in the accumulation of foreign currency. Foreign currency reserves peaked at \$3.5 billion in April 1995.

Sixth, inflation eased. The rate of inflation was chronically high at around 10% until the end of the 1980s, but it averaged below 5% in the first half of the 1990s. The years 1993 and 1994 saw a marked improvement to below 2%, but this was mainly due to a substantial fall in rice prices, as discussed below. With the easing of inflation, the real deposit rate, which remained negative until the end of the 1980s, moved into positive territory for the first time during the 1990s, contributing to the aforementioned jump in the gross domestic saving rate.

Let us look at the development of the manufacturing sector, which was responsible for a rapid increase in private investment. The accelerated growth of the manufacturing sector, especially the large-scale manufacturing industry, began in the second half of the 1980s according to Table 1.2. It should be noted that it went into a high growth phase at almost 10% in the 1990s. On the other hand, the agricultural sector stagnated during the first half of the 1990s and recorded a negative growth rate in 1995, as discussed below. However, the 1995 GDP growth rate was sustained at 4.4% by the strong growth of the non-agricultural sector driven by the manufacturing industry. This was the first instance in the history of Bangladesh in which a negative agricultural growth rate did not result in a large drop in its economic growth rate.

The introduction of foreign capital had been encouraged since the Ershad era and finally began to gather speed in the 1990s. The total number of registered foreign corporations outside of export processing zones was 596 by June 1996, and 459 or 77% of which were set up in and after 1991. (Seventy-one and twenty foreign corporations respectively were operating in export processing zones in Chittagong and Dhaka.)

However, it must be pointed out that the growth of the large-scale manufacturing industry from the mid-1980s still had some major problems. The biggest problem was that high growth was achieved only in a small number of industries such as garments, pharmaceuticals, *bidhi* (popular tobacco), sugar, and chemical fertilizers, demonstrating that broad-based industrialization was yet to be realized (Table 1.6). Furthermore, the rapidly developing garment

Table 1.6: Bangladesh's manufacturing growth in the 1990s

	Growth rate					
Share	Over 10%	8–10%	6–8%	4–6%	0–4%	Negative growth
5% and above	Handlooms Pharmaceuticals		Chemical fertilizer	Tea processing		Jute Cotton
2–5%	*Bidhi*	Sugar		Leather	Tobacco	Paper
1–2%	Books & magazines Metal rolling Silk & rayon Compressed gas	Fish processing		Soap Leather shoes Milling	Dye & bleach Cement	
0.5–1%			Baking Lamps	Petroleum products Newspapers	Clay brick	Battery cells Motor vehicles Alcohol Ship building Ceramics Rubber shoes
0.25–0.5%	Salt Perfume & cosmetics		Cable Carpets & rugs	Polyvinyl chloride	Aluminum utensils Match	Cooking oil Electrical appliances TV Agrochemicals

Below 0.25%	Paint & varnish		Timber furniture	Vertical devices		Electrical devices
	Glassware			Soft drink		Metal processing
						Motorcycles
						Iron & steel
						Wooden ware
						Engines & turbines
						Weaving machines
						Electrical machines
Total	11	2	6	10	6	21

Note: The growth rate is based on the average growth rate for each category for 1989–96. The share is each category's share of the total added value of the manufacturing sector. The industry categories are based on the four-digit industry classification system.

Source: Centre for Policy Dialogue (1997: 293).

industry relied heavily on imported raw materials, with the ratio of domestically added value being about 30%. It has to be said that Bangladesh had not yet achieved fully fledged industrialization.

Finally, the agricultural (especially rice) sector tended to stagnate noticeably in the first half of the 1990s. The annual agricultural growth rate from 1990 to 1995 was a mere 1.0% and, in particular, the crop sector, which centered on rice, recorded a pitiful growth rate of 0.4%. The main reason for this was the falling price of rice. The nominal rice price dropped by about 30% over a period of nineteen months from September 1992 to February 1994 compared with the previous year. Reasons for this slump were said to include a massive amount of private stock that was released into the market after three consecutive years of bumper harvest and the loss of a balance between supply and demand caused by a sudden reduction in the amount of government-procured domestic rice from 960,000 tons in 1992 to 230,000 tons in 1993 and 150,000 tons in 1994. Moreover, a combination of soaring prices and a shortage of chemical fertilizers dealt a serious blow to dry-season irrigated *boro* rice cropping from the end of 1994; in particular, it caused a huge loss to STW owners selling irrigation water. Consequently, the pace of STW diffusion slowed and more farmers redirected their irrigation water from rice to wheat, vegetables, and potatoes.

In the mid-1990s, the government retracted its earlier declaration of rice self-sufficiency and resumed rice imports, which increased from almost zero in 1991 to 810,000 tons in 1995 and to 1.14 million tons in 1996. Wheat imports (including foreign aid) also increased rapidly from 890,000 tons to 1.76 million tons in 1995 and to 1.29 million tons in 1996. Thus, the share of rice and wheat as a proportion of the total import value rose from about 1% in 1992 to 8% in 1996, eating into precious foreign currency reserves.

The Awami League Administration Period (1996–2001)

Amid an intensifying confrontation between the ruling and opposition parties that started around 1994, Prime Minister Khaleda Zia was at last forced to dissolve the parliament in November 1995. Following a general election, the Awami League led by Hasina (the daughter of Mujibur Rahman) returned to power in June 1996 after twenty-one years in opposition.

Bangladesh's economic growth broke the 5% barrier and continued on a higher growth path during the second half of the 1990s (Table 1.2). As the population growth rate decreased further from 1.8% to 1.5%–1.6%, its per capita economic growth reached its highest-ever level in the range of 3% to 4%.

One reason for this high growth rate was a rapid recovery of the agricultural sector from a slump during the first half of the 1990s. Especially, production of the main crop of rice increased steadily. In 1998 Bangladesh was struck by a major flood as extensive as the one a decade earlier, which caused a serious loss in the *aman* rice crop. However, an unprecedented increase in dry-season *boro* production immediately afterwards resulted in an increase in the overall rice production of 2.2% over the previous year. In the following year, rice production increased by a remarkable 16.1% as the production of *aman* recovered. Although rice production followed exactly the same course of loss, recovery, and increase after a major flood disaster as in the case ten years earlier, the key difference this time was that the increase in *boro* production was achieved through an increased yield rather than an increased cropping area (by an expansion of irrigation). Food production returned to a steadily rising trend that substantially exceeded the rate of population growth of the 1980s and the real price of rice fell sharply, prompting the government to declare that the country had achieved food-sufficiency once again, just as it had done in the early 1990s. With per capita rice consumption leveling off in recent years, Bangladesh has been showing clear signs of shaking off the Ricardian Trap.[5]

In contrast to the strong performance of the agricultural sector, manufacturing growth slowed during this period compared with the BNP administration period. And the strains of aggressive fiscal policy, which is considered as the main cause of economic growth during the Awami League administration period, have gradually surfaced in recent times (after 2001). Exports of garments, which had reached as high as 75% of the total export value, began to slow and, together with a rapid expansion of imports during this period, caused a rapid depletion of foreign currency reserves. (After peaking at \$3.5 billion in 1995, Bangladesh's foreign currency holdings steadily decreased to \$1.54 billion at the end of 1997 and hit its lowest level at \$1.09 billion in October 2001 shortly after the September 11 terrorist attacks.)

The Bangladesh economy remained on a fairly high and stable growth path at an annual rate of 5% and appeared to be filled with an optimism that belied the gloomy conditions that had existed immediately after its independence. However, its path was somewhat distorted in that the growth was underpinned by the development of the tertiary sector rather than the manufacturing sector.

The Significance of the 1980s (and 1990s)

It is clear from the above overview that the 1980s was a very important period in the course of Bangladesh's economic growth. The agricultural sector underwent marked growth to achieve food (rice) sufficiency. Rising economic standards and mitigation of poverty in the rural area, where a majority of the population lived, boosted the consumer goods purchasing power considerably. To exaggerate slightly, the signs of macroeconomic stabilization and full-scale high growth of the economy, including the manufacturing sector, during the 1990s perhaps could not have emerged without this underlying support.

Although the situation during and after the 1990s provided Bangladesh with a great opportunity to begin full-scale and sustainable economic growth centering on the development of export-oriented manufacturing industries, it is difficult to say that its potential was fully realized. It is believed that there are two major reasons for this.[6] One is that the economy stagnated along the way for nearly a decade from the early 1990s (when an agricultural slump pushed it back slightly) to the late 1990s (when agriculture returned to the previous growth path and achieved food self-sufficiency again). The other, more serious reason is that the inflow of direct foreign investment slowed after peaking in 1998, constraining the development of export-oriented manufacturing industries that should have been driving the economy.[7] This slowdown in direct foreign investment can be regarded as a more serious problem because it was caused by distinctly structural factors such as the deterioration in the law and order problem (especially after the country's transition to civilian government), a spate of *hartar* (general strikes), underdeveloped infrastructure, and the problem of labor force quality.

These are very important issues to consider for the future development of Bangladesh's economy but I will refrain from discussing them further since they are outside the scope of this study.[8]

I would like to discuss in more detail the significance of agricultural development during the 1980s and a concomitant rise in rural economic standards by presenting specific data below.

Bangladesh has often been referred to as a typical case of 'absolute poverty structure' or 'stagnant Asia' (Watanabe 1982; 1985). It was described as a classic Malthusian world, or a typical low-level equilibrium world, in which an enormous force is at work to constantly pull down the populace to the level of bare subsistence (absolute poverty) because any increase in food production is swallowed up by a growing population that increases at around the same rate. This logic regards *population pressure* as the primary defining factor.

It is undeniable that the conditions that existed in Bangladesh until the end of the 1970s made Watanabe's logic appear somewhat reasonable. Let us go back to Figure 1.1. This graph shows a long-term downward trend in real wages of agricultural laborers to the end of the 1970s.

This trend becomes even more evident if we look back to the British colonial period. A comparison of wages (based on the amount of milled rice that could be bought with the daily wage) shows that it was four to six *seer* (one *seer* = 0.93 kilograms) in the early twentieth century (data from 1908 and 1918), and that it dropped dramatically to 1.5 *seer* in 1973/74 and 1.4 *seer* in 1974/75; it was 2.4 *seer* in 1975/76, 2.3 *seer* in 1976/77, 2.1 *seer* in 1977/78, 2.4 *seer* in 1978/79, 1.9 *seer* in 1979/80, 2.4 *seer* in 1980/81, and 2.2 *seer* in 1981/82 (Schendel and Faraizi 1984). Real wages in the late 1970s were floundering at an extremely low level, at around half of the early twentieth-century level. On the other hand, the population was literally exploding as it increased at an annual rate of more than 2.6% during the 1970s.

However, it is quite inconceivable that the classic mechanism whereby an increase in population is induced by even a small amount of surplus food production was operating in Bangladesh, even in those days. It would be more logical to think that the population explosion was mainly caused by a falling mortality rate, especially for infants, and was basically independent of changes in food production. It is reasonable to say that the fundamental error in the application of the classic mechanism has been proven sufficiently by subsequent trends such as the development of the economy, a slowdown in population growth, and a resultant reduction in the size of the population of absolute poor.

Boyce (1987), who tracked and analyzed an agrarian impasse in Bengal up to the end of the 1970s using detailed statistical data, adopted a different viewpoint from that of Watanabe and looked for a fundamental cause for stagnation in the agrarian structure, especially inequality in the land distribution structure, rather than the population. However, he was similar to Watanabe in his strong pessimism for the future of the Bangladeshi economy because he limited his analysis to the end of the 1970s. It is possible to say that this so-called agrarian structural constraint theory has also proven to be fundamentally erroneous by the historical fact that Bangladeshi agriculture achieved rapid growth without any major change in its structure during and after the 1980s.

Figure 1.2 shows long-term trends in the production of rice and wheat in Bangladesh. It is evident from the graph that the increase in food production accelerated after the late 1970s. Figure 1.3 shows movements in the real price of rice (using the consumer price index as the deflator) over the same period. The price of a kilogram of rice, using the 1997 figure as the base price, continued its downward trend from the Bangladeshi *taka* (Tk) 16–20 range at the end of the 1970s and the early 1980s to around Tk13 in the early 1990s, and then down to just over Tk10 at the end of the 1990s. This clearly declining real price of food indicates that agricultural growth from the 1980s was based on productivity improvement through technological innovation.

Also, the substantial drop in the real price of the staple food, rice, by itself would have had an enormous poverty reduction effect in light of the true state

Figure 1.2: Production trend of rice and wheat in Bangladesh

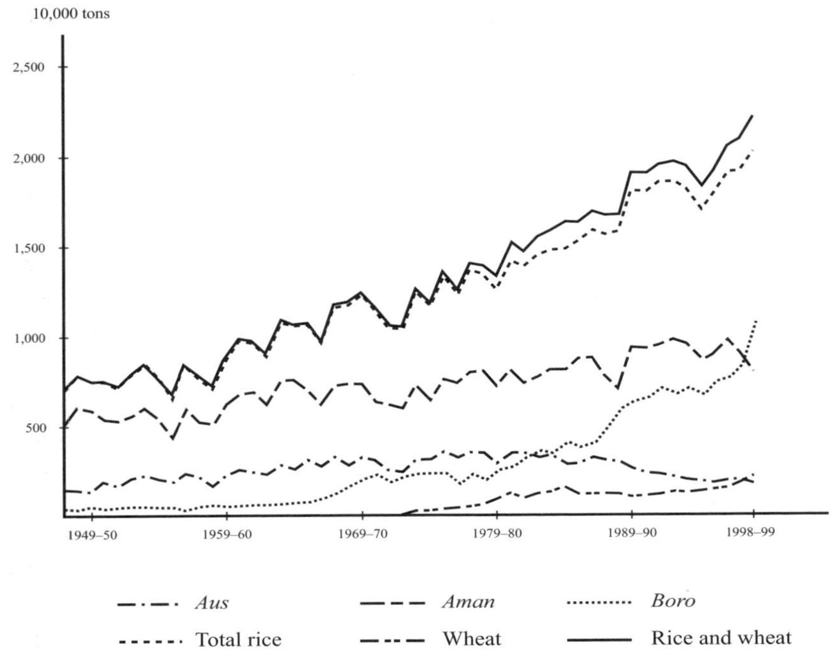

of household expenditure in Bangladesh, where the Engel coefficient was 58% (rural 64%, urban 46%) and the expenditure on grain alone was 26% (rural 31%, urban 14%), even in the mid-1990s (BBS 1998). One proof of this is the dramatic rise in real wages of agricultural laborers as shown in Figure 1.1. By the way, an estimate of the most recent wage in rice is around four *seer*, which means that it has almost recovered to the early twentieth-century level.

To summarize, Bangladesh has undergone structural changes in its economy that were solid enough to eradicate the image of *absolute poverty structure* or *stagnant Asia* from the 1980s as it experienced advancements in agricultural technological innovation, particularly in the rice sector, and marked growth in the non-agricultural sector a little later. In the rural area, highly (land) intensive and (land) productive farming was carried out despite further fragmentation and shrinking of farm size, and, at the same time, it became more common for a majority of rural households, including landless households and small farming units, to shift their main sources of income from purely farming to various rural non-farming activities, such as farm product processing and marketing and rural

Figure 1.3: Real rice price in Bangladesh (1997)

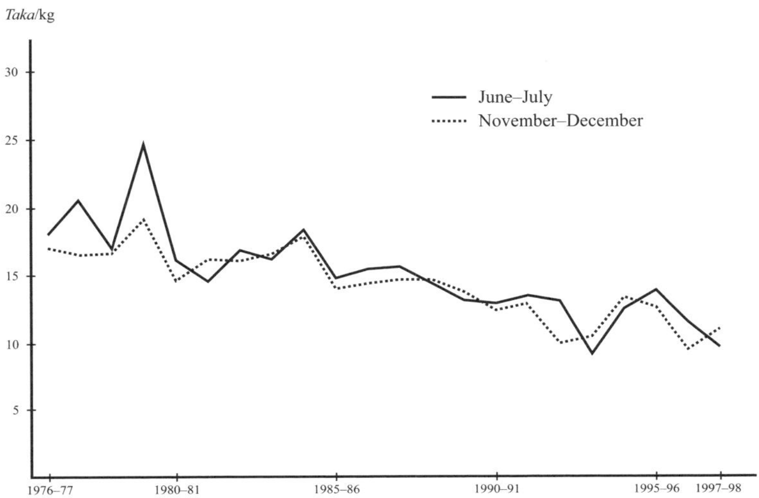

consumer goods distribution. As mentioned in the introduction, the current study presents the viewpoint that these structural changes were fundamentally underpinned, and induced, by agricultural growth mainly based on the Green Revolution in the production of the major grain crop of rice from the 1980s.

Part I
The Green Revolution and Rural Class Structure

2
The Formation of the Groundwater Market and Rural Income Distribution: The Emergence of Waterlords

The Groundwater Market as the Key

Before embarking on a thorough discussion about the groundwater market for irrigation, I would like to devote some space to explain why it is an important issue in the context of Bangladeshi agriculture.

The bulk of Bangladeshi farmland is located in one of the largest tropical deltas in the world. Reclamation and development is historically slower in deltas than in more upstream riverine areas because of difficulty with water control and, especially, because it is difficult to secure both habitable space during the wet season and water for domestic use during the dry season (Takaya 1987). As with the three big tropical deltas in Southeast Asia (the Chao Phraya Delta in Thailand, the Ayeyarwaddy Delta in Myanmar, and the Mekong Delta in Vietnam), the Bengal Delta is no exception in this regard.

However, the Bengal Delta is distinct from the three big Southeast Asian tropical deltas in at least one aspect. As reported by Andō and Uchida (1994: 24), the Bengal Delta forms an ecological environment that is greatly different from that of, say, the Chao Phraya Delta in that its topography 'is abundant with micro-topographic undulations such as natural embankments and back swamps with a notable presence of clay soil in low lands and arable soil consisting of sand, silt and loam in higher lands that are suitable for upland farming.' The Bengal Delta was reclaimed much earlier than the three big Southeast Asian tropical deltas and, because of its distinct ecological environmental conditions, experienced the evolution of a complex farming system consisting of rice farming (which is also quite diverse and complex) and upland farming.

Yet, agriculture in the Bengal Delta was developed only through more passive human adaptation to seasonal fluctuations in the hydrological environment ('agronomic adaptation' according to Ishii 1975) due to the technological difficulty with water control, which was common to all tropical deltas but particularly serious in the Bengal Delta. From another perspective, it was an environment that was susceptible to a certain type of 'agricultural involution' (Geertz 1963). It had to follow a development path that was clearly different from the agricultural development that took place in, for example, the Punjab region, another British Indian province, which was triggered by large-scale investment in the canal irrigation system ('engineering adaptation').

The Green Revolution began in Asia in the mid-1960s but initially bypassed the Bengal Delta because water control was an essential condition for the diffusion of the seed-fertilizer technology. What happened in the Bengal Delta was an agricultural involution-type technological change in which the cultivation of *aus* rice, which was traditionally grown in higher lands in the early wet season, expanded into low lands and gave rise to double cropping with transplanted *aman* rice or mixed cropping with broadcast *aman* rice.[1]

This does not mean that there has never been water control in the Bengal Delta. Traditionally, *boro* rice was cultivated in the lowest-lying lands with residual water from the wet season, and was irrigated by manual pumping of surface water at times of water shortage. When the Green Revolution technology represented by high-yielding varieties (HYVs) became available in the late 1960s, trials of dry-season irrigated rice cultivation (*boro*) using diesel oil-powered pumping of surface water were started. At the same time, the government began to install DTWs in some areas in an attempt to introduce dry-season irrigated rice cultivation in higher lands. However, the very slow progress of this initiative prompted vigorous debates about its motives (this phenomenon of slow irrigation progress was common to Bangladesh and eastern India, the poverty-stricken rice-growing regions).

Arguments about possible reasons for the slow pace of tubewell investment include the following. First, it was argued that a land consolidation program for small and fragmented farmlands was essential in realizing economies of scale of the tubewell irrigation technology, and the lack of advancement in this process was hindering investment in tubewells.[2] The seriousness of this problem was much the same for STWs, with a maximum irrigation capacity of fifteen to twenty acres (around ten acres in reality), and DTWs, with a larger capacity of sixty to eighty acres, due to the smallness of the average farm size and the extreme fragmentation of farmland in the rice-growing regions of the eastern Indian subcontinent, including Bangladesh.

The second argument was the *capital constraint hypothesis*, which claimed that farmers did not have sufficient capital to invest in expensive tubewells.[3] The third argument sought to locate fundamental reasons in the agrarian structure or semi-feudal mode of production that determined the first and second factors at higher levels. The eastern part of the Indian subcontinent, including Bangladesh, was characterized by inequalities in its land ownership structure that divided the rural population into two opposite groups: relatively large landlords (one group) and small farmers, tenant farmers, and landless agricultural laborers (the other group). It was argued that, as long as the former group *exploited* the latter through marketing of agricultural products and finance, it was natural that farmland consolidation and the introduction of tubewells were slow because a cooperative relationship between the two groups was absolutely vital for implementing these programs.[4] It was also argued that landlords were the main thwarters of new technologies because their introduction would improve the economy of the poor and thereby remove the very condition that had enabled exploitation of the poor by the wealthy.[5]

Regardless of these arguments, however, the actual situation changed dramatically in an unexpected direction in the 1980s. The introduction of tubewells, especially STWs, began to spread rapidly and marked agricultural development (based on the adoption of dry-season irrigated rice production) took place in a wide area. This development easily defeated at least the first argument, above, since it was achieved with almost no land consolidation.

So, what brought about the rapid dissemination of STWs?[6]

First, there is no doubt that a substantial decline in the (real) price of STWs played an important role. In Bangladesh, diesel engines for tubewells were supplied exclusively by Japanese farm machinery manufacturers such as Yanmar, Kubota, and Mitsubishi from the 1970s to the mid-1980s. As a secondhand market for these Japanese engines developed gradually, and as Korean and Chinese engines arrived on the market, the tubewell price dropped substantially and became affordable for farmers. This situation became firmly established, especially under the Bangladeshi government's import liberalization policy for engines, which was implemented immediately after the devastating flood of 1988.

In addition, it is impossible to disregard the fact that, in order to cover a shortage of funds when Japanese engines had a market monopoly, the government set up a low-interest rate loan program for farmers who wished to invest in tubewells. The role of the policy-oriented finance as a pump-priming measure up to that point cannot be understated, even though many farmers went on to fund the purchase of tubewells by themselves, without relying on a bank loan, once the tubewell price declined as mentioned above. In other words, the aforementioned capital constraint hypothesis appears to have been at least partially valid.

So, how was the problem of farmland fragmentation overcome? Selling water was the answer. The key to the solution was not co-purchase and co-ownership of tubewells by small farmers but the establishment of a relationship in which certain wealthy upper-class farmers purchased and installed tubewells and sold irrigation water as a commodity to poor farmers who cultivated the farmlands surrounding the tubewells. The emergence of such a groundwater market enabled poor farmers to adopt irrigated farming, instantly spreading dry-season irrigated rice cultivation and achieving rapid development of agriculture. The groundwater market played an extremely significant role for agricultural development in this region.

However, at least two questions arise here. The first question is how terms for groundwater sales, especially the water price, were set and how they influenced income distribution between tubewell owners and non-owners.[7] This question is concerned with the criticism that exorbitantly high water prices allowed tubewell owners to dominate rural areas as *waterlords* rather than as landlords. The second question relates to the fact that groundwater was a very special commodity that had *externality*, even though water trading became widespread. Its technical properties and the social relationship between the seller and the buyer had significant impacts on the conditions and outcomes (for example, efficiency and income distribution) of the transaction. Is it possible to say that to deal with irrigation water as a pure commodity is an optimal (or at least appropriate) choice?

As is commonly known, the rise of neoliberalism worldwide since the 1980s has popularized the view that the market mechanism provides the most desirable solution in terms of efficiency and equality. Does it also apply to groundwater? A specific discussion of this question would be of great value, since irrigation is the key input for the diffusion of Green Revolution technologies. This is therefore the topic for discussion for the whole of Part I of this book, as well as this chapter.

In this chapter, the rapid development of the groundwater market until it reached 'saturation' in the early 1990s is analyzed through a case study of one village in northwestern Bangladesh. In Chapter 3, based on a case study of multiple villages in the same region, the transformation of the groundwater market by further expansion of tubewell investment after saturation and its significance are discussed. Finally, Chapter 4 looks towards a village in the neighboring Indian state of West Bengal in order to examine groundwater market issues under different policy and institutional conditions and the agro-ecological environment.

In the next section of this current chapter, net irrigation surplus and other analytical concepts for the groundwater market are explained. In the following section, after a brief overview of the study village, a step-by-step economic analysis of the groundwater market is undertaken. The last section presents a conclusion.

Determination of Irrigation Water Charges: Analytical Concepts for the Groundwater Market

How is the irrigation water charge determined when a farmer installs a tubewell and sells his water to other farmers who cultivate the surrounding farmlands? For the time being, let us assume a plausible situation of a seller's monopoly in which there is one water seller and several water buyers.[8]

Where π represents a profit gained by the tubewell owner during an irrigation season, A represents the acreage of the water sold (assuming that all the water is sold), c represents the variable cost per acre for tubewell operation (mainly fuel cost), F is the fixed capital cost, and w is the water charge per acre, the following relationship exists.

$$\pi = wA - cA - F$$

Assuming profit-maximizing behavior on the part of the tubewell owner, the equilibrium water charge w^* is determined as follows. Here, e represents the price elasticity of the demand for water.

$$w^* = e/(e-1) \times c$$

Figure 2.1 is a diagrammatic representation of the above. D is the demand for irrigation water, which is derived from rice production. Size of water sales area A^* is limited to the intersection point of the marginal revenue (MR) curve and the marginal cost (MC) curve derived from water demand function D, which in turn determines water charge w^*. A surplus represented by the shaded area is called the net irrigation surplus (NIS). NIS is calculated by subtracting the (actual) cost of irrigation and all non-irrigation costs (current input cost and labor cost) from the gross value of rice production. Theoretically, it is composed of land rent and profit, which are distributed to landowners and the tubewell owner respectively. Shah (1993) regarded the value of $e/(e-1)$ ($= w/c$) as a good indicator of the monopolistic power of the tubewell owner.

An Analysis of the Groundwater Market: The Case of Aira Village

Agriculture and Irrigation in the Study Village

Aira village is located on a diluvial plateau called the Barind Tract in Bogra district in northwestern Bangladesh. It had 209 households and 435 acres of land at the time of the 1992 survey. The Barind Tract had long been known

Figure 2.1: Water charge rate determination and net irrigation surplus

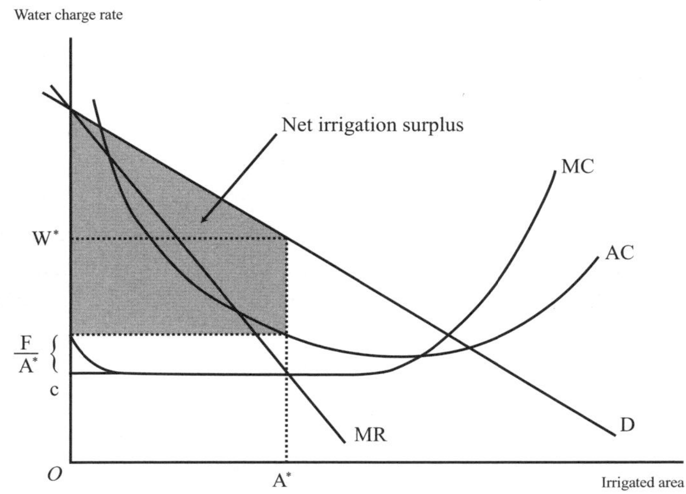

as a single-cropping area of wet-season transplanted *aman* rice until the rapid dissemination of STWs during the 1980s (Table 2.1), which boosted the irrigated area ratio to 90% by the early 1990s and established the double-rice cropping of transplanted *aman* and dry-season irrigated *boro* as the major cropping pattern (Table 2.2).

The acceleration of STW installation from the latter half of the 1980s, as shown in Table 2.1, was brought about under the following circumstances. The STW was an expensive piece of machinery, which cost around Tk30,000, because only Japanese-made diesel engines were permitted into the country until the mid-1980s. As a secondhand market for these Japanese imports developed, and after the importation of cheap Korean and Chinese diesel engines was liberalized in 1988, the nominal price of a STW was halved to around Tk15,000. The decline in price was even more substantial in real terms, given an annual inflation rate of around 10%. Two of the early STW buyers used bank loans but all subsequent purchases were in cash. It is clear that the decline in price made the STW affordable to farmers, especially upper-class farmers.

In Aira village there was no notable industry other than farming, and its social stratification was relatively clear-cut, with appreciable division between the farmer class and the agricultural laborer class (Table 2.3). Upper-class farmers were more enthusiastic about the introduction of STWs, with twenty-

Table 2.1: Introduction of STWs in Aira village

YEAR	NEW	TOTAL
1981	1	1
1982	0	1
1983	0	1
1984	3	4
1985	1	5
1986	0	5
1987	2	7
1988	3	10
1989	7	17
1990	6	23
1991	5	28
1992	2	30

Source: Compiled by the author based on the 1992 field survey.

Table 2.2: Agricultural use of land in Aira village

CROPPING PATTERN	AREA (ACRE)	SHARE (%)
Transplanted *aman–boro*	367	84
Aus–Transplanted *aman–khira*	14	3
Aus–Transplanted *aman–boro*	12	3
Boro	10	2
Others	33	8
Total	436	100

Note: *Aus* rice is cultivated in the early wet season, transplanted *aman* in the late wet season, and *boro* in the dry season. *Khira* is a type of cucurbitaceous vegetable.

Source: Compiled by the author based on the 1992 field survey.

two of thirty STWs in the village owned by thirty-four upper-class farmers whose landholdings were two-and-a-half acres (one hectare) or more.

Mode of Water Transaction

Table 2.4 lists the thirty STWs and their respective irrigated areas. The STW basically consists of an imported diesel engine and domestically produced

Table 2.3: Class composition, employment structure and asset holdings in Aira village

Class by land holdings (acre)	Households	Major occupation of household head					Farmland owned (acre)	Farmland operated (acre)	STWs owned
		Farming	Agricultural Labor	Trade	Service	Other			
0	102	18 (18%)	6 (67%)	6	1	9	0	28.6	0
0.01–0.49	34	15 (44%)	9 (27%)	4	–	6	7.2	16.7	2
0.50–0.99	14	8 (57%)	4 (29%)	–	–	2	9.7	21.4	2
1.00–2.49	25	18 (72%)	1 (4%)	1	2	3	34.2	40.5	4
2.50–4.99	17	13 (77%)	–	–	3	1	56.8	62.2	8
5.00–	17	14 (82%)	–	–	2	1	123.1	119.0	14
Total	209	86 (41%)	82 (39%)	11	8	22	231.0	288.4	30

Source: Compiled by the author based on the 1992 field survey.

pipes. In Aira village all but one were six-horsepower diesel engines, eight of which were new Japanese-made units; fourteen were secondhand Japanese units, seven were new Korean or Chinese units, and one was a secondhand Chinese-made unit. All were powered by diesel oil, since the village had no electricity. The irrigation coverage per STW in 1992 ranged widely from 5.3 acres to 20.0 acres, with an average area of 10.3 acres.[9]

The mode of water transactions can be classified into three broad categories (Table 2.4). The first category contained lands that were owned and cultivated with irrigation water by STW owners themselves; it also contained a very small proportion of land that was seasonally exchanged and consolidated between STW owners. It accounted for 35% of the total irrigated area.

The second category involved the leasing of other people's lands by STW owners during the dry season for the purpose of irrigated rice growing. This arrangement was called *chaunia* and, at 42%, represented the largest share of the irrigated area. It was common practice for STW owners to pay landowners a rent in kind at the rate of three *maund* (one *maund* = 37.3 kilograms) of paddy per *bigha* (one *bigha* = one-third acre) or, infrequently, four *maund* for very productive land. Since the average yield of *boro* rice in the village was thirteen *maund*/*bigha*, the land rent amounted to 20% to 25% of gross production.

The third category was the sale of water, which accounted for 24% of the irrigated land. This could be classified into three types depending on the mode of water charge payment: crop sharing, fixed cash rate per area, and a combination of crop sharing and cash payment. Crop sharing was the most common system and accounted for 14% of the irrigated land. The STW owner's share was either 33% or 40%, with six out of eleven cases using the former rate and five using the latter. This mode of water charge payment was equivalent to Tk3,000–Tk3,500 per acre depending on the yield. On the other hand, the fixed cash rate was Tk2,100–Tk2,400 per acre. While irrigation water was supplied in installments during the season, cash payment was basically made in advance, with only a portion of it being paid later in the season. In the combined payment mode, a portion of the water charge was paid in advance by cash and the remainder was paid by a share of the harvested crop. In general, the cash portion was Tk300 per acre and the STW owner's share of the crop was 33%. Under the water sales contract, the STW owner was responsible for digging irrigation channels prior to each season and water was usually supplied on a rotation basis.

In summary, farmers who did not own STWs basically had two options. One was to purchase water and operate irrigated rice cropping by themselves. The other was to lease their land to STW owners in the dry season and receive a rent. As mentioned below, the key determining factor for the choice between the two would be their ability to come up with working capital for irrigated rice cropping.

Table 2.4: STW-irrigation coverage and breakdown by transaction mode

				Breakdown of irrigation coverage				
						Water selling (acre)		
STW No.[a]	Model[b]	New/ Used	Irrigation coverage (acre)	Self-cultivated (acre)	*Chaunia* (acre)	Share-cropping	Cash + share-cropping	Cash
1	Yan 6HP	New	10.0	2.3	7.0		0.7	
2	Yan 6HP	New	18.0	1.3	9.7	7.0		
3	? 6HP	Used	9.3	5.0	2.3	2.0		
4	Mit 6HP	New	9.7	2.0	6.3			1.3[e]
5	Yan 6HP	Used	13.3	3.3	5.0	5.0		
6	Yan 6HP	Used	17.0	7.7	9.3			
7	Yan 6HP	New	6.7	5.0			1.7	
8	Yan 6HP	Used	11.0	4.3	4.3	2.3[c]		
9	Mit 6HP	New	12.0		11.3			0.7[f]
10	Yan 6HP	New	10.0	4.7	3.3	2.0		
11	Yan 6HP	Used	11.3	2.7	4.3	4.3		
12	Miy 6HP	New	5.7		2.0	3.7[c]		
13	Mit 6HP	Used	8.7	3.9	4.8			
14	Don 8.5HP	Used	10.0	8.3		1.7		
15	Yan 6HP	New	11.3	7.7		3.7[c]		
16	Miy 6HP	New	6.3	1.0	2.0		3.3	
17	Miy 6HP	New	6.7	1.0	2.0			3.7
18	Miy 6HP	New	12.3	9.0			3.3	
19	Mit 6HP	Used	10.7	2.0	8.7			
20	Yan 6HP	New	20.0	4.7	6.0	9.3[c]		
21	Miy 6HP	New	12.0	4.7	6.3		1.0	
22	Yan 6HP	Used	8.7	3.3	4.7			0.7
23	Yan 6HP	Used	8.0	5.0		3.0		
24	Don 6HP	New	10.0		8.0	2.0[c]		
25	? 6HP	Used	8.3	2.7	4.0			1.7
26	Mit 6HP	Used	6.7	2.0		4.7		
27	Yan 6HP	Used	11.7	4.3	6.7		0.7	
28	Miy 6HP	New	9.0		7.0		2.0[d]	
29	Yan 6HP	Used	5.3	4.2			1.2	
30	Yan 6HP	Used	7.8	4.3	2.7		0.8	
Total			307.5	106.4	127.7	44.4	21.0	8.1
Average			10.3 (100%)	3.5 (35%)	4.3 (42%)	1.5 (14%)	0.7 (7%)	0.3 (3%)

Table 2.4 continued

Notes:
a: Listed chronologically by purchase date.
b: Yan: Yanmar, Mit: Mitsubishi, Miy: Miyanton (Korean), Don: Donfing (Chinese).
c: The tubewell owner's share was 40% in these cases; 33% in the other cases.
d: The tubewell owner's share was 900 *taka* per acre plus 33%; 300 *taka* per acre plus 33% in the other cases.
e: Water charge rate was 2,400 *taka* per acre.
f: Water charge rate was 2,400 *taka* per acre; 2,100 *taka* per acre in the other cases.
Source: Compiled by the author based on the 1992 field survey.

Determination of the Water Charge

At which level was the water charge (*w*) for water sales determined in Aira village? Let us compare it with the variable irrigation cost (*c*) and the average cost (*ac*), which is a total of the variable irrigation cost and the depreciation cost of fixed capital.

Table 2.5 lists the estimated values of *w*, *c*, and *ac* for each STW as of 1992. In the case of payment by crop sharing or the combined payment mode, *w* was estimated by converting the payment in paddy into money based on the rice price. The variable irrigation cost comprised the costs of fuel, lubricant, spare parts, repairs, and labor, and the labor cost included wages for laborers employed for irrigation channel excavation and STW operation and night watchmen to prevent equipment theft. The depreciation cost was calculated using the straight-line method, assuming a useful life of ten years for new Japanese engines and five years for others (secondhand Japanese and new/secondhand Chinese and Korean engines).

The ratio of water charges to the variable irrigation cost varied greatly (Table 2.5), but, even after allowing for capital depreciation, only one of the shallow tubewells operated at a loss.

It was found from the estimation that *w/c* ranged widely from 1.13 to 6.18, with an average of 2.59. STW No. 25 produced the smallest *w/c* value of 1.13 and was the only case operating at a loss, with the value of *w/ac* being less than unity.

Now, let us compare the estimated *w/c* value above with data from other case studies. Table 2.6 is a summary of earlier studies in Bangladesh and shows the lowest average *w/c* value as 1.16 and the highest as 2.53. Aira's average of 2.59 is a little bit higher than the highest value in this range and also very high when compared with estimates from India.[10] It means that the level of competition was quite low in the groundwater market of Aira village. However, it would be rash to conclude that the market was highly monopolistic based only on the value of *w/c* without analyzing the rate of return on STW investment. Accordingly, distribution of NIS is analyzed in the next section.

Table 2.5: STW operating cost and water charge rate (*taka*/acre)

STW No.[a]	Variable cost: Fuel and lubricant	Parts & repairs	Labor	Sub-total (*C*)	Depreciation cost	Total (*AC*)	Water charge (*W*)	*W/C*	*W/AC*
1	1,149	220	248	1,617	328	1,945	3,000	1.86	1.54
2	578	0	106	684	122	806	3,450	5.04	4.28
3	904	215	81	1,200	323	1,523	3,080	2.57	2.02
4	1,043	247	116	1,406	306	1,712	2,250	1.60	1.31
5	1,096	276	150	1,522	165	1,687	3,220	2.12	1.91
6	624	78	55	757	165	922			
7	1,209	200	313	1,722	224	1,946	3,900	2.26	2.00
8	1,032	259	145	1,436	273	1,709	3,312	2.31	1.94
9	989	565	131	1,685	125	1,810	2,400	1.42	1.33
10	950	252	225	1,427	280	1,707	3,450	2.42	2.02
11	714	33	0	747	345	1,092	4,620	6.18	4.23
12	1,119	142	118	1,379	807	2,186	3,240	2.35	1.48
13	622	78	54	754	276	1,030			
14	1,008	194	264	1,466	400	1,866	3,300	2.25	1.77
15	945	238	207	1,390	389	1,779	3,168	2.28	1.78
16	1,314	343	305	1,962	730	2,692	3,160	1.61	1.17
17	1,067	0	149	1,216	448	1,664	2,100	1.73	1.26
18	972	64	143	1,179	285	1,464	2,940	2.49	2.01
19	995	266	210	1,471	243	1,714			
20	776	25	67	868	140	1,008	3,864	4.45	3.83
21	1,115	180	150	1,445	250	1,695	2,720	1.88	1.60
22	929	264	115	1,308	414	1,722	2,100	1.61	1.22
23	810	533	220	1,563	550	2,113	3,450	2.21	1.63
24	950	0	160	1,110	360	1,470	3,456	3.11	2.35
25	1,528	325	0	1,853	361	2,214	2,100	1.13	0.95
26	779	190	0	969	418	1,387	3,680	3.80	2.65
27	855	145	192	1,192	410	1,602	3,900	3.27	2.43
28	1,096	143	0	1,239	411	1,650	2,740	2.21	1.66
29	1,531	306	283	2,120	679	2,799	3,660	1.73	1.31
30	1,297	277	0	1,574	487	2,061	3,500	2.22	1.70
Weighted average[b]	920	191	128	1,240	366	1,606	3,210	2.59	2.00

Notes:

a: Listed chronologically by purchase date.

b: The weighted average using the irrigation coverage as the weight.

Source: Compiled by the author based on the 1992 field survey.

Table 2.6: Examples of groundwater market analyses in Bangladesh

	Samples	Average irrigated area (acre)	Method of collecting water charge (%)			Capital cost (*taka*)	Costs per acre (*taka*)		
			Fixed	Sharecropping	Others		Operation & maintenance (*C*)	Water charge (*W*)	*W/C*
(1) STW	41	11.2	49	17	34	22,000	515	1,264	2.45
(2) LLP	61	37.8	82	–	18	31,250	390	667	1.71
(3) DTW	36	62							
Fixed charge (electricity)	29	64	100	–	–	130,000	407	839	2.06
Sharecropping (diesel)	7	54	–	100	–	130,000	807	1,680	2.08
(4) DTW	18	49							
Fixed charge	5	59	100	–	–	130,000	681	793	1.16
Sharecropping	13	45	–	100	–	130,000	861	2,122	2.46
STW	37	11.6	–	100	–	30,000	1,025	2,380	2.32
LLP	5	20.3	–	100	–	21,160	831	2,099	2.53
(5) DTW	26								
Including fuel cost		63.3	100	–	–	130,000	795	980	1.23
Excluding fuel cost		45.6	100	–	–	130,000	288	459	1.59
LLP	17	32.4	82	–	18	28,750	433	728	1.68

Note: STW: shallow tubewell, DTW: deep tubewell, LLP: low lift pump.

Source: Table Fujita (1990b: 73).

Table 2.7: Distribution of net irrigation surplus (*taka*)

	CHAUNIA LANDOWNER	WATER BUYER FARMER	STW OWNER	TOTAL	PER AREA (*TAKA*/ACRE)
Rent	265,446	150,750	218,507	634,703 (49%)	2,064
Capital interest on cultivation cost	–	41,772	139,064	180,836 (14%)	588
Capital interest on irrigation cost	–	3,927	65,238	69,165 (5%)	225
Profit (surplus)	–	2,052	408,710	410,762 (32%)	1,336
Total	265,446 (20%)	198,501 (15%)	831,519 (64%)	1,295,466 (100%)	4,213

Source: Compiled by the author.

Distribution of NIS

As mentioned earlier, NIS is the remainder of the gross production value of a crop after deducting irrigation cost, current input cost, and labor cost. (Note that the irrigation cost is the actual irrigation cost incurred by the STW owner, not the water charge paid to him.) The irrigation cost varied from one STW to another, as shown in Table 2.5, and so did the current input cost and the labor cost. The rice yield (and the selling price) also varied according to input level and soil quality of the irrigated land. The size of NIS therefore varied depending on the STW, and the manner of distribution of NIS to the STW owner, the landowner (in a *chaunia* arrangement), and the farmer (who bought irrigation water) naturally varied depending on the mode of water transaction. Table 2.7 shows the total NIS and its distribution for all thirty STWs. The total NIS was just under Tk1.3 million, 20% of which was distributed to *chaunia* landowners, 15% to farmers who bought water and carried out irrigated rice farming, and the remaining 64% to STW owners. Note that their shares of the total land ownership were 42%, 24%, and 35% respectively.

The above is the personal distribution relationship. Since the distribution to the factors of production is more important in economic analysis, let us next convert this personal distribution into the functional distribution.

First, the whole of the *chaunia* landowner's share of the surplus is considered to be a land rent. It establishes the average land rent as equal to Tk2,064 per acre. Next, the water buyer farmer's share must also be a (self-cultivating) land rent only, given that NIS is arrived at after deducting the current input cost and the labor cost (including family labor). This leaves an average surplus of Tk650 per acre in the hands of the water buyer farmer, even after deducting the imputed land rent at the aforementioned rate. It is somewhat unjustifiable to treat this as the operator's surplus. It is perhaps more plausible to consider it as the capital interest on working capital comprising the current input cost and the labor cost (including a portion of the variable irrigation cost).[11] Based on the prevailing short-term interest rate in the village of 100% per annum, and if we assume a borrowing period of two months, [12] the water buyer farmer's surplus would disappear almost completely, as shown in Table 2.7. Similarly, the STW owner's share can be broken down into a (self-cultivating) land rent, interest on working capital, and profit. It is clear that the profit gained by STW owners was substantial.

Now, is it possible to say that this profit in the hands of STW owners represented a fair return? Table 2.8 shows a profit from each STW, with an average profit per STW of Tk13,624. This equates to a rate of return on initial investment of 69% per annum.[13] In Aira village there is a long-term tenancy system with advance rent payment called *khaikhalashi*. Let us compare the return on investment of 69% with the effective interest rate realized under *khaikhalashi*. Under this system, the tenant gains the right to use a piece of farmland for a period of seven years in exchange for the payment of Tk10,000–Tk15,000 per acre and he is not liable to repay a principal at the end of the tenancy period. In other words, the value under *khaikhalashi* is equal to the discounted present value of the land rent over seven years. Based on the estimated annual land rent for the average farmland in Aira village of Tk6,354 per acre (Table 2.10), the interest rate under *khaikhalashi* would range from 38% to 61% per annum (with a median rate of 50%). This means that the return on STW investment of 69% was considerably higher than the return under *khaikhalashi*.[14]

The high rate of profit is considered a fundamental factor for the continued introduction of new STWs even after irrigation coverage reached the saturation level (as we will see in Chapter 3), and it would be reasonable to conclude that STW owners enjoyed quite a high level of monopoly in Aira village's groundwater market in 1992.

Thus, the functional distribution of NIS is estimated to be 49% to rent, 19% to capital interest, and 32% to profit (Table 2.7). Figure 2.2 illustrates these factor shares that have been converted into monetary amounts per acre of land. The bottom half of the figure shows the personal distribution of NIS for the *chaunia* system, water sale by share cropping, and water sale by fixed cash payment. The *chaunia* landowner received land rent only. The water buyer farmer in a share-cropping arrangement received capital interest on current input cost and labor cost, as well as land rent. In addition, the water buyer farmer in a fixed cash payment arrangement also received capital interest on variable irrigation cost.[15] Looking at this from a different angle, to farmers who did not own STWs,

Table 2.8: Rate of return on STW investment

STW No.[a]	Surplus for water buyer farmer (taka/acre)	Profit for STW owner (taka)	Capital cost (taka)	Rate of return on investment (%)
1	–789	1,832	32,800	5.6
2	675	53,692	22,000	244.1
3	310	15,191	15,000	101.3
4	–599	128	29,644	0.4
5	593	22,367	11,000	203.3
6		16,575	14,000	118.4
7	152	12,599	15,000	84.0
8	–804	8,700	15,000	58.0
9	–41	8,059	15,000	53.7
10	177	17,303	28,000	61.8
11	1,504	50,120	19,500	257.0
12	692	3,535	23,000	15.4
13		7,547	12,000	62.9
14	938	20,352	20,000	101.8
15	–1,192	4,198	44,000	9.5
16	–480	–28	23,000	–0.1
17	–460	2,527	15,000	16.8
18	–1,446	3,752	17,500	21.4
19		12,201	13,000	93.9
20	–187	48,388	28,000	172.8
21	–1,623	–7,447	15,000	–49.6
22	3,000	28,434	18,000	158.0
23	1,170	14,727	22,000	66.9
24	–299	16,222	18,000	90.1
25	138	44	15,000	0.3
26	1,208	17,033	14,000	121.7
27	1,331	35,680	24,000	148.7
28	–2,578	–8,291	18,500	–44.8
29	285	4,118	18,000	22.9
30	–143	8,877	19,000	46.7
Average	28	13,624	19,798	68.8

Note:
a: Listed chronologically by purchase date.
Source: Compiled by the author.

Figure 2.2: Cost composition for irrigated *boro* cropping in Aira village

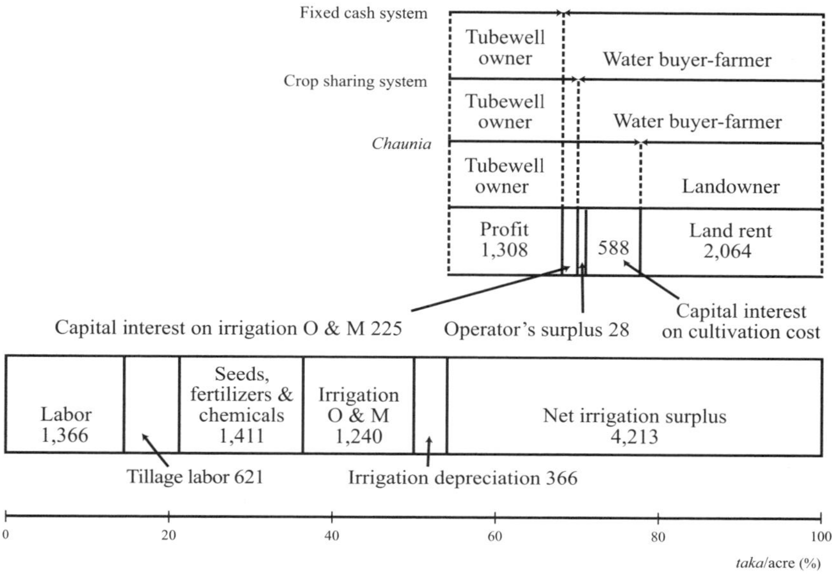

the question of how much working capital they could bear would be one of the important factors in determining whether they would purchase water and operate irrigated rice farming by themselves (and, in this case, whether to pay water charges in cash, by crop sharing, or by using a combined method) or lease their land to STW owners through *chaunia*.

Raising of Working Capital by STW Owners

Given the established *chaunia* system, STW owners in Aira village need to raise substantial amounts of money for working capital. Table 2.9 shows estimated working capital requirements ranging from Tk10,000–Tk110,000, with an average amount just below Tk55,000. Since twenty-seven people owned thirty STWs, three of them owned two STWs each and the total amount for two STWs is shown in the table for these cases. Considering that land rent from five acres of farmland is only just over Tk30,000 per annum, this working capital requirement was no small figure, even for wealthier farmers.

The table also shows STW owners' borrowings. Note that some STW owners let their plots for *khaikhalashi* and used a portion of rent to cover working capital, but these cases are not included in the table. The average amount of borrowing per person was Tk7,600, which represented 14% of working capital, and the degree of dependency on borrowed money was as high as 60% in some cases.

Table 2.9: STW owner's working capital requirement and dependency on borrowings (*taka*)

STW No.[a]	Share of irrigation operation and maintenance	Cultivation cost: Own land	Cultivation cost: *Chaunia* land	Total working capital	Borrowings	Borrowing ratio	Average interest rate[b]
1	15,955	7,590	23,100	46,645	0		
2	12,300	4,719	35,211	52,230	1,000	2%	100%
3	11,160	16,875	7,763	35,798	5,920	17%	120%
4	10,720	5,670	17,861	34,251	13,000	38%	100%
5	31,625	14,245	23,625	69,495	12,000	17%	16%
6	19,419	42,630	51,818	113,867	0	0%	
7	11,030	19,875	0	30,905	0	0%	
8	15,800	13,868	13,868	43,535	12,000	28%	16%
9	18,540	0	33,561	52,101	32,000	61%	70%
10	13,665	15,369	10,791	39,825	0	0%	
11	17,065	23,805	35,745	76,615	32,000	42%	48%
12	7,865	0	6,150	14,015	2,000	14%	100%
13							
14	14,660	27,141	0	41,801	0	0%	
15	15,710	26,565	0	42,275	0	0	
16							
17	380	3,240	6,480	10,100	7,000	69%	100%
18	13,515	34,425	0	47,940	0	0%	
19	15,745	6,480	28,188	50,413	3,000	6%	100%
20	21,340	16,004	20,430	57,774	20,000	35%	200%
21	17,040	16,920	22,680	56,640	20,000	35%	0%
22							
23	12,500	15,975	0	28,475	3,000	11%	16%
24	11,100	0	23,400	34,500	6,000	17%	120%
25	11,810	8,303	12,300	32,413	15,000	46%	100%
26	6,490	7,170	0	13,660	2,000	15%	100%
27	13,740	14,319	22,311	50,370	10,000	20%	100%
28	9,350	0	19,425	28,775	6,000	21%	100%
29	10,873	14,490	0	25,363	0	0%	
30	12,040	15,158	9,518	36,715	1,500	4%	100%
Average	13,757	13,735	27,492	54,983	7,645	14%	77%

Notes:
a: Listed chronologically by purchase date. Figures for No. 13 STW were combined with those for No. 6 as they were owned by one person. Similarly, No. 16 was combined with No. 5 and No. 22 with No. 11.
b: The weighted average using the amount as the weight.
Source: Compiled by the author based on the 1992 field survey.

And interest rates were markedly high. While commercial banks charged a loan interest rate of 16% per annum, only a few people could use their facility and a majority of STW owners had to rely on moneylenders who charged a rate of 100% to 120%, or occasionally 200%, per annum. Many of these moneylenders were traders who lived in Sherpur city (capital of the *thana*), about seven to eight kilometers from Aira village, and some were Hindu moneylenders who had been active during the British colonial era and were still operating. In this way, a portion of NIS flowed out of the village in the form of capital interest.

Factor Bias of Technological Change

Finally, let us estimate factor shares of dry-season *boro* rice production and examine any bias of technological change through a comparison with wet-season transplanted *aman* rice production. In Aira village, production of HYVs was relatively common, even for wet-season rice cultivation, because the village was free from flood damage due to its diluvial plateau location. Consequently, the following is actually a comparison between post-Green Revolution wet-season rice production and dry-season rice production rather than a direct discussion of bias of technological change caused by the Green Revolution. However, approximate discussion of bias is possible since factor shares, especially land share, of wet-season rice production has not changed very much since the Green Revolution.

Table 2.10 shows the result of this comparison. The variety of transplanted *aman* rice used for the cost estimates is *BR11*, which is the HYV with the largest planting area.[16] For both *BR11* and *boro* rice, capital interest on current input cost, labor cost, and variable irrigation cost was calculated at a rate of 100% per annum for a period of two months. Although transplanted *aman* rice is a wet-season crop, it occasionally requires supplementary irrigation in the later stages of its growth and farmers have to buy water from STW owners at a fixed rate cash payment per acre. Land rent paid to the landowner by the crop-sharing tenant farmer was calculated at a rate of 50% (it was common practice for the landowner to receive one-half of the harvested crop without any cost outlay). This led to an operator's surplus of almost zero, indicating the appropriateness of the estimation.

Looking at the table, the share of land for *boro* rice production is 22%, which is markedly lower than 50% for transplanted *aman* rice production.[17] On the other hand, the share of labor is slightly lower and the share of capital (a total of capital interest and profit) is markedly higher for *boro* rice. It would be possible to conclude that Green Revolution technology, which was developed in the form of an expansion of irrigated *boro* rice cropping through groundwater development in Bangladesh, had, at least initially, a strong land-saving and capital-using bias. This has very serious implications, some of which are discussed below.

Table 2.10: Cost of rice production in Aira village (*taka*/acre)

	TRANSPLANTED *AMAN*	*BORO*	TOTAL
Materials cost	1,240 (14)	3,020 (33)	4,260 (24)
– Irrigation component[a]	300 (3)	1,610 (18)	1,910 (11)
Labor cost	2,280 (26)	1,990 (22)	4,270 (24)
– Tillage labor component	1,320 (15)	620 (7)	1,940 (11)
Capital interest[b]	590 (7)	810 (9)	1,400 (8)
Profit[c]	–	1,300 (14)	1,300 (7)
Land rent[d]	4,470 (52)	2,050 (22)	6,520 (37)
Total[e]	8,580 (100)	9,170 (100)	17,750 (100)

Notes:
a: STW operating cost + depreciation cost.
b: Capital interest on materials cost including STW operating cost and labor cost for a period of two months at an annual interest rate of 60%.
c: Profit to the STW owner calculated by subtracting all costs other than profit from gross production value.
d: Land rent for transplanted *aman* is calculated by subtracting all costs other than land rent from gross production value. For *boro*, it is seasonal tenancy (*chaunia*) rent.
e: For transplanted *aman*, calculation was based on yield at 39 *maund*/acre, price at 210 *taka/maund* and straw byproduct at 390 *taka*/acre. For *boro*, yield at 40 *maund*/acre, price at 220 *taka/maund* and byproduct at 370 *taka*/acre.
1 *maund* = 37.3kg.

Source: Compiled by the author based on the 1992 field survey, except data for transplanted *aman*, which are from Rashid (1994: 35).

First, the relative importance of land, which had been the foundation of domination by upper-class farmers in rural areas for a long time, declined and the economic value of capital increased. However, since a majority of STW owners were upper-class farmers and the *chaunia* arrangement accounted for the largest share of the farmland in Aira village, much of the increased capital share accrued to upper-class farmers. It would be reasonable to say that lower-class farmers and landless laborers hardly received any benefit other than the creation of year-round employment opportunities and some increase in wage rates. Still, the increased economic value of capital means, at least potentially, an expansion of opportunities for landless agricultural laborers and lower-class farmers to move upwards. In fact, some lower-class farmers and landless households are starting to purchase and install STWs or receive capital interest by lending working capital to STW owners at high interest rates in certain areas, especially in villages with a developing non-farm sector.[18] And the rural non-farm sector has a tendency to expand in response to the Green Revolution.

Forward and backward linkage effects and final demand effects of the Green Revolution create more room for small-scale commercial activities, which are mainly taken up by the landless and lower-class farmers. It has to be said that implications for income distribution are not that simple.

Even in Aira village, which was hopelessly lacking non-farm employment opportunities, the rapid development of rice double cropping began to manifest the underlying labor shortage, which prompted an influx of seasonal laborers from faraway villages during the busy season. This suggests that the economic conditions of landless laborers have also improved. One piece of evidence for this can be found, although indirectly, in the flow of *khaikhalashi* funds shown in Table 5.13 in Chapter 5. Mortgage transactions such as *khaikhalashi* and *bondak* were historically a means by which the poor in financial distress borrowed money from the wealthy, and such transactions were regarded as a significant factor in the disintegration of the peasantry.[19] However, it is clear that the opposite situation was happening in Aira village at the beginning of the 1990s, at which time credit was flowing from the poor to the wealthy (and land was flowing from the wealthy to the poor).[20] This can be seen as strong evidence for the increasing economic power of the lower class.

Second, the vulnerability of *boro* rice production to falling rice prices should be noted. There is the risk of a dramatic reduction in the planted area of *boro* rice if STW owners stop the operation of their wells in response to a small drop in the rice price. Assuming a *chaunia* land rent fixed at the current level for the time being, STW owners would be forced to cease operation if the rice price declined to the level where it squeezed out their profits and depreciation costs and began to eat into their variable irrigation costs. According to Figure 2.2, this level would be Tk1,674 per acre, or a decline in the rice price of 18%. Although the effect would be milder because the land rent would be adjusted to some degree in reality, its low resistance to rice price fluctuations is undeniable when compared with transplanted *aman* rice production, which has a greater land share.[21]

Summary

The objective of this chapter was to examine how the water charge was determined in the groundwater market of rural Bangladesh and the corresponding income distribution structure based on the case of Aira village in Bogra district. Based on the well-established system of farmland lease to tubewell owners called *chaunia*, the prevailing land rent was ascertained and a full picture of the factor shares of irrigated rice production became clear. The analysis revealed that interest on working capital was charged at a rate as high as 100% per annum and therefore much of NIS was distributed to capital interest, as well as to land rent and profit. The estimated rate of return in STW investment was substantially higher than the long-term interest rate, suggesting some adverse effects of monopoly in the groundwater market.

Irrigated rice farming has resulted in a dramatic decline in land share, a dramatic rise in capital share, and a minor decrease in labor share. This technological bias is generally expected to work in favor of wealthy farmers in the village who own more capital. As discussed in more detail in Chapter 5, however, the reality is not that simple. While the increased share of capital was falling into the hands of wealthy farmers in Aira village and outside moneylenders, there were some signs in some villages that the lower class was beginning to receive part of the increased capital share by lending large sums of irrigation working capital to the upper class. In particular, it has become possible for the lower class in villages with abundant non-farm employment opportunities to accumulate some capital. In this context, the Green Revolution was able to provide a stimulus for a type of change that was opposite to polarization. It is possible to say that the increased share of capital meant, at least potentially, more opportunities for the villages' lower class to move upwards. This would be largely attributable to the fact that the merging of capital and land was minimal in the case of the STW, which was the main form of irrigation in Bangladesh, compared with the case of canal irrigation. If this view is correct, the same situation may be also happening in the vast rice-growing area of eastern India, where the STW irrigation system spread rapidly in the 1980s and where, perhaps, an urgent study is warranted.

3
The Transformation of the Groundwater Market during the 1990s

The state of the groundwater market at the beginning of the 1990s was analyzed, based on the case of Aira village in Bogra district, in the previous chapter. Findings can be summarized into four major points:

1. STW ownership was strongly biased towards wealthy farmers.
2. In addition to water sale by STW owners, accumulation of land through *chaunia* (seasonal tenancy of land by payment in kind at a fixed rate) was widespread.
3. The water charge for irrigation in a crop-sharing arrangement was very high at 33% to 40% of a harvest (paddy) and it squeezed the share of land rent. In other words, irrigated farming exhibited a strong tendency towards capital-using, land-saving technology.
4. Return on STW investment was substantially higher than the prevailing interest rate charged in long-term informal finance transactions within the village, indicating an ill effect of the monopolistic state of the groundwater market.

In this chapter the transformation of the groundwater market during the 1990s is discussed based on its structural characteristics observed at the time of the 1992 field survey and on the results of another survey conducted in the same area from 1999 to 2000. The market transformation occurred, in short, as the groundwater market went through a new phase in its development. During this phase, construction of large numbers of new tubewells continued, even after the irrigation area exceeded 90% and tubewell investment appeared to reach saturation level in the early 1990s. The number of tubewells almost doubled by the end of the 1990s. Unlike the previous chapter, which focused on rural income distribution in the groundwater market, this chapter presents a full analysis of irrigation efficiency and examines changes in income distribution following the market transformation.

A few existing studies about irrigation efficiency are worth mentioning. Kurosaki (1997) suggests the possibility that water price determination exceeding the marginal irrigation cost can coexist with resource allocation efficiency by presenting criticism of our paper (Chapter 2), which is based on a classical monopoly model, and proposing an alternative model. Kurosaki (1996,

1998) also demonstrates that Pakistan's groundwater market is efficient in that there is no significant difference in crop yield for tubewell owners and non-owners, but it is inefficient in the sense that there is a significant difference in cropping intensity, especially for wet-season crops (mainly rice, which is highly dependent on irrigation). It is possible to consider that the findings of a similar study of Pakistan's groundwater market efficiency by Meinzen-Dick (1996) are mostly the same as Kurosaki's.[1] However, this chapter attempts to adopt a slightly different viewpoint and discusses groundwater market efficiency by focusing on the capacity utilization rate of irrigation facilities and the economic behavior of tubewell owners and water buyer farmers that influence it.[2] As mentioned later, the water distribution behavior of the tubewell owner is a key determinant of irrigation-dependent cropping intensity and crop yield level. In this sense, even though the end result may be the same, the distinctive feature of this chapter is this broader perspective that includes the farmer's tubewell investment behavior, which is a (slightly longer-term) determinant of the capacity utilization rate of irrigation facilities.

This chapter is structured as follows. In the first section, as an introduction to the analysis of survey data, the development process of irrigation in Bangladesh is briefly outlined, with particular emphasis on the new phenomenon of *overinvestment* in tubewells that unfolded during the 1990s. In the second section, the state of groundwater market transformation during the 1990s is explored, with a special focus on overinvestment in tubewells, declining real water charges, and changes in the water charge payment modes. This second section is based on slightly crude survey results from two villages in Bogra district for which previous survey data are available.

In the third section, a full economic analysis of irrigation efficiency and income distribution is presented, based on a detailed survey of all tubewell owners in a study village (Titkle village) in Bogra district. An outline of the village and the process of tubewell introduction are presented, followed by a revenue and expenditure analysis of tubewell operation. This section demonstrates that a majority of tubewells (65% of diesel-powered STWs, the most common type of tubewell) were operating at a loss and that the main reason for the loss is that they were unable to secure sufficient irrigation coverage. It is hypothesized that this situation might have been caused by a vicious cycle of the tubewell owner's selfish water distribution behavior and the water charge payment avoidance behavior of water buyer farmers. In view of this situation, it is established that the economic behavior of individual new entrants to STW ownership was not necessarily irrational and that a deficit from STW operation was likely to have been compensated by additional production of irrigated crops, such as potato and mustard, and an increase in yield of irrigated rice (*boro*). It is argued, however, that society as a whole was in a state of inefficiency despite this economic rationality at the individual level. Finally, it is revealed that land rent began to rise again as the real water charge dropped, and the significance of the groundwater market transformation during the 1990s for income distribution is explained. The conclusion summarizes the main points of this chapter.

Development of Irrigated Agriculture

Until the End of the 1980s

Let us go back to Figure 1.2, which shows the trend in Bangladesh's rice and wheat production for more than half a century from the 1947 India–Pakistan Partition to recent times.

The production of dry-season irrigated *boro* rice shows a sharp increase from the 1980s, which represents none other than the trend of groundwater irrigation following the diffusion of tubewells. It coincided with the beginning of market deregulation and privatization in relation to modern agricultural inputs. Low lift pumps (LLPs) and DTWs, which came into common use in the 1960s, were owned by the Bangladesh Agricultural Development Corporation (BADC) and leased to farmers. Even repairs and servicing were undertaken exclusively by BADC technical officers. However, STWs, which gradually spread from the first half of the 1970s, were sold to individual farmers from the beginning, and LLPs and DTWs were also sold to the private sector from the end of the same decade.

Thus, the first half of the 1980s witnessed a rapid expansion of groundwater irrigation, mainly using STWs. Still, irrigation equipment was initially sold through designated sales channels and packaged with bank financing. LLPs and DTWs, especially the latter, were preferentially sold to farmers' cooperatives, retaining a strong element of government control. Tubewell owners had to continue to rely on BADC for repairs and servicing of their irrigation facilities, since there were few private contractors offering such services. The government then devised regulatory measures such as restrictions on spacing between tubewells as it became concerned with the disorderly installment of STWs. Combined with the emerging problem of nonperforming bank loans in relation to irrigation equipment sales, these factors slowed down the dissemination of irrigation facilities temporarily in the mid-1980s.

Major floods in 1987 and 1988 caused severe damage to wet-season rice crops. The government decided to adopt a bold deregulation and liberalization policy in an effort to restore rice production by increasing *boro* rice cultivation. It specifically entailed a freeze on the tubewell spacing regulation, the abolition of regulatory standards for STW diesel engines, and the liberalization of diesel engine imports. Cheap Chinese-made engines flooded into the country to compete with expensive Japanese-made engines and, together with the development of a secondhand Japanese engine market and an irrigation facility repairs and service market, the dissemination of STWs picked up its pace once again. From this point on, an overwhelming majority of STW purchases were made by farmers using their own funds instead of bank loans.[3]

As seen in Figure 1.2, total rice production jumped in 1989–90 as the production of wet-season *aman* rice recovered. This not only contributed to the achievement of self-sufficiency (in the sense that rice imports were close to zero) but also led to an oversupply of rice and a sharp decline in the rice price shortly after.

The 1990s

The wholesale price of rice in Bangladesh spiraled downwards after reaching Tk1,207 (per 100 kilograms) in April 1992. It went below Tk1,000 to Tk967 in October 1992, and remained low (at Tk800–Tk900) for one-and-a-half years before recovering to Tk1,035 in February 1994. The lowest price during this period was Tk769, which was recorded in July 1993.[4]

It is considered that the prolonged slump in the rice price was caused by the private sector's release of surplus (which had accumulated over the previous three consecutive years of bumper harvests) and large quantities of wheat import.[5] On the other hand, the diesel oil price surged on the back of the 1991 Gulf War and remained at high levels, even after a ceasefire (Figure 3.1; the diesel oil price has been substituted by the kerosene price for which statistics are readily available). Given that a majority of STWs were powered by diesel fuel, farmers who had bought tubewells were directly hit by the deteriorating terms of trade. This was the fundamental cause of slowing grain production in the early 1990s, as shown in Figure 1.2. At the same time, dry-season *boro* rice was replaced by wheat, potato, and other vegetables, which were selling for better prices.

In 1994–95, however, a decline in *aman* rice production (due to a drought) and a slump in *boro* rice production (due to rising prices and a shortage of chemical fertilizers, especially urea[6]) caused a drop in the overall rice production and thereby a rapid recovery in the price (Figure 3.1). Meanwhile, the diesel price tended to decrease during this period, improving terms of trade. Grain production recovered quickly in the second half of the 1990s under these conditions.[7]

Figure 3.1: Nominal price indices for rice, urea and kerosene in Bangladesh

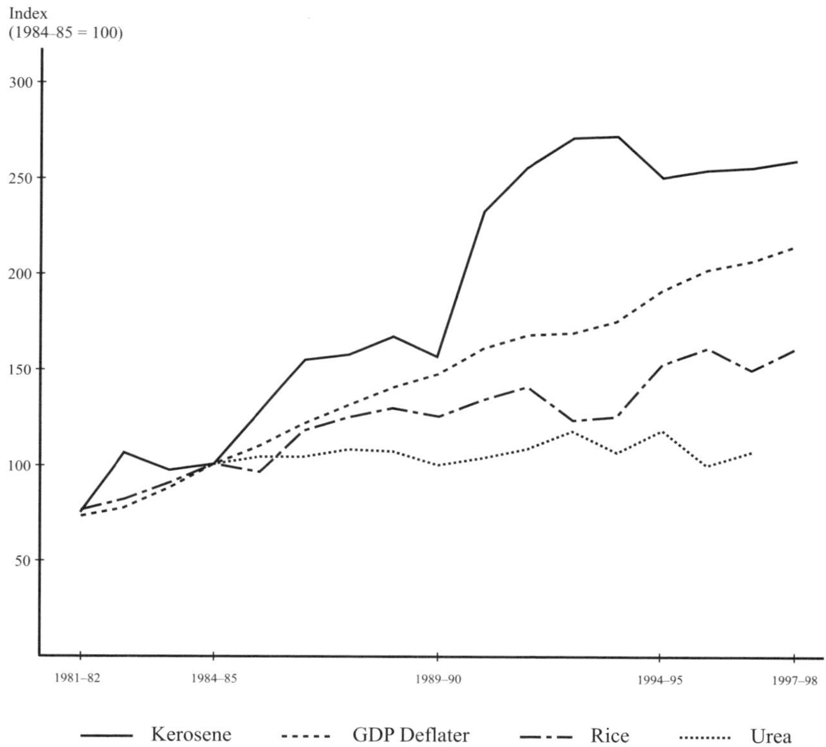

The main reason for increased rice production can generally be attributed to an increase in the planting area and an increase in yield per acre. It is clear that the increased rice production in the latter half of the 1990s was quite different from that at the end of the 1980s in that the former was mainly caused by an increase in yield of *boro* rice whereas the latter was mainly caused by an increase in *boro* rice planting area.[8]

Figure 3.2 shows changes in the STW irrigation area and the planting areas of the main irrigated crops of *boro* rice and wheat from the mid-1980s. Considering that it is possible to ignore changes in the irrigation area supplied by irrigation facilities other than STWs, the figure shows a seemingly odd phenomenon in which the planting areas for *boro* rice and wheat stagnated during the 1990s, whereas the irrigation area steadily increased. Of the two lines representing the irrigation area statistics in the figure, the National Minor Irrigation Census (NMIC) series is more reliable than the Bangladesh Bureau of Statistics (BBS) series.[9] It is likely that the BBS series was estimated by multiplying a priori

Figure 3.2: Changes in the irrigated area in Bangladesh

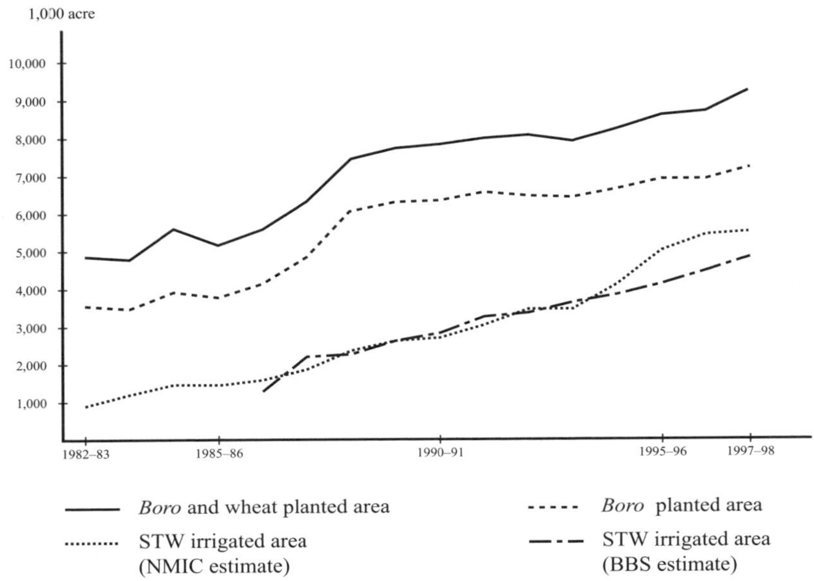

irrigation area per STW by the number of STWs. However, the NMIC series has exactly the same defect up until 1992–93, as the irrigation area was estimated using a unit irrigation area of ten acres per STW.[10]

In any case, it is conceivable that the average irrigation area per STW might have continued to decrease throughout the 1990s. This may be the reason why the planting areas of *boro* rice and wheat stagnated, while the number of STWs increased. Since the number of STWs increased, the total STW irrigation area appeared to increase in statistics because it was estimated by simple multiplication. If this hypothesis is correct, it is quite likely that the introduction of STWs was *excessive* during the 1990s and gave rise to inefficiency in the sense that their capacity utilization rate decreased.[11]

The next section examines this situation empirically based on field surveys.

From a Quick Rural Survey

Bogra district is located in the northwestern part of Bangladesh and is known as one of the most advanced irrigated rural areas. The city of Bogra boasts the country's best retail area selling STWs and other irrigation equipment.[12] The surrounding rural area experienced a rapid dissemination of irrigation facilities from the 1980s, which made the region a major commercial rice-growing region supplying Dhaka.

A simple survey conducted in December 1999 focused on changes in the groundwater market during the 1990s in Tetulia village and Aira village (the study village discussed in Chapter 2), which are located on the outskirts of Bogra city, and detailed field surveys that had been conducted by Japanese scholars[13] (Figure 3.3).

Table 3.1 shows the number of STWs, irrigation rate of farmland, and the average irrigation coverage per STW (for *boro* rice) in both villages where the STW was the sole means of irrigation. It is clear from the table that, although the irrigation rate had already exceeded 90% by the end of the 1980s or the beginning of the 1990s in both villages, the installation of STWs continued,

Figure 3.3: Bogra city and survey villages in the outskirts

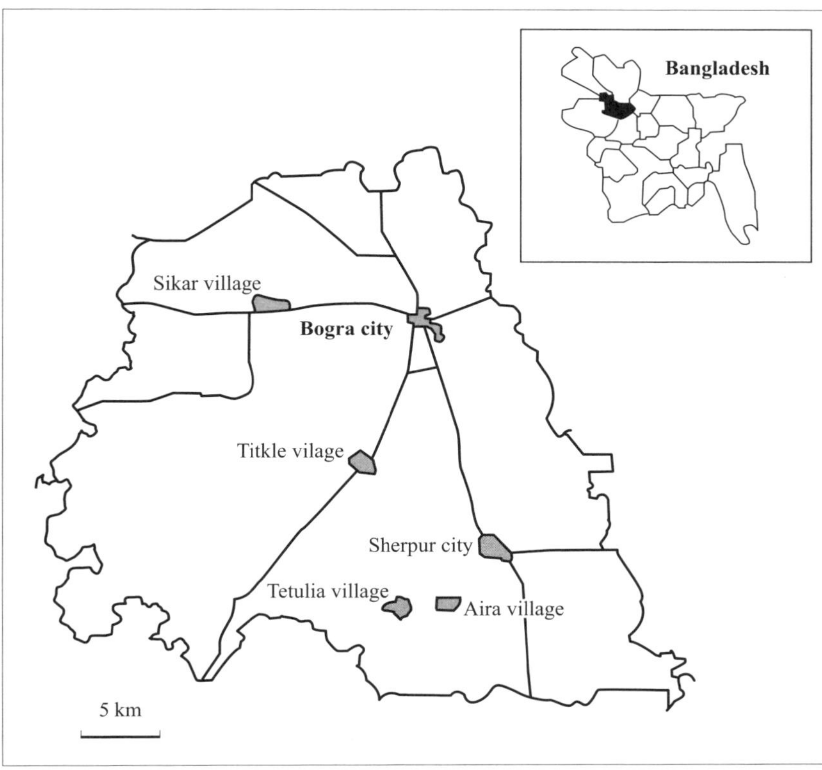

Source: Prepared by the author based on BBS 1988.

with their numbers rapidly increasing by 2.1 times from thirty-eight in 1987 to eighty in 1999 in Tetulia village and by 1.7 times from thirty in 1992 to fifty-two in 1999 in Aira village. Consequently, the average irrigation coverage per STW fell sharply from ten to twelve acres (actual) to six to seven acres (estimate). Also, as discussed later, a detailed survey of Titkle village found that the average diesel STW irrigation coverage was just 6.1 acres, suggesting the occurrence of the same phenomenon even though no past data were available for comparison.

Table 3.2 shows changes in the water charge rate. The water charge for the diesel STW in Tetulia village increased by 40% to 60% from Tk1,500 per acre in 1987 to Tk2,100–Tk2,400 in 1999. It means that the price of diesel oil (substituted with kerosene) rose by about 70% over the same period (as shown in Figure 3.1) and the water charge rose by almost as much. In Aira village, however, the water charge did not change during the period between 1992 and 1999. This is also consistent with the movement of the oil price shown in Figure 3.1. In other words, the water charge rate exhibited its sensitivity to the price of diesel oil, which was a major cost component of irrigation.

The real price of diesel oil decreased from 1991, hence it is reasonable to expect that the real water charge would have come under downward pressure. In fact, the nominal water charge remained constant in Aira village, which means that the real water charge decreased by 35%, since the inflation rate over that period was about 35%. It is also conceivable that the intensifying competition prompted by the rapid increase in the number of STW installations spurred this decline in the real water charge.

It is likely that the above decline in the equilibrium water charge (and an increase in the land rent on the reverse side of the same coin, as discussed below) induced the following systematic changes in the groundwater market.

First, in Tetulia village, *chaunia* (the seasonal tenancy of farmland in which rent was paid in kind at a fixed quantity per acre) accounted for 67% of groundwater transactions[14] in 1987, but this type of transaction had decreased dramatically by 1999 and water sale by fixed-rate cash payment had become predominant in the groundwater market. Land rent under the *chaunia* arrangement was unchanged at nine *maund* of paddy per acre between 1987 and 1999. It appears that the land rent increased by the amount of the increase in the rice price but not as much as the amount of decrease in the water charge. In other words, it is plausible that the water charge deviated from the equilibrium under the *chaunia* system and that this was the main cause for its decline.[15]

Similarly in Aira village, the *chaunia* arrangement represented 65% of groundwater transactions in 1992, but had declined by 1999 and given way

Table 3.1: STW irrigation in two villages in Bogra district

	NUMBER OF STWS	IRRIGATION RATE (%)	IRRIGATION COVERAGE PER STW (ACRE)	*BORO* YIELD (*MAUND/BIGHA*)
Tetulia village (1987→99)	38 → 80	94 → 100	12.0 → 6.1	10–11 → 12–15
Aira village (1992→99)	30 → 52	90 → 100	10.3 → 6.6	13 → 16

Note: 1 *bigha* = 0.33 acre, 1 *maund* = 37.3 kg.

Source: Based on the author's December 1999 survey.

Table 3.2: Changes in the water charge in three villages in Bogra district

	BASE YEAR	1999
Tetulia village (STW)	1,500 (diesel)	2,100–2,400 (diesel) 1,800 (electric)
Aira village (STW)	2,100–2,400 (diesel)	2,100–2,400 (diesel)
Titkle village		1,386 (DTW, electric) 1,500 (STW, electric) 1,800 (STW, diesel)

Note: The base year for Tetulia village is 1987 and Aira village 1992.

Source: Based on the author's December 1999 survey.

to water sale by fixed-rate cash payment. And the water charge payment arrangement by crop sharing (including the combined crop sharing and cash payment method), which accounted for 32% of the groundwater market in 1992, had completely disappeared by 1999. It is likely that the expensive water charge represented by the tubewell owner's crop share of 33% or 40% was the main cause of its demise.[16] Under the crop-sharing system, the water charge would have reflected not only an increase in the rice price but also an increase in crop yield of about 20% (Table 3.1).[17]

Finally, I would like to provide a supplementary explanation of Table 3.2. Looking at regional variations, the water charge in 1999 was substantially lower in Titkle village than in Tetulia or Aira. The difference in diesel STW water charges reached 15% to 25%. This is likely to reflect the favorable terms of trade for irrigated rice production enjoyed by Titkle village, since transport costs were lower there than in the other villages due to its location on a major highway.[18]

From an Intensive Rural Survey: The case of Titkle Village, Bogra District

So far it has been found that the introduction of STWs continued at a fast pace in rural areas on the outskirts of Bogra city, even after almost full irrigation coverage was achieved, resulting in a sharp drop in the average irrigated area per STW.[19] What was the context behind this phenomenon? A detailed field survey was conducted in a selected village in December 1999 (and a supplementary survey in September 2000) in order to answer this question. The findings from this survey follow.

Outline of the Village

Titkle village is located approximately ten kilometers south-southwest of Bogra city (Figure 3.3). It comprises one large *para* (hamlet) and one small *para*, and had a total land area of 496 acres, 194 households,[20] and a population of 877 people as of August 1996 when the study on the impact of the Grameen Bank was conducted by the Overseas Economic Cooperation Fund (presently Japan Bank for International Cooperation).[21] A majority of households were Muslim and only fourteen were Hindu. The landless represented a substantial proportion of the households, with eighty-one households (42%) being landless and thirty-four households (18%) being *functionally* landless (owning less than half an acre of land). Despite having good access to Bogra city, the village had relatively few non-farm employment opportunities, which included day labor (mainly in farm work), small business, and rickshaw pulling. It had one *madrasa* (Islamic school), one elementary school, and one public medical clinic, and held a small periodical market on Mondays and Thursdays on the south side of the road from the smaller hamlet to the main highway. The Grameen Bank, the Bangladesh Rural Advancement Committee (BRAC), and Thengamala Mohila Shabuj Sangha (TMSS) began to run microcredit programs, mainly for landless households, in 1991.

The total farmland area owned by villagers was just over 206 acres, with an average area per household (except landless households) of 1.83 acres. Distribution of farmland was considerably skewed, with 131 acres (64%) being occupied by twenty-four households (12%), each owning two-and-a-half acres or more.

Just like Aira village, Titkle village was positioned on the diluvial Barind Tract and outside the regular flood hazard area. Approximately one-quarter of its farmland was located on high lands and the rest on midlands. At the time of the 1999 survey, double rice cropping of transplanted *aman* and *boro* was the major cropping pattern, and triple cropping of transplanted *aman–rabi–boro* was spreading to about 14% of its farmland. *Rabi* means dry-season (non-rice)

Figure 3.4: Titkle village's cropping calendar (1999)

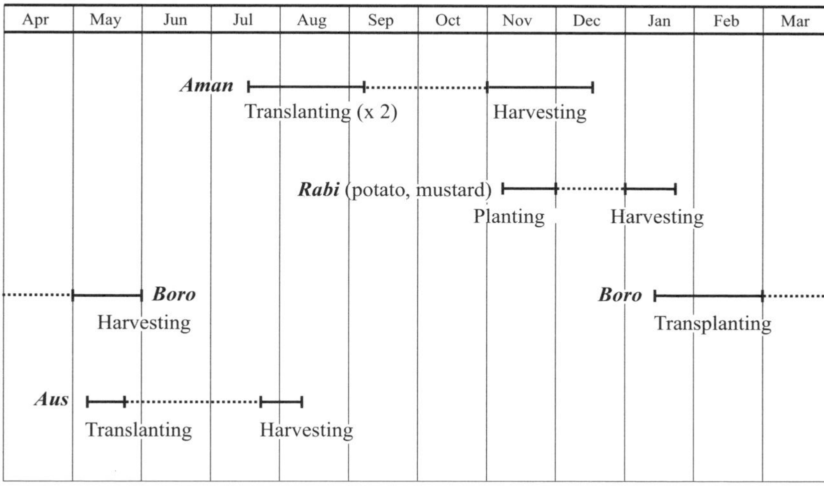

crops, and they were mainly potato and mustard in the case of Titkle village (see agricultural calendar in Figure 3.4). There were twenty-four STWs, two DTWs, and nine power tillers in the village as of August 1996. The irrigation coverage was already close to 100%. Table 3.3 shows that distribution of this agricultural machinery was highly skewed to upper-class farmers. It is notable, however, that STW ownership was also widespread among middle-class farmers who had one to two-and-a-half acres of land.

Tubewell Introduction Process

According to Mr. A., a *madrasa* teacher in the village, irrigation was introduced to Titkle village in 1982. Mr. A. and two co-owners purchased a diesel-powered STW, which provided an irrigation coverage of about fifty *bigha* (16.7 acres) at a fixed-rate cash payment water charge of Tk1,500 per acre. It appears that *chaunia* was never practiced in this village, even though it was observed widely in Tetulia village and Aira village.[22]

The water charge remained the same until the end of the 1980s. It increased by about 20% to Tk1,800 in the 1990s (probably due to the Gulf War-induced oil price surge), and has remained at that level. The price of diesel oil was Tk1,500 per barrel in 1982 and Tk2,740 (an increase of about 80%) at the time of the 1999 survey. If the nominal water charge actually rose by only 20%, the rate of return on diesel-powered STW investment must have tended to decline as competition intensified.

Table 3.3: Class profile of Titkle village residents

Land ownership (acre)	Number of households	Population	Average size of household	Total farmland area (acre)	Area per household	STWs	DTWs	Power tillers
0	81	305	3.77	0	0	1		2
–0.49	34	139	4.09	9.07	0.27			
0.50–0.99	17	93	5.47	12.33	0.73	1		
1.00–2.49	38	167	4.39	54.29	1.43	6		
2.50–4.99	14	98	7.00	54.35	3.88	6	0.5	1
5.00–7.49	5	45	9.00	29.71	5.94	6	1	4
7.50–	5	30	6.00	46.58	9.32	4		2
Total	194	877	4.52	206.33	1.83	24	1.5	9

Note: Landless households were excluded from the calculation of average farmland area per household.

Source: Compiled by the author based on the Study on the Impact of the Grameen Bank by the Overseas Economic Cooperation Fund (August 1996).

Table 3.4 shows the process of introduction of irrigation facilities into Titkle village based on data collected in interviews with all existing tubewell owners.[23]

Instead of going into a detailed explanation of this table, I shall point out just two things. First, it is likely that the five diesel STWs, one electric STW, and two electric DTWs that were introduced between 1990 and 1992 would have been most severely affected by the aforementioned slump in rice prices (and soaring oil prices) from the second half of 1992 to early 1994. Second, rapid introduction of diesel STWs occurred during the 1980s prior to the rice price crash and in the second half of the 1990s after the recovery.

Table 3.5 is a list of tubewells at the time of the 1999 survey arranged by each owner's farmland area from small to large. There were twenty-three diesel STWs (twenty were in operation), two electric STWs, and two electric DTWs.

Profitability of Tubewell Investment and Operation

The main crop for irrigation was *boro* rice, and some irrigation was provided for *rabi*, as well. Transplanted *aman* rice was a wet-season crop and not usually irrigated.

Let us look at the *boro* rice irrigated area per tubewell in Table 3.5. The average coverage for diesel STWs in operation was 6.1 acres; of the two electric STWs, one irrigated 11.7 acres and the other 17.3 acres; and of the two electric DTWs, one irrigated 36.7 acres and the other 78.8 acres. It is clear that the

Table 3.4: The process of tubewell introduction in Titkle village

	STW (DIESEL)		STW	DTW
	NEW	REPLACEMENT	(ELECTRIC)	(ELECTRIC)
1982	1			
1983	1			
1984	1			
1985	4			
1986		2		
1987	2			
1988		2		
1989	1			
1990	1	2		
1991			1	1
1992	1	1		1
1993	1	1		
1994	4	1	1	
1995	1	1		
1996		2		
1997	1	2		
1998	2	2		

Note: Compiled from data collected in interviews with the existing tubewell owners only.
Source: Based on the author's December 1999 survey.

irrigation coverage per diesel STW was at a low level, similar to that in Tetulia village and Aira village.

Table 3.6 shows income and expenditure in relation to tubewell operation, compiled for diesel STWs (also grouped into profitable units and loss-making units based on net profit as discussed later), electric STWs, and electric DTWs. These were estimated on the following bases.

Income

There were five broad types of irrigated farmland: self-cultivated land, (temporarily) exchanged land, mortgaged land (pledged), leased land, and water sale land. Exchanged land was farmland temporarily exchanged between tubewell owners. Mortgaged land was acquired usually for seven years through a type of usufructuary mortgage called *khaikhalashi*.[24] Leased land was either *potton* (seasonally leased land for a single crop) or *sompotton* (yearly leased land) (either way, rent was paid by cash at a fixed rate in advance). As mentioned earlier, *chaunia* (seasonal tenancy of farmland by payment in kind) was not found in Titkle village. Finally, water sale land was farmland to which the

Table 3.5: List of tubewells and their owners

Farmer number[a]	Tubewell number	Farmland owned (acre)	Farmland owned in 1996	Tubewell type	Year introduced	Origin	New or used	Horse-power (HP)	Initial investment (*taka*)	Irrigation area: *Rabi*[b]	*Boro*	*Aus*	*Brinjal*[c]	Remarks
No.14	S①	0	0	STW (D)	1998	China	New	?	12,500	0	[2.83]	0	0	Went back to DTW after a single water supply (non-operational).
No.15	S②	0.50 (divided)	1.65	STW (D)	1995	China	Used	8.5	12,100	0	1.66	0	0.33	Newly introduced.
No.1	S③	1.00	1.00	STW (D)	1993	Japan	Used	6	15,500	0	4.66	0	0	Second unit; initial introduction in 1990.
No.12	S④	1.17	1.17	STW (D)	1995	Japan	Used	?	14,500	0.55	12.66	0	0	Replaced many times since initial introduction in 1985.
No.11	S⑤	1.50	1.50	STW (D)	1994	China	New	8.5	16,000	0.32	2.00	0	0	Second unit; initial introduction in 1993.
No.9	S⑥	1.67 (purchased)	0.99	STW (D)	1998	China	New	8.5	15,000	1.33	4.33	0	0	Second unit; initial introduction in 1997.
No.18	S⑦	1.73	1.73	STW (D)	1997	Japan	Used	6.5	7,500	1.54	4.82	1.67	0	Introduced one unit each in 1992 & 1993.
No.16	S⑧	2.00	2.00	STW (D)	1992	China	New	7	9,000	0.33	5.16	0	0	Third unit; initial introduction in 1985; replaced in 1990.
No.19	S⑨	3.00	3.00	STW (D)	1996	China	New	6.5	13,460	5.34	3.33	0	0	Third unit; initial introduction in 1985; replaced in 1990.
No.20	S⑩	3.40	3.40	STW (D)	1998	China	New	?	10,400	1.57	5.31	0	0	Newly introduced.
No.3		4.33	4.33	STW (D)	1985	Japan	Used	5.5	12,500	0	0	0	0	For sale (non-operational).
	S⑪			STW (D)	1998	China	New	5.5	12,800	0	10.66	0	0	Newly introduced.
No.8	S⑫	4.67	4.67	STW (D)	1994	China	New	?	13,500	1.33	9.99	0	0	Newly introduced; co-ownership; currently leased.
No.17	DTW②	4.90	4.90	DTW (E)	1992	Korea	New	30	212,000	0	36.67	0	0	Newly introduced.
No.7	S⑬	5.00	5.00	STW (D)	1987	Japan	Used	6.5	21,500	0	6.50	0	0	Newly introduced.
No.13	S⑭	5.00	5.00	STW (D)	1994	China	New	6	14,000	1.08	4.66	0	0	

No.6	S⑮	5.00	5.00	STW (D)	1996	China	Used	6	7,750	9.50	10.00	0	0	
	S⑯			STW (D)	1997	China	Used	6	7,250					Initial introduction in 1982; replaced in 1987, 1988 etc.
No.4	S⑰	5.28	5.28	STW (D)	1984	China	Used	6.5	25,500	9.84	11.67	0	0	Newly introduced.
	DTW①			DTW (E)	1991	India	New	25	216,000	0	78.84	0	0	
	SE①			STW (E)	1994	Bangladesh	New	5	19,400	0	11.67	0	0	Initial introduction in 1986; replaced in 1988.
No.21		5.68	5.68	STW (D)	?	?	?	?	?	0	0	0	0	Unused for 2 years; declined an interview.
No.2	S⑱	6.00	6.00	STW (D)	1994	China	New	?	13,090	0.82	4.17	0	0	Initial introduction in 1983; sold after 1 year.
No.5	S⑲	8.67 (purchased)	7.42	STW (D)	1994	China	Used	8.5	7,500	1.25	4.89	0	0	Newly introduced.
No.10	S⑳	10.00	10.00	STW (D)	1987	China	New	6.5	10,800	0	7.34	0	0	Sold; replaced in 1999.
	S㉑			STW (D)	1989	Japan	New	6.6	38,500	2.49	8.33	0	0	
	SE②			STW (E)	1991	Bangladesh	New	5	28,100	0	17.33	0	0	
Total										37.29 (14.0%)	266.65 (100%)	1.67	0.33	

Note:
a: Farmer numbers were assigned in the order of interviews conducted. They were rearranged in the order of size of farmland owned in this table.
b: *Rabi* indicates non-rice crops grown in winter.
c: In Bangladesh eggplant is called *brinjal*.

Source: Based on the author's December 1999 survey.

Table 3.6: Profitability of tubewell irrigation investment and operation (*taka*)

Type	STW (diesel), unprofitable			STW (diesel), profitable		STW (electric)	DTW (electric)
Sample size		13			7	2	2
Crop	*Rabi*	*Boro*	Others	*Rabi*	*Boro*	*Boro*	*Boro*
Irrigation area (acre)	1.78	5.03	0.15	2.03	8.11	14.50	57.76
Self-cultivated	0.73	1.74	0	0.91	2.02	2.84	1.50
Exchanged	0.03	0	0	0	0	0	0
Mortgaged	0.01	0.24	0	0	0.36	0.84	0
Leased	0.48	0.97	0.15	0.36	0.36	1.50	4.59
Water sale	0.53	2.09	0	0.76	5.38	9.33	51.67
Water sale price (*taka*/acre)	390	1,776	360	626	1,801	1,500	1,386
Revenue (*taka*)	694	8,933	54	1,271	14,606	21,750	80,055
Costs (*taka*)							
Diesel/electricity	128	4,782	28	289	5,388	9,250	34,500
Lubricant		386			524	0	0
Tubewell maintenance & management		1,468			971	1,100	0
Tubewell shed		632			464	1,000	2,400
Hired labor		2,235			3,143	5,625	12,000
Family labor		2,792			1,647	0	0
Interest on working capital		623			621	849	2,445
Depreciation		706			646	792	6,420
Total cost		13,780			13,693	18,616	57,765
Net profit (revenue – cost)		–4,099			2,184	3,134	22,290
Income (net profit + family labor)		–1,307			3,831	3,134	22,290
Fuel efficiency (fuel cost/acre)	72	951	187	142	664	638	597
Initial investment (*taka*)		14,027			14,757	23,750	214,000

Note: The above figures are average values per tubewell.

Source: Based on the author's December 1999 survey.

tubewell owner supplied water in exchange for the payment of a water charge by the farmer. In Titkle village the water charge was paid by cash at a fixed rate per acre. The going water price for *boro* rice cropping was Tk1,386 per acre for electric DTWs, Tk1,500 for electric STWs, and Tk1,800 for diesel STWs, and the water charge was generally paid in two installments (after transplanting and after harvesting). The going rate for *rabi* cropping was Tk100 per acre for each water supply.

The total irrigated area of 305.94 acres (Table 3.5) consisted of 61.23 acres (20.0%) of self-cultivated land, 0.40 acres (0.1%) of exchanged land, 7.40 acres (2.4%) of mortgaged land, 37.93 acres (12.4%) of leased land, and 198.98 acres (65.0%) of water sale land. Water sale was clearly the predominant form of transaction in Titkle's groundwater market at the end of the 1990s.

Income was calculated by multiplying the total irrigated area (including self-cultivated land, exchanged land, mortgaged land, leased land, and water sale land) by the water charge. Where the actual water price was not available due to the absence of water sale land, an estimated water price (supplied by tubewell owners) was used.

Expenditure

Expenditure was broadly divided into current expenditure and fixed cost. Current expenditure included expenses for fuel (diesel or electricity), lubricant oil, spare parts/repairs/service of the tubewell, rebuilding and maintenance of the tubewell shed, and labor (for channel excavation, tubewell operation, operation assistance, and night watch). Where family labor was used instead of employed labor, an estimated labor cost (supplied by tubewell owners) was used. Given that the water charge was paid in two installments, capital interest on current expenditure was calculated and added on at the interest rate of 5% per month[25] for a period of one month.

Fixed cost was a depreciation cost of investment in equipment. Equipment included engines, pipes and filters, and hand-operated pumps[26] for diesel STWs, and motors (including pipes and filters), transformers, electricity connection, and tubewell sheds for electric STWs or DTWs. In terms of the depreciation cost, it was necessary to consider the fact that the useful life of the tubewell was longer than commonly expected and that the residual (resale) value of diesel STWs varied widely in the very active secondhand market; also, they tended to fetch prices higher than one would imagine or even higher than the original purchase price in some cases. Interviews with tubewell owners revealed that they had to spend large sums of money on maintenance and management of their tubewells (especially STWs) and, consequently, tubewells themselves did not depreciate in value very much. Since zero depreciation would clearly be an underestimation, however, the depreciation cost was calculated using the straight-line method on the basis of the residual value for DTWs being one-quarter of the original price and that for STWs being one-half of the original price. The depreciation cost also took into account a useful life of twenty-five years for DTWs, fifteen years for new Japanese-made electric STWs, and ten years for the rest.

Net profit

Let us look at net profit figures calculated on the above basis in Table 3.5. Of the total of twenty-four cases (excluding S1, which had ceased operation), fourteen cases were operating at a loss and ten cases were making a profit. When we look at diesel STWs only, the proportion of loss-making tubewells was even higher, with thirteen out of twenty cases in the red and seven cases in the black.

One cause of the losses would be low fuel efficiency. As shown in Table 3.6, the average diesel oil cost per acre of *boro* rice irrigation was Tk664 in the case of profitable STWs and Tk951 in the case of unprofitable STWs. If the average fuel cost for unprofitable STWs was reduced to Tk664, their net profit figure would improve from negative Tk4,099 to negative Tk2,655.[27] One likely cause of low fuel efficiency would be topography such as hilly terrain. Unfavorable conditions should basically be compensated by higher water charges (which would be accepted by water buyer farmers) and should not become the cause of a deficit. Basically, low fuel efficiency would have to be a matter of the managerial capability of the tubewell owner.

Another possible cause of the loss was the assessment of family labor. Unprofitable STWs tended to use more family labor in their operations compared with profitable STWs. Farmers tended to overestimate the family labor cost in a community with few other employment opportunities. It is therefore likely that the loss would be slightly smaller.

However, neither of these factors is likely to be the primary cause of unprofitable operation. Table 3.6 shows the average irrigated area for each of the profitable and unprofitable operation groups. Looking at the main irrigated crop of *boro* rice only, there is a clear gap between the size of 5.03 acres for the unprofitable STW group and 8.11 acres for the profitable STW group. Since the realized irrigation area corresponds to the capacity utilization rate of tubewells, it is reasonable to say that the low capacity utilization rate is the primary cause of the unprofitable operation. This is because, given the fixed nature of costs relating to tubewell maintenance and management, shed building (rebuilt yearly), and labor, as well as depreciation, the smaller the realized irrigation area, the more squeezed the profit.

Figure 3.5: Diesel STW irrigation area and investment profitability in Titkle village

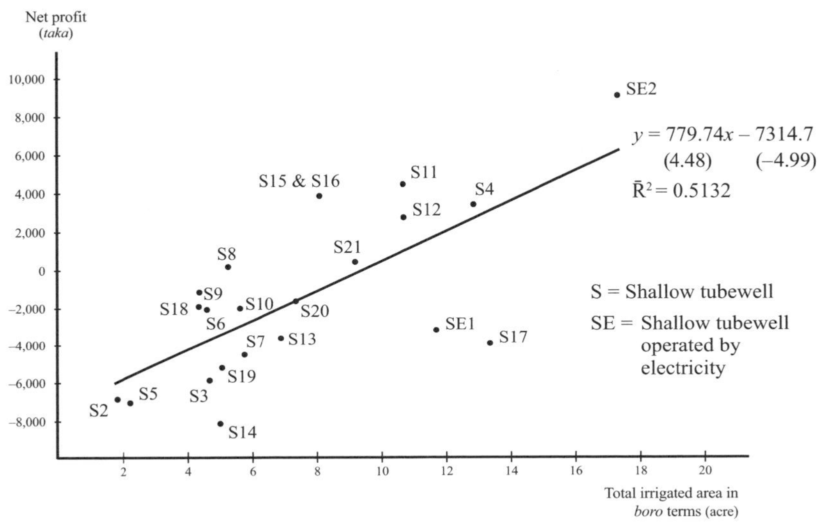

Note: The numbers in brackets are t-values.

Figure 3.5 shows the relationship between the net profit and the annual aggregate irrigated acreage, which is a water charge-weighted sum total of *boro* rice irrigated areas.[28] The diagram demonstrates that there is a statistically significant relationship between net profit and acreage, and that the break-even point is found at just over nine acres.

Inefficiency in the Groundwater Market and its Cause

It may be possible to say that the high rate of return on tubewell investment identified in the previous chapter was the fundamental reason for new investment in tubewell installations. The question is why new tubewell investment continued to the point that a majority of tubewells fell into the red. And why was the water charge different between electric DTWs, electric STWs, and diesel STWs? These two questions are linked, as discussed below.

When villagers were asked the latter question, many of them mentioned the ‘lower (operating) cost’ of electric tubewells. Yet, just like diesel STWs, electric DTWs and electric STWs were operated privately and it would be better for the owners to sell water for higher prices regardless of cost. Therefore, the lower cost does not really explain the situation. I shall examine its real cause a little later.

Figure 3.6: Map of Titkle village and tubewell installation sites

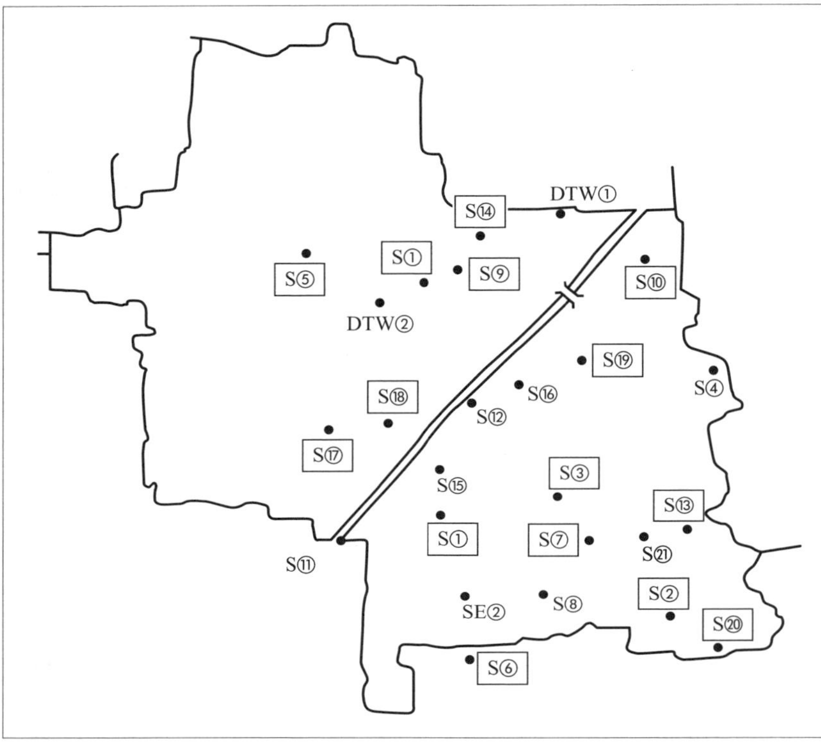

Source: Prepared by the author based on the December 1999 survey.

Note: DTW: deep tube well (electric); SE: shallow tubewell (electric); S: shallow tubewell (diesel). Boxed tubewell numbers denote unprofitible operations.

In order to explore the first question more specifically, the position of each tubewell has been plotted in Figure 3.6. The map was prepared in the 1910s during the British colonial period and shows a considerably different picture of the area. Its farmland has since become highly fragmented, so it was rather difficult to identify where tubewells were located but there was no other option.

What was even more problematic was that tubewell locations on this map were limited to those tubewells owned by the villagers. It would be reasonable to think that there were many cases of *beyond village boundary* installations, as in the case of the S6 tubewell, which was owned by a Titkle village household but located on farmland inside a neighboring village to the south. It was also confirmed in interviews that there were many tubewells owned by non-residents in the empty space in the western part of the village on the map.

The following argument is made based on the above limitations. The tubewell numbers of unprofitable tubewells are boxed in Figure 3.6. Let us consider why they were unprofitable.

First, five STWs (S1, S9, S10, S14, and S19) within the command area (which extended to the eastern side of the highway via a channel underneath the road: see Figure 3.6) of DTW1, installed in 1991, were operating in the red. S1 was an example of *odd* failure; it was installed in 1998 but, after supplying water for *boro* rice cropping only once, it ceased operation when its customers (and its owner) dropped out and reverted to water purchase from DTW1. S10 (1998), S14 (1994), and S19 (1994) entered the market after DTW1 was installed. They were operating in the red presumably because they failed to secure sufficient irrigated area because farmers were able to buy water from DTW1 for a water charge that was more than 20% cheaper. S9 began operation in 1985 and it would have fallen into the red when it did not withdraw from the groundwater market after the installation of DTW1 in the vicinity.

Second, S18 entered the market in 1994. It is likely that it was unprofitable because it failed to secure sufficient irrigated area due to its location between two earlier entrants, DTW2 and S17.

Third, SE1 was operating in the red because of the presence of S15 nearby on the north side, as well as because of its low power efficiency (discussed in Note 27). SE1 was installed in 1994 and failed to take a sufficient irrigated area away from S15, even though its water charge was about 17% lower. S15 had been operated for many years by Mr. A, a *madrasa* teacher with five acres of farmland, and it is likely that his political power won out.

Fourth, S2, S3, S7, and S13 were unprofitable STWs which (except for S13) entered the market later than S21 and failed to secure a sufficient irrigated area in competition with S21. (S21 was still operating in the black but its profitability would have decreased due to a reduced irrigated area.)

It is clear from the above analysis that many of the unprofitable STWs *forced* their way into the command area of the existing tubewells. The first and second cases, especially, are examples of less cost-effective diesel STWs entering into the command area of an electric DTW, and such economic behavior of new entrants is particularly puzzling.

This question was raised directly with these new entrants. Their replies were mostly the same: 'The DTW owner did not supply water properly; he made irrigation arrangements to suit his own convenience.' They said that they had become fed up with the situation and purchased and installed their own STWs.

When DTW owners were asked for their side of the story, they replied, 'Water buyer farmers have a tendency to default on payment of their water charge;

why should I supply water to them according to their demand?' Owners of relatively low lands, especially, showed a strong tendency to refuse payment, since irrigation water flowed in from the surrounding fields. It can be regarded as the free-rider problem associated with externalities of irrigation.[29]

One DTW owner commented as follows:

> New entrants still come in even when I sell water for as low as Tk1,385. If I raise the water charge, more people will enter the market (by purchasing and installing STWs). I am selling water for a price even lower than Tk1,386 to one farmer who has tried to enter the market. I don't want you to tell others about this...

The problem is likely to lie in the so-called high transaction cost of water sales. There were large numbers of cases in which the tubewell owner's water distribution behavior was *selfish* and farmers were unable to obtain enough water when they wanted. One reason for such behavior was the water buyer farmer's tendency to avoid water charge payments. The low quality of irrigation service and the unwillingness to pay the water charge are in a mutually defining relationship that forms a vicious cycle.[30]

It was also discovered in interviews that this situation was widely applicable to STWs, not just DTWs. In this case, the new entry of unprofitable STWs into the market cannot necessarily be defined as irrational at the individual level. It is likely that the tubewell operating loss, itself, was compensated by benefits derived from the improved quality of water distribution realized by tubewell ownership.

One of the possible benefits is an increased yield of *boro* rice. An unstable supply of water would result in a lower yield of *boro* rice for the water buyer farmer than for the tubewell owner. A supplementary survey was carried out in September 2000 for the purpose of verifying this point. However, the interview survey found that there was basically no difference in yield and, if there was, it was only a small difference of about 2%.[31] Of course, even a difference of 2% would translate to just below Tk800 in monetary terms,[32] which would not be entirely negligible.

What is considered more important would be a difference in the planting rate of *rabi* (which is the ratio of *rabi* planting acreage to *boro* rice planting acreage; the planting rate of *boro* rice was almost 100%, with no difference between tubewell owners and water buyer farmers). It is the question of how much *rabi* crops can be cultivated in the gap between double rice cropping of transplanted *aman* and *boro*. Using data from Table 3.6, the *rabi* planting rate among water buyer farmers was 6.5%, whereas the rate among tubewell owners amounted to 31.5%. There was a clear difference. In other words, a disadvantage of unstable water supply was most clearly demonstrated by the difference in the ability to grow *rabi* crops that required irrigation.

Of course, the realized higher *rabi* planting rate has already been taken into account in calculating the operating loss from these unprofitable tubewells, therefore it cannot be regarded as a fundamental factor that can eliminate a deficit. However, the net profit (land rent) of *rabi* crops shown in Table 3.7 could not have been realized without tubewell irrigation; therefore, it should be regarded as a quasi-rent that was obtained only from the ownership of a tubewell. This is the point of difference between *rabi* and *boro* rice, which had been long established as an irrigated crop. In that case, it should be considered that an additional income of Tk3,333 per acre (the average net profit from potato and mustard crops in Table 3.7) for 25.0% of the tubewell owner's land (*boro* planting area)—being a difference between 31.5% and 6.5%—was earned by owning a tubewell.

Table 3.7: Production cost and income for major crops

	BORO		TRANSPLANTED *AMAN*		POTATO		MUSTARD	
Sample size	8		7		4		3	
Average planting area (acre)	4.35		4.60		1.23		1.06	
Unit yield (ton/ha)	4.49		3.23		14.53		0.69	
Price (*taka/maund*)	250		269		121		633	
Revenue (*taka*/acre)	12,916	(100%)	10,544	(100%)	19,800	(100%)	4,750	(100%)
Paddy	12,147		9,366					
Straw	769		1,179					
Costs (*taka*/acre)	6,563	(51%)	4,453	(42%)	14,142	(71%)	3,743	(79%)
Seeds	288	(2%)	183	(2%)	3,855	(19%)	168	(4%)
Fertilizers	1,430	(11%)	751	(7%)	3,817	(19%)	1,517	(32%)
Chemicals	67	(1%)	0	(0%)	807	(4%)	0	(0%)
Irrigation	1,637	(13%)	0	(0%)	743	(4%)	150	(3%)
Rental of machines	394	(3%)	1,064	(10%)	1,080	(5%)	640	(13%)
Hired labor	2,151	(17%)	2,051	(19%)	1,366	(7%)	380	(8%)
Family labor	0	(0%)	0	(0%)	1,781	(9%)	710	(15%)
Interest on working capital	597	(5%)	405	(4%)	509	(3%)	178	(4%)
Net profit (*taka*/acre)	6,353	(49%)	6,092	(58%)	5,658	(29%)	1,007	(21%)

Source: Based on the author's December 1999 survey.

Since the average *boro* rice planting area of unprofitable STW owners was 2.95 acres, the additional income from the difference in the *rabi* planting rate would amount to just below Tk2,500. When combined with an additional income of Tk800 from an increased yield of *boro* rice, the total additional income would be just over Tk3,200, which would compensate for most of the operating deficit.[33] This would mostly explain the reason why the entry of new STWs continued, even if their owners knew that the operation of the STW itself might not be profitable.

Turning to the second question, the water charge was different between different types of tubewells because, based on the abovementioned comments made by DTW owners, the cost advantage of electric DTWs and electric STWs enabled the owners to lower the water charge in order to discourage existing water buyer farmers from installing their own diesel STWs.[34]

In any case, it is highly likely that the groundwater market in Titkle village was rational at the individual level even though it appeared irrational. However, there was the problem of social cost benefit. Let us suppose that tubewell owners kept close communication with water buyer farmers and supplied water properly and that water buyer farmers paid water charges properly. First, the *rabi* planting acreage and the *boro* yield would increase for the water buyer farmers and their economic surplus would expand. Second, the excessive entry of new tubewells would stop and the irrigation coverage per tubewell would increase, expanding the existing tubewell owners' economic surplus as well. Titkle's groundwater market was therefore inefficient from a social point of view.

The question is why the uncooperative behavior of both the tubewell owners and the water buyer farmers could not be curtailed adequately. In view of the aforementioned externalities associated with irrigation and subtle differences in the cropping schedule between different farming plots within one command area (due to the lie of the land, how widely dispersed the fields were, the availability of labor, the crop variety, and other factors), the technological cost of coordination between the two would certainly be high.

However, a more decisive structural factor appears to be the fact that this rural community has never had, in its history, an institutionalized forum where potential or actual conflicts of interests between farmers were mediated so that a compromise could be reached (that is, there was a definite lack of accumulated social capital). For this reason, the cost of coordination would inevitably be high, not only technologically but also institutionally.[35] It seems that this situation has to be recognized as a *cultural* characteristic at this stage[36] and I would hope that future studies in the field of historical research will explore the reason why Bangladesh's rural society has evolved without developing an institutionalized mechanism for coordination of conflicting interests.

Decreasing Water Charge and Changing Factor Shares of Irrigated Agriculture

Finally, let us discuss the distributive implications of a decline in the real water charge. In other words, whether it is necessary to make some modifications to the argument (presented in Chapter 2) that STW irrigation exhibited a marked bias towards land-saving and capital-using technology in the face of the aforementioned transformation of the groundwater market. To find an answer to this question, a crop production cost survey was conducted. Due to limitations of time, however, this was carried out only as a supplement to the main survey of tubewell owners.[37] The results are summarized in Table 3.7.

Income here is a total value of main crops and byproducts such as rice straw. Cost is a total of current input (seeds, fertilizer, agricultural chemicals, and irrigation) cost, employed labor cost, family labor cost,[38] and fixed capital cost (a total of maintenance cost, depreciation cost, and capital interest cost) substituted with capital interest on working capital. Per acre values are used in the following discussion.

First, data for the main irrigated crop of *boro* rice was collected from eight farming households. Based on the yield of between 4.2 and 4.6 tons per hectare, the gross income of just below Tk13,000, and the cost of Tk6,560, their net income was approximately Tk6,350. Interest on working capital was calculated on the basis of a monthly interest rate of 5% and a borrowing period of two months (as per Note 25).

What is most notable here is the share of water charge in the gross production value. It was 13% on average. In Aira village, studied in 1992 (Chapter 2), the median share of water charge was 33% to 40% (under the crop-sharing system), with a slightly higher share under the *chaunia* system and a slightly lower share under the fixed-rate cash payment system. The burden of water charge was substantially lower in Titkle village in 1999 than in Aira village in 1992. This reconfirms the decline in the real water charge that was discussed earlier and also draws our attention to the fact that the share of net profit in gross production value increased considerably to 49% as the water charge fell.

Now, net profit should consist of land rent and operator's surplus in theory. Let us make a comparison with the actual land rent payment. It would be most appropriate to compare it with the land rent for seasonal leasing (*potton*) for *boro* rice. The going rent was between Tk3,600 and Tk4,500.[39] It appears to be considerably lower than the net profit of Tk6,350. However, land rent is paid in advance and therefore interest should be taken into account. So, the figure would be between Tk4,320 and Tk5,400 based on a monthly interest rate of 5% and a borrowing period of four months. In general, the difference between Tk6,350 and this land rent would be interpreted as the operator's surplus.

During this interview survey, a strong impression emerged that the rent for seasonal leasing for *boro* rice cropping might be below the equilibrium rent level. In fact, the practice of seasonal leasing for *boro* rice cropping was quickly disappearing, and some people even said that no farmers would offer fields for seasonal leasing for the next dry season. Perhaps the rent for seasonal leasing for *boro* rice cropping, which had been set at a rational level when the real water charge was still quite high, had upward rigidity for some reason and therefore deviated considerably from the equilibrium as land rent rose in response to a fall in the real water charge. It appeared that its return to the equilibrium was taking place through the new practice of *sompotton* (year-round leasing). This is demonstrated below. Please note that income from crops other than *boro* rice also has to be taken into account in the case of year-round leasing.

Let us look at the production cost of transplanted *aman* rice first (Table 3.7). In contrast to *boro* rice, the yield varied widely between farms (from 2.7 to 4.3 tons per hectare).[40] The average gross income was about Tk10,550 and the average cost was about Tk4,450, which left just below Tk6,100 as a net profit. It means that the share of net profit in gross production value was as high as 58%.

Income from *rabi* cropping in some of these farms has to be taken into account. According to Table 3.5, the proportion of the *rabi* planting area to the *boro* rice planting area was 14% on average, and the ratio of potato and mustard was almost even in Titkle village. Assuming each was cultivated in 7% of farmland, a net profit from *rabi* cropping would be Tk470 based on the surveyed production costs (notwithstanding the small sample size) shown in Table 3.7.

Consequently, the total annual net profit earned from an acre of farmland would be approximately Tk12,900, consisting of Tk6,350 from *boro* rice, Tk6,100 from transplanted *aman* rice, and Tk470 from *rabi* crops.[41] The going rent for year-round leasing in Titkle village was Tk9,000–Tk9,900,[42] which became Tk12,600–Tk13,860 when interest on working capital was added at 5% per month for eight months[43] as mentioned earlier. The two amounts are more or less consistent.[44]

One of the more productive farmers, when asked if the rent for year-round leasing was considered expensive for transplanted *aman* rice alone, replied, 'from a tenant's point of view, a loss from transplanted *aman* rice cropping could be made up for by *boro* rice cropping.' This reinforces our hypothesis that the current situation can be construed as the process of adjustment towards the equilibrium rent through converting to year-round leasing.

A rent of Tk12,600–Tk13,860, including interest, amounts to 50% to 55% of gross production value (about Tk25,180 on average, including transplanted *aman*, *rabi*, and *boro*), which is a very large factor share.[45] However, there was a cool-headed economic principle working in the background, as we have seen above, and it was not the case of landlords making undue profits.

Thus, it is possible to say that the relative share of irrigated farming factors in Bangladesh returned to the pre-irrigation level as land rent increased sharply in response to a fall in the real water charge, which was caused by the transformation of the groundwater market during the 1990s. The fall in water charge and the rise in land rent might not have changed the relative factor shares substantially for many tubewell owners who were wealthy farmers (large-scale landowners). Yet, self-cultivating farmers not owning tubewells would have had a substantial increase in their net income.

Summary

The major points of this chapter are summarized as follows.

First, Bangladesh's groundwater market underwent a quite extensive structural change throughout the 1990s. This was clearly reflected in a decline in the water charge caused by a fall in the real price of diesel oil and intensifying competition between tubewells. And the adjustment to the water charge involved some institutional changes (at least in some rural area) such as transition from seasonal tenancy (*chaunia*) to water sale by tubewell owners or transition from the fixed-rate payment in-kind system to the fixed cash payment system for water purchases.

Second, intense competition between tubewells resulted in a dramatic decline in the irrigation coverage of each tubewell (from ten to twelve acres down to six to seven acres for diesel STWs), which reduced profitability of tubewell investment and operation and pushed many tubewells into the red. The power of tubewell owners, who were once labeled as waterlords, appeared to have been lost almost completely.

Third, this *overinvestment* in tubewells accompanied some improvements in the *rabi* planting rate and the *boro* yield, which likely compensated for a loss from tubewell operation. In other words, it was likely to have been economically rational behavior on the part of individual farmers who made an investment. However, it is considered to have contributed to social inefficiency in the sense that the production efficiency of irrigated farming by water buyer farmers remained low. At the same time, the tubewell capacity utilization rate continued to fall.

Fourth, the likely cause of this inefficiency was the tubewell owner's *selfish* water distribution behavior and the water buyer farmer's nonpayment of the water charge—two factors that were on the opposite sides of the same coin. Further, the absence of a coordination mechanism to regulate and control uncooperative behavior in rural society was a contributing factor. However, this conclusion that attributes the production inefficiency to a cultural factor requires a thorough discussion and remains an issue to be addressed in future studies, even though there is no other explanation at this point in time.

Fifth, the falling water charge pushed up land rent, which had dropped dramatically during the diffusion process of tubewell irrigation up to the end of the 1980s and had benefited land owners. The share of land rent (including interest paid in advance) in the gross production value reached 50% to 55%.

Finally, one issue remains to be pointed out. It was not possible to include the other important factor driving the rural economy—the labor market condition—in the survey this time. Bangladesh's economic growth accelerated during the 1990s and the per capita income increased at a high rate of 3% to 4%, especially in the latter half of that decade. Yet, the real wage rate in rural areas hardly improved[46] and this is why the labor share in agriculture is believed to have changed little, as indirectly shown in this chapter (in the sense that a fall in the water charge resulted in a rise in the land rent). This is an extremely important point, as it is deeply linked to the economic wellbeing of the rural landless people. There is a need for deeper analysis in the future in order to find out why the accelerated economic growth and the stagnation of the real wage rate coexisted.

4
Irrigation and Agricultural Development in West Bengal, India

This chapter discusses the development of groundwater irrigation and the attendant transformation of agriculture in the Indian state of West Bengal, which is adjacent to the western side of Bangladesh. The previous two chapters followed the process of emergence and transformation of the groundwater market in Bangladesh. This chapter looks at the same process in West Bengal and is based on a village survey conducted from 1999 to 2000.

The Green Revolution in India began in the mid-1960s in the northwestern region, mainly in the state of Punjab, but was not in full swing until the 1980s. Marked growth in agricultural production was initially limited to certain areas and certain crops and only spread to other parts of the nation and a wide range of crops (not only wheat) during the 1980s. From then on, India established a decisive lead on sub-Saharan African countries in terms of national nutrition standards.[1]

A particularly notable feature of India's agricultural development from the 1980s was the development that took place in eastern India (which had been a sluggish region described as semi-feudal), especially the growth of the staple rice sector. It is considered that the development was mainly underpinned by the development of groundwater irrigation through tubewell construction by individual farmers.[2]

The first aim of this chapter is to demonstrate this hypothesis using data from West Bengal in eastern India. This empirical approach based on a single-village survey has been adopted, despite obvious limitations, mainly due to critical lack of statistical information at the semi-macro level.[3]

The state government of West Bengal has been under the rule of the Communist Party since the late 1970s. Perhaps because of this, there has been a strong tendency to publicize its rapid agricultural and rural development from the 1980s as the fruit of agrarian land reform (redistribution of farmland, a government policy to strengthen tenancy rights named *Operation Barga*, and so on) and *panchayat* (local government) reform.[4] This tendency has also been deeply entrenched in the state's academia in the field of the social sciences.[5] This chapter attempts to mildly refute the commonly accepted view by arguing that the primary cause of agricultural development was technological innovation triggered by tubewell development by the private sector (such as by wealthy farmers) and therefore was not directly linked to the aforementioned policies of the state government.

As in the case of Bangladesh, there is the criticism that the development of privately owned tubewells has created a new ruling class—the *waterlords* instead of the landlords—in rural areas. The existence of waterlords would be unacceptable to those who have promoted agrarian land reform. However, this criticism is not grounded in the realities of tubewell irrigation water transactions.[6]

The second aim of this chapter is to overturn the waterlord argument through detailed analysis of the realities of the groundwater market at the village level. In this sense, this chapter can be regarded as a West Bengal version of Chapter 3, which made a similar attempt with regard to Bangladesh.

However, the situation surrounding tubewell irrigation in West Bengal is far more complex and interesting than in Bangladesh. It entails, for example, the existence of the state-operated DTW, a transition from the standard STW to the new 'mini deep' type of submergible STW, and the issue of subsidies for the electricity supplied to tubewells. These points are discussed in detail below. While keeping the issue of waterlords in view, this chapter presents and analyzes the complex realities as much as possible.

The composition of this chapter is briefly explained here. In the first section, the agricultural sector in West Bengal and its development mechanism are outlined and the location of the study village is defined. The following section concentrates on the study village, and traces and reconstructs the history of the agricultural development of the study village as far as possible (back to the mid-1960s when state-operated DTWs were drilled). The process of change in the village's agriculture was prompted by the introduction of tubewells, as well as by the process of transformation of the groundwater market. This section also analyzes tubewell operation based on a census survey of the owners of privately owned STWs, then pays attention to the true state of irrigated agriculture and to an economic analysis based on a crop production cost survey. A close examination of various determinants of the village's groundwater market then follows. These determinants include the issues associated with state-operated DTWs, power subsidies, and nonpayment of water charges for privately owned tubewells. The final section presents a summary, including some findings and implications.

An Outline of Agricultural Development in West Bengal

Based on a detailed examination of agricultural statistics, J. K. Boyce (1987) conducted a quantitative analysis of agricultural development in the Bengal region (Bangladesh and the Indian state of West Bengal) up to the end of the 1970s and defined it in one word—impasse. He attributed this to the failure to take cooperative action in controlling water during the wet season and the inequalities in the agrarian structure that had created an unfortunate division between labor and land.[7] Ironically, however, Bengali agriculture began to develop rapidly just after the end point of Boyce's analysis period.

At the start of the 1980s, West Bengal suffered rice crop failures due to drought. After that, however, it achieved a remarkable and sustained increase in rice production. By the end of the 1980s, its rice production increased by about 3.7 million tons, or 50%, from around seven million tons to ten to eleven million tons. This was an annual increase of about 4.4%.[8] Acceleration of agricultural growth was obvious to everyone when compared with the fact that the agricultural growth rate from 1965 to 1980 remained at 2.3%, which was only marginally higher than the population growth rate according to Boyce's estimation.

Bengal's staple food—rice—included three types: wet-season *aus*, which was harvested in the middle of the wet season; a wet-season *aman*, harvested at the end of the wet season; and a dry-season *boro*. In contrast with Bangladesh, where *aus* rice was relatively important, *aman* rice was the predominant type in West Bengal. Prior to the development of irrigation, hardly any *boro* rice was cultivated in either region, with only small amounts being produced in wetlands using residual water from the wet-season rains. West Bengal's traditional cropping pattern was single wet-season cropping of *aman* rice or double cropping of *aman* rice and dry-season drought-resistant pulses.

Very simply stated, agricultural development in West Bengal was, as far as rice was concerned, realized by either an increase in the yield of wet-season *aman* rice or an expansion of the planting area of dry-season *boro* rice through the development of irrigation.[9] The aforementioned increase in the state's rice production of about 3.7 million tons during the 1980s consisted of 2–2.8 million tons of *aman*, 0.8–1.2 million tons of *boro*, and 0.3–0.4 million tons of *aus* (expressed as ranges due to widely fluctuating production from year to year).

The state's rice production reached just over thirteen million tons at the end of the 1990s and achieved a further increase of about three million tons over the next decade (2.7% per annum). A major expansion of *boro* rice production was the primary contributor to this increase over the period, while *aman* rice recorded only a minor increase, and *aus* rice production actually decreased.

In other words, growth in the yield of *aman* rice was still a major contributor during the 1980s but the *boro* rice planting area was already expanding rapidly and became the only factor in increasing rice production during the 1990s. Tubewell irrigation development was the background factor for this.

Some may argue that the commonly accepted view about the success of agrarian land reform and local government reform cannot be dismissed because more than half of the increase in rice production during the 1980s was attributable to *aman* rice production. However, such an argument cannot escape the criticism of crudeness at the empirical level.[10] Unless they investigate the technological advancements and diffusion that were involved in the increase in the yield of *aman* rice, by meticulously following changes in the rice variety and management practices and technologies (including supplementary irrigation to ensure high and stable yield), and establish the direct and indirect effects of agrarian land reform and local government reform on the dynamics of these technological changes, their argument cannot be convincing.[11]

Irrigation in West Bengal can be broadly grouped into the gravity flow canal system and the pumped groundwater irrigation system.

The development of the canal system was undertaken in conjunction with the Damodar Valley project in 1948, immediately after independence, and subsequent large-scale river development projects such as the Mayurakshi project and the Kangsabati project.[12] It ended by the mid-1970s and the irrigated area has not increased very much since then, when it reached around 2.7 million acres. The system supplies irrigation water to Burdwan, Birbhum, Bankura, Hooghly, and Medinipur districts (Figure 4.1). It is mainly used for supplementary irrigation for *aman* rice but also supplies irrigation for *boro* rice if abundant water still remains in the dry season.

On the other hand, groundwater irrigation by tubewell construction developed in the southern, western, and northern (except northernmost) parts of the state, including Medinipur, South 24 Parganas, North 24 Parganas, Nadia, Murshidabad, Malda, and West Dinajpur districts. Table 4.1 shows changes in the *boro* cropped area from the 1980s. Districts registering a marked expansion of the *boro* rice area mostly correspond to districts that experienced dissemination of tubewell irrigation. The study village was located in Nadia district, which was one of the main areas of groundwater irrigation.

Irrigation Development and Agricultural and Rural Transformation in the Study Village

Nadia district had a land area of 3,927 square kilometers, a population of 3.85 million people (as of 1991), and an annual rainfall of 1,474 millimeters, 88% of which fell during the wet season from May to October. The rain provided enough water for wet-season rice cropping but irrigation was essential during the dry season.

Figure 4.1: The state of West Bengal and the village of Gontra

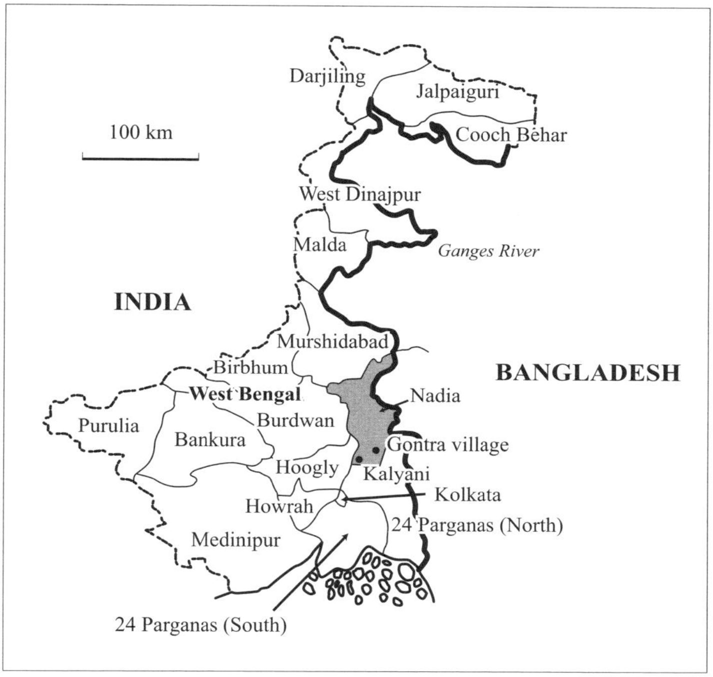

The study village, Gontra village (*mauza*), is in Chakda block, southern Nadia. The town of Kalyani is a two- to three-hour drive north from the state capital of Kolkata, and Gontra village is another hour's drive northeast from Kalyani (Figure 4.1).

A preliminary survey in November 1999 was followed by a main survey in September 2000.[13] It was estimated that the village had 250 households and a land area of 900 acres, 650 acres of which were farmland. The irrigation rate was almost 100%. Double rice cropping of wet-season transplanted *aman* and dry-season *boro* was the predominant cropping pattern,[14] but the cultivation of banana and various vegetables was introduced to some highlands and earned good returns. While irrigation was essential for *boro*, transplanted *aman* only needed supplementary irrigation in years with insufficient rainfall. Horticultural crops in the highlands also required irrigation but they occupied a very small proportion of the total farmland. An excellent agricultural cooperative was active in four villages in the area, including Gontra village, and was playing a major role in improving agricultural production and rural living standards.[15]

Table 4.1: Changes in *boro* cropping in West Bengal by district

DISTRICT	*BORO* PLANTED AREA ('000 ACRE) 1980–81	1985–86	1990–91	1993–94 (A)	NET SOWN AREA (1994–95) (B)	(A)/(B) × 100	*BORO* YIELD (AVERAGE TON/ACRE 1989/90–1991/92)
Burdwan	232.0	240.9	293.8	390.4	1,171.0	33.3%	1.19
Birbhum	58.6	46.2	91.7	141.3	766.0	18.4%	1.23
Bankura	13.8	35.8	101.6	107.2	937.0	11.4%	1.16
Medinipur	118.1	257.2	486.0	533.7	2,069.7	25.8%	1.15
Howrah	15.8	57.3	113.7	129.7	194.0	66.9%	1.24
Hooghly	140.6	122.8	170.7	192.2	565.9	34.0%	1.15
24 Parganas (North)	70.7	123.8	190.5	210.0	643.9	32.6%	1.30
24 Parganas (South)	14.1	35.8	97.4	124.8	1,009.9	12.4%	1.13
Nadia	*66.5*	*140.8*	*232.5*	*239.7*	*742.0*	*32.3%*	*1.32*
Murshidabad	55.8	91.9	137.1	157.2	1,007.4	15.6%	1.28
West Dinajpur	14.6	36.6	132.7	165.3	1,110.2	14.9%	1.21
Malda	54.6	74.9	138.1	152.2	706.9	21.5%	1.34
Jalpaiguri	0.2	0.2	1.7	4.9	794.4	0.6%	1.15
Darjeeling	–	–	0.5	1.0	354.3	0.3%	1.21
Cooch Behar	0.2	1.0	19.0	26.7	615.0	4.3%	1.02
Purulia	0.5	0.5	7.2	5.7	812.9	0.7%	0.91
West Bengal	856.1	1,265.7	2,214.2	2,582.0	13,500.5	19.1%	1.19

Source: Prepared by the author based on Bureau of Applied Economics and Statistics 1995.

At the time of the main survey in September 2000, there were thirty-one STWs within the village's boundaries, plus two DTWs owned by the state of West Bengal. There were three types of STWs: three diesel-powered STWs, eighteen electricity-powered STWs, and ten submergible STWs (SMs). The submergible tubewell was so called because a motor was lowered into the ground and submerged in groundwater at a depth of about sixty feet. The STW extracted water from an aquifer at a depth of sixty to seventy feet, the DTW from 400 feet, and the SM from a mid-range at 180 to 200 feet, which was why it was called the 'mini deep' locally. The SM appeared on the market in response to falling groundwater levels, as discussed below.

History of Irrigation and Agricultural Development

An interview survey conducted at the Minor Irrigation Department, in Kalyani, which was in charge of management and operation of state-run DTWs, as well as interviews with village leaders (mostly the president and directors of the cooperative), revealed a general outline of the history of agricultural development in Gontra. It is divided into four periods for ease of understanding: the mid-1960s to the mid-1970s, the mid-1970s to mid-1980s, the mid-1980s to mid-1990s, and after the mid-1990s.

The Mid-1960s to Mid-1970s

It was April 1964 when the excavation of two DTWs was completed in Gontra village.[16] The initial investment must have been a very large sum, since the DTWs were powered by electric motors and connected to newly constructed networks of underground irrigation pipes. The underground pipe system meant that, to a considerable degree, the irrigation coverage was fixed from the start and that there was no need for maintenance and management work for water channels. The state government of West Bengal paid for the whole initial investment, managed and operated them directly by assigning one operator and two assistants (full-time public servants) to each DTW, and paid all expenses such as electricity charges and machinery maintenance costs from the budget of the state government's Minor Irrigation Department. Beneficiary farmers merely paid water charges at a fixed rate per acre (with high subsidies as discussed below) to the state government. A beneficiary committee was formed by representatives of beneficiary farmers, tubewell operators, technical officers from the Minor Irrigation Department, and the presidents and members of *gram panchayat* (administrative villages) in order to carry out necessary coordination and communication and to resolve problems.

The combined irrigation coverage of the two DTWs was approximately 150 acres, which amounted to about 23% of the village's farmland. The village had few ponds for irrigation. In any case, the planting area for *boro* rice was limited. Most fields were used for single cropping of *aman* rice and either lay fallow or grew low-return pulses such as grass pea during the dry season.

The Mid-1970s to Mid-1980s

The situation changed around 1972–74 when farmers began to introduce diesel STWs. Pumping of irrigation water from ponds using these diesel engines also spread and expanded the *boro* cropping area. According to estimations of informed people in the village, the irrigation rate reached 50% to 60% by the mid-1980s. What is notable here is the fact that, at this time, STW owners leased fields from farmers (only during the dry season) to cultivate *boro* rice instead of farmers buying irrigation water from STW owners for *boro* cropping. The going rent that STW owners paid farmers was three *maund* of paddy per *bigha*.[17] The yield of *boro* at the time was about eighteen *maund* per *bigha*.

The Mid-1980s to Mid-1990s

At the start of the 1980s, West Bengal suffered consecutive years of poor rice harvest due to droughts. The state government came up with various measures for the promotion of agriculture and especially emphasized electrification of rural areas using a 'cluster system.' When at least six STWs were installed in one zone under consideration for electrification, the zone was referred to as a cluster and given priority for electricity connection. This program was introduced in Gontra village from the mid-1980s and prompted electrification of diesel STWs, as well as installation of many new electric STWs. Increased availability of long-term finance from the Land Development Bank also contributed to the diffusion of STWs.[18] By the start of the 1990s, the use of electric STWs spread to almost cover the whole village, except those areas irrigated by DTWs. Dry-season cropping of *boro* rice expanded to nearly all parts of the village.

The mode of irrigation water transactions gradually changed around this time. More farmers began to buy irrigation water from STW owners to cultivate *boro* rice themselves. It is said that the number of self-cultivating farmers exceeded the number of farmers seasonally leasing their fields by the end of the 1980s.

From the Mid-1990s

However, a major problem arose during this process of irrigation expansion. Declining groundwater levels caused a shortage of irrigation water and the situation became serious when tubewells ran dry in March and April at the end of the irrigation season. People had no choice but to introduce SMs or the mini deep, which was capable of pumping groundwater from deeper aquifers.

Table 4.2 shows the number of tubewell installations by year, and is compiled from the results of the census survey of tubewell owners in the village. According to the table, SMs were introduced in 1992, when two were installed, and a further seven units were installed between 1995 and 1997. The SM was introduced as a substitute for the electric STW. It had an irrigation capacity of 120 *bigha*, which was much larger than the capacity of a standard STW of forty to fifty *bigha*. A new problem that arose in association with this is discussed later. The conversion to SMs did not bring about any change to the double rice-cropping pattern with transplanted *aman* and *boro*.

At the time of the survey, the practice of seasonal tenancy by tubewell owners had disappeared and all farmers were buying irrigation water. One background factor for this was that the *boro* rice production technology became standardized and widespread, minimizing its risks. Another factor was the fact

Table 4.2: The process of STW diffusion in Gontra village

	Diesel STW	Electric STW	SM
1982	2		
1983	4		
1984	1	2	
1985	1	1	
1986	1	2	
1987		6	
1988		4	
1989		2	
1990			
1991			
1992		1	2
1993	1		
1994	1		
1995			3
1996		2	2
1997			2
1998			
1999			
2000			
Total (existing)	3	13	9

Source: Prepared by the author based on the September 2000 field survey.

that the Green Revolution, with the expansion of *boro* rice as its core activity, improved the standard of living for the villagers, which in turn improved their financial condition. Farmers needed working capital if they were to carry out *boro* cultivation by purchasing irrigation water, which suggests that ordinary farmers might have been unable to buy STWs of their own but had sufficient financial capacity to conduct irrigated *boro* cultivation.[19] One STW owner commented that no one was willing to offer fields even if he wanted to lease them, emphasizing that the change had come mainly from the farmers who did not own STWs. It is likely that a fall in the real water charge that resulted from intensifying competition among the increasing number of tubewells (to be discussed later) was also an important factor in promoting self-cultivation with purchased water.

Actual State of Tubewell Operation

As stated above, there were two DTWs, three diesel STWs, eighteen electric STWs, and ten SMs in Gontra village at the time of the September 2000 survey.

The two DTWs were state-operated, one SM was operated by the agricultural cooperative, and the remaining thirty tubewells were privately operated. The census survey of these privately owned tubewells had to exclude five electric STWs and one SM because they were owned by people living outside the village. Accordingly, twenty-five tubewells, including three diesel STWs, thirteen electric STWs, and nine SMs (including one operated by the agricultural cooperative) were surveyed. One household owned two electric STWs and one SM, and another household owned one electric STW and one SM. For the rest, each household owned one tubewell each. Besides the agricultural cooperative, the total number of households with tubewells in the survey was twenty-one.

The survey results are as follows. First, Table 4.2 shows the process of diffusion of tubewells in Gontra village. The table was a compilation of the information gathered in the interviews with farmers with tubewells. It is consistent with the history of irrigation gleaned from the interview survey of the village leaders, except for a slight discrepancy in the timing of diesel STW diffusion. The diffusion of diesel STWs started from 1982 according to Table 4.2, whereas the village leaders stated that it started from the mid-1970s. It is unclear which information is correct.

Next, Table 4.3 shows the farmland size distribution of tubewell owners. The average farmland size held by the owners of electric STWs and SMs was almost seven acres; that of diesel STW owners was more than two-and-a-half acres. There were no tubewell owners with a land holding of less than one-and-a-half acres. The largest farmland was fifteen acres (held by the owner of two electric STWs and one SM) and the second largest was 11.7 acres (held by the owner of one SM). It is clear that ownership of tubewells, especially more-expensive tubewells, was the exclusive domain of upper-class farm households.[20] This is consistent with the facts reported in Webster (1999) and mentioned in Note 6.

Table 4.4 shows the average income and expenditure figures by tubewell type (diesel STW, electric STW, and SM) based on twenty-one of the twenty-five surveyed tubewells for which financial data were available. Data for four tubewells were unavailable because two were out of service and two owners declined to provide information. Profit for each tubewell was plotted in Figure 4.2, with the total irrigation area in terms of *boro* acres on its horizontal axis. The *boro* acre is the weighted sum of the irrigation acreage of different crops using the weight factor, which is the water charge for each crop divided by the water charge for *boro* being 100.

The above survey results led to the following findings. First, despite the fact that the bottom line figures were somewhat overestimated due to the exclusion of depreciation cost on the initial investment in tubewells and interest on working

Table 4.3: The size of farmland owned by tubewell owners

FARM AREA CLASS (ACRE)	DIESEL STW	ELECTRIC STW	SM
0			
0.01–1.49			
1.50–2.49	1	3	
2.50–4.99	2	2	3
5.00–9.99		6	3
10.00–		2	2
Agricultural Cooperative			1
Total	3	13	9
Average farm size (acre)	2.72	6.54	7.00

Note: One household owning 8.67 acres and another owning 15.00 acres owned two electric STWs and SMs respectively. They have been simply added up.

Source: Prepared by the author based on the September 2000 field survey.

capital from the expenditure calculation,[21] standard STWs (not only diesel but also electric) were generally operating at a loss, hence tubewell investment was far from a lucrative investment opportunity. In short, standard STWs were operating at a loss because they did not have sufficient irrigation coverage (that is, they had low-capacity utilization rates). Figure 4.2 indicates that a tubewell must supply irrigation to at least twenty-five to thirty *bigha* (eight to ten acres) in order to operate profitably. The break-even point was just over nine acres in the case of Bangladesh, as discussed in Chapter 3.

Second, four of the eight SMs were operating in the black, two were operating in the red, and two were just breaking even. It is clear that the command area again played a critical role in determining the profitability here. However, even the four profitable SMs produced rather modest profits of Indian rupees (Rs) 10,000–15,000 per year. Assuming that the useful life of the SM was twenty years, depreciation expense calculated by the straight-line method would be about Rs3,000, which would leave a (net) profit of Rs7,000–Rs12,000. Even if interest on working capital was assumed to be zero, the rate of return on investment would only be 12% to 21% per annum. A waterlord accusation appears to be far removed from reality.

How did this situation arise? Explanations for each tubewell type based on tubewell locations in Figure 4.3 are presented here.

First, three existing diesel STWs were introduced in 1985, 1986, and 1993 respectively. Their capital value per unit was Rs10,000–Rs15,000 (historical price). They generally had small command areas, with two supplying five *bigha*

Table 4.4: Income and expenditure for tubewell operation in Gontra village

	Diesel STW		Electric STW				SM		
Valid sample	2		11				8		
Initial investment (Rs)	12,500		13,158				56,388		
Average irrigated area (*bigha*)	2.5 (*boro*)	2.5 (veg)	14.7 (*boro*)	7.7 (*aman*)	0.5 (*aus*)	0.9 (veg)	32.5 (*boro*)	16.7 (*aman*)	1.9 (veg)
Self-cultivated	2.5	2.0	6.4	2.5	0.4	0.4	9.5	6.4	0.5
Water sale	0	0.5	8.3	5.2	0.1	0.5	23.0	10.3	1.4
Water sale price (Rs/*bigha*)	350	300	395	58	100	300	351	110	150
Gross income (Rs)	1,625		6,130				13,375		
Expenditure (Rs)									
Diesel oil/Electricity	2,050		4,273				4,501		
Maintenance & management	750		1,280				1,759		
Family labor	860		2,845				2,588		
Hired labor	0		382				1,125		
Total expenditure	3,660		8,780				9,973		
Net income (Rs)	–2,035		–2,650				3,402		

Note: 1 *bigha* = 0.33 acres, US$1 = 44.9 Rs (rupees) (as at Sept 2000), veg = vegetables.

Source: Prepared by the author based on the September 2000 field survey.

Figure 4.2: Tubewell irrigated area and profitability in Gontra village

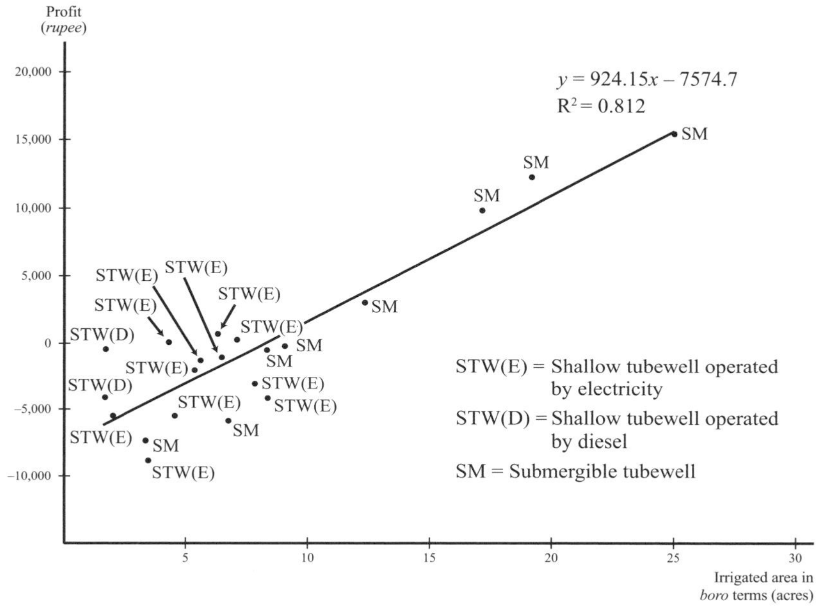

and one supplying eight *bigha*. The first two did not sell irrigation water. They can be regarded as marginal tubewells to provide small-scale irrigation to their owners' self-cultivated fields, which were located on higher parts of the village field and could not obtain irrigation water from nearby tubewells.

Second, thirteen existing electric STWs were installed in 1984 (one), 1985 (one), 1986 (two), 1987 (three), 1988 (three), 1992 (one), and 1996 (two). Their historical prices at the time of purchase ranged from Rs10,000–Rs20,000, which was similar to the prices of diesel STWs. The STW newly installed by farmer No.8 in 1996 was used to irrigate six *bigha* of his own land and was considered to fall in the same category as the abovementioned diesel STWs, as was the STW owned by farmer No. 7. The STW installed by farmer No. 15 in 1988 was out of service at the time of the survey because it had lost some command area to a new STW built in close vicinity by farmer No. 5 in 1994. The STW installed by farmer No. 20 in 1987 suffered a reduction of its command area to eight *bigha* when the neighboring STWs were rapidly converted to SMs.

Excluding these four units as special cases, the command area for *boro* rice of the remaining nine units ranged from twelve to twenty-five *bigha*. The average area of 16.4 *bigha* (five-and-a-half acres) is a very low-capacity utilization rate in view of their irrigation capacity of forty to fifty *bigha*.

Finally, the historical price of nine SMs ranged from Rs50,000–Rs60,000, which was much higher than STW prices. The SM of farmer No. 10, which had been converted from a standard STW in 1997, failed to secure a sufficient command area due to competition with two adjacent SMs (farmer No. 2, who converted in 1995, and farmer No. 8, who converted in 1996) and was out of service at the time of the survey. The SM owned by farmer No. 21 had a markedly small command area of ten *bigha* (*boro*) for no obvious reasons. Except for these two, the remaining seven SMs had *boro* irrigated areas ranging from twenty to fifty *bigha* and were not achieving very high capacity utilization rates in view of their irrigation capacity of 120 *bigha*.

Thus, it would be possible to argue that the generally declining profitability of tubewell operation was caused by a reduction in the command area per tubewell due to indiscriminate introduction of tubewells—essentially the same situation as in the case of Bangladesh (Chapter 3). It is likely that returns on tubewell investment gradually declined over time and a majority of tubewell operations had fallen into the red by the time of the survey. However, a difference between the situations in Gontra village and Bangladesh was the possibility that Gontra was in a state of some kind of disequilibrium in the sense that it was in the middle of an adjustment process involving conversion from the standard STW to the SM in the face of declining groundwater levels. It is not easy to predict to what extent this state of disequilibrium would be corrected through the conversion from the standard STW to the SM or the withdrawal of the STW in the future.

Since the irrigation capacity of the SM was three times more than that of the standard STW, a large-scale shake-out would be inevitable. Yet, there were few signs of coordinated response on the part of tubewell owners or the village leaders. The only noticeable response was a passive one in the form of suspension of operation when a deficit reached an intolerable level.

This appears to speak volumes about the clear limitations of adjustment through a pure market mechanism in irrigation, which has a strong externality arising from the contiguity of farmland, and, despite this, about the absence of non-market adjustment, at least in the Bengal region.

Profit Structure of Irrigated Agriculture

Let us move on to a profitability analysis for irrigated agriculture founded on water purchased from tubewell owners. Table 4.5 shows the analysis for the two major irrigated crops of *boro* rice and transplanted *aman* rice. Data were collected in a supplementary survey to the census survey of tubewell owners.[22] The sample size was eleven owners for *boro* rice and nine owners for *aman* rice.

The average yield per *bigha* was 15.9 *maund* for *boro* rice and 14.3 *maund* for transplanted *aman* rice (4.40 tons/hectare and 3.95 tons/hectare respectively).

Table 4.5: Rice crop production cost and income in Gontra village

	TRANSPLANTED *AMAN*	(SHARE)	*BORO*	(SHARE)
Sample	9		11	
Yield (*maund*/acre)	42.9		47.7	
Gross income (Rs/acre)				
Paddy	8,853		10,140	
Paddy straw	837		750	
Total gross income	9,690	100%	10,890	100%
Expenditure (Rs/acre)				
Current input				
Seedlings	519		618	
Urea	279		501	
TSP[a]	180		366	
MP[b]	165		207	
Other chemical fertilizers	159		150	
Manure	0		654	
Agricultural chemicals	204		207	
Subtotal current input	1,506	15.5%	2,703	24.8%
Labor cost				
Land preparation	921		942	
Transplanting	570		597	
Weeding	831		678	
Harvesting	1,458		1,659	
Others	243		243	
Subtotal labor cost	4,023	41.5%	4,119	37.8%
Water charge	309	3.2%	1,185	10.9%
Total expenditure	5,838	60.2%	8,007	73.5%
Operator's surplus (Rs/acre)	3,852	39.8%	2,883	26.5%

Notes:
1 *maund* = 37.3 kg
a: TSP means trisodium phosphate.
b: MP means muriate of potash.

Source: Prepared by the author based on the September 2000 field survey.

There was a significant difference between their production costs,[23] with those for *boro* rice being considerably higher, whereas their labor expenses were very similar. The irrigation cost represented a small proportion of the gross production value in both cases, and was only 11% for *boro* rice. It is clear that the irrigation cost was not a heavy burden, even in *boro* rice production, not to mention transplanted *aman* rice production.

However, it would be impossible to understand how heavy the irrigation cost burden of 11% was unless it was compared with something else. Two cases are provided for comparison.

The first one is a comparison with the historical data on Gontra village itself. Due to difficulty in obtaining past data, this estimation is made based on somewhat strong assumptions. As mentioned earlier, the rent was three *maund* of paddy per *bigha* when seasonal tenancy of farmland by tubewell owners was predominant in Gontra village. Credible information puts the yield at a much higher rate in those days (about eighteen *maund*) than at the time of the survey. Assuming that the value of rice straw byproduct was proportional (7.4% of the main crop, the same as at the time of the survey), the land rent would have been 15.5% of the gross production value in those days. Also assuming similar production costs and labor costs (24.8% and 37.8% of gross production value), the surplus in the hands of tubewell owners would have amounted to about 22% of gross production value. This would represent the real irrigation cost in those days, which was twice the level at the time of the survey.[24]

Second, let us use the case of Titkle village in neighboring Bangladesh for comparison. Table 3.7 in the previous chapter shows data from the December 1999 survey, which was conducted at around the same time as the Gontra village survey. The Titkle case was different from Gontra in that a majority of farmers bought water from diesel STWs, but the irrigation cost was very similar to that of Gontra at 12.7% of gross production value. It became clear in Chapter 3 that the real water charge decreased substantially due to intensifying competition in the groundwater market. There is little doubt that the same situation occurred in Gontra village.

The following is somewhat superfluous to the current discussion, but the operators' surplus from transplanted *aman* rice and *boro* rice production was almost equal to the market rent, indicating that the land lease market was competitive in Titkle village in Bangladesh. What was the situation in Gontra village?

Going back to Table 4.5, the operators' surplus per acre was Rs3,852 from *aman* and Rs2,883 from *boro*. On the other hand, the market rent was Rs3,000–Rs4,500 for transplanted *aman* and Rs3,000–Rs3,600 for *boro* (both were paid in advance) according to the interview survey.[25] While they were almost the same for transplanted *aman*, there was a rather substantial discrepancy in the case of *boro*. This situation appears to be related to the fact that the rice price was somewhat abnormally depressed in Gontra village immediately after a year of booming rice export to Bangladesh in 1998 (due to major flooding there). A possible explanation is that a land rent of Rs3,000–Rs3,600, which had been reasonable at the previous rice price level, became slightly expensive when the rice price fell. In other words, it would be possible to argue that the land lease market was also functioning well in Gontra village.

As another superfluous point, a comparison of Table 4.5 and Table 3.7 reveals one important fact—a marked difference in the labor share of rice production (and the land share on the reverse side of the same coin) between the two areas. The labor share was 20% to 30% in Titkle village, Bangladesh, whereas it reached about 40% in Gontra village.[26]

The reason for this is not fully understood. The wage rate for eight hours of labor, including payment in kind, was about Tk40 in Bangladesh and Rs40–Rs45 in West Bengal. After adjusting for the exchange rate of one rupee to Tk1.21, the difference in the wage rate would be 35% at most, which would not fully explain the difference in labor cost between the two areas. The difference was particularly large in *boro* rice cropping. It can only be assumed that rice farming (especially *boro*) in Titkle village, Bangladesh, had a strong labor-saving tendency for some reason. This issue has to be left for future studies.[27]

For whatever reasons, the land share of rice production was considerably higher in Bangladesh than in West Bengal, and this fact would have extremely important implications on the economic wellbeing of the rural landless and small farmers. While irrigated agriculture developed through the dissemination of tubewells in the same manner in both Bangladesh and West Bengal within the Bengal region, the two areas stood in stark contrast on a vital point, which was the distribution between the most important factors of production: labor and land.[28]

The Groundwater Market

Finally, a few notable features of Gontra village's groundwater market are discussed.

State-operated DTWs

First, the issue of irrigation subsidies should be addressed. The water charge for irrigation from the state-operated DTWs was Rs80 per *bigha* for *boro* rice and Rs20–Rs25 for *aman* rice. In view of the market rates for private tubewell irrigation (Rs350–Rs400 and Rs100 respectively), the public irrigation charges were highly subsidized. Even if the state government had charged the private owner's rates, it would have been far from breaking even since it paid its tubewell operators and assistants exceptionally well. The true cost to the state government would far outweigh the subsidy.

The problem was that the full-time operator and two assistants assigned to each DTW were actually not doing any work, and farmers jointly employed another operator and shared the cost pro rata according to the size of their irrigated land. A substantial portion of the subsidy for minor irrigation was wasted on the totally useless salary payment.

Many of the state-operated DTWs were nearing the end of their useful lives. What would happen when they stopped operating? Since this problem had not yet surfaced in Gontra village, the case of a nearby village is presented.

A survey was conducted in the nearby village of Birahi, which is located en route from Kalyani to Gontra. A thirty-five-year-old DTW had reached the end of its usefulness and fairly extensive rehabilitation work had just been completed. While some useable parts of the facility (such as the underground water pipe network) were retained, a large amount of money (about Rs475,000, but the exact amount was unknown to farmers) was invested in works such as re-excavation of the well and replacement of the motor and had to be repaid over five years following a repayment grace period of two years (during which interest only was payable at 16%). The control of the facility was transferred to the local farmer group, which became responsible for the costs of tubewell operation and maintenance. It paid a monthly electricity charge of Rs9,000–Rs11,000 for six months of the year and also hired an operator.

The irrigated area was about fifty acres for *boro* rice and more than 130 acres for transplanted *aman* rice. The water charge per *bigha* was set at Rs500 for *boro*, Rs60 for transplanted *aman*, and Rs100 for jute. Since the water charge for the state-operated DTWs was Rs80 for *boro*, Rs20 for transplanted *aman*, and Rs20 for jute, these charges represented a sudden increase in the financial burden on farmers. The group was hoping to expand the command area for *boro* rice cropping (a substantial number of farmers had converted to water purchase from private STWs prior to the rehabilitation of the DTW as its performance had gradually deteriorated) but its leaders could not hide their apprehension about prospects of repayment when they were interviewed.

In short, it is clearly the policy intention of the West Bengal state government to transfer full control of rehabilitated DTWs one by one to farmer groups. However, success or failure of this policy depends on whether farmer groups can secure proper maintenance and repair services for their DTWs, and, moreover, whether they can operate them in a financially viable manner.

The Issue of Power Subsidies for Agriculture

In West Bengal, just as in other states in India, there is an issue about power subsidies for agriculture (and households). The electricity charge for agriculture consists of a flat-rate base charge, which is set at a very low level. Shah

(1993) recognizes the role of the flat-rate charge system in restraining tubewell water sale prices and boosting the economic wellbeing of lower-class farmers who do not have tubewells, while admitting that it keeps the marginal cost of groundwater pumping at a very low level, which, in turn, leads to the serious environmental problem of over-extraction of groundwater. Shah also recommends that the state electricity board should raise the base charge substantially, while keeping the flat-rate system in order to resolve its management problem.

The state government moved to raise electricity charges (effective from 26 January 1999) by issuing a notice from the undersecretary of the Ministry of Power on 24 December 1998. This was the first revision in seven years since October 1991. The main points of the revision were as follows.

1. The nominal base charge was increased by 1.9 times and the flat-rate system was retained for STWs (three to five horsepower). There had been no distinction between SMs and standard STWs prior to the revision, but a separate charge for SMs was introduced under this revision and was about 1.5 times the charge for standard STWs. Thus, the annual electricity charge increased from Rs1,700 to Rs3,284 for standard STWs and to Rs4,932 for SMs.
2. The metered-rate system, not the flat-rate system, had been used for DTWs and river lift pumps prior to the revision. Under the revision, both types were classified into the five- to fifty-horsepower motor category and the unit price for one kilowatt hour was increased from Rs55 to Rs123, or by 2.24 times.

However, the above increases did not actually amount to real charge increases when inflation was taken into account. The general wholesale price index (1970–71 = 100) in Kolkata city was 510 in 1990–91 and 1,008 in 1998–99, which means an inflation rate of 98% over the period.[29] The nominal charge increase was 93% for standard STWs, 190% for SMs, and 124% for DTWs and the river lift pumps, which translates into real increases of negative 5%, 92%, and 26% respectively.

Although the electricity charge for SMs was raised substantially, it is understood that a majority of SMs were falsely registered as standard STWs with the state electricity board and that their owners did not pay at the revised rate. This was verified by the fact that there was little difference in the electricity charge between electric STWs and SMs in Table 4.4.

In short, it is likely that the electricity charge revision in West Bengal at the end of 1998 did little to reduce the power subsidy for agriculture. However, it is clear from the financial analysis of tubewell operation that the power subsidy was fully reflected in the low level of water charges paid by lower-class farmers without tubewells. The benefit of the power subsidy trickled down sufficiently.

Other Issues

The conversion from standard STWs to SMs that was prompted by declining groundwater levels during the 1990s has already been mentioned. However, just as in the state of Punjab, which was going through the same phase, this response was a temporary fix and simply deferred the problem. Although the causal relationship has not been established sufficiently, it has been suggested that the groundwater irrigation development caused arsenic contamination of groundwater. In fact, significant numbers of people showed symptoms of arsenic poisoning in the village.[30]

Apart from the above environmental issue, there was another problem associated with declining groundwater levels and the conversion to SMs. The problem—of adjustment to the command area, which has been mentioned previously—stemmed from the fact that SMs had an irrigation capacity three times greater than that of standard STWs. It would require some kind of coordination between tubewell owners, guided by the village leadership.

Finally, the problem of nonpayment of the water charge by farmers who had fields in lowlands should be touched upon. The problem would become especially serious with regard to *aman* rice cropping, which might or might not require irrigation depending on the weather. Since water flows into lowlands from the surrounding lands naturally, even if owners do not buy irrigation water, owners of lowlands who receive demands for water charge payments from tubewell owners can insist that they never agreed to buy water. Needless to say, this problem originates from the externality of irrigation. Just as in the case of Titkle village in Bangladesh, such opportunistic behavior of water buyer farmers contributed to a squeeze on the profitability of tubewell investment.

Summary

This chapter has discussed the development of irrigated agriculture prompted by the diffusion of tubewells and the transformation of the groundwater market, and associated issues based on the case of Gontra village in Nadia district, West Bengal. The main findings are as follows.

First, the primary cause of agricultural development from the 1980s can be attributed to the development of groundwater irrigation by tubewell construction, at least in Gontra village, rather than to agrarian land reform or local government reform. Among the policy measures under the Communist Party administration, the promotion of rural electrification, which supported the development of privately owned tubewell irrigation, is noteworthy as an accelerator factor.

Second, it was observed also in Gontra village that tubewell ownership was heavily weighted towards upper-class farmers. Yet, this did not necessarily mean that they were waterlords who monopolized profits from irrigated agriculture. The reality was the reverse. Water prices fell so low as to put tubewell operation under strong pressure and the benefits of the Green Revolution reached farmers who conducted irrigated farming with water bought from tubewell owners. It is possible to at least conclude that the waterlord argument has become a relic of the past.

Third, the power subsidy for agriculture in West Bengal was not reduced by the revision of electricity charges at the end of 1998. Still, the subsidy sufficiently benefited water buyer farmers rather than tubewell owners.

Fourth, it was clear that the land share of rice farming (especially irrigated *boro* rice farming) tended to be lower and the labor share tended to be higher in Gontra village, West Bengal, than in Bangladesh. Although the reason for this is yet to be explored, it is possible to conclude that the benefits of the Green Revolution have, to a large degree, pervaded not only the lower-class peasantry but also the landless labor class.

Fifth, there is an urgent need for detailed socioeconomic research in order to evaluate the government policy to transfer the total control of rehabilitated state-operated DTWs to farmer groups.

Sixth, the problem of declining groundwater levels is becoming serious. In relation to this issue, it would be desirable to devise some measures to reduce frictions that arise in the process of conversion from standard STWs to SMs. Also, groundwater arsenic poisoning is a dire problem that requires urgent investigation into its causes so that appropriate measures can be taken.

Part II
The Changing Agrarian Structure and Finance

5
Credit Flow from the Wealthy to the Poor

Failure of Formal Finance and Transformation of Informal Finance

Formal finance facilities available in rural Bangladesh included loans from the Bangladesh *Krishi* (Agricultural) Bank (BKB) and commercial banks (mainly for upper-class farmers), loans from agricultural cooperatives (mainly for small farmers), and loans from NGOs and the Grameen Bank (for landless laborers and marginal farmers). The expansion of formal finance into the rural area advanced at a fast pace from the mid-1970s and through the 1980s in Bangladesh. The change was triggered by the Special Agricultural Credit Program, which began in 1977. Under this program, financial institutions were subjected to strong administrative guidance and expanded their branch networks into rural areas in an effort to achieve their lending targets in the agricultural and rural sector. As a result, the number of regional branches of the BKB and six government-run commercial banks (Sonari, Janata, Agrani, Rupali, Pubali, and Uttara—the latter two were later privatized) increased 3.8 times, from 854 to 3,225, over an eight-year period between 1975 and 1983, and the size of their agricultural credit grew 8.1 times from Tk467 million in 1975/76 to Tk3,772 million in 1983/84 (the real value deflated by the agricultural input price; the base year of 1975/76) (Hossain, M. 1985a). The rapid credit expansion was owed largely to the provision of short-term crop loans without land collateral that became available under the program.

The abovementioned cooperatives for small farmers refer to the cooperatives in the Comilla Model two-tier system, which achieved a certain level of success in the Comilla area under the guidance of the Bangladesh Academy for Rural Development (BARD) in the early 1960s before it was implemented on a national scale.[1] Primary cooperatives were formed at the village level and a federation of cooperatives was organized at the *thana* level, both of which have been under the supervision of the Bangladesh Rural Development Board (BRDB) since 1983. Primary cooperatives included original-type farmers' cooperatives for small farmers (*Krishi Samabaya Samity* (KSS)), women's cooperatives (*Mohila Samabaya Samity* (MSS)), and assetless cooperatives (*Bittohin Samabaya Samity* (BSS)). As at the end of 1990/91, the numbers of primary cooperative societies (with their members in brackets) were 66,899 for the KSS (2.46 million), 6,840 for the MSS (0.33 million), 14,592 for the BSS (0.41 million), and 9,958 for other types of cooperative societies (0.11 million)—a total of just under 100,000 cooperatives with 3.3 million members (average 33.6 members per cooperative) (BRDB 1992). There were 59,990 *mauza* (revenue villages) nationwide, which translated to 1.64 primary cooperatives in each *mauza*. Primary cooperatives collected shares and savings deposits from their members and received funds from one of the nationalized commercial banks, the Sonari Bank. The federation of cooperatives at the *thana* level acted as a sub-lender of funds from the Sonari Bank to primary cooperatives. Among loans furnished through cooperatives, the size of loans for agricultural purposes increased rapidly in the first half of the 1980s with government support. It dramatically expanded from Tk258 million (only 6.4% of the total agricultural lending by all financial institutions) in 1981/82 to Tk4,065 million (65% of the same) in 1982/83 and Tk3,228 million in 1983/84. The Comilla-type cooperative system was able to grow rapidly on the back of the abovementioned rural expansion of commercial banks because of the characteristic of its finance mechanism based on sub-lending of Sonari Bank loans.

Although rural formal finance grew rapidly from the late 1970s to the early 1980s as described above, the rate of growth began to slow considerably from the mid-1980s due to the sluggish and worsening rate of financial recovery. The recovery rate was already below 50% in 1980/81, dropped below 40% in 1984/85, and fell further to 25% when the freezing of new lending was declared in 1985/86. Thus, rural formal finance collapsed and the amount of lending has remained at the 1982/83 level of Tk6–Tk7 billion in nominal terms since then. With the annual inflation rate of about 10%, the sector has effectively continued to shrink considerably (Fujita 1993a: 64–8). In short, the main culprit for the collapse of rural formal finance in the mid-1980s was the Comilla-type cooperatives. Accordingly, the provision of funds to these cooperatives was severely curbed, rapidly decreasing from Tk3–Tk4 billion at the peak to Tk1.22 billion in 1984/85 and Tk0.60 billion in 1985/86 (World Bank 1993). Like the *classic* cooperatives mentioned in Note 1, many of these primary cooperatives have been inactive since then.[2] Cooperatives have failed to become the leading players in rural formal finance. The upper-layer *thana* federations of cooperatives have barely continued their activities, which are funded mostly by margins on the sub-lending of meager loans from the Sonari Bank to primary cooperatives.

By the way, the debt default problem has not improved very much since then, despite various policy measures devised by the authorities such as the reinforcement of proceedings to enforce payment, the reinforcement of customer management measures (for example, the issuing of passbooks), and the establishment of the finance court for facilitation of conflict resolution.[3]

The aforementioned Grameen Bank is a special financial institution for the rural poor (especially women), which was launched by Professor Mohammad Yunus of the Faculty of Economics, Chittagong University, at that time, as an action research project in 1976 and which achieved rapid growth following government legislation as a bank in 1983.[4] The word *grameen* means 'of the village' in the Bengali language. The main characteristics of its operation are as follows. The bank provides loans without collateral to members of landless households and marginal landholders with less than half an acre, and the borrowers are required to make weekly repayments over one year. The bank's officers pay weekly visits to villages so that members can carry out their banking activities without having to visit the bank branch. A loan is issued to the individual but the borrower must be part of a group of five members who are jointly responsible for the loan. The Grameen Bank was the pioneer of microcredit, which was earnestly promoted in Bangladesh, mainly by NGOs, after the aforementioned collapse of formal finance in the mid-1980s.[5]

In 1987 the first large-scale finance survey of rural areas across the country was carried out by the Bangladesh Bureau of Statistics (BBS), which was in the midst of a rural finance transition during which NGOs replaced banks and cooperatives as the main players in formal finance.[6] The survey found that formal finance accounted for only a small portion (about one-third) of rural finance (Table 5.1). In other words, the special financial institution BKB, commercial banks such as the Sonari Bank, quasi-government agencies, cooperatives, NGOs, and the Grameen Bank together represented only 28% of the total borrowing transactions by rural households and 36% of the total loan amount. The rest was represented by informal finance, which mainly comprised loans from professional moneylenders, friends, and relatives. Of course, it is common knowledge that these types of statistics can be unreliable in Bangladesh. It may be more so for a sensitive topic such as finance, about which respondents may be reluctant to provide honest answers. The possible existence of sub-lending of funds from formal finance to informal finance on a scale that cannot be ignored would also make the situation more complicated.[7] However, the finding that informal finance was the main means for borrowing, and that it accounted for roughly two-thirds of rural finance, has been verified, though fragmentarily, by the accumulated rural micro-studies from various parts of the country.[8]

By the way, the mainstream understanding of rural informal finance in the Indian subcontinent, including Bangladesh, has been as follows. Lenders in informal finance (besides town-based professional usurers) are landlords and wealthy farmers, and borrowers are lower-class farmers, tenant farmers, and

Table 5.1: Composition of rural finance lenders in Bangladesh

	% OF TRANSACTIONS	% OF VALUE	VALUE PER TRANSACTION (*TAKA*)
Bangladesh *Krishi* Bank	11	17	5,275
Sonari Bank	3	5	5,878
Other banks	3	5	5,331
(Semi-)government agencies	2	2	3,809
Subtotal	*19*	*29*	*5,225*
Cooperatives	5	4	2,749
NGOs	1	1	3,157
Grameen Bank	3	2	3,109
Subtotal	*9*	*7*	*2,914*
Moneylenders	29	27	3,265
Friends & relatives	39	34	3,070
Other	4	3	2,546
Subtotal	*72*	*64*	*3,119*
Total	100	100	3,509

Source: Prepared by the author based on BBS 1989.

landless laborers. The existence of high interest rates prevents the latter from escaping poverty and acts as a powerful factor to promote differentiation of peasantry.

Atiur Rahman's following comment draws our attention as a typical expression of this 'commonly accepted view' of credit flow in informal finance.

> Moneylenders we interviewed included people from various classes of land ownership but a majority were clearly large-scale landholders...We have found that the usufructuary mortgage system, together with professional moneylenders, drove farmers into distress sale (of land) and played a significant role in increasing the number of landless households, and that this is still happening today (Rahman 1986: 166).

Professor Hideki Esho lists thirteen common features of 'non-institutional rural credit markets,' with Indian rural areas in view, and states:

> Borrowers can be broadly divided into the farmer group (large/middle/small farmers, tenant farmers, agricultural laborers) and the non-farmer group (traders, especially village retailers, handicraftsmen, rural industrial laborers) but the chief

> borrowers are people in the low income bracket, which include small farmers, tenant farmers, agricultural laborers and the non-agriculturalists...lenders include professional moneylenders, agriculturalist moneylenders, landlords, traders, commission agents, friends, neighbors and relatives, and the first five types of lenders charge high interest rates while the latter three charge the effective interest rate of zero or even below zero (Esho 1987: 19–20).[9]

Again, lending from the wealthy to the poor is considered self-evident.

Bhaduri's famous semi-feudal model took a hint from the *actual condition* of rural areas in eastern India adjacent to Bangladesh. According to this model (in which the landlord acts to maximize his combined income that consists of the rent from the tenant and the interest on a consumer loan, which he furnishes to the tenant regularly), the landlord tries to obstruct the introduction of new technologies, since it reduces the tenant's need for a consumer loan and reduces the landlord's total income (Bhaduri 1973). It seems that the theory of exploitation and control of tenant farmers, lower-class farmers, and agricultural laborers by landlords and upper-class farmers through usury has become deeply entrenched as a commonly accepted view.

It appears, however, that this commonly accepted view of rural informal finance is, in fact, not sufficiently supported by empirical research. Or, at least, the fact that this financial sector underwent some kind of major structural change after the 1980s is not recognized widely. For example, Bardhan and Rudra (1978) revealed that many of the assumptions used in Bhaduri's semi-feudal model, including the tenant's chronic indebtedness to the landlord, have, in fact, diverged from the actual condition of rural areas in eastern India.

This chapter argues that the above commonly accepted view is very unlikely to be valid and, based on two rural field surveys in Bangladesh at the beginning of the 1990s, presents the fact that the position of the lender and the borrower of informal finance has *reversed*—with the poor in the lower classes with newly acquired savings power lending funds to the wealthy in the upper classes at high interest rates. This chapter also examines the actual condition of informal finance in detail from the viewpoints of inter-class flows, terms and conditions such as interest rates, loan periods and collaterals, its association with formal finance, and purposes for which the borrower uses the loan, and discusses the resultant policy implications.

The composition of this chapter is as follows. In the first section, the characteristics of land ownership and agricultural production and the structure of off-farm employment in the two study villages are outlined. It becomes clear that the two villages have contrasting characteristics in terms of the structure of land ownership and the development of off-farm employment. Then, the actual condition of inter-class flow of informal finance is analyzed. The analysis has found that a common fact in both villages was that the lower class in terms of landholding size was the credit entity and the upper class was the deficit entity in finance, which contradicted the commonly accepted view. Terms and conditions such as interest rates in informal finance are also discussed.

The second section considers counterarguments that are expected to be raised against the proposition about credit flow from the poor to the wealthy. One is the possibility that differences in landholding size do not correspond perfectly with differences in household income and wealth. The other is the possibility that the impact of the Grameen Bank on the poor has reached the informal finance sector. This section demonstrates that these cases are unlikely. The third section examines how the upper class was using the funds borrowed at high interest rates, and reveals that there was much demand for working capital for tubewell operation, as well as for small businesses in the agricultural and other commodities marketing sector.

Finally, the above survey findings are summarized and the economic background leading to the generation of the credit flow in informal finance that contradicted the commonly accepted view is hypothesized and its policy implications are discussed.

The Condition of Rural Informal Finance: From Two Village Surveys

An Outline of the Study Villages

The necessary information about the study villages is presented first. Important facts in understanding the actual condition of finance include the class composition based on landholding size and the associated employment structure, especially the condition of off-farm employment. The condition of agricultural production is also important. The two villages are compared on these points in the following discussion.

One of the survey villages was Daskin Chamuria village in Kalihati *thana*, Tangail district, which is sixty to seventy kilometers northwest of the capital Dhaka by direct distance. It takes about three hours to travel from Dhaka by bus and about another thirty minutes on foot. The other village was Aira village in Sherpur *thana*, Bogra district, 130 to 140 kilometers northwest of Dhaka by direct distance (see Chapter 2). The survey was conducted prior to the completion of the Jamuna Bridge and a trip from Dhaka to Aira took a whole day (six to seven hours), including between two and two-and-a-half hours on a ferry across the Jamuna River, one of the world's major rivers. The remote village was another seven to eight kilometers off the main bus route, and the access road became so muddy in the wet season that even a four-wheel-drive vehicle would dare not enter.

The two villages were different in agricultural ecology. Daskin Chamuria village was located in the deep flooding area in the middle of a vast floodplain on the eastern bank of the Jamuna River, whereas Aira village was sitting on the Barind Tract outside the regular flood-prone area.

The two villages were similar in that the introduction of tubewells progressed rapidly during the 1980s (Table 5.2), which enabled the spread of the new cropping system that centered on dry-season irrigated cropping of *boro* rice.[10] The introduction of tubewells during the 1980s quickly boosted the irrigation coverage to 80% to 90% in both villages, and double cropping with traditional wet-season rain-fed *aman* rice and irrigated *boro* rice became the main cropping pattern (Table 5.3). (Triple cropping with *rabi* crops such as mustard between these two rice crops was predominant in Daskin Chamuria village.)

However, the differences in the ecological conditions were reflected in large differences in rice yield. Especially with *aman* rice, BR-line[11] HYVs were commonly grown in Aira village, which yielded over forty *maund*/acre (one *maund* = 37.3 kilograms, forty *maund*/acre = approximately 3.69 tons/hectare);

Table 5.2: Process of STW diffusion in the study villages

	Daskin Chamuria village		Aira village	
	New	Cumulative total	New	Cumulative total
1975	2[a]	2	–	–
1980	–	2	–	–
1981	1	3	1	1
1982	2	5	–	1
1983	3	8	–	1
1984	1	9	3	5
1985	2	11	1	5
1986	–	11	–	5
1987	3	14	2	7
1988	3	17	3	10
1989	1	18	7	17
1990	3	21	6	23
1991	2	23	5	28
1992	–	23	2	30

Note: a = the deep tubewell (DTW).

Source: Prepared by the author based on the field survey.

Table 5.3: Farmland uses in the study villages

Cropping systems[a]				Daskin Chamuria village (1991/92)		Aira village[b] (1992/93)	
				Area (acre)	Share	Area (acre)	Share
	Aman		- *Boro*	99	31%	367	84%
	Aman	- *Rabi* crops	- *Boro*	108	34%	4	1%
Aus/Jute		- *Rabi* crops		36	11%	–	–
			Boro	32	10%	–	–
Aus	- *Aman*	- *Rabi* crops		–	–	14	3%
Aus	- *Aman*		- *Boro*	–	–	12	3%
	Aman			6	2%	10	2%
Other cropping patterns				40	12%	29	7%
Total				320	100%	436	100%

Notes:
a: *Rabi* is the collective name for dry-season non-rice crops.
b: The *rabi* crop in Aira village is a cucurbid vegetable called *khira*.
Source: Daskin Chamuria village—Prepared by the author based on the field survey. Aira village—Rashid (1994: 54).

the yield in Daskin Chamuria village was below twenty *maund*, less than half of Aira's. The *boro* rice yield was over forty *maund* in Aira village, while it was below forty *maund* in Daskin Chamuria village. Consequently, the annual total production per acre from double cropping of rice in Aira village was as much as 1.4 times that in Daskin Chamuria village.

Let us compare the population pressure on land. According to Table 5.4, the population density of Daskin Chamuria village was 1,433 people per square kilometer, which was more than three times greater than the 453 people per square kilometer in Aira village. However, about half of Aira village's farmland was owned by residents of other villages and the real population pressure on farmland was about twice the above figure. Since the average population density of Bangladesh, including urban areas, was 716 people per square kilometer, Daskin Chamuria village's population density was very high.[12]

Table 5.5 shows the class composition by landholding size and the distribution of farmland in each village. The following points are notable.

First, the difference in the population density was reflected in a large difference in the average farmland holding per household for all households, including landless households. It was 0.69 acres in Daskin Chamuria village and 1.11 acres in Aira village.

Second, inequality in land distribution was far greater in Aira village than in Daskin Chamuria village. It should suffice here to point out the ratio

Table 5.4: Area and population of study villages and local administrative units

	AREA (KM²)	NUMBER OF HOUSEHOLDS	POPULATION (PERSONS)	POPULATION DENSITY (PERSONS/KM²)	NUMBER OF LOWER ADMINISTRATIVE UNITS INCLUDED
Daskin Chamuria village	1.9	538	2,665	1,433	–
Shahabhuti *union*	19.2	4,563	26,108	1,359	21 villages
Kalihati *thana*	301.2	65,035	354,959	1,178	12 *unions*
Tangail district	3,414.0	571,000	3,000,000	879	11 *thanas*
Aira village	2.0	209	906	453	–
Mirzapur *union*	39.9	7,175	34,876	875	36 villages
Sherpur *thana*	296.3	45,258	229,005	773	9 *unions*
Bogra district	2,920.0	516,000	2,670,000	914	11 *thanas*
Bangladesh	148,000	1,940,000	106,320,000	716	64 districts

Source: BBS (1993b) except data on Daskin Chamuria and Aira villages, which are based on the field survey June–August 1992.

Table 5.5: Class composition and farmland distribution in the study villages

LANDHOLDING SIZE (ACRE)	DASKIN CHAMURIA VILLAGE			AIRA VILLAGE		
	NUMBER OF HOUSEHOLDS	OWNED LAND (ACRE)	OPERATED LAND (ACRE)	NUMBER OF HOUSEHOLDS	OWNED LAND (ACRE)	OPERATED LAND (ACRE)
0	206 (38)	0.0 (0)	29.6 (9)	102 (49)	0.0 (0)	28.6 (10)
0.01–0.49	132 (27)	29.1 (8)	47.0 (14)	34 (16)	7.2 (3)	16.7 (6)
0.50–0.99	84 (16)	58.8 (16)	50.0 (15)	14 (7)	9.7 (4)	21.4 (7)
1.00–2.49	78 (14)	121.4 (33)	106.4 (32)	25 (12)	34.2 (15)	40.5 (14)
2.50–4.99	24 (4)	83.2 (22)	49.8 (15)	17 (8)	56.8 (25)	62.2 (22)
5.00–	8 (1)	77.7 (21)	50.0 (15)	17 (8)	123.1 (53)	119.0 (41)
Total	538 (100)	370.3 (100)	332.8 (100)	209 (100)	231.0 (100)	288.4 (100)
Area per household		0.69	0.62		1.11	1.38

Note: Numbers in brackets show %.

Source: Prepared by the author based on the field survey.

of the landless (49% in Aira and 38% in Daskin Chamuria) and the ratio of households with more than two-and-a-half acres (16% in Aira and 5% in Daskin Chamuria).

Third, and especially applicable to Aira village, the scale of farmland transfer through tenancy or mortgage was relatively small given the large number of landless households.[13] In other words, large landholders tended to operate their own farms using employed laborers instead of leasing their land to tenant farmers. Even in Daskin Chamuria village, with relatively more small farms, the hired-labor type operation was more common than the family-labor type operation.

Finally, let us make a comparison of the employment structure. Suppose we use the term 'agricultural dependency' to describe the ratio of households whose heads work mainly in farming or agricultural labor to all households: it was 56% (Table 5.6) in Daskin Chamuria village, whereas it reached 80% (Table 2.3) in Aira village. The agricultural dependency was especially low for the lower class in Daskin Chamuria village—at only 38% for the landless and 51% for the group with less than half an acre. Daskin Chamuria village had a rural industry in the form of small handloom factories, unskilled work at *bidhi* (tobacco) factories scattered in neighboring towns, and employment in services such as teaching and rickshaw or *ban* pulling. Small businesses were also readily available,[14] whereas Aira village had very few employment opportunities outside of agriculture.

To sum up, Daskin Chamuria village had slightly lower agricultural productivity and a uniformly small scale of operation, but it had abundant off-farm employment opportunities in hand-weaving and other industries. Aira village was purely a farming village and almost entirely dependent on highly productive farming, and exhibited a clear differentiation between large-scale farmers and agricultural laborers.

The Reverse Flow *of Informal Finance*

Finance-related data were collected as part of the baseline survey, which was a census survey of all households conducted in each survey village from June to August 1992.[15] The survey was conducted by the well-trained staff (villagers) of the project, who visited each household to gather data. All households in each village were asked to provide the following details about their outstanding loans (either borrowed or lent) at the time of the survey.

1. Borrowings from formal financial institutions (name of the financial institution, loan period, loan amount, interest rate, collateral, and purpose).
2. Borrowings through informal finance (name and household number of the lender, relationship with the lender, time of borrowing, amount, interest rate, and purpose).
3. Lending through informal finance (name and household number of the borrower, relationship with the borrower, time of lending, amount, interest rate, and collateral). (This question was excluded from the Aira village survey.)

Table 5.6: Employment structure in Daskin Chamuria village—main occupation of the household head

Landholding size (acre)	Number of households	Farming	Agricultural wage labor	Weaving wage labor	Small business	*Bidhi* factory	Teachers & other services	*Rickshaw* driver	Other
0	206	11 (5)	69 (33)	48 (23)	23 (11)	19 (9)	6 (3)	11 (5)	20 (10)
0.01–0.49	138	21 (15)	49 (36)	22 (16)	18 (13)	8 (6)	6 (7)	4 (3)	8 (6)
0.50–0.99	84	51 (60)	12 (14)	2 (2)	7 (8)	2 (2)	6 (7)	–	5 (6)
1.00–2.49	78	67 (85)	1 (1)	1 (1)	2 (3)	2 (3)	5 (6)	–	1 (1)
2.50–4.99	24	19 (79)	–	1 (4)	–	–	3 (13)	–	1 (4)
5.00–	8	5 (63)	–	–	–	–	3 (38)	–	–
Total	538	173 (32)	131 (24)	74 (14)	50 (9)	31 (6)	29 (5)	15 (3)	35 (7)

Note: Numbers in brackets show %.

Source: Prepared by the author based on the field survey.

The survey results relating to informal finance are presented first and the actual condition of formal finance is discussed later. The results are summarized in Table 5.7 and Table 5.8.

In Table 5.7 all households in Daskin Chamuria village are divided into four categories: lenders, lender-cum-borrowers, borrowers, and others (households not involved in informal finance). Households in each category are further divided into landholding classes. The total amount of lending (the average amount per household in brackets), the total amount of borrowing, and the current balance for each class are also included.[16] Table 5.8 shows the same data for Aira village. The following points are notable in these tables.[17]

First, the number of households that were involved in informal finance was extremely high. The percentage of households involved in either lending or borrowing or both was 79% in Daskin Chamuria village and 61% in Aira village. What is especially noteworthy is the high percentage of lenders (46% in Daskin Chamuria and 34% in Aira), rather than the high percentage of borrowers (56% in Daskin Chamuria and 39% in Aira). There existed a complex financial market consisting of numerous borrowers and almost equally numerous lenders.

Second, comparison of the percentage of households involved in informal finance between different landholding classes reveals that the percentage of lenders was similar between the lower class and the upper class, whereas the percentage of borrowers was clearly lower in the lower class than the upper class.

Third, the average amounts of lending and borrowing per household were quite considerable. The average lending was Tk8,212 and the average borrowing was Tk8,569 in Daskin Chamuria village; in Aira village they were Tk10,679 and Tk7,861. Considering that the wage rate for agricultural day labor ranged from Tk30–Tk40, including payment in kind, these amounts were almost as much as the annual income of an agricultural laborer. Informal finance involved not only high percentages of villagers but also quite large amounts of money.

Fourth, further comparison between landholding classes reveals that inter-class differentials in the amount of lending per household were relatively small, whereas the amount of borrowing per household tended to be higher for the upper class. The lower class tended to lend large and borrow small, while the upper class tended to lend and borrow large. This was because members of the lower class with no (or small) landholding tended to use small, short-term loans instead of large, long-term loans that usually required transfer of a usufructuary right to their farmland.

Table 5.7: Finance by landholding class in Daskin Chamuria village

Landholding size (acre)	Number of households	Lenders[a]	Lender–borrowers[a]	Borrowers[a]	Other[a]	Lending amount[b] (taka)	Borrowing amount[b] (taka)	Balance (taka)
0	206	66 (32)	22 (11)	43 (21)	75 (36)	575,150 (6,536)	196,310 (3,020)	378,840
0.01–0.49	138	37 (27)	35 (25)	49 (36)	17 (12)	601,100 (8,349)	361,920 (4,309)	239,180
0.50–0.99	84	11 (13)	26 (31)	36 (43)	11 (13)	269,880 (7,294)	468,750 (7,560)	–198,180
1.00–2.49	78	9 (12)	23 (29)	40 (51)	6 (8)	317,350 (9,917)	691,270 (10,973)	–373,920
2.50–4.99	24	2 (8)	7 (29)	14 (58)	1 (4)	82,200 (9,113)	480,300 (22,871)	–398,100
5.00–	8	2 (25)	3 (38)	2 (25)	1 (13)	121,220 (24,244)	372,200 (74,440)	–250,980
Savings association	–	–	–	–	–	28,500	–	28,500
Total	538	127 (24)	116 (22)	184 (34)	111 (21)	1,995,400 (8,212)	2,570,750 (8,569)	–575,350

Notes:

a: Numbers in brackets show %.

b: Numbers in brackets are the amount per household.

Source: Prepared by the author based on the field survey.

Table 5.8: Finance by landholding class in Aira village

Landholding size (acre)	Number of households	Lenders[a]	Lender–borrowers[a]	Borrowers[a]	Other[a]	Lending amount[b] (taka)	Borrowing amount[b] (taka)	Balance (taka)
0	102	19 (19)	7 (7)	17 (17)	59 (58)	199,671 (7,680)	43,505 (1,813)	156,166
0.01–0.49	34	9 (26)	5 (15)	9 (27)	11 (32)	134,744 (9,625)	34,577 (2,470)	100,167
0.50–0.99	14	3 (21)	3 (21)	5 (36)	3 (21)	36,620 (6,103)	51,900 (6,488)	–15,280
1.00–2.49	25	8 (32)	3 (12)	9 (36)	5 (20)	71,600 (6,509)	104,225 (8,685)	–32,625
2.50–4.99	17	1 (6)	6 (35)	9 (53)	1 (6)	170,825 (24,404)	176,187 (11,746)	–5,362
5.00–	17	4 (24)	4 (23)	6 (35)	3 (18)	155,419 (19,427)	242,062 (24,026)	–86,643
Total	209	44 (21)	28 (13)	55 (26)	82 (39)	768,879 (10,679)	652,456	116,423

Notes:
a: Numbers in brackets show %.
b: Numbers in brackets are the amount per household.

Source: Prepared by the author based on the field survey.

Fifth, the lending/borrowing balance by classes reveals that the bottom two classes had credit balances (credit entities) and the upper four classes had debit balances (deficit entities). In Bangladesh, landless households and smallholding farm households (less than half an acre) in the lower two classes were generally regarded as the poor and were eligible for policy support by the government. The fact that these classes were credit entities in the informal finance market is very interesting. It contradicts the previous commonly accepted view and it was applicable not only to Daskin Chamuria village (with relatively equal land distribution and abundant off-farm employment opportunities) but also to Aira village (with unequal land distribution and high agricultural dependency).

So far, the flow of informal finance between rural classes based on Table 5.7 and Table 5.8 has been discussed. The fact that the net flow of finance was moving from the lower class to the upper class has been presented and its implications discussed. However, an argument reliant on the balance between the amount of lending and the amount of borrowing alone may be slightly problematic.

In order to supplement and reinforce my argument, I present a matrix of inter-class flow of informal finance, albeit only for the case of Daskin Chamuria village.

Table 5.9 is a matrix of long-term finance called *bhograhani* (to be discussed later) and Table 5.10 is a matrix of short-term finance other than *bhograhani*. Please note that, due to the nature of a matrix chart, the tables cover only the intra-village part of finance, and finance transactions with outside parties had to be excluded.

The results are summarized below. First, it is possible to point out that most long-term finance transactions are found in the bottom left part of the matrix below the italicised figures (45° line). In other words, it is possible to conclude, with a reasonable certainty, that finance flowed from the lower class to the upper class.

Second, short-term finance transactions are distributed to both sides of the 45° line, confirming that the market structure was not so simple even though the net flow was moving from the lower class to the upper class. What can be seen as a general tendency, however, is the fact that loans from the lower class to the upper class were in quite large amounts, whereas loans from the upper class to the lower class were in small amounts. This suggests a widespread situation in which the lower class could not obtain finance in the first place due to lack of credit, except for some credit-worthy people (readers may recall the percentage of households that were neither borrowers nor lenders was higher in the lower class in Tables 5.7 and 5.8), or they could only obtain small, short-term loans from the upper class through their patron–client relationship.

Table 5.9: Inter-class finance flow matrix in Daskin Chamuria village (long-term finance)

	Lender													
	0		0.01–049		0.50–0.99		1.00–2.49		2.50–4.99		5.00–		Total	
Borrower	Loans	Amount (*taka*)	Loans	Amount (*taka*)	Loans	Amount (*taka*)	Loans	Amount (*taka*)	Loans	Amount (*taka*)	Loans	Amount (*taka*)	Loans	Amount (*taka*)
0	*1*	*4,000*	1	2,500									2	6,500
0.01–0.49	20	47,050	*20*	*61,200*	6	21,500	8	32,400					54	162,150
0.50–0.99	21	85,800	20	93,500	*10*	*36,300*	9	32,500	4	15,500			64	263,600
1.00–2.49	27	108,350	27	118,900	10	49,000	*11*	*48,600*	3	13,000			78	337,850
2.50–4.99	17	85,500	10	49,300	8	63,000	6	29,000	*1*	*9,000*			42	235,800
5.00–	10	46,500	14	55,400	3	8,400	10	69,400	2	7,500	*1*	*5,000*	40	192,200
Total	96	377,200	92	380,800	37	178,200	44	211,900	10	45,000	1	5,000	280	1,198,100

Source: Prepared by the author based on the June–August 1992 survey.

Table 5.10: Inter-class finance flow matrix in Daskin Chamuria village (short-term finance)

	LENDER													
	0		0.01–049		0.50–0.99		1.00–2.49		2.50–4.99		5.00–		TOTAL	
BORROWER	LOANS	AMOUNT (*TAKA*)	LOANS	AMOUNT (*TAKA*)	LOANS	AMOUNT (*TAKA*)	LOANS	AMOUNT (*TAKA*)	LOANS	AMOUNT (*TAKA*)	LOANS	AMOUNT (*TAKA*)	LOANS	AMOUNT (*TAKA*)
0	*37*	*69,500*	20	30,500	11	10,405	9	9,700	2	2,700	7	12,000	86	134,805
0.01–0.49	19	26,700	*14*	*20,000*	8	7,660	7	5,800	1	2,000	4	1,300	53	63,460
0.50–0.99	13	13,500	12	14,600	*8*	*9,800*	4	5,000	1	1,000	1	1,500	39	45,400
1.00–2.49	16	17,100	11	18,300	4	4,800	*4*	*3,250*	3	7,500	1	5,920	39	56,870
2.50–4.99	6	10,000	2	2,500	–	–	2	8,000	–	–	1	7,000	11	27,500
5.00–	6	38,000	3	11,500	1	10,000	4	27,000	–	–	–	–	14	86,500
Total	97	174,800	62	97,400	32	42,665	30	58,750	7	13,200	14	27,720	242	414,535

Source: Prepared by the author based on the June–August 1992 survey.

Modes of Transaction and Interest Rates in Informal Finance

Let us examine the contents of informal finance. Many different types of informal finance transaction were observed in the survey of the two villages. They can be broadly divided into two types: transactions involving transfer of a usufructuary right (usufructuary mortgage) and all other transactions. In the former type of transaction, farmland is transferred from the borrower to the lender in exchange for a loan, and the lender acquires a usufructuary right to the borrower's farmland. It can be further divided into the type requiring repayment of the principal loan and the type not requiring repayment.

With the type requiring repayment, the creditor continues to hold the usufructuary right to the farmland until the loan principal is repaid. Its distinctive feature is that interest on the loan is offset by the use of the usufruct year after year. It was the predominant mode of transaction in Daskin Chamuria village and it was called *bhograhani* locally or *bondak* more generally. In Daskin Chamuria village it was customary for the debtor to sell his farmland and use a portion of the proceeds for repayment if he could not repay the principal rather than the creditor taking ownership of the farmland.[18]

With the type of informal finance transaction not requiring repayment, the debt automatically expires after a period of time stipulated in the contract and the usufruct is returned to the debtor. This mode of transaction, called *khaikhalashi*, was predominant in Aira village. The contract period used in Aira village was seven years in most cases. In this sense, *khaikhalashi* can be considered a long-term tenancy contract with advance payment of a seven-year rent. However, the land owner's primary objective is to obtain a sizeable sum of money, not to lease the land to a tenant farmer, and therefore *khaikhalashi* should be considered a type of financing vehicle.

The amount of loan required for the acquisition of a usufructuary right to one acre of land ranged from Tk15,000–Tk25,000 for *bhograhani* in Daskin Chamuria village, and Tk10,000–Tk15,000 for *khaikhalashi* in Aira village, depending on the fertility of land. The rate of return realized in these transactions should theoretically be equal to the annual net income from the farmland (land rent) as a percentage of the loan principal in the case of *bhograhani*; in the case of *khaikhalashi* it should be equal to the discount rate at which the present value of the net income from the farmland (land rent) over seven years equals the loan principal. In both cases, the land rent needs to be estimated in order to estimate the rate of return.

Table 5.11 and Table 2.10 (Chapter 2) have been prepared for this purpose.[19] Based on these, the land rent per acre in Daskin Chamuria village was Tk5,860

Table 5.11: Production costs in Daskin Chamuria village (*taka* per acre)

	AMAN		MUSTARD		*BORO*		TOTAL	
Materials cost	410	(8)	1,000	(23)	1,850	(24)	3,260	(19)
Irrigation[a]	200	(4)	–		1,000	(13)	1,200	(7)
Labor cost	1,950	(41)	1,200	(28)	2,900	(37)	6,050	(35)
Plowing labor	600	(13)	800	(19)	1,000	(13)	2,400	(14)
Capital interest[b]	240	(5)	220	(5)	460	(6)	920	(5)
Profit[c]	–		–		910	(11)	910	(5)
Land rent[d]	2,150	(45)	1,880	(44)	1,830	(23)	5,860	(34)
Total[e]	4,750	(100)	4,300	(100)	7,950	(100)	17,000	(100)

Notes:
a: Operating cost plus depreciation cost of the tubewell.
b: Capital interest on materials cost, including tubewell operating cost, plus labor cost for two months at 60% per annum.
c: Profit to the tubewell owner derived after capital interest on tubewell operating cost and irrigation cost is deducted from the tubewell owner's share of gross production (1/4 = 1,900 *taka*).
d: The balance after deducting all costs other than land rent from gross production value.
e: Calculated on the basis of: yield 20 *maund*/acre, output price 220 *taka*/*maund*, straw byproduct 350/acre for *aman*; yield 8 *maund*/acre, output price 530/*maund*, byproduct 60 *taka*/acre for mustard; and yield 40 *maund*/acre, output price 190 *taka*/*maund*, straw byproduct 350 *taka*/acre for *boro*.
Numbers in brackets show %
Source: Prepared by the author based on the field survey.

for triple cropping (*aman*–mustard–*boro*) and Tk3,980 for double cropping (*aman*–*boro*),[20] and Tk6,520 for double cropping (*aman*–*boro*) in Aira village. These figures translate into a rate of return on a long-term financing vehicle of about 25% in Daskin Chamuria village and 39% to 63% in Aira village. These were the long-term interest rates effected in these villages.[21]

Let us look at the type of informal finance that does not require transfer of the usufructuary right to farmland. This is a standard loan with interest payment and generally a short-term loan for up to several months that does not require collateral. However, the two villages had different interest payment practices. In Aira village the loan was advanced in cash, and both the principal and the interest were paid in cash in many cases. In Daskin Chamuria village the loan was advanced and repaid in cash but the interest was paid by paddy in the vast majority of cases.

The most common rate of interest was 8.3% per month (100% per annum) in Aira village, but it was as high as 120% to 200% per annum if a loan was obtained from moneylenders based in towns seven to eight kilometers outside the village. Some moneylenders demanded precious metals as collateral. On the other hand, the interest on a loan principal of Tk1,000 was two to three

Table 5.12: Long-term and short-term informal finance—Daskin Chamuria village (*taka*)

LANDHOLDING SIZE (ACRE)	*BHOGRAHANI* (LONG-TERM) LENDING	BORROWING	BALANCE	OTHER (SHORT-TERM) LENDING	BORROWING	BALANCE
0	353,850 (27,600)	19,000 (0)	334,850 (27,600)	175,900 (17,800)	142,410 (34,900)	33,490 (–17,100)
0.01–0.49	396,700 (72,000)	158,750 (63,400)	237,950 (8,600)	96,900 (35,500)	78,970 (60,800)	17,930 (–25,300)
0.50–0.99	180,700 (30,500)	259,200 (148,250)	–78,500 (–17,750)	42,680 (16,000)	45,400 (15,900)	–2,720 (100)
1.00–2.49	212,100 (30,500)	353,400 (228,500)	–141,300 (–198,000)	56,750 (18,000)	56,870 (52,500)	–120 (–34,500)
2.50–4.99	45,000 (22,000)	224,800 (196,000)	–179,800 (–174,000)	15,200 (0)	30,000 (29,500)	–14,800 (–29,500)
5.00–	15,000 (12,000)	190,200 (95,500)	–175,200 (–83,500)	26,220 (68,000)	86,500 (0)	–60,280 (68,000)
Savings association	2,000 (0)	0 (0)	2,000 (0)	26,500 (0)	0 (0)	26,500 (0)
Total	1,205,350 (194,600)	1,205,350 (731,650)	0 (–537,050)	440,150 (155,300)	440,150 (193,600)	0 (–38,300)

Note: Intra-village transactions are in the top line and inter-village transactions are in brackets.

Source: Prepared by the author based on the field survey.

maund (Tk200–Tk220/*maund* in 1991/92 prices) of paddy in Daskin Chamuria village, which would translate to a rate of return of 50% to 60% per annum. These were the short-term interest rates in these villages.

Now, Table 5.12 and Table 5.13 describe the flow of finance arranged under the long-term finance (usufructuary mortgage) and short-term finance (all other types) categories for Daskin Chamuria village and Aira village respectively. Intra-village transactions are shown on the top line and external transactions are shown in brackets on the bottom line.

The first thing that attracts attention is the overwhelmingly large share of the long-term finance involving usufructuary mortgage by value in both villages. It is particularly noticeable for intra-village finance, with long-term finance amounting to 73% in Daskin Chamuria village and 95% in Aira village. Even for external finance, long-term loans accounted for 56% to 79% in Daskin Chamuria village and about 50% in Aira village.

Table 5.13: Long-term and short-term informal finance—Aira village (*taka*)

LANDHOLDING SIZE (ACRE)	*KHAIKHALASHI* (LONG-TERM)			OTHER (SHORT-TERM)		
	LENDING	BORROWING	BALANCE	LENDING	BORROWING	BALANCE
0	136,400	9,825	126,575	133,650	9,170	4,480
	(49,62)	(0)	(49,621)	(–)	(24,510)	(–24,510)
0.01–0.49	103,649	27,887	75,762	6,620	590	6,030
	(24,475)	(3,600)	(20,875)	(–)	(2,500)	(–2,500)
0.50–0.99	18,300	28,400	–10,100	1,870	0	1,870
	(16,450)	(10,500)	(5,950)	(–)	(13,000)	(–13,000)
1.00–2.49	45,450	73,300	–27,850	2,400	4,000	–1,600
	(23,750)	(22,925)	(825)	(–)	(4,000)	(–4,000)
2.50–4.99	65,025	130,887	–65,862	0	9,000	–9,000
	(105,800)	(21,575)	(84,225)	(–)	(14,725)	(–14,725)
5.00–	63,912	162,437	–98,525	220	2,000	–1,780
	(91,287)	(38,425)	(53,162)	(–)	(39,500)	(–39,500)
Total	432,736	432,736	0	24,760	24,760	0
	(311,383)	(96,725)	(214,658)	(–)	(98,235)	(–98,235)

Note: Intra-village transactions are in the top line and inter-village transactions are in brackets. However, information about inter-village short-term lending was not collected and not included in the table.

Source: Prepared by the author based on the field survey.

Second, the share of external transactions in informal finance was 18% of lending and 36% of borrowing in Daskin Chamuria village, and 40% of lending and 30% of borrowing in Aira village. Financing across village borders accounted for about 20% to 40%. It is also clear that some of the usufructuary rights flowed out of the village because the amount of borrowing exceeded the amount of lending in Daskin Chamuria village, whereas in Aira village some usufructuary rights were acquired from other villages because the amount of lending exceeded that of borrowing.

In summary, it has been found that long-term finance rather than short-term finance was the main form of informal finance and hence usufructuary mortgage was most common in both study villages, that the short-term interest rate was twice as high as the long-term interest, and that interest rates in Aira village were nearly twice as high as those in Daskin Chamuria village. Considering that the inflation rate was about 10%,[22] that the most prevalent interest rate in formal finance was 16% per annum, and that the transaction costs of borrowing in formal finance were very high,[23] it would be reasonable to think that there were some good economic reasons for a long-term interest rate of 25% to 60% and a short-term interest rate of 50% to 120%, even though they were high.

Is the *Reverse Flow* of Informal Finance a Sham?

Validity of Landholdings as the Basis for Income and Wealth Brackets

The next issue to consider is that classification such as the lower and upper classes is based on the size of landholding and does not necessarily correspond directly to the level of income and wealth. If landholding classes are not consistent with income and wealth classes, policy implications derived from the above proposition (the flow of finance from the lower to upper classes) will be completely different. Since farmland fragmentation and increasing off-farm employment opportunities generally work to reduce the importance of landholding in income and wealth creation, the examination of this issue is especially relevant to the case of Daskin Chamuria.

Let us look at Table 5.14, which shows the relationship between the income and wealth level and the landholding size in Daskin Chamuria village. Since it was difficult to estimate the income of the rural household, for convenience the table shows the relationship between the landholding size and the non-land asset (house and consumer durable goods) ownership as an approximation of the income level. Upon close examination of individual survey sheets from Daskin Chamuria village, it was decided that it would be most appropriate to include the following assets.[24]

First, a *chula* (cooking stove) was a symbol of an independent household, and whether it had a roof or walls to keep out the wind and rain (hereinafter called a *cooking shed*) was one indicator of wealth. In rural Bangladesh a fireplace for cooking was directly dug in the ground outside the house. An outdoor stove was used during the dry season and a stove set up in a simple cooking shed was used during the wet season in most cases. Cooking sheds in Daskin Chamuria village were built with materials such as jute hurds, *kash* leaves,[25] rice or wheat straws, synthetic fiber chemical fertilizer bags, and tin plates, and usually cost Tk200–Tk300, or Tk500–Tk700 for high-quality construction (these and the following were current prices at the time of the survey between June and August 1992). Households without a cooking shed were considered very poor. They had to ask their relatives or neighbors to let them use their cooking sheds or *chouka* (portable stoves) in the house. As we can see from Table 5.14, nearly 30% of households did not have cooking sheds.

Table 5.14: Correspondence between landholding and wealth in Daskin Chamuria I

LANDHOLDING (ACRES)	NUMBER OF HOUSEHOLDS	POINTS[a] 0	1[b]	2[c]	3[d]	4[e]	5	6	7	AVERAGE POINTS
0	206	98	64	32	9	2	–	1	–	0.82
0.01–0.49	138	35	56	24	13	6	4	–	–	1.36
0.50–0.99	84	10	20	27	20	5	–	1	1	1.99
1.00–2.49	78	2	15	18	17	16	6	3	1	2.83
2.50–4.99	24	–	–	3	2	6	7	5	1	4.50
5.00–	8	–	–	–	–	2	1	2	3	5.75
Total	538 (100)	145 (27)	155 (29)	104 (19)	61 (11)	37 (7)	18 (3)	12 (2)	6 (1)	1.67

Notes:
a: The total number of points based on one point being awarded for ownership of either a cooking shed, a bed, a table (or two chairs), a guest room, a radio, a black and white television or a bicycle, and no points for non-ownership of these items.
b: Of 155 cases, 119 had a cooking shed, 25 had a bed and seven had a radio.
c: Of 104 cases, 60 had a cooking shed and a bed, 13 had a cooking shed and a table, 12 had a cooking shed and a guest room, and eight had a cooking shed and a radio.
d: Of 61 cases, 30 had a cooking shed, a bed and a table, 11 had a cooking shed, a bed and a guest room, and 10 had a cooking shed, a bed and a radio.
e: Of 37 cases, 19 had a cooking shed, a bed, a table and a guest room and 10 had a cooking shed, a bed, a table and a radio.
Numbers in brackets show %.

Source: Prepared by the author based on the field survey.

The second item was the bed. An adequate bed could be made for a cost of Tk300–Tk500. Without beds, a family had to sleep on a dirt floor. It can get quite cold in Bangladesh during the dry season and it would be difficult to sleep on a dirt floor. The table shows that about 30% of households could afford to have a cooking shed but not beds.

The third item was the table (or two or more chairs). A table, mainly used as a study desk for school-age children, would cost Tk100–Tk150 and a chair would cost about Tk100, both of which could be made or bought at a bazaar or a *hat* (periodical market). About 20% of households with a cooking shed and a bed could not afford to own a table (or two or more chairs).

The fourth item was the guest room (which was a separate building). There were varying levels of luxury but a guest room could be built for Tk2,000–Tk3,000 if there was spare space. The ownership of a guest room was a symbol of substantial wealth. About 10% of households with a cooking shed, a bed, and a table (or two or more chairs) did not have a guest room.

The fifth item was electrical or durable consumer goods such as a radio, a black and white television, a ceiling fan, or a bicycle. All were literally symbols of wealth and the ownership rate in Daskin Chamuria village was very low.

Based on the asset ownership distribution in Table 5.14, there is indeed a strong correlation between asset ownership and landholding size. Table 5.15 shows the percentages of the poor, middle, and wealthy classes in each landholding class. The definition of these income classes are stated in the note to the table but, in broad terms, the poor class includes households without a rainproof cooking shed and households with a cooking shed but no beds. The middle class includes households with a cooking shed and a bed and a table (or two or more chairs) in some cases, but no guest room. The wealthy class includes households with a guest room and a radio, a black and white television, a ceiling fan, or a bicycle. Seventy-four per cent of the landless and households with less than 0.50 acres of land belonged to the poor, 51% of households in the 0.50–0.99 acre bracket and the 1.00–2.49 acre bracket belonged to the middle class, and 84% of households in the 2.50–4.99 acre bracket and the over 5.00 acre bracket belonged to the wealthy.

The above result leads to the conclusion that land ownership was the overwhelmingly important factor in defining a household's income creation ability in Daskin Chamuria village.

A further analysis is not conducted here, but the importance of land ownership is expected to have been greater in Aira village, which was a more purely farming village than Daskin Chamuria village.

The Impact of Formal Finance on Informal Finance

The above discussion has confirmed that the flow of funds in informal finance moved from the poor to the middle and the wealthy in the income-based class system, which corresponded to the landholding-based class system.

The next issue for consideration is how much impact the rapid spread of formal finance (especially by the Grameen Bank), which has been available to the poor in recent years, has had on the informal finance flow structure. If it is merely an expression of direct and indirect effects of this special form of formal finance, it will have completely different policy implications again. The impact of formal finance led by the Grameen Bank in each village is examined below.

Daskin Chamuria Village

The sources of formal finance observed in Daskin Chamuria village included the Comilla-type cooperative societies, the *dekhi* project (*dekhi* is a

Table 5.15: Correspondence between landholdings and wealth in Daskin Chamuria II (%)

LANDHOLDING CLASS	POOR CLASS	MIDDLE CLASS	WEALTHY CLASS	TOTAL
Class I	73.5	22.7	3.8	100
Class II	29.0	50.6	20.4	100
Class III	–	15.6	84.4	100
All landholders	55.8	30.7	13.6	100

Notes:
Class I includes the landless and landholders of 0.01–0.49 acres.
Class II includes landholders of 0.50–0.99 acres and 1.00–2.49 acres.
Class III includes landholders of 2.50–4.99 acres and over 5.00 acres.
The poor, middle and wealthy classes correspond to the point ranges of 0–1, 2–3 and over 4 in Table 5.14 respectively.

Source: Prepared by the author based on the field survey.

traditional foot-operated rice-husking implement), the BKB and commercial banks, and the Grameen Bank. Table 5.16 shows households with outstanding loans from these financial institutions for each landholding class.

There were two assetless cooperatives (BSS), one farmers' cooperative (KSS), and one women's cooperative (MSS) in Daskin Chamuria village. One BSS was established in 1980 (with forty-five members, forty of whom were villagers) and the other BSS in 1981 (with forty-six members, forty-one villagers); the MSS was established in 1987 (with forty members, thirty-two villagers) and the KSS in 1987 (all twenty-five members were villagers). Cooperative finance was composed of sub-lending of loans from the Sonari Bank, as mentioned earlier. Cooperatives were required to build up savings deposits for several years before receiving loans from the bank and to wait several years again for the next advancement of funds. Furthermore, not all members were eligible for loans and the individual loan amount was limited to Tk500–Tk1,500 per person (Tk2,000–Tk3,000 for some people).[26] It was not large enough to influence the flow of funds in informal finance. The *dekhi* project was a type of loan program to increase employment and income for rural women, and was set up by an NGO called Swanirvar; however, like cooperative finance, it had the following limitations. In Daskin Chamuria village, twenty-five of its forty-two members obtained loans in 1989 but the amount was limited to Tk1,500 per person and the program had been abolished by the time of the survey.

Table 5.16: Borrowers of formal finance in Daskin Chamuria village

Landholding	Number of	Cooperatives				*Dekhi*	BKB/ commercial	Grameen Bank	
size (acres)	households	KSS	MSS	BSS (1)	BSS (2)	project	banks	1992	1994
0	206	– (2)	4 (10)	8 (18)	1 (9)	11 (12)	5	44	89
0.01–0.49	138	– (8)	2 (8)	1 (15)	1 (13)	2 (3)	3	36	52
0.50–0.99	84	– (2)	2 (3)	1 (4)	– (10)	8 (12)	2	16	26
1.00–2.49	78	– (4)	– (4)	1 (2)	3 (7)	4 (10)	2	11	18
2.50–4.99	24	– (8)	2 (5)	– (1)	– (2)	– (3)	3	1	2
5.00–	8	– (1)	– (2)	– (0)	– (0)	– (2)	1	–	–
Total	538	0 (25)	10 (32)	11 (40)	5 (41)	25 (42)	16	108	187

Note: For cooperatives and the *dekhi* project, member numbers are shown in brackets.

Source: Prepared by the author based on the field survey.

As for the BKB and commercial banks, only sixteen households (3%) in Daskin Chamuria village replied that they had outstanding loans. There were eight loans (total Tk105,700) from the BKB, eight loans (Tk65,200) from the Rupali Bank, and one loan (Tk10,000) from the Sonari Bank. Seven of these loans were taken out before 1985 and only six loans were obtained in the 1990s (an average loan of Tk5,083). Again, it could not possibly have a large impact on the flow of funds in informal finance.

Finally, the Grameen Bank has a short history. It was in February 1990 that a branch was set up next to the office of the *union* (administrative village) to which Daskin Chamuria village belonged, and the first center (the bank's customer management unit comprised up to eight five-member groups) was organized in Daskin Chamuria village in June 1990. Another center was formed in December 1990, another in January 1991, another in March 1992, and two more in 1993. The Grameen Bank membership had grown rapidly to 108 members (107 households) by the time of the August 1992 survey and to 187 members (183 households) by 1994. These figures represent 19.9% and 34.8% of the total households. As we can see from Table 5.14, a majority of members were women in the landless and below 0.50 acres class according to the nature of its program.

And the amount of loans from the Grameen Bank grew dramatically. It lent Tk58,000 to twenty-eight people (an average of Tk2,071) in 1990, Tk163,000 to sixty-seven people (average Tk2,433) in 1991, and Tk469,500 to 108 people (average Tk4,347) in 1992. The average loan amount jumped suddenly in 1992 because the bank introduced various types of loans such as seasonal loans, hand-tubewell loans, toilet loans, and housing loans, in addition to the previously available general loan. It also enabled members to take out more than one loan simultaneously.[27]

In Daskin Chamuria village, formal finance had been available only to certain people prior to this, but it appears that the Grameen Bank removed such barriers altogether. According to a very rough estimation, the share of formal finance in the demand for finance in Daskin Chamuria village increased from 10% to 15% prior to 1990 and to about 25% in 1992. It is likely that the share increased further after 1993, when both the membership and the average loan amount of the Grameen Bank recorded a sudden increase.

Let us return to the first question and consider the extent to which formal finance determined the flow of funds in informal finance based on the above data. Was the emergence of the lower class as the credit entity in informal finance merely a consequence of the rapidly increasing credit extended to the lower class by the Grameen Bank? Let us examine this point based on Table 5.17, which shows the lending–borrowing balance in informal finance of nonmembers of the Grameen Bank (as of August 1992).

Table 5.17: Lending–borrowing balance for nonmembers of the Grameen Bank—Daskin Chamuria village

LANDHOLDING SIZE (ACRES)	NUMBER OF HOUSEHOLDS	LENDING (TAKA)	BORROWING (TAKA)	BALANCE (TAKA)
0	162	397,000	119,500	277,500
0.01–0.49	102	473,000	247,970	225,030
0.50–0.99	68	201,900	402,850	–200,950
1.00–2.49	67	264,950	533,920	–268,970
2.50–4.99	23	60,200	458,800	–398,600
5.00–	8	121,220	372,200	–250,980
Total	430	1,518,270	2,135,240	616,970

Source: Prepared by the author based on the field survey.

The result is clear. The two lower classes again had a credit balance and the four upper classes had a debit balance. It would be difficult to say that the reverse flow of informal finance contradicting the commonly accepted view was a direct product of the Grameen Bank.

Aira Village

Let us look at the case of Aira village. Villagers used formal finance through the BKB and commercial banks and the Grameen Bank only.[28] Table 5.18 shows borrowers of these financial institutions in each landholding class.

The BKB and commercial banks were used more widely than in Daskin Chamuria village (twenty-seven households or 12.9%). And except for 1981, 1983, and 1987, for which one loan was taken out in each year, and two loans that were drawn in unknown years, many loans were taken out more recently, such as eleven in 1991 and ten in 1992. The average loan amount was quite high at Tk11,770 (Tk8,048 for 1991 and 1992 only). According to the table, the distribution of these bank loan users was skewed heavily towards the upper classes.

The Grameen Bank, on the other hand, had only one center in the village (founded in March 1990), with a membership of thirty-six (17.3%), which was smaller than that in Daskin Chamuria village. However, the average borrowing per member increased at a higher pace from Tk1,813 in 1990 to Tk3,000 in 1991, Tk5,556 in 1992, and Tk15,560 in 1993.[29] The distribution of the Grameen Bank members was again skewed heavily towards the lower classes.

Thus, the share of formal finance in the demand for finance appeared to

Table 5.18: Borrowers of formal finance in Aira village

LANDHOLDING SIZE (ACRES)	NUMBER OF HOUSEHOLDS	BKB/ COMMERCIAL BANKS	GRAMEEN BANK
0	102	–	21
0.01–0.49	34	1	7
0.50–0.99	14	2	1
1.00–2.49	25	3	4
2.50–4.99	17	13	1
5.00–	17	8	2
Total	209	27	36

Source: Prepared by the author based on the field survey.

Table 5.19: Lending–borrowing balance for nonmembers of the Grameen Bank—Aira village

LANDHOLDING SIZE (ACRES)	NUMBER OF HOUSEHOLDS	LENDING (*TAKA*)	BORROWING (*TAKA*)	BALANCE (*TAKA*)
0	81	193,946	39,560	154,386
0.01–0.49	27	125,794	30,052	95,742
0.50–0.99	13	36,620	38,250	–1,630
1.00–2.49	21	71,600	78,125	–6,525
2.50–4.99	16	170,825	152,312	18,513
5.00–	15	155,419	174,787	–19,368
Total	173	754,204	513,086	241,118

Source: Prepared by the author based on the field survey.

be greater in Aira village than Daskin Chamuria village. According to a very rough estimate, it was around 20% before the Grameen Bank arrived and reached 35.4% after its arrival.

Table 5.19 shows the informal finance balance of nonmembers of the Grameen Bank in Aira village. Again, the poor formed the credit entity whose lending exceeded borrowing. However, the situation in this village was slightly different from that in Daskin Chamuria village in that the deficit amounts of the upper class were smaller and much of the surplus fund of the lower class flowed out of the village.

The Economic Role of Informal Finance

The above discussion has so far suggested that the accumulation of surplus funds by the rural lower class (the poor) was not attributable to the activity of the Grameen Bank and that it should be recognized as a phenomenon generated by more fundamental changes in the rural economy.

The question is, how did the lower class become capable of accumulating surplus funds? It cannot be explained by the special condition in Daskin Chamuria village alone (the presence of the hand-weaving industry) because the same phenomenon was happening in Aira village, which lacked such a condition. I propose a hypothesis that advancements in rice production technologies and dramatic increases in rice production (the Green Revolution) could be the underlying factors that brought about these changes. One pathway for a trickle-down effect to the lower class would, of course, be an increase in employment within the agricultural sector. The introduction of double rice cropping and the progress of the Green Revolution triggered by the rapid dissemination of tubewells during the 1980s stimulated the demand for labor in the agricultural sector. The demand for labor increased substantially in Daskin Chamuria village when labor-extensive dry-season field crops (*rabi*) such as pulses, oilseeds, and coarse grains were replaced by irrigated rice crops (*boro*) and the practice of wet-season rice transplanting began after the introduction of tubewell irrigation. The demand for labor at least doubled in Aira village when dry-season fallow land was transformed into irrigated rice-growing land. (See the labor costs in Table 5.11 and Table 2.10.) This is more evident in the case of Daskin Chamuria village, but the Green Revolution stimulated the growth of the off-farm sector within a rural area through inter-industrial linkage effects and final demand effects and substantially expanded employment there. The development of rural infrastructure, which progressed generally in Bangladesh during the 1980s, was important as one of the driving forces behind such advancements (although the development of small-scale infrastructure was inadequate, as emphasized later in Chapter 7, the development of arterial roads and large bridges progressed remarkably). The combination of these factors led to rising real wages in the rural area during the 1980s (Chapter 1).

What we need to remember here, however, is that the emergence of the situation in which the poor class of rural Bangladesh accumulated considerable surplus funds and lent them to the upper class in the village does not necessarily mean that its economic condition improved considerably—as clearly demonstrated by the level of poverty among the lower class in Daskin Chamuria village based on the earlier data about the ownership of non-land assets. It appears that members of the lower class were still at the stage where they had to give priority to securing rice for their own consumption rather than building up their assets. The strategic importance to the lower class of securing rice for consumption was indicated by the very fact that the predominant part of informal finance was in the form of long-term usufructuary mortgage and that the interest on short-term finance was paid in paddy even in Daskin Chamuria village where the proportion of long-term finance was relatively low. The appropriate interpretation here would be that the lower class had moved on from its slightly unstable condition (in which its members were buying rice with daily wage income) to the level where there was some money to spare.

Now, let us put aside the issue of the lender for a while and consider the purpose for which the borrower needed to acquire funds at high interest rates. This question could be answered by analyzing the uses of funds in the baseline survey questions about finance, but, unfortunately, there were not enough responses for analysis. There were responses here and there nominating straightforward consumption, as well as land purchase, children's education, ceremonial occasions, or medical treatment, as the purpose for borrowing, but this question was generally left unanswered; in particular, there were hardly any answers about the purpose of long-term finance through *bhograhani* and *khaikhalashi*.

Accordingly, the following section focuses only on the demand for productive funds and examines the lending–borrowing balance in informal finance by comparing villagers who operated small businesses that were potentially in need of funds and other villagers in an attempt to approach the question indirectly.

Daskin Chamuria Village

Small businesses that were likely to be in need of funds in Daskin Chamuria village included tubewell owners, hand-weaving factory owners,[30] and traders of agricultural produce and rural consumer goods (including larger businesses with shops and smaller petty traders). There were 119 households (22.1%) with one or more members engaged in these businesses. These people are called 'small business operators' hereafter.

Table 5.20 shows the positions of small business operator households and other households in informal finance. The following points are notable.

First, the ratio of lenders to borrowers tended to be lower for the small business operator group than the other group. The lender ratio was 38% for small business operators and 47% for the rest, and the borrower ratio was 69% for the former and 52% for the latter (these figures include people who were the lender-cum-borrowers).

Second, small business operators were large deficit entities in short-term finance. In other words, they had large working capital requirements.

Table 5.20: Finances of small business operators in Daskin Chamuria village (*taka*)

	Lenders	Lender–borrowers	Borrowers	Other	*Bhograhani* (long-term) Lending	*Bhograhani* (long-term) Borrowing	*Bhograhani* (long-term) Balance	Other (short-term) Lending	Other (short-term) Borrowing	Other (short-term) Balance
Tubewell owner	2	5	6	1	44,100	171,700	–127,600	78,800	160,150	–81,700
Retailer/tailor	2	3	6	3	24,600	66,000	–41,400	32,420	39,500	–7,080
Handloom owner	3	2	3	2	37,000	5,200	31,800	18,500	36,400	–17,900
Fishnet business	2	8	10	1	22,800	101,200	–78,400	31,000	74,500	–43,500
Clothing business	–	1	2	2	3,200	13,500	–10,300	0	3,600	–3,600
Rice business	3	5	9	5	57,900	12,700	45,200	14,300	18,400	–4,100
Egg/vegetable/ fruit business	4	1	11	2	41,600	34,500	7,100	15,950	39,500	–23,550
Other business	1	4	7	3	37,000	44,000	–7,000	18,000	11,200	7,600
Total: small business operators	17 (14%)	29 (24%)	54 (45%)	19 (16%)	268,200	448,800	–180,600	209,770	383,600	–173,830
Total: others	110 (26%)	87 (21%)	130 (31%)	92 (22%)	1,131,750	1,488,200	-356,450	385,680	250,150	135,530

Source: Prepared by the author based on the field survey.

Third, small business operators also had larger deficits in long-term finance by *bhograhani* on average than did the rest. Small business operators had Tk180,600 or 33.6% of the village's total *bhograhani* deficit of Tk537,050, which was much higher than their 22.1% share of the total number of households in the village.

The above findings indirectly confirm the existence of demand from small business operators for working capital, mainly in the informal financial market. Table 5.21 also shows that the landholding size of the small business operator group was considerably larger than average; tubewell owners, especially, were heavily skewed towards the upper class.

The reason for tubewell owners' requirements for large working capital is as follows.

Daskin Chamuria village experienced a rapid diffusion of tubewells and a dramatic transformation of farming practices during the 1980s. The irrigation coverage exceeded 80% and dry-season irrigated *boro* rice became the main crop. STWs had a capacity to supply irrigation to about thirteen acres on average, but fragmentation of farmland meant that there were no households that were capable of owning and operating such a large tract of land. This gave rise to a groundwater market. It enabled farmers without STWs to buy water from tubewell owners to cultivate *boro* rice. It also spawned the crop-sharing system for water charge payment. Farmers who bought water from tubewell owners handed over a quarter of their harvest as the water charge.

The crop share system gave water buyer farmers the benefit of a deferred water charge payment, but it meant that tubewell owners had to pay tubewell operating expenses such as wages and electricity charges out of their own pockets until they were recovered at harvesting time. This must have created demand for substantial funds among tubewell owners, and they had to borrow funds from the lower class at high interest rates due to the underdevelopment of the formal financial system. It was customary for tubewell owners to borrow funds in December or January at the start of *boro* rice cultivation, to pay interest in paddy in May or June at the time of harvesting, and to repay the principal in cash in August or September. Let us take one large landholder (eight acres) who owned and operated three tubewells as an example (Table 5.22). The table shows that this large landholder raised funds from a wide range of lenders in the lower class, such as from agricultural laborers and handloom weavers.

Yet, business must have been viable for tubewell owners despite high interest rates. They must have allowed for the high capital interest in the water charge rate of a quarter of harvested crops. And the water charge they received in paddy corresponded well with the interest they paid in paddy, resulting in savings in transaction costs that would be incurred if they had to buy or sell paddy.

Table 5.21: Distribution of small business operators by landholding size in Daskin Chamuria village

	Number of households	0	0.01–0.49	0.50–0.99	1.00–2.49	2.50–4.99	Over 5.00	Average size (acres)	Grameen Bank members
Tubewell owner	14	2	1	1	2	5	3	5.32	1
Retailer/tailor	14	4	2	3	3	1	1	1.28	4
Handloom owner	10	1	3	2	2	2	–	1.11	3
Fishnet business	21	4	3	9	4	1	–	0.79	5
Clothing business	5	3	–	–	2	–	–	0.55	1
Rice business	22	12	5	3	2	–	–	0.30	4
Egg/vegetable/fruit business	18	6	9	2	1	–	–	0.22	8
Other business	15	4	5	1	5	–	–	0.58	3
Total: small business operators	119 (22%)	34 (17%)	28 (20%)	21 (25%)	21 (27%)	9 (38%)	4 (50%)	1.19	29 (27%)
Total: other	419 (78%)	172 (83%)	110 (80%)	63 (75%)	57 (73%)	15 (62%)	4 (50%)	0.54	79 (73%)

Source: Prepared by the author based on the field survey.

Table 5.22: Borrowings and fund sources in the case of one tubewell owner—Daskin Chamuria village (*taka*)

Landholding size of fund source households (acres)	Number of households	Borrowing amount		
		Bhograhani	Other	Total
0	9	29,000	38,000	67,000
0.01–0.49	7	18,400	11,500	29,900
0.50–0.99	2	400	10,000	10,400
1.00–2.49	5	9,400	27,000	36,400
2.50–4.99	1	7,500	–	7,500
5.00–	–	–	–	–
Other villages	3	27,000	–	27,000
Total	27	91,700	86,500	178,200

Source: Prepared by the author based on the field survey.

Aira Village

Aira village is a far simpler case than Daskin Chamuria village due to the lack of off-farm industries. The main small business that required productive funds was tubewell operation, besides which there was a small number of businesses trading in rice, eggs, meat, and cosmetics. A total of forty-two households (20.1%) were small business operators.

Table 5.23 shows the positions of small business operator households and other households in informal finance. It is possible to point out that small business operators were larger deficit entities in short-term finance also in Aira village. However, tendencies were opposite to those in Daskin Chamuria village on the following points. First, there were more lenders among small business operators and more borrowers among the rest. Second, small business operators were large credit entities in *khaikhalashi*.

As shown in Table 5.24, a majority of tubewell owners were upper-class farmers and had a proactive attitude to expanding the scale of farm operation through *khaikhalashi*. As discussed in Chapter 2, tubewell owners in Aira village tended to try to expand irrigated land through seasonal tenancy (*chaunia*) rather than water sale, and the accumulation of farmland through *khaikhalashi* can be considered a part of their strategy.

However, this operation expansion strategy inevitably increased their requirement for working capital. As discussed in Chapter 2, they borrowed funds at a high interest rate of 100% to 120% per annum from professional usurers (many of whom were also traders) in towns seven to eight kilometers

Table 5.23: Finances of small business operators in Aira village (*taka*)

					Khaikhalashi (long-term)			Other (short-term)		
	Lenders	Lender–borrowers	Borrowers	Other	Lending	Borrowing	Balance	Lending	Borrowing	Balance
Tubewell owners	9	14	4	2	399,923	174,300	225,623	1,940	65,725	–63,785
Small traders	4	2	4	3	53,275	31,775	21,500	8,100	3,470	4,630
Total: small business operators	13 (31%)	16 (38%)	8 (19%)	5 (12%)	453,198	206,075	247,123	10,040	69,195	–59,155
Total: others	31 (19%)	12 (8%)	47 (32%)	77 (52%)	290,921	323,386	–32,465	144,720	53,800	–39,080

Source: Prepared by the author based on the field survey.

Table 5.24: Distribution of small business operators by landholding size in Aira village

	Number of households	0	0.01–0.49	0.50–0.99	1.00–2.49	2.50–4.99	Over 5.00	Average size (acres)	Grameen Bank members
Tubewell owners	29	1	2	2	5	7	12	4.19	0
Small traders	13	7	4	–	1	–	1	0.83	5
Total: small business operators	42 (20%)	8 (8%)	6 (18%)	2 (14%)	6 (24%)	7 (41%)	13 (76%)	3.15	5 (14%)
Total: other	167 (80%)	94 (92%)	28 (82%)	12 (86%)	19 (76%)	10 (59%)	4 (24%)	0.59	31 (86%)

Source: Prepared by the author based on the field survey.

away rather than from lenders within the village, and the groundwater market was functioning to cover the cost of this high capital interest.

It must be reiterated, however, that the lower class was still the credit entity and the upper class the deficit entity in informal finance as a whole in Aira village. Upper-class farmers were divided into tubewell owners and non-tubewell owners. There were households among the latter that had large deficits in informal finance and it is likely that they were the borrowers of long-term funds, mainly through *khaikhalashi*. Lower-class members provided loans to these upper-class farmers in the village (in addition to lending to residents of other villages) and secured rice for their own consumption for a period of seven years.

Summary and Implications

Economic Significance of the Reverse Finance Flow

The commonly accepted view that landlords and upper-class farmers are lenders and that landless laborers and small farmers are borrowers in Bangladesh's rural informal finance has been very dominant. However, an examination of the (net) flow of funds in informal finance in one of the study villages, Daskin Chamuria village, has revealed that, contrary to the commonly accepted view, landless laborers and small farmers were credit entities and middle and upper-class farmers were deficit entities. Upper-class farmers were not completely deficit entities in Aira village, but landless laborers and small farmers were credit entities, as was the case for Daskin Chamuria village. In other words, it has been observed in both villages that the lower class accumulated substantial surplus funds, which were lent at high interest rates through the informal financial market instead of through modern financial institutions.

The above survey result is quite astounding and some people may be skeptical about its representativeness and universality. However, Suda's study of the Comilla district (Suda 1991) is notable in that it pointed out the flow of long-term credit from the lower class to the upper class through *bondak* at an early stage. The case study of Ashora village in the same Comilla district (Chapter 6) also supports this finding. The following survey by the Japanese NGO Shapla Neer (1995) produced almost the same result.

The Shapla Neer survey was conducted in three villages in the southern part of Ishwarganj *thana*, Mymensingh district. Out of a total of 613 households, 380 households, mostly with a landholding of less than one acre, were included in the sample[31] and were surveyed in relation to their education standards, health and hygiene, living standards, and gender, as well as debts and savings (for the

Table 5.25: Informal finance of target households in the Shapla Neer survey villages

	NEEJEGAON VILLAGE	SHATIHALI VILLAGE	BAGBEL VILLAGE
Total number of target households	111	148	121
Number of valid responses	109	146	121
Informal finance borrowers	63%	51%	59%
Total borrowing (*taka*)	224,567	270,551	211,452
Average borrowing (*taka*)	3,254	3,656	2,978
Informal finance lenders	27%	36%	25%
Total lending (*taka*)	216,676	454,449	199,800
Average lending (*taka*)	7,472	8,575	6,660

Source: Prepared by the author based on Shapla Neer (1995: 16–19).

purpose of this chapter, saving is hereafter called lending). The survey was conducted in August and September 1994.

Table 5.25 shows the survey results. Comparison of the total amount of borrowing and the total amount of lending in informal finance of the target households (lower class = the poor) reveals that the borrowing amount was slightly larger in Neejegaon village and Bagbel village, while the lending amount far exceeded the borrowing amount in Shatihali village. Only the result from Shatihali village was consistent with the two survey villages of this chapter, but the results from Neejegaon village and Bagbel village did not completely contradict the findings of this chapter, since the lending amount almost matched the borrowing amount in these villages. In fact, it generally reinforces the finding in the sense that the lower class was beginning to accumulate substantial savings, which were about to surpass the total borrowings. The inter-class finance flow was not yet reversed in Neejegaon village and Bagbel village, perhaps because they were purely agricultural villages and very late in introducing irrigation.

Finally, I would like to provide additional explanations about the fact that lending of funds at high interest rates to the upper class by the lower class did not mean that the lower class became powerful enough to *exploit* the upper class.

First, it should be emphasized that the lower class had managed to accumulate substantial surplus funds but at the same time did not own very basic durable consumer goods such as beds (as we have seen in the case of Daskin Chamuria village). Members of the rural lower class were merely following a strategy to secure a stable supply of rice for their own consumption by using surplus funds for lending instead of for purchasing consumer durables. In other words, they were just emerging from a vulnerable subsistence in which they had to buy rice with their daily wages. The situation was far from the stage where more favorable and stable off-farm employment opportunities were widely available, and the correlation between the landholding size and the level of income and wealth no longer existed. It is not difficult to imagine that the lower class of Aira village was in an even tougher situation due to lack of non-agricultural job opportunities.

Second, how the upper class invested the funds financed by the lower class, albeit at high interest rates, was an important question. In the case of small businesses, as discussed earlier in this chapter, it was highly likely that the upper class was, on average, earning profits at higher rates than the interest rates being paid. In this sense, the structure of *exploitation* of the lower class by the upper class remained unchanged. Even with a portion of funds used for nonproductive purposes other than small business, if they were invested in human capital, such as children's education, medical treatment, or overseas work, they would bring much larger returns to the upper class in the medium to long run, and hence there was perhaps nothing revolutionary about the reverse flow of funds from the lower class to the upper class.[32] Whereas Japan absorbed surplus funds from the general public through the postal savings system efficiently and invested them in the national strategic sectors in the process of its economic development, funds were circulating directly through the informal financial market in the case of Bangladesh only because it had failed to construct a financial system to absorb surplus funds from the general public. The essence of the matter might not be so different between the two countries.

Policy Implications

At the moment, a fierce debate is taking place on the subject of the actual state of rural finance and associated policy issues in developing countries. In short, it is a challenge posed by a new way of thinking to a traditional way of thinking. The traditional way of thinking:

> approaches the problems of the rural informal financial market exclusively from the demand side (on the presumption that sufficient supply of funds to match the demand cannot be achieved within such a market), and therefore believes that the expansion and entry of formal credit at concessional rates into rural areas was absolutely imperative and that it will automatically dissolve the two-tier financial structure in developing countries and lead to increased productivity in agriculture...[which is the]...argument for external fund injection [so to speak] (Esho 1987: 14).

On the other hand, the new way of thinking advocated by the school led by Professor Adams of the Ohio State University focuses on savings mobilization on the supply side and treats finance as a process of social intermediation of funds. It therefore regards the effects of external fund injection in a negative way, since it leads to poor debt recovery rates and inequality of access, and reduces the independence and equity of the financial market.[33]

As stated at the beginning, Bangladesh attempted to extend formal finance to the rural area according to the traditional way of thinking espoused by the 'external fund injection argument' from the mid-1970s, but this strategy was frustrated by the mid-1980s due to the poor debt recovery rate. On the other hand, surplus funds were generated in rural areas by economic growth driven by the Green Revolution and, due to high transaction costs of savings, filled demands in rural areas directly without passing through modern financial institutions. In other words, an independent rural financial market was born and began to function unbeknown to policy makers. Although interest rates were high at 20% to 60% for long-term finance and 50% to 120% for short-term finance, it satisfied the demand for funds and provided a place for surplus funds to go.

Thus, the findings discussed in this chapter support the new way of thinking in principle and suggest the need to give more importance to savings mobilization on the supply side, even in the rural financial policy of the least-developed countries such as Bangladesh. Financial institutions must endeavor to reduce savings-related transaction costs by eradicating problems such as the traveling distances to their outlets, complex procedures for the opening of accounts, psychological barriers towards bank officers, and a sense of distrust of the banking system.[34]

On the other hand, the rapid growth of the Grameen Bank in recent years and its success in subsuming the rural poor while achieving a near 100% fund recovery rate should lead to the reassessment of the external fund injection argument. The achievements of the Grameen Bank in making formal finance available to the rural poor, who could not even write their own names (especially women, who were socially vulnerable), thus reducing poverty should be highly commended. This chapter has focused on the aspect of surplus funds being generated by the rural poor but it is also true that they had to rely on usurious consumer finance and that there was a certain segment of the poor that even usurers would not deal with. The presence of the Grameen Bank was very significant to these people if they could gain access to its services. And it is highly likely that the Grameen Bank would help support the segment of the poor that was generating surplus funds and clearly trying to escape from poverty.

However, this *success* of the Grameen Bank has prompted almost too much attention to the development approach of using low-interest finance for the rural poor in Bangladesh in recent years. Its negative aspect, or, more precisely, conditions for more effective functioning of the Grameen Bank for the poor, is discussed in the following Addendum and in Chapter 7 of this book.

Addendum to Chapter 5
The Fallacy and Reality of Microcredit

As at the end of December 1994, the Grameen Bank (hereafter referred to as GB in this addendum) covered 34,913 *gram* (villages), or about 40% of all villages in the country, and had a total membership of more than two million people; each *gram* had an average of 1.72 centers (customer management units comprised up to eight groups with five members in each group) and fifty-eight members (Grameen Bank 1995). In addition, similar microcredit programs of leading NGOs such as the Bangladesh Rural Advancement Committee (BRAC) and the Association for Social Advancement (ASA) are expanding considerably. The government-affiliated Bangladesh Rural Development Board (BRDB) is trialing a loan provision method that is similar to that of GB in its integrated rural development projects such as RD12. The World Bank has set up the *Palli Karma-Sahayak* Foundation (PKSF), which receives funding from it and provides microcredit through small NGOs to members of the rural poor who are not covered by the aforementioned organizations.

In this way, microcredit is about to sweep across rural Bangladesh, and it goes without saying that the success of GB is behind this phenomenon. From its modest beginnings as an action research project under the initiative of Professor Mohammad Yunus of Chittagong University in 1976, GB became an authorized bank in 1983 and has since achieved phenomenal growth. Many studies about GB's impacts that were accumulated in the early stages of its development generally recognized the significant role it played in reducing rural poverty.[1] It was claimed that GB members' income was found to increase by 30% to 40% within two to three years of their participation.

The basic hypothesis of Professor Yunus at the start of his action research project was that 'if the poor are able to acquire funding under reasonable terms and conditions, they are able to create productive self-employment opportunities without any other assistance.' It was the premise that the rural landless poor had the potential to be entrepreneurs and the provision of affordable credit would allow their talents to blossom, leading to the success of income generating (IG) projects and the escape from poverty. This has been the basic hypothesis underpinning the microcredit development strategy to date.

However, it is rather unreasonable to expect that anyone who acquires a certain amount of funding under favorable terms and uses it as seed money can set up an IG project to generate permanent income. It is more sensible to think that only a small proportion of these people have such enterprising spirit.

This subchapter presents new findings about the poverty reduction mechanism of microcredit, based on a survey of GB loans in Daskin Chamuria village, Tangail district, and discusses their policy implications.

The Illusion of the Income Generating Project

In Daskin Chamuria village the establishment of GB occurred in quick succession: the first center opened in June 1990 and was followed by the second center in December, the third center in January 1991, the fourth center in March 1992, and two more centers in 1993. My November 1992 survey covered a total of 108 GB members who belonged to three of these centers. Twenty per cent of the village's total 538 households were members of GB.

The general loan could be drawn only once a year. It was repaid weekly in small installments over a year and, upon full repayment, a new (increased amount of) loan became available. The seasonal loan was a new type of lending to coincide with the cropping season and a small, fixed amount of repayment was made weekly, with the balance becoming payable after harvesting. GB began to provide hand-tubewell loans for drinking water and housing loans, as well.

Table 5A.1 shows the numbers and amounts of all GB loans for different purposes drawn by 108 GB members from June 1990 (the time of the introduction of GB to Daskin Chamuria village) to the time of the survey in November 1992. Let us focus our attention on the general loan for the moment. Frequent borrowers had completed two borrowing-repayment cycles and had already drawn their third loans. There was a total of 198 loans from the first draw to the third draw, and the total amount of borrowing was just over Tk520,000. The number of loans for the purpose of productive investment in trade activities, livestock, hand-weaving, and transport (for example, rickshaw and *ban* pulling) was 102, which was only 52% of the total loans. The ratio would barely reach 55%, even when five loans for cultivation were added. The remaining 45% of loans were used for consumption, marriage funds, medical treatment, house renovations, loan repayments, and land mortgage lending and other sub-lending. It is notable that there were 68.5 loans (0.5 loan means one loan was used for more than one purpose) for land mortgage lending, other sub-lending, and loan repayment, which represented a large share of the total loans at 34.6% (to be discussed later).

Another problem was that those funds borrowed for productive purposes were seldom invested in the activities of housewives who were GB members. Weaving and transport (for example, rickshaw and *ban* pulling) were men's work. Even in trade activities, women might be involved in production and processing of their products (for example, the rice business involved parboiling of purchased paddy, husking, cleaning, and selling), but actual trade activities at periodical markets were done by men. More specifically, trade activities entailed various businesses as listed in Table 5.20 (Chapter 5) and only the rice, fishnet, and egg/vegetable/fruit businesses likely had women's involvement at the production and processing stage. Even with the addition of the purchasing and growing of livestock such as cattle (dairy or beef), goats, and chicken, in which women played the leading role, the reality was that investment in productive activities only accounted for a little more than half of the total borrowings, as mentioned above.

Thus, it would be reasonable to say that the presumption that most GB loans were invested in IG projects as policy intended was an illusion to a large extent. Further, many of the trade activities were mainly men's occupations under the *purdah* custom,[2] and women's activities were traditionally limited to the parboil processing of paddy, rice husking and cleaning, fishnet manufacturing, livestock rearing, and vegetable growing. Even when borrowed funds were invested in IG projects, actual activities were undertaken by men other than GB members (that is, their husbands or sons) in many cases.[3]

Of course, some effects of GB loans were observable. An employment survey of all 538 households in Daskin Chamuria village revealed that twenty-eight of the 108 GB member households (26%) had at least one family member engaged in the running of a hand-weaving factory or a general store, manufacturing and sale of fishnets, or other self-employed activities, whereas the ratio was only seventy-seven to 430 households (18%) for non-GB members. It is also possible to say that the ratio is merely a quarter of GB members, however.

Table 5A.2 is an example of the rates of return on investment for IG projects using GB loans. They were measured in Tangail district in about 1982 when GB was still in the experimental stage. The following points are notable. First, more businesses in the processing and manufacturing sector had negative returns or very low returns compared with the trading sector. Second, in a comparison between female and male members, the rate of return for women was a large negative figure.

In other words, IG projects in processing and manufacturing, which were traditionally undertaken by women, generally produced low rates of return and often negative returns.[4] Based on this economic analysis, it is not surprising that GB loans were seldom invested in this sector in Daskin Chamuria village.[5]

Land Mortgage Lending and Other Sub-lending

Now, let us discuss land mortgage lending and other sub-lending and loan repayment, which accounted for a high proportion of GB loan use purposes.

Table 5A.1: Purposes of Grameen Bank loans in Daskin Chamuria village

	General loan								Seasonal loan		Other loans	
	First		Second		Third		Total					
Trading	38.5 (36%)	86.50	28.5 (38%)	88.00	5 (33%)	19.50	72 (36%)	194.00	7 (13%)	15.50	–	–
Livestock	13.5 (13%)	29.50	8.5 (11%)	25.00	2 (13%)	8.00	24 (12%)	62.50	2 (4%)	5.00	–	–
Cultivation	3 (3%)	7.00	2 (3%)	5.50	–	–	5 (3%)	12.50	18 (34%)	39.00	–	–
Handloom	2 (2%)	5.00	1 (1%)	3.00	–	–	3 (2%)	8.00	–	–	–	–
Transport (rickshaw etc.)	2 (2%)	4.50	1 (1%)	3.50	–	–	3 (2%)	8.00	–	–	–	–
Land mortgage lending & other sub-lending	27.5 (26%)	58.25	21 (28%)	62.00	4 (27%)	16.00	52.5 (27%)	136.25	10 (19%)	24.00	–	–
Loan repayment	6 (6%)	13.00	7 (9%)	23.50	3 (20%)	11.50	16 (8%)	47.75	6 (11%)	14.50	–	–
House renovation	5 (5%)	10.50	0.5 (1%)	1.50	–	–	5.5 (3%)	12.00	3 (6%)	7.00	1 (5%)	12.00

Hand tubewell	–	–	–	–	–	–	–	–	1 (2%)	2.00	19 (95%)	41.50
Consumption	6.5 (6%)	14.75	3.5 (5%)	10.75	–	–	10 (5%)	25.50	2 (4%)	3.50	–	–
Marriage fund	1 (1%)	2.00	2 (3%)	6.00	1 (7%)	4.00	4 (2%)	12.00	2 (4%)	5.00	–	–
Medical treatment	2 (2%)	5.00	–	–	–	–	2 (1%)	5.00	–	–	–	–
Unknown	1 (1%)	2.00	–	–	–	–	1 (1%)	2.00	2 (4%)	5.00	–	–
Total	108 (100%)	238	75 (100%)	228.5	15 (100%)	59	198 (100%)	525.5	53 (100%)	120.5	20 (100%)	53.5

Note: Number of loans in the left column; Amount in thousand *taka* in the right column.

Source: Prepared by the author.

Table 5A.2: An example of investment profitability in IG projects

	PROFITABILITY
Processing and manufacturing	
Cane work and bamboo ware	–83%
Pottery	42%
Rice hulling and cleaning	–126%
Oil press	–50%
Carpet weaving	–113%
Handloom	22%
Dairy products	47%
Average	–38%
Trading	
Rice	62%
Seasonal farm produce	91%
Livestock and forestry products	102%
Cottage industry products	–50%
Urban industry products	145%
Peddling	–56%
Shopkeeping	86%
Average	61%
Male	57%
Female	–87%

Source: Prepared by the author based on Hossain, M. (1985b).

Land mortgage lending refers to the *bhograhani* system under which lending of about Tk15,000–Tk25,000 per acre can secure the lender a usufruct right to the borrower's farmland until the loan is repaid in full. The fund borrowed from GB is sub-lent to a landowner in exchange for the tillage right to the land. In this case, revenue generated from the usufructuary right (land rent) is the interest on the principal from which the interest on the GB loan is paid, and any residual amount becomes the profit margin of the sub-lending. Loan repayment is included in this discussion because a considerable number of loans were used for loan repayment to clear land mortgages.

As we have seen in Chapter 5, the lower class in terms of landholding comprised the main lenders in *bhograhani* in Daskin Chamuria village. It was therefore common for them to self-cultivate the land acquired through *bhograhani*, and the main purpose for their lending against land mortgage was to secure rice for their own consumption. The flow of funds through *bhograhani* from the lower class to the upper class was fundamentally a phenomenon that occurred independently from the intervention by GB. We should take the view that this large flow of funds had already existed by the time GB appeared on the scene, and part of GB's funds moved with the flow into investment in land mortgage.

In Daskin Chamuria village the estimated annual land rent for the double rice cropping pattern with *aman* and *boro* (practiced on 31% of the village's land) was about Tk4,000, and the estimated annual land rent for the triple cropping pattern with *aman*, mustard, and *boro* (34%) was just under Tk6,000, therefore the annual rate of return for *bhograhani* was about 25%.[6] This was only slightly higher than the interest rate on GB loans (16% at that time), but it was a relatively safe investment opportunity and favorable in the sense that lenders were able to secure income for their own labor cost incurred in cultivation.

The fact that much of the funds borrowed from GB were flowing into mortgage lending was also pointed out by Todd (1996), who conducted a detailed participatory observation of GB members in Tangail district. Todd apparently had difficulty eliciting the truth from members, since land mortgage lending was regarded as *on-lending* of a loan and was not approved by GB as a legitimate investment at the time of her survey. The situation was the same in Daskin Chamuria village. (I should add that it has become an approved investment now.)

Land mortgage lending is slightly different in character from blatant on-lending in the sense that it is the same as the acquisition of the right to cultivate the land by the poor. However, the land mortgage lending and other sub-lending category in Table 5A.1 does include the case of more blatant on-lending. It is the short-term loan with interest payment in kind (two to three *maund* of paddy are received as the interest on a loan of Tk1,000), which we saw in Chapter 5. The interest rate in this case amounted to 50% to 60% per annum, which was a large profit margin over GB's interest rate of 16%.

The Poverty Reduction Mechanism of the Grameen Bank

GB provided the rural poor with access to loans, which contributed to poverty alleviation. This point is almost certainly a fact and its achievement is extremely significant. However, it must be said that it is highly unlikely that the mechanism of poverty alleviation was brought about through the success of IG projects as publicized by GB itself.

Then, what is the poverty alleviation mechanism of microcredit offered by GB and others? It cannot be explained by the abovementioned profit margins gained by sub-lending alone. To state the conclusion first, it is likely that the loans induced poor households, especially men, to develop a 'thrift and saving' habit by acting as 'advances for savings' (Rutherford 1998).

Here is a clear example. Among the landless and petty landholders of Daskin Chamuria village, there were many weaving factory wage laborers (men) who worked in handloom factories in the village or neighboring villages. In seventy (20.3%) of the total 344 households in the landless and landholding below half-an-acre class, the main occupation of the household head was as a weaving factory wage laborer (Table 5.6 of Chapter 5). As Table 5A.3 shows, there was a high concentration of GB members among the wives of weaving factory wage laborers.

Weaving factory wage laborers were guaranteed stable employment for much of the year. They worked on a piece-rate basis and their wages increased as their skill levels increased. Their wages were slightly higher than those of agricultural laborers and were paid weekly. They were able to expect quite a stable flow of 'decent' regular income. According to several villagers, weaving factory wage laborers used to go to the town together on weekly paydays, enjoy amusements such as movies, and come home late at night. This changed when their wives became GB members. They refrained from spending on such amusements and worked longer hours to earn more wages. They were, of course, trying to earn money for weekly repayments to GB. The weekly wage cycle and the weekly GB repayment cycle happened to coincide perfectly.

From this viewpoint, GB loans indeed played the role of 'advances for savings' for them. The wives of weaving factory wage laborers successfully drove their husbands to 'thrift and savings.' If this was the case, it would not matter at all what GB loans were used for, to put it in extreme terms. Whether they invested in a business and failed, or spent all on consumption, they were able to make repayments as long as they earned more from the regular income source they already had.

Weaving factory wage laborers were, of course, in a very fortunate position. There were many poor households without such stable, regular income. However, even in these households, when the wife became a GB member, the husband was forced to maintain repayments of 'advances for savings' by maximizing his labor input into his pre-existing unstable work opportunity. If he failed and she fell behind in repayment, she would be advised by her fellow members of the five-member group and the GB staff to resign voluntarily and would eventually be forced to drop out. Itō (1999) and others have already demonstrated that GB was able to maintain its astonishingly high repayment rate because problems were 'dealt with' through this mechanism before they came into the open.[7] It is easy to imagine that the risk of dropping out was higher for poor households without stable and regular income.

Table 5A.3: Main occupations of household heads and Grameen Bank participation rates in Daskin Chamuria village

	Grameen Bank members		Non Grameen Bank members	
	Number of households	%	Number of households	%
Farming	9	11.3	25	9.5
Agricultural wage labor	21	26.3	97	36.7
Weaving wage labor	27	33.8	47	17.8
Bidhi factory labor	3	3.8	22	8.3
Business	14	17.5	25	9.5
Rickshaw driving	3	3.8	11	4.2
Service	0	0.0	13	4.9
Other	3	3.8	24	9.1
Total	80	100	264	100

Note: Landless households and households with less than 0.50 acres of land only.

Now, these savings that were forced upon the poor through the provision of GB loans were actually used for purposes listed in Table 5A.1. Among these potential investments, land mortgage lending and other sub-lending would be the safest and most secure investment. Sub-lending can be considered as a type of asset investment, since the capital is recovered intact at the expiry of the term (albeit with some loss of value from inflation). Sub-lending other than land mortgage lending is also asset investment in a financial asset.

It is clear from Table 5A.1 that the ratio of loans for land mortgage lending and other sub-lending and loan repayment to the total general loans was on the increase, and rose from 31.1% for the first time, to 37.3% for the second time, and to 46.7% for the third time in Daskin Chamuria village. In other words, more and more GB members went into asset investment with each passing year. If the acquisition of livestock was to be considered a type of asset building, the importance of asset building clearly increased at an accelerating pace.

To sum up, the poverty alleviation mechanism of GB can be roughly explained as follows. GB loans act as advances for savings and force poor households, especially their male members, to maximize labor input into pre-existing work opportunities in order to ensure repayment. This encourages thrift and saving, while savings are used mainly for asset investments, which generate relatively secure profits, which in turn increase the household income. The proportion of loans used for asset investment increases as household financial situations improve with each passing year. Those GB members who manage to keep up with weekly repayments without dropping out of the program gradually see the prospect of escape from poverty.

The above process of escape from poverty usually takes more than several years. According to M. Hossain (1988: 60, Table 30), the amount of per capita 'social investment' in such things as housing, education, and hygiene increased rapidly from Tk662 within one year of joining GB to Tk989 in one to two years, to Tk1,656 in two to three years, and to Tk3,541 after three years. This fact in itself would be a good indicator of poverty alleviation. Asset investment is followed by even longer-sighted social investment, which offers very high profitability in the medium to long term. By the fifth year of GB membership, members can feel certain that they have managed to escape from poverty.[8]

In any case, I would like to reiterate the dubiousness of the *commonsense* premise that the repayment of GB loans is covered by earnings from the investment of GB loans.

Policy Implications

If the poverty alleviation mechanism of GB works in the way that has been discussed in this addendum, it will lead to several important policy implications.

First, it is highly unlikely that policy guidance to make poor households direct their microcredit to productive investment will generate desirable effects. In this sense, the microcredit delivery method used in India's Integrated Rural Development Program (that is, provision in goods such as livestock) deserves reconsideration.

Second, in the South Asian context, it is highly unlikely that microcredit is beneficial for the poorest of the poor, especially households lacking any male workers (such as widowed households). Without a fundamental means to generate income, which acts as a vital source of savings, these households are unlikely to make effective use of advances for savings.

Third, more attention should be paid to the issue of 'dropouts' (Karim and Osada 1998). While the success of microcredit is underpinned largely by the praises for a high repayment rate, we must not forget the fact that there are considerable numbers of households that are judged to be ineligible for membership or member households that are forced to drop out.

Fourth, microcredit cannot be expected to lead the way to economic growth. Rather, it should be recognized as an effective means for spreading the benefits of steady economic growth to the lower class.

Lastly, it should be remembered that there had been strong doubts about the effectiveness of microcredit before the success of GB was widely recognized.[9] These criticisms are still valid today as long as microcredit is perceived as something that should be supported by high profitability of IG projects. This is another reason why it is extremely important to understand the poverty alleviation mechanism of microcredit correctly.

6
Transformation of the Potato-marketing System and Finance

This chapter examines one aspect of the recent change in Bangladesh's rural finance based on the specific phenomenon of transformation of the potato-marketing system. Potato is a growth crop that has been raising its status in the local diet amid the country's economic development and urbanization, especially since the spread of cold storage made year-round shipment possible.[1] Potato production increased from a mere 200,000 tons or so in the mid-1950s to 500,000 tons by the mid-1960s, reached one million tons in the early 1980s, and recently exceeded 1.5 million tons.

However, large seasonal variations in the price of potato still remain because of the high cost of cold storage. These seasonal price variations from the mid-1990s to the year 2000/01 are plotted on Figure 6.1. It shows that potato prices were at their lowest in March, immediately after harvesting, at Tk130–Tk200 per *maund*, and peaked in November, just before sowing, at around Tk350 per *maund*.[2] The price difference over the whole period was usually more than Tk150, meaning that the price rose by 10% to 15% per month. As discussed later in the chapter, the net cost of cold storage was considerably lower than this. In other words, there were opportunities to make large economic gains in the potato-marketing process and it would be interesting to discover which economic entities (farmers, traders, cold storage owners, and so on) were seizing them.

Yet, these seasonal price variations were smaller than expected in some years, as typified by the lines representing 1997/98 and 2000/01 in Figure 6.1, for example. It means that the risk would be quite high, since those economic entities that have invested in the potato-marketing business would suffer a loss. In other words, investment for the purpose of economic gains in potato marketing would fall in the high-risk–high-return category.

D. J. Lewis (1991), an anthropologist, conducted a detailed field survey of the potato-marketing system in the rural area in the mid-1980s. His study area was a new potato-producing region in Comilla district in eastern Bangladesh. The establishment of a cold storage there in 1982 started a process of major transformation of the rural areas through potato production. The cold storage was an investment by an urban entrepreneur and Lewis focused his attention on this case as a typical example of the invasion of urban capital into the rural

Figure 6.1: Seasonal fluctuations in the urban wholesale price of potato

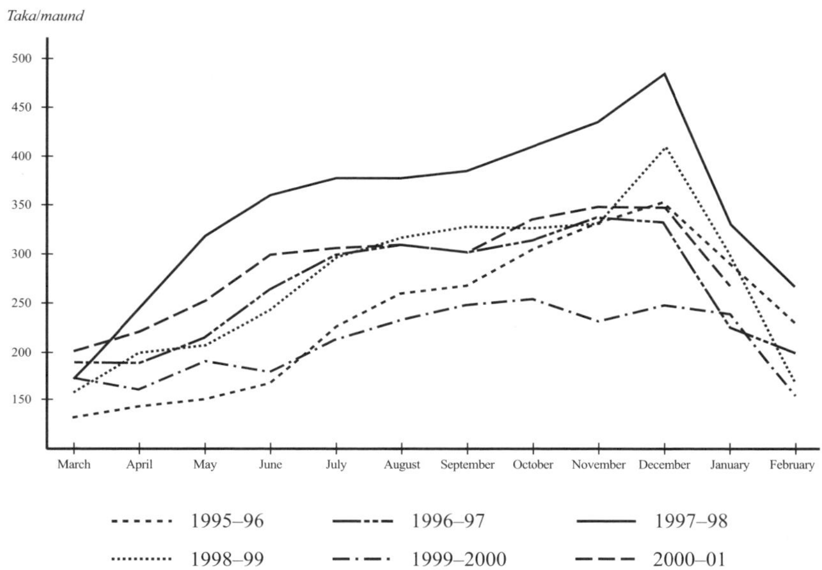

area. The rural area was still very poor at the time, and the urban entrepreneur's economic capacity overwhelmed everyone else. The cold storage bought 60,000 bags of potatoes (two *maund* or about seventy-five kilograms per bag) initially in 1982, which was half its total storage capacity, and suffered a major loss when the potato price happened to crash that year. The cold storage stopped buying potatoes after that. Instead, it found customers among traders and wealthy farmers by adopting a system under which it provided a loan of Tk70 per *maund* to large customers with a trading volume of over 100 *maund* and by making marketing efforts such as the introduction of deferred payment of the storage charge (Tk55 per *maund*). Part of the loans provided to traders was sub-lent to small to medium potato farmers in the form of a *dadan* (advance payment). The cold storage owner directed his effort to the popularization of the potato variety (Diamond) that was suitable for cold storage.

The same urban entrepreneur went on to build a jute factory next to this cold storage facility. Having witnessed this urban entrepreneur's active investment in the rural area, Lewis characterized the situation as the deepening of 'dependency capitalism.'

However, this type of *exploitative* relationship in the agricultural marketing chain was not limited to potato. For example, Crow (1989) and Crow and Murshid (1994) point out the existence of exploitative relationships (tied transactions) based on advance payment between petty traders and local merchants or wholesalers in rice marketing. It is understood that domination of the agricultural marketing chain by capital owners and the resultant unequal distribution of economic profits had been the norm in Bangladesh at least up to the 1980s, and, in fact, it did appear to be the case.

This chapter presents an analysis of the transformation of the potato-marketing system from the mid-1980s based on an intensive survey conducted intermittently between 1999 and 2003 in a village near Lewis's study area in Comilla district. To state the conclusion first, investment by urban entrepreneurs in cold storages and jute factories contributed much to the economic development of the surrounding rural areas but the end result was not the deepening of dependency capitalism as predicted by Lewis. It was rather a decline in relative economic dominance by the urban entrepreneurs due to trickle-down effects. Traders grew as the main player in investment in the cold storage of potatoes and, at the same time, stopped providing advances to farmers. Farmers, traders, and cold storage owners ended up performing only their respective *primary* functions of potato production, marketing, and cold storage service. The direct cause of this change was an intensifying competition between increasing numbers of cold storage facilities, but the more fundamental reason was a rise in the income of rural residents prompted by the economic development (including an expansion of off-farm employment opportunities) in the study area. Farmers became wealthier in relative terms and no longer required advances for potato production.

In the first section below, the agricultural and employment structures of the study village are briefly explained. The second section provides an overview of the potato cold storage and marketing system. The third section presents a cost-return analysis in relation to farmers, traders, and cold storage owners involved in potato production and marketing for the survey year (2000/01). The fourth section attempts a more general analysis of the potato market by expanding the scope from a single year to multiple years. The fifth section presents the conclusion.

Agricultural and Employment Structures of the Study Village

The survey was conducted in Ashora village in Debidwar *upazila* (subdistrict), Comilla district. Comilla district was a major potato-producing region representing 19% of the total production (1997), second only to Munshiganj district (35%). The village was on an arterial road linking the capital Dhaka and Chittagong via Comilla, and only two kilometers from the seat of the municipal government of the neighboring Chandina *upazila*, which had a large permanent market (Chandina Market), as well as bank branches, a post office, and communication facilities. Another slightly smaller permanent market (vegetables only) was four kilometers from the village. Chandina Market also held *hat* (periodic markets) twice a week. There were as many as three potato cold storages within a five kilometer radius of the village. One was the cold storage, built in 1982, that was studied by Lewis. Next to this storage was the aforementioned jute factory, which was an important source of employment for the village's residents. All in all, the village was very favorably located.

Geographically, Ashora village was located more or less on highlands and free from regular flooding. Three DTWs were constructed in the latter half of the 1970s but they have been under the ownership and management of farmer groups since they were transferred from BADC under the privatization policy at the beginning of the 1980s. DTWs supplied irrigation to about 70% of the village's farmland. The introduction of STWs began at the end of the 1980s and accelerated from the mid-1990s. About twenty STWs were in operation at the time of the survey. The rate of farmland irrigation was 100% and the village practiced a highly intensive quadruple cropping pattern based on triple rice cropping with *aus*, *aman*, and *boro*, plus potato cropping between *aman* and *boro*. Bullocks were no longer used for cultivation, and tractors were used for plowing and soil preparation on all fields. The scale of farm operation was very small, and a majority of farmers grew rice for their own consumption and their main cash crop was potato. Even larger farm households hardly sold any rice because they carried the large burden of feeding their wage laborers (three meals per day for seasonal migrant laborers and two meals for local laborers).

The village consisted of four *para* (hamlets). The census survey was conducted in the east *para* and the middle *para*, and collected data from a total of 106 households.[3] Table 6.1 shows the employment structure (main occupations of household heads) for these households classified according to the size of farmland holdings. There are four classes of landholding sizes: landless, small farm (below 0.50 acres), medium farm (0.50 to 1.49 acres), and large farm (1.50 acres and over). It was reflective of the small scale of farmland holding in this village that a landholding over an acre-and-a-half was classified as a large farm.

The first notable feature of Table 6.1 is that few household heads in the landless and small farm classes engaged in farming[4] and very few were agricultural wage laborers. Many engaged in off-farm employment such as factory labor, overseas work, service (among small farm households), and trading other than potato trading. The second feature is that many household heads in the medium

Table 6.1: Farmland distribution and employment structure by the farmland holding class in Ashora village

Farmland holding class (acre)	Number of households	Main occupation of the head of household[a]								Farmland holding area (acre)
		Farmer	Agricultural wage laborer	Factory worker	Overseas worker	Service[b]	Potato merchant	Other merchant[c]	Other[d]	
0	27	5	2	9	7	0	0	2	2	0
		(19)	(7)	(33)	(26)	(0)	(0)	(8)	(7)	
0.01–0.49	40	12	2	4	5	9	1	5	2	8.5
		(30)	(5)	(10)	(13)	(22)	(2)	(13)	(5)	
0.50–1.49	25	14	1	0	1	3	4	2	0	21.5
		(56)	(4)	(0)	(4)	(12)	(16)	(8)	(0)	
1.50–	14	7	0	0	2	1	4	0	0	39.6
		(50)	(0)	(0)	(14)	(7)	(29)	(0)	(0)	
Total	106	38	5	13	15	13	9	9	4	68.6
	(100)	(36)	(5)	(12)	(14)	(12)	(9)	(8)	(4)	(100)

Notes:
a: Numbers in brackets are percentages.
b: Service (*chakkri*) means permanent salaried occupations in the public and private sectors.
c: Other merchants are in very labor-intensive trades such as molasses, hosiery and clothing.
d: Other occupations include rickshaw and minibus drivers.

Source: Prepared based on the field survey in June and July 2000.

and large farm classes engaged in farming but considerable numbers were working overseas, in service or potato trade. Factory laborers were working at the aforementioned privately owned jute mill in the neighboring village. Agricultural labor in the village was mainly performed by seasonal migrant laborers who came all the way from northern Bangladesh.

Overseas employment began in the early 1980s, and the workforce initially flowed from the medium and large farm classes to oil-producing Middle Eastern countries, but they had to return home when the Gulf War broke out in 1991. Overseas work resumed after the war but workers from the medium and large farm classes shifted their destinations to Southeast Asian countries such as Singapore and Malaysia, and the workforce from the landless and small farm classes went to the Middle East this time.[5]

In short, the study village had highly developed off-farm employment opportunities, including overseas employment, despite its purely rural location. Small farm and landless households in the rural low-income class, in particular, were increasing the so-called 'quit-agriculture' tendency. Some accumulated capital through off-farm employment and used it to acquire farmland through mortgage or tenancy to carry out farming operations, while farm labor was performed mainly by seasonal laborers from afar.

Lastly, let us look at the inter-class flow of informal finance in Ashora village (Table 6.2 and Table 6.3), as we have done in Chapter 5. The two tables show a clear flow of long-term finance on *bondak* (farmland mortgage) from the lower class to the upper class, indicating the existence of the observable inter-class 'reverse flow.' In short-term finance, funds flowed between the upper and lower classes in indeterminate directions (although it is not immediately obvious from the tables), especially when loans from cold storages are excluded.

The Potato Cold Storage and Marketing System

Potato yield largely depends on the quality of seed potatoes. It was BADC that dealt in certified seeds and sold to authorized dealers. BADC used to import expensive seed potatoes from the Netherlands but began to produce its own second-generation seeds from the imported first-generation seeds from 1986 (Lewis 1991: 322–3). It was possible to propagate further generations of seeds from BADC's certified seeds but the yield would drop sharply after two years, making it uneconomical. Cheap seeds propagated from certified seeds at the farm level (Tk350–Tk400 per *maund*) were in wide circulation and were bought by many farmers.[6] However, BADC's certified seeds gave them higher yields, even though they were more expensive (Tk500–Tk750 per *maund*).

Table 6.2: Farmland holding class and informal finance in Ashora village

Farmland holding class (acres)	Number of households	*Bondak* (*taka*)				Short-term finance other than *Bondak* (*taka*)			
		Lender	Lender & borrower	Borrower	Other	Lender	Lender & borrower	Borrower	Other
0	27	10	0	2	15	0	8	12	7
0.01–0.49	40	11	4	9	16	6	13	15	6
0.50–1.49	25	2	0	13	10	2	8	11	4
1.50–	14	1	4	5	4	2	6	2	4
Total	106	24	8	29	45	10	35	40	21

Source: Moazzem (2004).

Table 6.3: Informal finance balance by the farmland holding class in Ashora village

Farmland holding class (acres)	Number of households	*Bondak*				Short-term finance other than *Bondak*			
		Lending amount	Borrowing amount	Balance	Balance per household	Lending amount	Borrowing amount	Balance	Balance per household
0	27	407,500	62,000	345,500	12,796	81,925	319,085	–237,160	–8,784
0.01–0.49	40	434,000	182,000	252,000	6,300	158,000	705,880	–547,880	–13,697
0.50–1.49	25	88,000	602,000	–514,000	–20,560	553,236	798,685	–245,449	–9,818
1.50–	14	232,000	265,000	–33,000	–2,357	1,508,190	1,598,200	–90,010	–6,429
Total	106	1,161,500	1,111,000	50,500	476	2,301,351	3,421,850	–1,120,499	–10,571

Source: Moazzem (2004).

Farm-propagated seeds were harvested in February and March and had to be stored in cold storage for the next season of production (sowing in November and December).

The potato-marketing channel is shown in Figure 6.2. 'S' denotes seed potatoes and 'NS' denotes non-seed potatoes (for consumption). The main marketing channel for the latter is as follows. The farmer sold non-seed potatoes to the *bepari* (local trader), who immediately transported and sold some to the consumption region and stored the rest in a rural cold storage facility. From around July to November, the local trader gradually withdrew potatoes from the storage as required and sold them to the *paikar* (wholesaler) in the city. (The *khuchra bikreta* (retailer) then sold them to consumers.) Potatoes produced in the study area were mostly transported to Bangladesh's second largest city, Chittagong, and consumed there.

I elaborate on the marketing system further. Farmers harvested their potatoes in February and March. They had three options at that point. One, they could sell them to local traders as soon as they were harvested.[7] Two, they could store them at home (not in cold storage) for two to three months after harvesting, then sell to local traders. They would take this option in anticipation that the potato price would be somewhat higher then than immediately after harvesting. (Potatoes would not keep for more than two to three months without refrigeration.) Three, they could store them in the cold storage and withdraw and sell to local traders at appropriate times.

At the time of sale by the first option, local traders actively visited villages to purchase potatoes. In general, upper-class farmers tended to sell directly to local traders at the farmyard, while lower-class farmers tended to take their potatoes to Chandina Market, two kilometers away, to sell to waiting traders. One reason was that local traders would not visit the farmyards of small growers for purchasing, but the main reason was that farmers could get slightly higher prices at the market.

Local traders were extremely busy at harvest time. They hired extra staff, and traveled a large area for twelve hours a day, measuring, bagging, and transporting purchased potatoes. And they were generally full-time potato dealers. They had much work to do outside of the harvesting season as they watched potato price movement, actively participated in the resale of potatoes stored in cold storages (in the form of certificate sales, to be discussed later), and gradually withdrew their own refrigerated potatoes for shipment to urban areas.

A majority of local traders were upper-class farmers, as well, and they generally had invested in STWs and farm machinery, such as tractors, to carry out water sale or plowing service operations. Some local traders, especially those over the age of fifty, were former government-authorized dealers of agricultural

Figure 6.2: Potato marketing channel

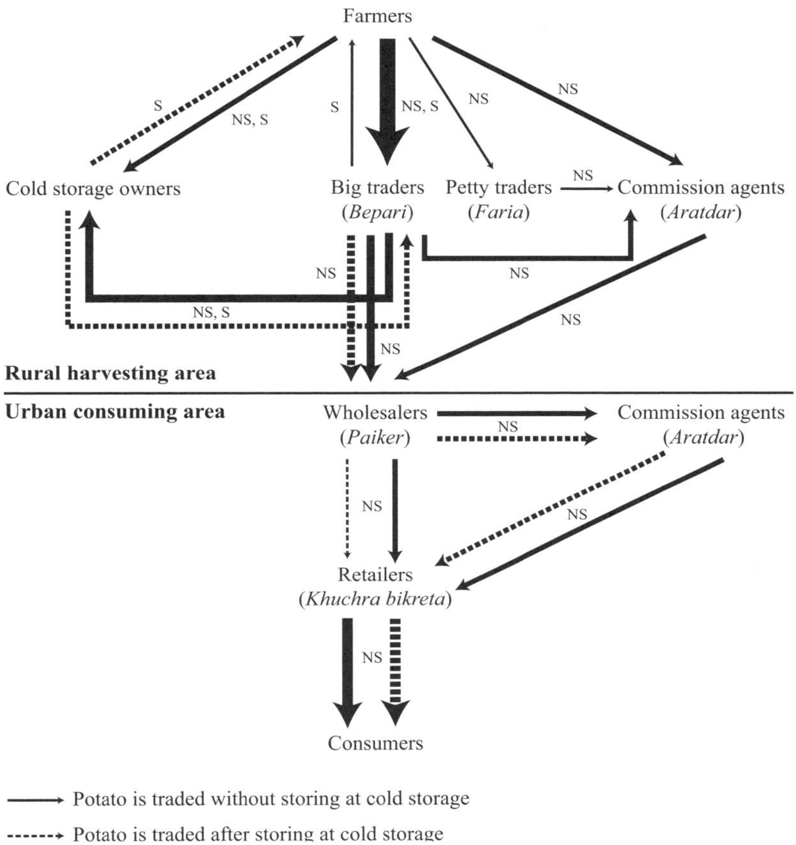

Note: NS and S indicate non-seed and seed potato respectively. Thickness of arrow indicates approximate transaction through different sources.

Source: Prepared by the authors 2000.

input materials (such as chemical fertilizers) and rationed goods when the market was under strict control (up to the end of the 1970s).

Chandina Market was a major potato-marketing center. There were several *aratdar* (commission agents) who had their shops at this municipal market. Their primary job was to act as middlemen for other traders for a commission, but they also worked as local potato traders by themselves. Unlike other local traders, however, they did not hire people to visit villages and pick up purchased potatoes. They generally advanced funds required for collection of potatoes to *faria* (petty traders) and waited for them to bring them in (Figure 6.2). Although many *faria* were operating in rice marketing, they were rather scarce in the potato-marketing system, under which the aforementioned direct collection by large local traders was more common.

While these petty traders, local traders, and commission agents were rural-based, cold storage owners were urban residents (as mentioned earlier). These urban entrepreneurs employed managers to run the day-to-day operation of their storages. At the time of the survey, there were three cold storages with storage capacity of 60,000 bags, 75,000 bags, and 100,000 bags each. The aforementioned cold storage built in 1982 had the smallest capacity and the other two were relatively new warehouses built in the 1990s. The largest one was also the newest, and was built in 1999. The capacity utilization rate at the time of the survey was 100%, 95%, and 25% respectively. There was another cold storage near the study village but it was closed for rehabilitation at the time of the survey. It was built in the latter half of the 1980s, closed in 2000, and reopened in 2003 after rehabilitation. As was the case with the aforementioned jute factory, cold storage owners were generally urban entrepreneurs who had other major business operations such as banking and export.

Employed managers of these cold storages were mainly responsible for maintaining the warehouse temperature at the optimum range between 2° and 4° centigrade and keeping potatoes in good condition by re-stacking jute-bagged potatoes two to three times a season for adequate aeration. It was not easy to maintain a constant room temperature, since the electricity supply was unreliable in rural Bangladesh. Potato spoilage due to power outage reportedly occurred frequently in the mid-1980s (Lewis 1991). The bad publicity about such an incident would spread widely in the area and might cause great damage to the business.

The cold storage would accept a minimum of ten *maund* of potatoes (two *maund* in a bag) for storage. The storage charge was Tk80 per *maund* regardless of the length of storage. The storage would lend Tk100–Tk150 per *maund* (Tk150 for largest customers) to large customers with over 200 *maund* of potatoes. The system has not changed since the time of Lewis's survey. Customers who had received loans were able to discard stored potatoes in the worst case if the potato price did not rise as expected. In this sense, the system of lending by the warehouse acted as the guaranteed minimum price for potato. However, if the loan recipients decided to withdraw their potatoes, they were obliged to repay the loans, as well as to pay the storage charge plus an additional Tk5 (a total of Tk85 per *maund*). Although the nominal interest on the loan was zero, the additional charge of Tk5 was, in fact, an interest on the loan. The effective interest rate varied according to the length of storage period (to be estimated later).

Finally, another player in the potato cold storage and marketing system should be mentioned—the salaried workers in the urban and rural areas. They belonged to the so-called middle class but, come harvest season, they purchased potatoes through commission agents at the municipal market, stored them in a cold storage facility, and received storage certificates issued by the cold storage operators. Because certificates were transferable, they would sell the certificates when they secured sufficient price appreciation or when they needed funds. They were called the *stockist* in the local language. Cold storages issued a certificate to any owner of stored potatoes, and therefore farmers, local traders, and commission agents were also actively involved in the certificate transaction market. The *stockist* was merely one of the players.

The Cost and Return Structures of the Economic Entities

Let us analyze how much profit the economic entities in the potato storage and marketing chain were deriving.

The survey was conducted mostly in August and September 2000 and there were two more months before all potatoes were withdrawn from cold storage and sold. Although this would leave the analysis incomplete for that part, economic analysis of costs and return for the year 2000/01, including data from the subsequent supplementary survey, is presented below. According to Figure 6.1, the potato price was about Tk200 per *maund* at the harvest time (March), which was the highest level in the previous several years;[8] it continued to rise rather sharply to Tk300 per *maund* by June, then leveled off[9] and reached only Tk350 per *maund*, even in November. It moved in an unusual pattern that was very different from the normal price movement. I would like to state here that the following analysis is based on the potato price movement in this particular year.

The Farmer

Fifteen farmer samples were selected as proportionally as possible to the population of 106 census-surveyed households based on the farmland holding size. All fifteen were purely farmers, and were not local potato traders. Seven of the fifteen households, about half, were also producing seed potatoes. The total production volume of these fifteen households included 262 *maund* of seeds and 1,276 *maund* of potatoes for consumption.

Table 6.4 shows the average production costs for seeds and non-seed potatoes expressed in *taka* per *maund*. The production cost per *maund* was Tk139 for seeds and Tk131 for non-seeds. The yield per acre for seeds was 168 *maund*,

Table 6.4: Cost of potato production in Ashora village

	NON-SEED POTATO	SEED POTATO
Sample number	15	7
Cost (*taka/maund*)		
Operating expenses	89 (64%)	87 (67%)
Seed	36	40
Chemical fertilizer	33	30
Agricultural chemicals	7	6
Irrigation	6	5
Plowing & soil preparation (by tractor)	7	6
Labor expenses	25 (17%)	24 (18%)
Plowing & soil preparation	1	1
Planting	7	6
Ridging	6	5
Fertilizing & spraying	3	2
Harvesting	8	10
Land rent	25 (17%)	20 (15%)
Total cost	139 (100%)	131 (100%)
Average farmland holding size (acres)	1.29	1.63
Average potato planting area (acres)	0.65	0.22
Yield (*maund*/acre)	144	168

Notes: 1 *maund* = 37.3 kilograms. US$1 = 53 *taka* (at the time of survey).

Source: Based on the survey in August and September 2000.

which was 17% higher than 144 *maund* for non-seeds, but there was little difference between their production costs, since the cost per acre for seeds was similarly higher. The sale price of seeds was Tk179 per *maund* according to Table 6.6, which was not very different from the price of non-seeds (Tk166–Tk183).

One notable point in Table 6.4 is the high levels of current input costs in potato production. In particular, the expenses on seeds and chemical fertilizers alone reached 50% of the total production cost for non-seed potatoes and 53% for seed potatoes. This fact was the reason why many farmers were obtaining credit from chemical fertilizer dealers and potato traders in the mid-1980s, when Lewis conducted his survey.

Table 6.5 shows the potato production volume and selling pattern for each of the fifteen farm households. ‘A1’ and ‘A2’ denote immediate sale after

Table 6.5: Potato sale by sample households in 2000/01

No.	FHS[A] (ACRES)	POTATO PLANTING AREA (ACRES) NON-SEED	SEED	POTATO SALE QUANTITY (*MAUND*) NON-SEED A1	A2	A3	A4	TOTAL	SEED B1	B2	TOTAL
1	0	0.27	0	4	4	6	0	14	0	0	0
2	0	0.51	0	6	53	0	12	71	0	0	0
3	0	0.60	0	1	76	0	6	83	0	0	0
4	0	0.23	0.07	20	0	0	10	30	0	10	10
5	0.05	0.51	0.15	6	34	0	10	50	0	16	16
6	0.06	0.30	0.00	0	35	0	0	35	0	0	0
7	0.45	0.35	0.04	8	36	0	0	44	0	6	6
8	0.45	0.30	0.00	15	20	0	0	35	0	0	0
9	0.72	0.24	0.00	50	0	0	0	50	0	0	0
10	0.72	0.03	0.30	0	4	0	0	4	14	6	20
11	0.90	0.48	0.12	12	46	30	20	108	0	30	30
12	1.08	0.75	0.00	34	25	16	34	109	0	0	0
13	1.20	0.83	0.18	57	0	0	0	57	0	40	40
14	2.14	1.86	0.00	0	150	0	100	250	0	0	0
15	8.14	2.48	0.70	336	0	0	0	336	0	140	140
Total				549	483	52	192	1,276	14	248	262
Ratio				43%	38%	4%	15%	100%	5%	95%	100%

Notes: FHS = Farmland holding size. No. 8 and No. 10 households bought 10 *maund* of seed potatoes and stored in the cold storage in addition to self-produced potatoes.
Source: Based on the survey in August and September 2000.

harvesting ('A2' means sale after two weeks of drying at home, see note 7), 'A3' denotes sale after two to three months of storage at home, and 'A4' denotes sale after cold storage in a warehouse. 'B1' and 'B2' are for seed potatoes. 'B1' denotes immediate sale to traders after harvesting and 'B2' denotes sale after cold storage.

First, the ratio of each selling pattern in the total production volume for the fifteen households in the case of non-seed potatoes was 43% for A1, followed by 38% for A2, 15% for A4, and 4% for A3. In the case of seed potatoes, B1 accounted for only 5%, whereas B2 had the overwhelming share at 95%. Farmers tended to sell non-seed potatoes immediately without cold storage, but they generally stored seed potatoes in cold storages. Seeds were used for potato production for the following year in most cases, but they could be sold for cash by resale of storage certificates if money was needed urgently. As mentioned earlier, 2000/01 was somewhat of an unusual year in that the potato price was quite high at the time of harvesting. It is possible that farmers might have shown a stronger tendency than usual to sell non-seed potatoes to traders immediately after harvesting because of this.

It is also true that almost half the number of farmers (seven out of fifteen households) kept some potatoes in cold storage (the ratio of cold-stored potatoes for seven households ranged from 7% to 40%, with an average of 27%), even in the case of non-seed potatoes. It was found in their interviews that this had a strong aspect of savings for when they needed cash to fund *aus* rice and *aman* rice production or for other purposes, as well as an aspect of investment for profit. The stored volume for farmer No. 2 was only six *maund*, which was below the warehouse's minimum quantity of ten *maund*. This indicates that he used cold storage jointly with other farmers.

Table 6.6 shows the estimated profit for each selling pattern. In estimating the cost component, farmers using A3, A4, and B2 methods, for example, waited several months before they obtained all revenues and, therefore, the interest incurred during that period should be included in the cost. Please note, however, that it has been omitted from this table.

Let us look at the row marked 'net revenue (profit)' in the table. In the case of non-seed potatoes, A1, A2, and A3 earned relatively high net revenue. This is consistent with the aforementioned price movement of potatoes in 2000/01. In particular, farmers who stored their potatoes at home for two to three months under the A3 pattern gained a very large profit, reflecting the rapid price rise that continued until around June in that year. It is clear from Figure 6.1, however, that this selling strategy would not be successful in most years.

By contrast, farmers who stored their potatoes in cold storage were less successful, since it reduced their net revenue per *maund*. The table shows that farmers who adopted the A4 method received a profit of Tk12 per *maund*, but this would become a negative figure when interest on working capital for cold storage was taken into account (Tk21 based on 3% per month for five months).

The table also shows a high profit from cold storage of seeds (B2). It should be noted that seed potato production was not very attractive as a business because there was a considerable risk of disease damage due to contamination from non-seed potatoes stored in the same place, and the seed potato market was thin and more risky.

Cold Storage

It is generally very difficult to obtain financial data from cold storage managers. Special cooperation was obtained from the smallest storage facility (with a storage capacity of 120,000 *maund*) and the following analysis is based on this case only. Table 6.7 shows a summary.

Table 6.6: Income of sample households derived from potato production and marketing for 2000/01

	NON-SEED POTATO				SEED POTATO	
	A1	A2	A3	A4[a]	B1	B2
Sample number	12	11	3	7	1	7
Gross revenue (= sale price)	166	183	231	260	179	400
Costs						
Production cost	139	139	139	139	131	131
Marketing cost	0	8	13	109	8	124
Freight cost	0	0	0	3	0	6
Labor cost	0	0	0	0	0	8
Cold storage cost	0	0	0	80	0	80
Jute bag cost	0	0	0	10	0	10
Potato wastage	0	8	13	16	8	20
Total cost	139	147	152	248	139	255
Net revenue (= profit)	27	36	79	12	40	145
Income[b]	64	73	116	49	84	189
Standard deviation of net revenue[c]	25.6	38.7	73.7	56.6		

Notes:
a: A4 involves sale in August. Farmers generally sold certificates for their stored potatoes to merchants in August.
b: Income includes profit plus remunerations for family labor and rent for owned farmland.
c: Standard deviation of net revenue was not estimated for Seed B2 because the price was the same for all seven sample households.
Source: Based on the survey in August and September 2000.

This was the oldest cold storage, built in 1982 and surveyed by Lewis (1991). It was completely filled with potatoes and achieved a capacity utilization rate of 100% in 2000/01. The cold storage provided loans to large customers for about 104,000 *maund* (87%) of the total 120,000 *maund* of potatoes. The loan amount usually ranged from Tk100–Tk150 per *maund* but it was Tk100 across the board in this case.

Let us calculate the effective interest rate on this loan. Those who received loans were supposed to pay an additional storage charge of Tk5 per *maund* when they took out their potatoes from storage. It means that they would pay an interest of Tk5 on a loan of Tk100, but the loan period was the key. If potatoes were stored from March to November, the loan period would be eight months

Table 6.7: Estimated profit for the cold storage for 2000/01

Quantity of stored potatoes (*maund*)		120,000	
With loans		103,968	(86.6%)
Without loans		16,032	(13.4%)
Gross revenue (*taka*)		10,119,840	
Costs (*taka*)			
Labor cost	1,700,000		
Electricity cost	2,000,000		
Depreciation cost	600,000		
Other input cost	755,000		
Bank interest paid	831,744		
Miscellaneous cost	550,000		
Total cost		6,436,744	
Net revenue (*taka*)		3,683,096	
Interest on own working capital (unpaid)		266,933	
Profit (*taka*)		3,416,163	

Notes:
a: The storage capacity was 120,000 *maund.*
b: Depreciation cost was estimated on a useful life of fifty years and a total construction cost of 30 million *taka* in 1982.
c: Other input cost includes the costs of diesel oil, gas and repairs.
d: Bank interest paid was estimated on an annual interest rate of 16% and a loan period of six months.
e: Interest on own working capital was estimated on an annual interest rate of 16% and a period of four months.

Source: Based on the survey in August and September 2000.

and the interest rate would be 7.5% per annum. Similarly, the interest rate would be 8.6% for a loan period of seven months, 10% for six months, 12% for five months, 15% for four months, and 20% for three months. On the other hand, this cold storage borrowed working capital from a commercial bank at an annual interest rate of 16%.[10] Therefore, if a customer with a loan used the cold storage for four months or longer, the cold storage had to carry the difference between the interest rates. The longer the storage period, the larger the interest burden it had to bear.

In Table 6.7, a cold storage charge of Tk85 per *maund* paid by customers with loans was recorded as revenue, while the interest payable on borrowings from a commercial bank (16% per annum) was calculated on the basis of an average borrowing period of six months (storage from March to September). The depreciation cost was estimated on the 1982 fixed capital investment amount of Tk30 million and the useful life of fifty years using the straight-line method.[11]

Based on the above assumption, the net revenue of this warehouse was Tk3.68 million. After subtracting the interest on the working capital, a profit of Tk3.42 million was derived. A simple calculation of the rate of profit is problematic, since the fixed capital investment was made way back in 1982 and hence omitted here. In any case, a profit of more than Tk3 million was an enormous amount in Bangladesh.

Now, is it reasonable to think that the cold storage owner did not bear any risk under the system of a flat storage charge (Tk80 per *maund*), regardless of the storage period? The answer is no. The profit was highly sensitive to the capacity utilization rate. In the case of the survey storage, a simple calculation shows that the profit would become zero (breakeven point) at a capacity utilization rate of 64%, and it would be unable to recover variable expenses (shutdown point) if the utilization rate went below 58%.

According to one report, the number of cold storages operating across Comilla district in 1998 was thirty-two, which was excessive for the volume of potato production in the area, and, in fact, there was a total unused capacity of 27% (Modern Industries Ltd and Agricultural Marketing Department 1998). Competition was intensifying as more cold storages were constructed, and their owners had to make every effort to maintain and increase the capacity utilization rate. As discussed in the next section, potato traders suffered large losses in 2000/01. In the following year, more cold storages raised the minimum amount of loans from Tk100 to Tk125 per *maund*. The increased loans for large customers can be interpreted as one of their marketing efforts.[12]

The Local Traders

Finally, the costs and returns of local traders are estimated (Table 6.8). A total of nine traders were surveyed, including traders residing in Ashora village and those who resided in neighboring villages and collected potatoes in Ashora village.

Let us examine the transaction without storage first. In such a transaction, the trader purchases potatoes from farmers and immediately transports them, without cold storage, to the city to sell. The purchase price was Tk190 per *maund* and the selling price was Tk215 per *maund*, generating a gross margin of Tk25. After deducting expenses such as freight cost, employed labor cost, agent commission, jute bag cost, and the trader's own labor cost, a net margin of Tk5 is left in hand. The net margin rate is 2% to 3%. The return on capital is derived by this net margin rate multiplied by the capital turnover rate.[13]

Table 6.8: Estimated profit for local potato traders for 2000/01

	STANDARD TRANSACTION	TRANSACTION INVOLVING COLD STORAGE		
	NON-SEED	NON-SEED		SEED
	MARCH SALE	JULY SALE	AUGUST SALE	B1
Sample number	1	4	8	1
Gross revenue (*taka/maund*)	215	325	292	400
Costs				
Purchase cost	190	197	197	197
Marketing cost	20	125	128	132
Freight cost	2	3	3	6
Labor cost	4	8	8	8
Cold storage cost	0	85	85	80
Commission agent cost	4	0	0	0
Self labor cost	1	11	11	13
Jute bag cost	8	10	10	10
Potato wastage	0	6	9	15
Other	1	2	2	0
Total cost	210	322	325	329
Net revenue (profit)	5	3	–33	71
Income	6	14	–22	84

Source: Based on the survey in August and September 2000.

One potato trader said in the interview that his turnover rate was forty times a year. The return on capital would be 80% to 120% per annum based on this figure. However, a turnover of forty times a year would mean that one transaction would be completed within just under ten days. This would be a rather exceptional case, considering that it was common for traders to wait fifteen to thirty days before receiving payment from urban *paikar* (wholesalers) in potato marketing. In this analysis, for the time being, I will adopt a return on capital of 40% to 60% per year (3% to 5% per month) based on a capital turnover rate of twenty times as a more reasonable estimate, although it is somewhat arbitrary and without solid data.

On the other hand, Table 6.8 shows that every local trader who cold-stored potatoes suffered a loss. In particular, when they withdrew potatoes from cold storage and sold in August, they suffered a large loss of Tk33 per *maund* of potatoes.[14] The size of their loss would increase if the opportunity cost of interest on their own working capital was taken into account.

Table 6.9: Working capital required by traders for potato storage

No.	Quantity of stored potato (*maund*)	Average purchase price (*taka/maund*)	Working capital required (*taka*)		
			Total (A)	Credit given by cold storage owner (B)	Shortfall (A–B)
1	210	220	46,200	20,000	26,200
2	600	184	110,400	90,000	20,400
3	846	184	155,664	120,000	35,664
4	1,200	195	234,000	126,000	108,000
5	1,350	175	236,250	138,000	98,250
6	2,095	184	385,480	300,000	85,480
7	2,260	200	452,000	360,000	92,000
8	2,822	210	592,620	281,000	311,620
9	3,240	220	712,800	480,000	232,800
Average	1,625	197	325,046 (100%)	212,778 (65%)	112,268 (35%)

Source: Based on the survey in August and September 2000.

Table 6.9 shows the purchase price and quantity of cold-stored potatoes for each of the nine traders surveyed. Each trader's working capital requirement can be estimated from this table. It ranged from Tk46,200–Tk712,800, with an average of Tk325,046. The average amount of loan from the cold storage was Tk212,778, which was only 65% of the average working capital. The remaining 35%, or about Tk128,000, had to be raised from somewhere else, including their own fund (to be analyzed later).

Margin Rate in Potato Cold Storage and Marketing and the Rural Financial Market

I have so far conducted an economic analysis of potato marketing for the year 2000/01 during which the potato price remained low from July and the economic entities who used cold storage suffered a loss. Let us attempt a more general analysis, assuming that 2000/01 was a special case.

Table 6.10 has been prepared for the purpose of estimating the margin rate of potato cold storage and marketing for ten years from 1991/92 to 2000/01. Two assumptions were used in calculating the cost borne by the economic entity investing in cold storage of potatoes. One was about the storage charge.

Table 6.10: Seasonal variations in the potato price and trader's remunerations

Year	Potato price (*taka/maund*)			Cost (*taka/maund*)			Net margin	Profit rate	Merchant's
	March (A)	November (B)	Price difference (C = B – A)	Cold storage cost	Other costs	Total cost (D)	E = C – D	(% /month) F = C/A/8	income (*taka*)
1991–92	116	284	168	59	30	89	79	8.5	128,375
1992–93	128	303	175	61	31	92	83	8.1	134,875
1993–94	141	419	278	64	32	96	182	16.1	295,750
1994–95	171	301	130	66	35	101	29	2.1	47,125
1995–96	132	333	201	68	38	106	95	9.0	154,375
1996–97	192	338	146	70	38	108	38	2.5	61,750
1997–98	175	233	58	73	41	114	–56	–4.0	–91,000
1998–99	159	331	172	75	45	120	52	4.1	84,500
1999–00	173	436	263	77	47	124	139	10.0	225,875
2000–01	202	348	146	80	47	127	19	1.2	30,875
Average	159	333	174	69	38	108	66	5.8	107,250
Average from 1996/97–2000/01	180	337	157	75	44	119	38	2.8	62,400
SD of average value	29	60	64	7	6	13	66	6	107,690

Note: Cost does not include interest on working capital. Cold storage cost was prorated based on Lewis (1991) and other costs were calculated in proportion to the CPI.

Sources: Potato prices from 1991/92 to 1994/95 are from Modern Industries (Bangladesh) Ltd and Agricultural Marketing Department, Crop Diversification Program (1998), and prices from 1995/96 to 2000/01 are from BBS, *Monthly Statistical Bulletin*. Consumer price indices are from BBS (at the website of Bangladesh Bank, www.bangladesh–bank.org).

Time-series data of the storage charge was not available, except for Tk55 per *maund* for 1986/98 (Lewis 1991). It was therefore calculated by interpolation on the assumption that it increased year after year at the same rate up to Tk80 per *maund* for 2000/01. The other assumption was about expenses other than the storage charge (current input expenses such as freight cost, employed labor cost, jute bag cost, and so on). Since there were no available data at all, they were estimated on the assumption that they increased every year at the same rate as the inflation rate to the actual values surveyed in 2000/01. The consumer price index (national) was used for adjustment for inflation.

The net margin was calculated by subtracting the thus estimated cost from the gross margin (a price difference between March and November[15]). The table shows the monthly margin rate, which has been converted from the net margin earned over eight months. According to the calculation, the monthly margin rate ranged from negative 4.0% in 1997/98 to 16.1% in 1993/94, with a ten-year average of 5.8%. It was 1.2% in 2000/01. The monthly net margin of 5.8% can be considered a fairly high rate. However, the average net margin[16] for the latter half of the period (1996/97–2000/01) was rather low at 2.8%, suggesting a slightly downward trend in the net margin rate.[17] Still, it would be reasonable to consider that the net margin rates of potato cold storage and marketing were at around 3% to 4% per month, even if this downward trend was taken into account.

The monthly net margin ratio of 3% to 4% would amount to 36% to 48% per annum, which could still be regarded as quite a high figure. However, traders were not always able to retain the whole margin for themselves. That depended largely on how they raised their working capital and how much interest they paid if they acquired their funds from external sources. This point is examined next.

As we have seen from Table 6.9, on average 65% of the working capital requirement was borrowed from cold storages. As estimated earlier, the interest rate was structured to rise by small increments, where it was 7.5% per annum or 0.63% per month for a storage period of eight months, 0.72% for seven months, 0.83% for six months, and so on. In any case, the interest rate of well below 1% per month was a very low rate. It must be said that the merit of being able to raise more than 60% of the fund at low interest rates would be enormous.

Suppose, rather conservatively, 65% of the fund was financed at a monthly interest rate of 1%. If a net margin of 3% per month was to be earned on the total fund, what would be the maximum permissible monthly interest rate on the remaining 35% of the fund? According to my estimation, it would be 6.7% per month.

The focal point here is the actual cost of funding the remainder of the working capital requirement. In order to find out, we need to look more closely at the transaction practice and interest levels in Ashora village's informal finance.

Informal finance in Ashora village could be broadly divided into long-term finance on farmland mortgage and all other types of finance (generally short-term up to one year). The former was called *bondak*, by which the lender advanced about Tk100,000 for one acre of farmland and acquired the usufructuary right to the farmland until the loan was repaid in full. The effective interest rate in this transaction would depend on the land rent of the farmland, but it was estimated to be 15.3% per annum.[18] In the census survey of all 106 households, the *bondak*-related credit balance was Tk1.11 million in total, 78% of which was borrowed by medium to large farmers. Yet, the funds were borrowed mainly to finance overseas work and land purchase, and none was borrowed for the purpose of potato storage and marketing.

On the other hand, the total loan balance of Tk1.21 million was observed in the form of short-term finance other than *bondak*.[19] In addition, there were short-term borrowings from commercial banks worth Tk1.5 million. (There were several members of the Grameen Bank and NGOs with microfinance, such as the PEACE Foundation, in the village, but these organizations had no base in the village and exerted very limited influence.) Table 6.11 shows the percentage shares of the purposes of these short-term borrowings.

It is clear from the table that, first, half of commercial bank borrowings were used to finance crop production, then house renovations and consumption, and hardly any borrowed funds were used for storage and marketing of potatoes. Second, only 5% of informal finance was used for storage and marketing of potatoes, but the ratio was as high as 43% among large farmers. Short-term informal finance did play a role in storage and marketing of potatoes.

What was the level of interest rates in short-term informal finance? According to Table 6.12, as many as 114 of 127 transactions involved *haulat* (interest-free loans). Of 114 transactions, twenty-nine were credit purchases from village general stores or agricultural input dealers, twenty-two were borrowings from the wife's father or relatives,[20] and the remaining sixty-three were borrowings from village relatives and acquaintances (including jute factory colleagues).

Only six transactions were borrowings for potato storage and marketing, and none was an interest-free loan; interest was payable in the form of a share of profits. The lender's share was 33% in two of the transactions and 50% in four transactions. For example, if the borrower made a profit worth 3% per month, he had to pay 1% to 1.5% per month to the lender. However, this interest rate was much lower than the maximum limit of 6.7% per month and risks were shared between the borrower and the lender, therefore it could be considered a very favorable condition for potato traders.

It should be noted, however, that not all traders were able to raise working capital in the informal financial market in this manner and that the average

Table 6.11: Short-term borrowings and their uses by the farmland holding class in Ashora village

Farmland holding class (acres)	No. of house-holds	Credit type	Loan outstanding (*taka*)	No. of trans-actions	Fund use (%) Con-sumption	House renovation	Land lease	Overseas work	Farming	Dairy cattle purchase	Potato business	Other business	Loan repayment	Total
0	27	Formal[a]	24,040	4	25	25	0	0	25	0	0	25	0	100
		Informal	319,085	38	47	8	5	21	3	5	0	8	3	100
0.01–0.49	40	Formal	26,300	3	0	33	0	0	33	34	0	0	0	100
		Informal	705,880	58	53	7	0	16	14	2	5	3	0	100
			(579,880)[b]	(56)	(56)	(7)	(0)	(16)	(14)	(2)	(2)	(3)	(0)	(100)
0.50–1.49	25	Formal	186,960	10	20	20	0	0	60	0	0	0	0	100
		Informal	798,685	32	41	12	0	0	19	3	25	0	0	100
			(160,685)	(26)	(50)	(15)	(0)	(0)	(23)	(4)	(8)	(0)	(0)	(100)
1.50–	14	Formal	1,258,000	7	0	0	0	14	58	0	14	14	0	100
		Informal	1,598,200	19	5	11	0	0	0	0	79	0	5	100
			(153,200)	(7)	(14)	(29)	(0)	(0)	(0)	(0)	(43)	(0)	(14)	(100)
Total	106	Formal	1,495,300	24	13	17	0	4	50	4	4	8	0	100
		Informal	3,421,850	147	43	9	1	12	10	3	18	3	1	100
			(1,212,850)	(127)	(50)	(10)	(1)	(13)	(12)	(3)	(5)	(4)	(2)	(100)

Notes:

a: Formal finance means borrowings from banks and NGOs.

b: Numbers excluding borrowings from cold storage are shown in brackets.

Source: Based on the survey in June and July 2000.

Table 6.12: Interest rates on short-term loans

PURPOSE	AVERAGE LOAN AMOUNT (*TAKA*)	NUMBER OF TRANSACTIONS	INTEREST RATE					
			INTEREST-FREE	> 5%/MTH	5%/MTH	10%/MTH	PROFIT SHARE (1/3)	PROFIT SHARE (1/2)
Consumption	2,940	63	59 (23)	1	0	3	0	0
House renovation	8,573	13	13 (1)	0	0	0	0	0
Farming	2,168	15	14 (2)	1	0	0	0	0
Dairy cattle purchase	4,025	4	4 (0)	0	0	0	0	0
Land lease	2,500	2	2 (0)	0	0	0	0	0
Overseas work	32,171	17	16 (0)	0	0	1	0	0
Potato business	36,667	6	0 (0)	0	0	0	2	4
Other business	17,497	5	5 (3)	0	0	0	0	0
Loan repayment	4,100	2	1 (0)	0	1	0	0	0
Total	12,128	127	114 (29)	2	1	4	2	4

Notes: Numbers in brackets are accounts payable to shops. Profit share of 1/3 or 1/2 is the partner's share. Credit provided by cold storage owners are not included in this table.

Source: Based on the survey in June and July 2000.

borrowing for these six cases was just over Tk36,000, which was far below the working capital shortfall indicated in Table 6.9 (Tk112,000 on average).

To summarize, potato traders were, on average, able to borrow 65% of their working capital requirement from cold storages at a monthly interest rate of less than 1%, which was a very favorable condition. If they managed to finance the remaining 35%, they could expect a return of 6.7% per month on that portion as a conservative estimate. The informal financial market was rather limited but it was far from a market of rampant profiteering. It would be reasonable to conclude that a net margin rate of 3% to 4% per month was not highly favorable but was not bad for potato traders, even if a fairly high risk was taken into account.

According to Table 6.9, potato traders in the survey traded an average of 1,625 *maund* of cold-stored potatoes. Based on this figure, the net margin on potato storage and marketing in monetary terms would be Tk107,250 as the average over the ten years and Tk62,400 as the average over the latter five years (shown in the rightmost column of Table 6.10). These amounts would convert to US$ 2,024 and US$1,177 respectively at the then exchange rate of US$1 to Tk53, which were considerably large amounts by rural Bangladeshi standards.

One question that remains is why cold storage owners would not invest in the potato storage and marketing business themselves if they could expect to earn such high margin rates? One reason would be the increased need for skills or social capital that was specific to the potato-marketing business as the urban potato market expanded and matured. Local traders would receive orders from wholesalers in the consumer city of Chittagong by telephone, secure exact lots according to their orders, charter trucks, and deliver the goods to Chittagong by the next morning. The only negotiation that would take place at that time was about the delivery price, and all other matters such as the quality of potatoes, arrival time, and time and method of payment were unspoken, pre-agreed terms. Local traders would have made enormous efforts to build up such relationships with wholesalers, since it would take a very long time to forge trusting relationships. It would be reasonable to expect that cold storage owners had failed in this process.

The second reason would be that cold storage owners were forced to concentrate their efforts on the maintenance and improvement of the storage capacity utilization rate due to intensifying competition from new cold storages, as mentioned earlier. To cite a piece of corroborative evidence, cold storage owners invited local potato traders to their parties in February shortly before the harvest time and offered storage charges and loan amounts for the new season to check their responses (while seeing their competitors' moves, of course).

Another important point would be that urban entrepreneurs could not be bothered with a relatively small profit opportunity such as the potato storage and marketing business, since their cold storage businesses would be very busy dealing with customer services and complaints and they also had other businesses to run.

There is also a question about why more farmers would not embark on the potato-marketing business. The answer is relatively self-evident. As the need for special skills and accumulated social capital in order to succeed as a potato trader increased, only a handful of farmers survived through the ages to be viable traders. It follows that those farmers who had dropped out were no longer in business. At the same time, however, farmers have moved on from the circumstances of the 1980s in which they were short of funds for potato marketing, and basically they no longer need to receive advances from traders.

Conclusion

In closing, here are the main findings of this chapter. First, investment in cold storages and jute factories by urban entrepreneurs greatly contributed to the economic development in rural areas. Its consequence was, however, not the deepening of 'dependency capitalism' as predicted by Lewis (1991), but was, ironically, a relative decline in the economic dominance of urban entrepreneurs due to trickle-down effects to rural residents.

Second, the potato storage and marketing system has undergone a major transformation from how it used to be when cold storages were first established during the 1980s. This transformation is a result of a relative decline in the economic power of urban entrepreneurs who own the cold storages and a relative rise in that of local potato traders and farmers. In other words, the trader grew to become the main player in potato storage and marketing investment and, at the same time, no longer provided advances to the farmer. The farmer, trader, and cold storage owner have come to perform their respective *primary* functions only (that is, potato production, storage and marketing, and cold storage service).

Third, the economic entity that conducted the potato storage and marketing business, and carried its risks, comprised upper-class farmers who acted as traders. They ran their businesses with a relatively small amount of their own capital by taking advantage of low-interest rate loan facilities provided by cold storages for their large clients and earned a net margin of 3% to 4% per month.

Fourth, farmers used cold storage for seed potatoes but they sold a majority of non-seed potatoes to traders immediately after harvesting. Although the number of farmers who stored non-seed potatoes was not small, the quantity of cold-stored, non-seed potatoes was limited. The main purpose of cold storage of non-seed potatoes was to save a crop that could be easily converted to cash when money was needed urgently, rather than to save a crop for speculation on a rise in the potato price.

Fifth, a continued strengthening of the economic power of farmers since the 1980s had almost extinguished the need for *dadan* (advances) from cold storage owners or potato traders among farmers, even in potato farming, which required intensive current input (seeds, chemical fertilizers, and so on). The landless and small farm households were, in fact, lending their surplus funds earned from off-farm employment through *bondak* and acquiring farmland from medium and large farmers in exchange. Overseas employment in the Middle East after the Gulf War was significant as one off-farm employment opportunity.

Part III
Infrastructure, Government, and Rural Society

7
Local Administration of Infrastructure Development, Village Society, and Rural Classes

In Bangladesh 'rural development' generally means two things: microcredit (or microfinance in a broad sense) and rural infrastructure[1] development. The Bangladesh Rural Development Board (BRDB) has been undertaking integrated development programs consisting of these two types of activity and has split the country into several divisions for this purpose. A program called RD7 was underway in the division that included Aira village, Bogra district, the study village for discussion in this chapter.

Public investment in the form of infrastructure development is generally considered to have a double effect in Keynesian economics. One is the creation of effective demand (that is, employment generation). The other is the productivity effect of investment, meaning that infrastructure development stimulates economic activity in the region. Needless to say, the former is a short-term effect and the latter is a medium to long-term effect. The main objective of rural development in Bangladesh is to increase employment and income of the rural landless and small farmers, and rural infrastructure development has traditionally been expected to bring employment opportunities to the poor (that is, a short-term employment generation effect). This is attributable to the historical background of the country's infrastructure development, which was launched as a Rural Works Program (which was one of four components of the Comilla Model of rural development during the 1960s) and implemented as an emergency employment measure to fight severe economic prostration and deepening poverty shortly after independence in 1971.

However, the medium to long-term productivity effect of infrastructure development is no less important than the short-term employment effect, or is even more critically important once an emergency situation is over. Increasing population pressure and a spreading market economy in the rural area of developing countries generally increase the demand for rural infrastructure such as roads, bridges, irrigation, drainage, and markets. As demonstrated by Ahmed and Hossain (1990), the productivity effect of investment in rural infrastructure is quite high. Conversely, a slow pace of infrastructure development acts as an impasse that greatly frustrates rural economic development.

By the way, rural infrastructure often constitutes the 'local public goods,' a type of public goods for identifiable beneficiaries, and it has a high risk of undersupply or inadequate maintenance as the result of a so-called 'free-rider' problem observed in such cases. The problem tends to become serious, especially in the case of a road or a bridge. In the case of irrigation, the optimum level of investment is relatively easy to achieve with tubewells, especially STWs, which are suitable for private-sector investment, but the problem often arises with canal irrigation, which is a more common form of irrigation. Even with STW irrigation by private investment, the problem of inadequate functioning of the market mechanism arose in Bangladesh because irrigation was an input with strong externality, and coordination among farmers was lacking, as discussed in Chapter 3.

The main question here is which economic entities should take charge of construction and maintenance in response to an increase in the demand for local public goods that have significant economic effects? Due to their public nature, it cannot be left to the market mechanism (*laissez-faire* policy). Governments or communities must assume a leading role. Unlike those areas that have been addressed in this book so far, free economic activity of private individual entities and its trickle-down effect to the lower class cannot be relied upon in the case of rural infrastructure development.

This chapter attempts to consider and elucidate the actual state of provision of local public goods in rural Bangladesh and related issues based on the case study of Aira village, Bogra district, and its local administration. Based on the field survey conducted from 1992 to 1994, it specifically looks at how small-scale infrastructure was provided (or not provided) at the village level, and what role the local administration played (or did not play) in it. Further, the ability and potential of Bangladesh's village community to provide and maintain local public goods will be examined in a more vivid form through the experience of a small-scale infrastructure construction experiment, which was conducted as part of the action research project[2] by the Japan International Cooperation Agency (JICA). The examination of these subjects should highlight various issues associated with local administration and village society in Bangladesh.

This chapter deals with the issue of interface between the lower tier of administration and the village surrounding the provision and maintenance of small-scale rural infrastructure, and one of its features is an attempt to approach the issue mainly from the village side, whereas past studies tended to approach from the administration side.[3]

The composition of Chapter 7 is as follows. In the first section, the system of planning and implementation of governmental rural infrastructure development projects and its actual state are analyzed based on the cases of Sherpur *thana* (*upazila*) in Bogra district and Mirzapur *union* in Sherpur *thana*. The second section shifts the focus to the village to examine the social organizations and related resource mobilization system of Aira village, and explains the details of the aforementioned experiment. The third section presents the conclusion of this chapter.

Governmental Rural Infrastructure Development Projects and the Village

Outline of Governmental Rural Infrastructure Development Projects

Bangladesh's governmental rural infrastructure development projects are undertaken through the subdistrict (*thana* or *upazila*) and the administrative village (*union*) at the bottom of the local administrative organization. The following section uses the case of Mirzapur *union* in Sherpur *thana*, Bogra district, which contains the study village of Aira, in order to examine the actual state of infrastructure planning, selection, and implementation, with a special emphasis on its relationship with the *gram* (natural village). Data was gathered through interview surveys at relevant organizations of the *thana* and the *union*.

Let us begin with the size and population of each administrative unit in the study area (see Table 5.4, Chapter 5). In Bangladesh the standard population size is 200,000 to 300,000 for a *thana* and 20,000 to 30,000 for a *union*. All surveyed units were of more or less average size. Sherpur *thana* contained nine *union*, including Mirzapur *union*, and Mirzapur *union* contained fifty-two *gram*.

The state of governmental rural infrastructure development projects has been strongly influenced by the ups and downs of local government reform at the subdistrict level over the past fifteen years or so. After seizing full power in the March 1982 *coup d'état*, H. M. Ershad renamed the subdistrict from *thana* to *upazila*. He attempted to reinforce and expand the political and administrative organization at the *upazila* level by setting up a new council called *upazila parishad* (headed by an *upazila* chairman chosen in a popular election) and by transferring the lower administrative functions (such as agriculture, livestock, fishery, healthcare, family planning, public health engineering, rural development, cooperative society, education, and relief assistance) from the *zila* (district) to the *upazila*, which was overseen by administrative officials assigned from the central government agencies. The *upazila parishad* was provided with an *upazila* development subsidy, which could be expended at its discretion and was mainly spent on infrastructure development.[4] However, the subsidy began to decrease after the mid-1980s. After Ershad stepped down in 1990, the subsidy was renamed as the Annual Development Program (ADP) and was further scaled back under the administration of Khaleda Zia. The *upazila* chairman and the *upazila parishad* were abolished and the subdistricts were renamed again from *upazila* to *thana*. However, they were allowed to keep the reinforced functions as the lowest administrative organization.[5]

Jurisdiction over infrastructure development at the *thana* level was shared by two agencies: the Local Government Engineering Department (LGED) (within the Ministry of Local Government, Rural Development, and Cooperatives) and the Ministry of Relief and Rehabilitation. The chief administrative officer at the *thana* level was the *thana* engineer for LGED and the project implementation officer for the Ministry of Relief and Rehabilitation.

Table 7.1 lists infrastructure development programs in Sherpur *thana*, showing the title, type of infrastructure, budget size, and number of projects per year for each program at the time of the survey (1993). The main infrastructure programs were for the development of roads, schools, and markets, but they also included construction of *thana* and *union* office buildings and staff housing, as well as religious facilities such as mosques and *madrasa*. As the list shows, there were variously named programs with various budget sizes for different infrastructure. The aforementioned ADP, which had succeeded the *upazila* development subsidy, was just one of them.

Two centrally controlled programs, the Growth Center Connecting Roads (GCCR) and Rural Development Program (RDP), had specific foreign aid and therefore the *thana* had almost no authority over their planning and implementation.[6] The General Education Project (GEP) and the Prime Minister's Education Project (PMEP) were the centerpieces of the primary education development policy of Khaleda Zia's government, and were somewhat special in that they served the political agenda of completing the reconstruction, repairs, and fitting out (desks and chairs) of all primary schools (GEP for public schools and PMEP for private schools) within several years.

Other than the above, the main *regular* infrastructure development programs included ADP, the Cooperatives for American Relief Everywhere (CARE), the Food for Works Program (FFW), Test Relief (TR), and the Rural Maintenance Program (RMP).

ADP was a subsidy distributed by the central government to *thana* in a lump sum, as mentioned earlier, and Sherpur *thana* mainly allocated it to the construction of culverts[7] along minor roads (mainly rural roads R2 and R3: see Table 7.2), to repairs to school buildings, and to the refitting/upgrading of schools. CARE is the name of a leading NGO but it also refers to a bridge and culvert development program, which was one of the infrastructure programs that CARE was carrying out on behalf of its donors.[8] FFW was a civil engineering program (labor-intensive soil works, mainly embankment construction) that paid its laborers in aid wheat, and its donors included the World Food Program and

Table 7.1: Infrastructure programs in Sherpur *Thana*

INFRASTRUCTURE	TYPE OF WORK	BUDGET PER PROJECT[a] (THOUSAND *TAKA*)	PROGRAM NAME[b]	NUMBER OF PROJECTS PER YEAR PER *THANA*	ALLOCATION PER *UNION*
Major road[c]	Bridge	200–500	CARE	3	
	Culvert	150–300	GCCR	5–6	
			RDP(RD7)	3–4	
	Embankment	200–500	GCCR	1	
			RMP*	1	
			FFW	8–10	1
Minor road[d]	Culvert (box)	About 100	ADP	6	0–1
	Culvert (pipe)	30–60	ADP	6	1
			CARE	4	
	Embankment	9,000–15,000	TR	30–70	3–8
		About 30	RMP		3 parts
Market	Improvement	700–800	RDP(RD7)	1	
School	Rebuilding	300–400	GEP	1 (From 1993, 4)	1–2
			PMEP	6 (1992), 12 (1993)	
	Equipment	60–80	GEP	7	1
			ADP		
	Repair (major)	30–40	GEP	1	
			ADP	3	
	Repair (minor)	9,000–15,000	TR	20–40	2–4

Notes:

a: Where project funds were allocated in wheat, they were converted using the market price of wheat at six *taka*/kg.

b: CARE: Cooperatives for American Relief Everywhere.
GCCR: Growth Centre Connecting Roads.
RDP: Rural Development Program.
RMP*: Rural Maintenance Project.
FFW: Food for Works Program.
TR: Test Relief.
RMP: Rural Maintenance Program.
GEP: General Education Project.
RMEP: Prime Minister's Education Project.
ADP: Annual Development Program.

c: Mainly feeder road B and rural road R1 (see Table 7.2).

d: Mainly rural roads R2 and R3 (see Table 7.2).

Source: Prepared by the author based on information gathered at Sherpur *Thana* office in 1993.

Table 7.2: The road system in Bangladesh

Classification	Jurisdiction[a]	Link	Standard width (m)	Total length[b] (km)	Paved road ratio[c] (%)
Arterial road					
National road	RHD	Capital & major regional cities	12.20	2,835	98
Regional road	RHD	Between former district capitals	10.90	1,382	98
Feeder road					
A	RHD	Between *thana* offices & arterial roads	7.32	8,743	64
B	LGED	Between major markets & arterial roads	7.32	22,185	26
Rural road					
R 1	LGED	Between *thana* and *union*	4.87	36,235	2
		Between markets			
R 2	LGED	Between *unions*	3.66	113,725	–
R 3	LGED	Between villages			
		Between farm and village	2.44		

Notes:
a: RHD: Road and Highways Development, LGED: Local Government Engineering Department.
b: As of 1989/90.
c: Including semi-paved and brick-paved roads.
Source: Local Government Engineering Bureau (1992: 4–5).

CARE. TR also involved labor-intensive soil works, mainly for embankment construction, and paid wages in wheat, but its size was only a fraction of FFW. Lastly, RMP was a year-round maintenance program for particular sections of particular roads. A group of five women was assigned to each *ward* of a *union* (three groups per *union*). This program usually covered the roads that were constructed or upgraded under the FFW program.

The official process from the planning to implementation of infrastructure development projects comprised the following steps. First, the chairman and members of the *union parishad* would try to identify needs for infrastructure development and put them together into specific proposals. The *union* chairman would take these proposals to the Project Selection Committee at the *thana* level, chaired by the *thana nirbahi* officer (the chief administrative officer of the *thana*). Upon deliberation, the committee would decide which proposals to adopt. The committee comprised the *thana nirbahi* officer, *union* chairmen, the *thana* engineer of LGED, the project implementation officer of the Ministry of Relief and Rehabilitation, and chief administrative officers from various other departments. The *upazila parishad* used to play the role of the selection committee but the above provisional body took over when the *upazila parishad* was abolished. *Union* chairmen would attend the committee to represent the local interests of their constituents and to compete with one another.

Even though they competed, however, it appears that the actual allocation to the *union* had to be based on an egalitarian principle. The average numbers of projects allocated to each *union* per year were as per Table 7.1: one project for embankment (FFW) of major roads (mainly feeder roads B and rural roads R1: Table 7.2), one to two projects for construction of culverts (ADP or CARE) for minor roads, three to eight projects for associated embankment (TR), one to two projects for school renovations, two to four projects for minor school repairs (TR), and one project for provision of equipment to schools.

Once the allocation was decided, implementation was the next stage and was carried out by one of two broad approaches. One approach involved a public tender under the supervision of the *thana* engineer and the execution of works by the successful bidder (ADP and CARE, including bridge and culvert construction). The other approach involved the Project Implementation Committee (PIC) organized for each project, which directly hired laborers and executed works under the supervision of the project implementation officer. Since FFW and TR mainly consisted of simple embankment construction works that did not require specialized civil engineering technology, they used the PIC method. PIC was a subcommittee with four or five members, who were appointed by the *union* before the proposal was submitted to the *thana* Project Selection Committee. Responsibilities were divided between LGED and the Ministry of Relief and Rehabilitation: the former was responsible for sophisticated projects that required civil engineering expertise, and the latter was responsible for simple manual construction works.

PIC and the Village

Unlike building contractors, PIC was a group of amateurs in civil engineering who were charged with the important responsibility to execute and supervise the project, hire the labor force, and pay wages. Since PIC played a pivotal role at the interface between the local government and residents in governmental rural infrastructure development projects, its actual workings are examined in detail.

Table 7.3 shows the actual FFW projects allocated to Mirzapur *union* from 1987 to 1992. One project was awarded every year and all were allocated to road improvement projects, except one pond re-excavation project in 1992. The amount of wheat budgeted for each project was forty to ninety tons (equivalent to Tk250,000–Tk550,000), which would have paid for 5,600 to 12,600 labor-days if all was used for wage payment.[9] PIC for a FFW project had the power to dispose of a large amount of funds and the 'rights and interests' it conferred were quite substantial. Perhaps for this reason, information about PIC members was unable to be obtained; many visits to the *thana* office of the Ministry of Relief and Rehabilitation in Sherpur *thana* were met each time with a refusal to cooperate with the survey.

On the other hand, many small-scale projects were implemented under the TR program. The number of projects allocated to Mirzapur *union* was fourteen in 1987 (total budget in wheat, 26.5 tons; per project, 1.9 tons), twelve in 1989 (8.1 tons; 0.7 tons), forty-six in 1990 (28.0 tons; 0.6 tons), seven in 1991 (unknown), and fourteen in 1993 (25.5 tons; 1.8 tons). (Information for 1992 was unavailable.)

Table 7.4 shows all TR projects, their budget size, and the number and composition of PIC members for 1993. Mirzapur *union* was cooperative in disclosing such information. The projects included seven road improvement projects, four school improvement projects (including *madrasa*), one pond bank repair project, one cemetery repair project, and one *union* office building improvement project. The budget per project was 1.5 to 2.5 tons of wheat (equivalent to Tk9,000–Tk15,000), which corresponded to an employable labor force of 210 to 360 labor-days. PICs for these projects included people such as members of the *union parishad*, *matabbor*[10] (village leaders), school principals and teachers, *samaj sebak*[11] (village youths), and imams (religious leaders).

The main features of infrastructure development projects undertaken by PICs can be summarized as follows. First, the inclusion of *union parishad* members in PICs (especially for road improvement projects) indicates clear influences of political interests of the *union parishad* chairman and members. The fact that no TR project had been undertaken for many years in Aira village, which had had no representative on the *union parishad* for many years, could only be understood in this context. The list of PIC members provided to me did contain one *matabbor* from Aira village, but it was found that his name was included in the list without his recognition. It was obvious that there was no proper mechanism to gather the needs for infrastructure development from the grassroots (village) level through the administrative channel. It was a matter of common knowledge that the organizational and functional weakness of the *union parishad* was causing this situation. For example, the *union parishad* of Mirzapur consisted of one chairman, nine members, and one secretary who were appointed at the district level, and the security officers, including only two *dafadar* and five *chowkidar* (village security officers).[12]

Table 7.3: FFW projects allocated to Mirzapur *Union*

YEAR	PROJECT	DONOR	BUDGET (IN WHEAT TONS)
1987	Road improvement	WFP	70.00
1988	Road improvement	WFP	84.50
1989	Road improvement	CARE	61.00
1990	Road improvement	WFP	60.44
1991	Road improvement	WFP	47.90
1992	Pond dredging	WFP	42.04

Notes:
WFP: World Food Program
CARE: Cooperatives for American Relief Everywhere.

Source: Prepared by the author based on information gathered at the Sherpur office of the Ministry of Disaster Management and Relief (1993).

Second, and inextricably linked with the first point, generally, misappropriation of wheat was rife. Although no specific instances were discovered in this survey, the following misappropriation rates have been reported by one case study in Faridpur district: 10% at the *thana nirbahi* officer level, 10% at the level of *thana* staff overseeing the infrastructure project, 5% at the food warehouse manager level (including wastage), 10% at the *union parishad* level, and 5% at the PIC level (Arn 1989: 26–9). In other words, only around 60% of the allocated wheat would be available to cover the actual project costs.

Third, a project was not necessarily born of consensus of the village, even when one of the village leaders was on the PIC for that project. Since the Bangladeshi village basically had no practice of meeting other than for a conflict resolution forum called *bichar*, as discussed below, there were no procedures for discussion and selection of desirable projects in the village or for submission of proposals to the *union parishad*. Accordingly, it was quite common that ordinary villagers did not know the mechanism of FFW or TR or had never heard of PIC.

Sources of Funds for Governmental Rural Infrastructure Development Projects

As easily imagined from the above, governmental rural infrastructure development programs were funded entirely by the government (or donors) and there was no concept of development being partially funded by beneficiary residents by way of, say, labor contribution. There was no people's participation approach, so to speak. This fact was perhaps intimately linked to the origin of programs

Table 7.4: TR projects allocated to Mirzapur *Union* in 1993

	Project	Wheat (tons)	Number of PIC members	Chairman	Secretary	Members		
1	Road improvement	2.5	5	*Union* member (1)	*Matabbor*	Primary school principal	*Matabbor*	*Matabbor*
2	Road improvement	2.5	5	*Union* member (6)	*Union* member (4)	Primary school principal	*Matabbor*	*Matabbor*
3	Road improvement	1.5	5	*Union* member (6)	SW	*Union* member (4)	*Matabbor*	Principal
4	Road improvement	1.5	4	*Union* member (5)	*Union* member (4)	SW	SW	
5	Road improvement	1.5	5	*Union* member (8)	Teacher	*Matabbor*	*Matabbor*	*Matabbor*
6	Road improvement	2.0	Unknown					
7	Road improvement	1.5	Unknown					
8	Pond bank improvement	2.5	5	*Union* member (9)	*Matabbor*	SW	SW	Imam
9	Junior high school improvement	1.5	5	Junior high school principal	Primary school principal	*Matabbor*	SW	VDP
10	Junior high school improvement	1.5	Unknown					
11	Primary school improvement	2.0	5	*Matabbor*	Teacher	*Matabbor*	*Matabbor*	
12	*Madrasa* improvement	1.5	5	*Matabbor*	*Matabbor*	*Matabbor*	*Matabbor*	*Matabbor*
13	Cemetery improvement	1.5	5	SW	SW	SW	SW	SW
14	*Union* office improvement	2.0	4	*Union* member (7)	SW	SW	SW	

Notes: *Union* member's electorate number in brackets. SW: *Samaj Sebak* (see text). VDP: Village security officer. *Matabbor*: Village leader (see text).

Source: Prepared by the author based on information gathered at Mirzapur *Union* in 1993.

such as FFW and TR as relief and rehabilitation programs mainly to reduce unemployment and underemployment among the rural poor in Banlgadesh.[13]

How about indirect contributions by rural residents through taxation? Let us look at the available fiscal revenue and expenditure data of Mirzapur *union* for 1992 (Table 7.5).

The first thing to notice is the actual fiscal scale, which was only Tk130,000–Tk150,000 as against the initial budget of over Tk310,000. The main reason for this was chronic delinquency in *union* tax payment among residents. The *union* tax was assessed for each household based on its farmland holding size, house valuation, and the household head's occupation.[14] Table 7.6 shows assessed amounts of *union* tax on Aira village residents by farmland holding classes for 1991. The average assessed amount per household was Tk8.8 per year, except for those households not recorded in the tax register. At under Tk10 the *union* tax was very low, considering that a rural day laborer's wage was about Tk40. Nevertheless, the delinquency rate for the whole *union* was as high as 61% (Table 7.5). Consequently, the fiscal base of the *union* was so weak and unstable that it barely managed to raise funds for its 10% share of RMP agreed with the donor.

Table 7.5: Fiscal balance of Mirzapur *Union* in 1992

REVENUE			EXPENDITURE		
ITEM	BUDGET	ACTUAL	ITEM	BUDGET	ACTUAL
Union tax	132,000	51,478	Staff salary	147,282	94,827
Licensing fees	14,200	4,470	Tax collector expenses	22,496	7,547
Other fees & charges	1,500	0	Current expenditure	39,865	9,578
Lease	65,500	18,120	Development expenditure	79,640	17,040
Miscellaneous	8,500	99	Plantation & aquaculture	5,000	3,900
Central government			Drinking water	3,000	0
subsidy	89,770	54,082	Family planning	2,000	0
			Education facilities	10,000	0
			Road improvement	18,000	0
			RMP	13,140	13,140
			Government buildings	28,500	0
			Social welfare	8,000	2,635
			Culture & sports	5,000	13,801
			Miscellaneous	2,500	1,657
Total	311,470	128,549		311,783	149,085

Note: RMP (Rural Maintenance Program): The portion paid by the *union* (10 %).

Source: Prepared by the author based on information gathered at Mirzapur *Union* in 1993.

Table 7.6: *Union* tax by farmland holding class in Aira village (1991)

FARMLAND HOLDING CLASS (ACRES)	NUMBER OF HOUSE-HOLDS	REGISTERED HOUSE-HOLDS	ASSESSMENT (*TAKA*)						TOTAL AMOUNT	AVERAGE PER HOUSE-HOLD
			0	1–5	6–10	11–30	31–50	50–		
0	102	98	8	86	4				373	3.8
0.01–0.49	34	31		29	2				153	4.9
0.50–0.99	14	13		10	3				67	5.2
1.00–2.49	25	23		7	11	5			225	9.8
2.50–4.99	17	16			3	12	1		338	21.1
5.00–	17	17			1	6	8	2	595	35.0
Total	209	198	8	132	24	232	9	2	1,751	8.8

Source: Prepared by the author based on information gathered at Mirzapur *Union* in 1993.

It was permanently behind in payments of salaries and allowances[15] and had very few funds to spend on infrastructure development.

The fiscal base was weak also at the *thana* level. The most important of its independent revenue sources was the tax on traders who gathered at markets. Sherpur *Thana* had nine large periodical markets that were taxable, and the tax collection agent for each market was selected by public tender each year. Any surplus collected over and above the tender price would be the agent's income. The total tender price for the nine periodical markets was Tk629,500 in 1992, Tk763,460 in 1993, and Tk865,980 in 1994,[16] 35% of which had to be delivered to the central government. The *thana* was able to spend the remaining 65% freely, but it was instructed to use 25% of it for maintenance and upgrading of periodical markets. Records for the past few years show that the balance of the fund was used to pay for the *thana*'s share of infrastructure programs such as GCCR, RDP, and CARE. This means that, in the end, the entire taxation revenue from periodical markets was injected into infrastructure development.

On the other hand, the total amount of infrastructure development funds allocated by the central government (or donors) to the *thana* was about Tk14 million, as shown in Table 7.1, which meant that only 3% to 4% of the *thana*'s infrastructure development budget was self-funded. The *thana*'s degree of financial independence was very low, since its other non-infrastructure project budgets and staff costs were also funded by the central government.

As above, there was hardly any direct or indirect mobilization of local community resources for infrastructure development at either the *union* or *thana* levels, and almost all costs were covered by the central government or donors. Further, the land tax is another direct (national) tax applicable to rural residents besides the *union* tax but it has also become a token tax after a series of deferment and exemption measures over many years.[17]

The Resource Mobilization System and Social Organizations of Aira Village

As we have seen so far, governmental rural infrastructure development projects have weak connections with village residents in all aspects, including planning, implementation, and funding. Furthermore, the progress of infrastructure development at the village level has been very slow due to tight financial restrictions. Even under such circumstances, however, voluntary construction and maintenance of public facilities (although mostly religious facilities) by mobilization of the village's own resources have been taking place in Aira village to a certain extent. This section sheds light on the village's resource mobilization system and the social organizations that underpin it.

An Outline of Aira Village

Aira village is situated 7.8 kilometers southwest of Sherpur city (with a population of 16,000 approximately) along an unpaved rural road (R1) off an arterial road that links the capital Dhaka with Rangpur. It is purely a farming village on the Barind Tract and has a land area of just under 500 acres, a population of 906 people (including forty permanent live-in laborers), and 209 households.

Figure 7.1 is a sketch map of Aira village. The residential zone is located in the northeastern quadrant of the village and includes seven large and small *para* (hamlets). Two are Hindu *para*, one of which (Shatain *para*) is located in the middle of paddy fields far from all other *para* and has extremely difficult access during the wet season. The other six *para*, including five Muslim *para*, are almost directly linked to the rural road (R1) to Sherpur city. The village's main produce is rice, which is transported by carts pulled by two buffalos along this road. However, it is a terrible road made of clay endemic to the Barind Tract, which makes it difficult for walkers, buffalo carts, and rickshaws to pass (not to mention four-wheel-drive vehicles) during the wet season. There is no primary school in the village, but one is located in another village two to three kilometers further up the road to Sherpur city. A junior high school is located next to the primary school in that village and its principal at the time of the survey was a *matabbor* from Aira village. Although the number of children going to primary school has increased in recent years, the literacy rate in the population aged fifteen and over in Aira village was still 25% (male 34%, female 16%).

Figure 7.1: Illustrated map of Aira village

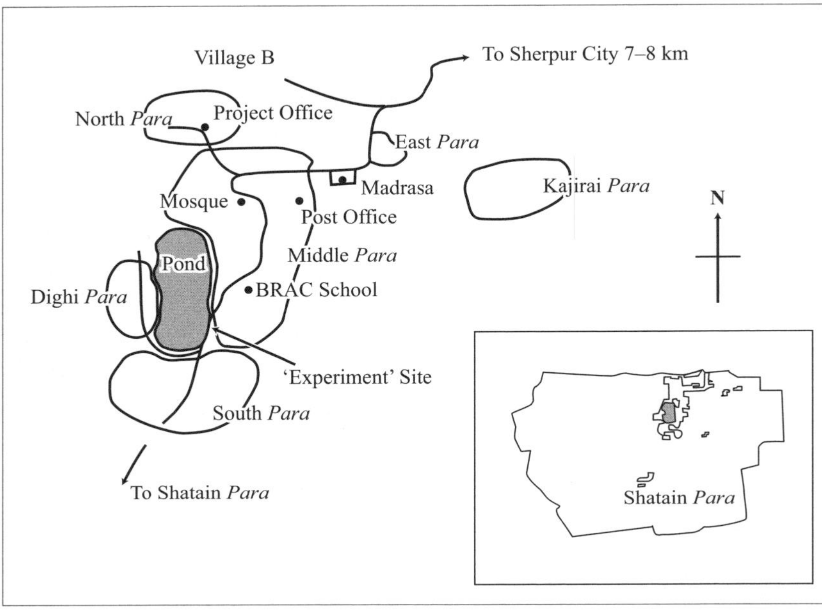

Source: Prepared by the author.

There was a newly established very small *hat* (periodical market) in the village but many villagers did their shopping at twice-weekly periodical markets in Sherpur city. There were many permanent shops, as well as public services such as hospitals and banks, in the city. Although there was a small town with the Mirzapur *union* office just south of the city along an arterial road, Aira villagers did not go there often, since it was less accessible from the village. Aira village had a post office, which was very unusual for a Bangladeshi village.[18]

The characteristics of each *para* are summarized in Table 7.7. The top five *para* are Muslim *para* and the other two are Hindu *para*. Figure 7.1 shows a large pond between Middle *para* and Dighi *para* (*dighi* means a pond). It is likely that the initial settlement took place around the pond (presumably at the end of the nineteenth century), since farmland holdings are concentrated among the residents of these two *para*.

In recent years, the village has experienced an influx of migrants from faraway villages in Shirajganj and Kurigram districts (due to river bank erosion there), and the influx was still continuing at the time of the survey. This is why almost half of the village's households did not belong to any *gusti* (patrilineal

Table 7.7: Hamlets (*para*) in Aira village and their basic data

HAMLET	NO. OF HOUSEHOLDS	POPULATION			HOUSEHOLD SIZE (PERSONS/ HOUSEHOLD)	OWNED FARM LAND (ACRES)	AVERAGE OWNED FARM LAND (ACRES)
		MALE	FEMALE	TOTAL			
North *para*	17	39	44	83	4.88	18.45	1.09
Middle *para*	86	202	169	371	4.31	126.56	1.47
Dighi *para*	15	31	25	56	3.73	34.21	2.28
South *para*	42	82	82	164	3.90	19.48	0.46
East *para*	8	18	12	30	3.75	2.02	0.25
Kajirai *para*	10	32	35	67	6.70	22.18	2.22
Shatain *para*	31	71	63	134	4.32	7.85	0.25
Total	209	475 (32)	430 (8)	906 (40)	4.33	230.75	1.10

Note: Figures in brackets are numbers of permanent attached laborers.

Source: Prepared by the author based on the 1992 field survey.

kinship group). Table 7.9 shows the time (generation) of settlement classified by the age of the household head. Of fifty non-*gusti* households who migrated to this village during the current generation, fifteen households settled in the 1970s, twenty-three households in the 1980s, and four households in the 1990s. It is likely that later settlers set up their homes on the fringes of the existing hamlets and gradually formed separate residential clusters, which came to be called South *para* and East *para* (see also Table 7.11). North *para* was one of the oldest *para* but many of the residents were migrants from a neighboring village to the north. Among Hindu *para*, Kajirai *para* had a small number of households but their land holdings were large, while Shatain *para* had many lower-caste residents who were landless and generally poor.

Agriculture was the predominant industry in the village. According to Table 2.3 in Chapter 2, which shows the main occupations of household heads for each farmland holding class, 80% of the household heads engaged in either farm operation or agricultural labor, and only small numbers were employed in service jobs (for example, as school teachers among the upper class) and in small business, handicraft, and begging (classified as 'other' in the table) among the lower class. Most of the sixteen households with no occupation were headed by women or elderly people.

The village's cultivated acreage was 436 acres, of which only 231 acres were owned by the villagers; the operated acreage, including tenanted (except seasonal tenancy) and mortgaged land, was still only 288 acres. The rest of the farmland was owned by residents of nearby villages who were basically small to medium-sized farmers who self-cultivated the land. It was not controlled by large absentee landlords who lived in the city or town. The degree of inequality in farmland distribution was high in Aira village, with 136 households with no land or with landholdings of less than half an acre representing 65% of the total number of households,[19] while thirty-four wealthy households with landholdings of two-and-a-half acres or more (16% of the total households) owned 78% of the farmland.

The traditional cropping pattern in the Barind Tract was single cropping of transplanted *aman* rice. When installation of STWs spread rapidly during the 1980s, the irrigation coverage jumped to more than 80% and the rice double-cropping system (with transplanted *aman* in the wet season (mostly rain-fed) and irrigated *boro* in the dry season) became predominant, except in some uplands and low wetlands. There were thirty STWs owned by villagers, twenty-two of which were owned by wealthy farmers with landholdings of two-and-a-half acres or more. The average command area per STW was about ten acres. Farmers without STWs either bought irrigation water from STW owners or leased their fields to STW owners during the dry season (for irrigated *boro* cultivation) (see Chapter 2). Irrigation channel excavation, repairs and maintenance, and water distribution were responsibilities of STW owners. Irrigation was principally carried out as a private economic activity and required little collaborative work.

Social Organizations and the Leaders

Consanguineous and Territorial Organizations

The most basic organizational unit in rural Bangladesh is the *khana* (household), which refers to the area in which a *chula* (cooking stove) and meals are shared. Aira village had 209 households (at the time of survey from June to August 1992). As shown in Table 7.7, the average household size was relatively small: 4.19 members for Muslims and 4.90 members for Hindus. They were basically nuclear families. There is another unit called the *bari*, which is usually a group of closely related households that sets up homes within grounds sharing a courtyard. In Aira village, 107 *bari* were observed: a majority comprised two or three households, and quite a few were single-household *bari*. No *bari* had more than ten households. The awareness of the existence and function of *bari* was not very high among the villagers.[20]

A more important consanguineous group in Aira village was the *gusti*, a patrilineal kinship group whose members shared the same paternal ancestors for several generations. However, almost half of the households did not belong to any *gusti* and the size of each *gusti* was relatively small. Table 7.8 is a list of Muslim *gusti*,[21] and shows that ninety-three households belonged to a total of fourteen *gusti*[22] and that the remaining seventy-five households did not belong to any *gusti*. The leading *gusti* in the village were N1, M1, M2, M3, and D1, and it is clear that they were superior in terms of farmland holding, education, and the number of member households. There were considerable disparities between households within each *gusti*, however, and not all households belonging to the same leading *gusti* were powerful. The *gusti* had a strong sense of ownership of the *gusti* farmland and tried to avoid loss of land through sale to outsiders.[23]

Table 7.9 shows the number of generations for which the household had lived in the village and the age group of the household head. As mentioned earlier, those households belonging to *gusti*, especially the leading *gusti*, settled in the village much earlier, while many non-*gusti* households migrated to the village during the current generation.[24]

Finally, Table 7.10 shows the relationship between the *gusti* and the *para*. It is clear that member households of a *gusti* were living in the same *para* in most cases and, except for Middle *para*, many of the *para* were formed with small numbers of *gusti* at the core and latecomer non-*gusti* households around them.

Social Organizations

A notable social organization in Aira village is the *sam*. I shall refer to it as *samaj* hereafter, since that is what it is generally called in Bangladesh.

The *samaj* is usually an organizational unit that conducts ceremonial events that are inextricably linked to religion, such as weddings, funerals, the Eid festival, and *musolmani* (the circumcision of boys). The *samaj*, for example, plays an important role in approving a matrimonial relationship or selecting guests for a wedding ceremony.[25] Its religious aspect is more notable with Muslims, as members of a *samaj* attend the same mosque and share the cost of maintaining and managing the mosque and paying the imam or *munshi* (religious leader). Yet, the *samaj* is not a religious congregation; it is primarily defined as a social organization that has authority to impose sanctions on deviations from social norms.[26] For example, disagreements between neighbors, disputes over land boundaries or ownership, and conflicts over crop damage by livestock, as well as violent incidents and violations of a moral code, such as extramarital sex, are mediated by the *matabbor*, the leader of a *samaj*, at a *bichar* or *salish*, which is a forum open to members.

In Aira village there was one Muslim *samaj*, and there was one Hindu *samaj* in each *para*. The survey found that they did perform the aforementioned functions

Table 7.8: *Gusti* of Muslim residents of Aira village and basic data

Gusti number[a]	No. of house-holds	Population	Owned farm land (acres)	Average owned farm land (acres)	Education: Primary school	Education: SSC or higher[b]	Education ratio[c] (%)
N1	3	23	12.3	4.11	5	8	100.0
N2	2	14	1.8	0.91	2	1	75.0
M1	13	74	44.5	3.42	10	2	28.6
M2	6	27	14.9	2.47	5	1	40.0
M3	9	44	15.2	1.69	4	4	29.6
M4	3	13	4.3	1.44	4	–	66.7
M5	8	31	8.5	1.03	4	–	21.1
M6	4	20	4.9	1.24	5	2	63.6
M7	10	37	8.8	0.88	4	1	20.8
M8	4	19	3.4	0.85	1	–	11.1
M9	5	16	3.2	0.63	2	–	20.0
M10	4	14	–	–	–	–	–
D1	17	68	45.2	2.66	12	1	39.4
S1	5	27	10.2	2.03	–	–	–
Gusti total	93	425	177.2	1.90	58	20	31.1
Non-*gusti*	75	280	23.6	0.31	13	2	9.0
Total	168	705	200.8	1.19	71	22	23.1

Notes:
a: N, M, D, and S were mainly residing in North *para*, Middle *para*, Dighi *para* and South *para*.
b: SSC (Secondary School Certificate) was a qualification given to those who passed the examination after completing primary school (five years) and junior high school (five years).
c: Education ratio = ratio of people with primary school or higher education in population aged fifteen and over.

Source: Prepared by the author based on the 1992 field survey.

such as mutual aid in ceremonial events, cooperation in religious activities, and the maintenance of social norms and order. However, the Hindu *samaj* in Shatain *para* was not functioning well and often relied on the Muslim *samaj* for dispute mediation. One example was a dispute over the right to fish in the pond. There was a medium-sized pond in Shatain *para* and the fishery right was shared by local residents. Members of one household, who had once migrated to India and come back to the *para* in mid-1993, claimed that they had registered the fishery right in their own name with the *union* before migrating to India. Residents of Shatain *para* were unable to resolve this issue among themselves and requested the Muslim *samaj* to make a ruling. Similarly, parties who were not satisfied with

Table 7.9: Length of residency in Aira village by household head's age group

	AGE OF THE HOUSEHOLD HEAD								
	10s	**20s**	**30s**	**40s**	**50s**	**60s**	**70s**	**80s**	**TOTAL**
Muslim									
Gusti									
Over 4 generations		1 (1)		2 (1)	3 (2)	1 (1)	1 (1)		8 (6)
3 generations		11 (4)	16 (8)	14 (11)	8 (4)	2 (1)			51 (28)
2 generations			8 (4)	4 (1)	2 (1)	2 (2)			23 (12)
Current generation		1 (1)	3	2	2				8 (1)
Unknown	1			1 (1)		1			3 (1)
Non-*gusti*									
3 generations		4	1						5
2 generations		7	5	4	3	1			20
Current generation		4	18	17	5	3	3		50
Hindu									
Over 4 generations				2	1	1			4
3 generations		4	4	2		1		1	12
2 generations		3	4	2		1			10
Current generation		1	5	2	2	3		1	14
Unknown			1						1
Total	1	43	65	50	26	17	5	2	209

Note: Figures in brackets are for leading *gusti* (N1, M1, M3, M4 and D1) only.

Source: Prepared by the author based on the 1993 field survey.

Table 7.10: Relationships between Muslim *gusti* and *para*

	N1	**N2**	**M1**	**M2**	**M3**	**M4**	**M5**	**M6**	**M7**	**M8**	**M9**	**M10**	**D1**	**S1**	**NON-*GUSTI***
North *para*	3	2	–	–	1	–	–	–	–	–	–	–	–	–	11
Middle *para*	–	–	13	6	8	3	4	2	7	4	5	4	5	–	25
Dighi *para*	–	–	–	–	–	–	1	–	–	–	–	–	11	–	3
South *para*	–	–	–	–	–	–	3	2	–	–	–	–	1	5	31
East *para*	–	–	–	–	–	–	–	–	–	–	–	–	–	–	5
Total	3	2	13	6	9	3	8	4	7	4	5	4	17	5	75

Source: Prepared by the author based on the 1992 field survey.

decisions of their own *samaj* would take their cases to the *union*, which was the lowest level organization of the official judicial system.[27] The number of such cases was increasing in Aira village.

However, the *samaj* in Aira village, especially the Muslim *samaj*, were powerful enough to play a certain role in the construction, maintenance, and management of local public goods. For instance, at the time of the survey the construction of a new *madrasa* was progressing; it had been initiated by the village's Muslim *samaj* after securing the cooperation of other Muslim *samaj* in neighboring villages. And a small *hat* was opened in Aira village in May 1993 as a result of the effort of the Muslim *samaj* to coordinate with the *samaj* and traders in neighboring villages.

Aira village also had some committees that were voluntarily operated without any involvement by the government, namely the mosque committee, the *madrasa* committee, and the *hat* committee. There was also the village development committee, members of which were selected by villagers under the guidance of the JICA project at the end of November 1992. The 'leaders' in Table 7.11 and Table 7.12 tentatively refer to the people who were members of three or more of these four committees. According to the tables, a majority of the leaders were from leading *gusti* such as N1, M1, M2, M3, and D1. It was found that the *samaj* leaders called *matabbor* who acted as dispute mediators and the leaders in this instance were mostly the same people. Table 7.13 shows personal attributes of these leaders and indicates that many of them were highly educated intellectuals from families with a long and distinguished history and financial wealth. The Muslim *samaj* and the committee structure founded on it can be characterized as coalitions of leading *gusti*. The committees were run by consultation among the *matabbor* or leaders. However, these committees did not hold any voluntary meetings for consultation, except for the village development committee, which was under the influence of the JICA project. This was a universal phenomenon observed in rural Bangladesh in general and not limited to the committees in Aira village.

Aira village's Muslim majority cooperated with one another in a single *samaj*, which appeared to be the main reason for the village's relatively high level of cohesion. Even in Aira village, however, *samaj* members were free to declare their withdrawal from the organization, and the *samaj* had no means to prevent former members from starting a new *samaj*. There was a constant risk for a *samaj* to split and become fractionalized. In the other *experimental village* of the JICA project (Daskin Chamuria village in Tangail district), for example, a *samaj* broke up as a direct result of problems such as a conflict over the distribution of ceremonial meat at the Eid festival, and ended up with more than twenty *samaj* in the village of 538 households (all of which were Muslim). When *samaj* fractionalize, disputes

Table 7.11: Composition of committee members by *para*

	No. of households	Mosque committee	*Madrasa* committee	Periodical market committee	Village development committee	Leaders
North *para*	17	2	5	5	3	3
Middle *para*	86	11	16	19	7	9
Dighi *para*	15	2	3	4	2	1
South *para*	42	1	2	4	1	1
East *para*	8	–	–	–	–	–
Kajirai *para*	10	–	–	2	1	1
Shatain *para*	31	–	–	2	1	1
Other villages	–	–	n.a.	18	–	–
Total	209	16	26	54	15	16

Note: Leaders mean those who were members of three or more committees; for Hindus, those who were members of the village development committee and the periodical market committee.
Source: Prepared by the author based on the 1993 field survey.

Table 7.12: Composition of committee members (Muslim only) by *gusti*

Gusti name	No. of households	Mosque committee	*Madrasa* committee	Periodical market committee	Village development committee	Leaders
N1	3	2	3	2	2	2
N2	2	–	1	1	1	1
M1	13	2	3	3	2	2
M2	6	2	3	4	2	2
M3	9	1	3	4	1	1
M4	3	1	1	1	1	1
M5	8	2	–	–	–	–
M6	4	–	1	1	–	–
M7	10	–	1	1	–	–
M8	4	–	–	1	–	–
M9	5	1	–	–	–	–
M10	4	–	–	–	–	–
D1	17	2	5	5	3	2
S1	5	1	1	2	1	1
Non-*gusti*	75	2	4	7	–	2
Total	168	16	26	32	13	14

Note: *Gusti* name is the same as Table 7.8.
Source: Prepared by the author based on the 1993 field survey.

Table 7.13: Profiles of 'leaders' in Aira village

	Para	*Gusti*	Education	Farmland holding (acres)	Age	Occupation	Length of residency	Remarks
4 committees								
1	North	N1	BA	3.00	55	Junior high school principal	3 generations	
2	North	N1	SSC	6.60	60	Not working	2 generations	
3	Middle	M1	SSC	8.66	45	Farmer	3 generations	
4	Middle	M1	class 10	8.00	35	Farmer	3 generations	
5	Middle	M2	SSC	4.00	43	Farmer	3 generations	
6	Middle	M2	class 3	–	36	Fisherman	3 generations	
7	Middle	M3	Title	6.00	38	*Imam*	3 generations	
8	Middle	M4	class 8	4.00	45	Farmer	2 generations	
9	Dighi	D1	class 8	12.00	50	Farmer	4 or more generations	
10	South	S1	–	6.35	65	Farmer	Current generation	
11	Kajirai	–	SSC	11.66	45	Farmer	2 generations	
12	Shatain	–	class 8	1.16	65	Farmer	3 generations	
3 committees								
13	North	N2	BA	1.00	35	Teacher	3 generations	not mosque committee member
14	Middle	D1	HSC	0.16	38	Farmer	3 generations	not mosque committee member
15	Middle	Non-*gusti*	SSC	3.33	40	Farmer	Current generation	not village development committee member
16	Middle	Non-*gusti*	SSC	2.66	35	Farmer	2 generations	not village development committee member

Note: SSC: Passed the certification examination after graduating from junior high school. HSC: Passed the certification examination after graduating from college (two years). BA: Graduated from university (four years) after graduating from college. Title: Islamic education equivalent of Masters Degree.

Source: Prepared by the author based on the 1992 field survey.

have to be mediated beyond the boundaries of individual *samaj* and are usually carried out by the *matabbor*, who has a larger sphere of influence.[28] Even in Aira village, the Muslim *samaj* broke up into three *samaj* in December 1993.[29]

The Resource Mobilization System

The committees in Aira village are notable in that they had a system for requisitioning and collecting their operating funds from villagers.

First, there were mosque-related finances.[30] The village had the most impressive mosque in the area. Two benefactors donated a quarter acre of land in the early 1970s and the building was completed on the site in September 1984. The enormous construction cost was mostly covered by a high official in Dhaka who was a former resident of the village, but individual villagers also contributed small amounts.

Following the completion, some farmland (which stood at 1.9 acres at the time of survey) was donated to the mosque (Table 7.14). These fields were being offered for share cropping or *khaikhalashi* and earned income for the mosque committee. Table 7.15 shows the revenue and expenditure of the mosque fund. Its revenue came from occasional donations from benefactors, donations at weddings, and proceeds from the sale of fruit growing on the mosque grounds, in addition to the aforementioned farmland income. Major expenditure items included religious meetings and maintenance and management of the mosque. The secretary of the mosque committee was responsible for the management of the fund.

Second, there were *madrasa*-related finances. Like the mosque, two benefactors donated 0.36 acres of land in March 1988 and the building was half-completed at the time of the survey (the work was suspended at the time due to a lack of funds). The *madrasa* also received a total of 1.17 acres of farmland in donations (Table 7.16), and tenancy rents from the farmland, together with donations from benefactors, formed the *madrasa* fund. The fund was managed by the secretary of the *madrasa* committee, who was also the secretary of the mosque committee. Table 7.17 shows the revenue and expenditure schedule of the fund. The main expenditure item to date was the cost of the land registration of the site.

As discussed later, there was a move to build a sports ground for the *madrasa* at the beginning of 1993 and contributions from villagers were called for. It is worthy of special mention that large donations totaling more than Tk30,000, as well as 0.52 acres of land, were promised.

Another notable resource mobilization method in relation to the mosque and the *madrasa* was contributions of *seccha sram* (gratuitous labor) from villagers. They were deployed in improvement works to the road adjoining the mosque and earth filling at the *madrasa* site, for example. However, the workload was not very heavy and a total of about seventy-five people were mobilized over two

Table 7.14: Land donations to the mosque

Year of donation	Land area (acres)	Attributes of donor household: Owned land (acres)	Attributes of donor household: *Gusti*	Remarks
About 20 years ago	0.125	4.00	M4	Construction site
About 20 years ago	0.125	3.33	Non-*gusti*	Construction site
1979	0.630	23.00	N1	Living outside of village
1982	0.340	8.25	D1	
1985	0.190	6.66	M1	
1986	0.080	6.04	M7	
1986	0.160	5.33	Non-*gusti*	
1988	0.330	23.00	N1	Living outside of village
1992	0.170	12.00	D1	

Source: Prepared by the author based on the 1993 field survey.

Table 7.15: Revenue and expenditure of the mosque fund (*taka*)

Year	Revenue: Tenancy rent	Revenue: Donation	Revenue: Wedding	Revenue: Fruit	Revenue: Other[a]	Revenue: Total	Expenditure	Term-end balance
until 1986								11,136
1987	1,131	1,714	384	931	12,000	16,340	20,329	7,147
1988	1,402		400	1,636		3,438	11,334	–759
1989	4,372	10	270	185		44,837	3,595	483
1990	8,112	1,485	360	3,115	4,000	17,072	4,921	12,634
1991	4,036	2,604	190	1,085		7,912	1,563	18,983
1992	3,916		860	997	2,000	7,773	4,626	22,130
1993[b]	1,575		200	153		1,928	246	23,812
Total	24,724	5,813	2,664	8,099	18,000	59,300	46,624	
Yearly average[c]	3,858	969	411	1,324	3,000	9,652	7,730	

Notes:

a: Donations from a high official who was a relative of a village *matabbor*.

b: Part year only.

c: Averages between 1987 and 1992.

Source: Prepared by the author based on the 1993 field survey.

Table 7.16: Land donations to the *madrasa*

YEAR OF DONATION	LAND AREA (ACRES)	ATTRIBUTES OF DONOR HOUSEHOLD		REMARKS
		OWNED LAND (ACRES)	*GUSTI*	
1986	0.250	–	–	Resident of another village
1987	0.180	4.00	M4	Construction site
1988	0.180	3.33	Non-*gusti*	Construction site
1989	0.160	6.35	S1	
1990	0.040	3.33	M3	
1991	0.180	12.00	D1	
1991	0.060	3.00	N1	
1992	0.120	4.00	M2	
1993	0.360	–	–	Resident of neighboring village

Source: Prepared by the author based on the 1993 field survey.

Table 7.17: Revenue and expenditure of the *madrasa* fund (*taka*)

YEAR	REVENUE			EXPENDITURE	TERM-END BALANCE
	TENANCY RENT	DONATION	TOTAL		
1991	371	2,885	3,256	1,410	1,846
1992	1,047		1,047	60	2,833
1993[a]	776		776	5,020	–1,411[b]

Notes:
a: Part year only.
b: Balanced by borrowing from the mosque fund.
Source: Prepared by the author based on the 1993 field survey.

days, each working half a day (four to five hours of actual work) in the case of mosque road improvement works.

Third, there was a fund in relation to dispute resolution by the *samaj*. While compensation was paid and received by only two parties involved in disputes such as crop damage by livestock, *jarimana* (penalties) imposed on violations of *samaj* precepts such as an act of violence were put into the *jarimana* fund. Although the amount was small,[31] the fund closely reflected the nature of the *samaj*.[32]

This *jarimana* fund was managed by the same person who managed the mosque and *madrasa* funds. Expenditures from the fund were considered by the *matabbor* first and decided by consent of members, when, for example, they gathered at the mosque for a service on Fridays.[33] Past expenditure items included the purchase of a large cooking pot for weddings, the purchase and repair of a tent for meetings and ceremonies, and the costs of law suits or certification at the *union* or *thana* level in relation to disputes over land. It should be noted that the fund was used to provide support for the informal education program of BRAC, a leading NGO, at the time of the survey. According to BRAC rules, the local community was responsible for the provision of land and the construction of school buildings, and BRAC would pay rents for these for the duration of its six-year program. The local community's share of costs was usually paid by individual benefactors but, in Aira village, it was decided that Tk2,500 should be expended from the *jarimana* fund as part of the school construction fund, and that the rents paid by BRAC in the latter half of the period (a total of Tk8,400 over forty-two months) would be put into the fund in return. Further, the landowner who offered to contribute his land for the school site also promised to continue to offer the school for public use after the completion of the program.

How were responsibilities for these various types of resource mobilization shared among villagers? Let us examine specifically the purchase of the *madrasa* sports ground site and the improvement of the mosque road for which data were available.

Table 7.18 shows the mobilization rates by religions and *gusti*. The first thing to notice is that the mobilization rate was only around 50%, with donations for the sports ground and contributions of labor for road improvement. It suggests that the social coercion power of the *samaj* for resource mobilization was not sufficiently strong. (However, both the mobilization rate and the amount of donations were highest for the leading *gusti*, followed by the non-leading *gusti*, and they were lowest for non-*gusti*; this indicates that some degree of social coercion did exist.) It is also notable that the Hindu residents also promised to make donations for the *madrasa* sports ground. It was perhaps because, although the *madrasa* was a Muslim educational facility, it was often converted into a general primary school and the sports ground would be used as a playground by Hindu children, as well.

Table 7.19 shows the mobilization rates by farmland holding classes. It is clear that the wealthier classes made greater contributions and that all donations of farmland were made by wealthy farmers.

The committee system and the resource mobilization system operating in Aira village based on its social organizations draw our attention as the case in which Muslim residents played a leading role in maintaining social order, providing mutual aid for ceremonial occasions, and collaborating in religious activity; they were also involved in the provision, maintenance, and management of associated local public goods to a certain extent. It is also noteworthy that the scale of resource mobilization required for the provision, maintenance, and management

Table 7.18: Resource mobilization for the provision of local public goods in Aira village I

		Contributions for the *madrasa* sports ground						Mosque road improvement		
	Number of households[a]	Cash (households)	Amount (*taka*)	Land (households)	Size (acres)	Participation rate (%)	Average amount[b] (*taka*/household)	Potential turnout[c] (households)	Actual turnout (households)	Turnout rate (%)
Muslim										
Leading *gusti*[d]	48	15	9,550	13	0.42	58.3	1,799	42	25	59.5
Non-leading *gusti*	45	19	5,800	4	0.10	48.9	705	43	23	53.5
Non-*gusti*	71	37	5,360	–	–	52.1	145	62	26	41.9
Hindu										
Kajirai *para*	10	–	–	–	–	–	–	–	–	–
Shatain *para*	29	13	796	–	–	41.4	66	–	–	–
Aira village subtotal	203	–	–	17	0.52	48.8	727	147	74	50.3
Nearby villages	5 villages		9,640							
Member of Parliament		1	2,000							
Total			33,146							

Notes:
a: The total number of households is different from Table 7.7 as five households moved out of the village after the 1992 field survey.
b: The land value was calculated on the basis of 97,200 *taka* per acre.
c: Households with at least one adult male.
d: N1, M1, M2, M3, D1.

Source: Prepared by the author based on the 1993 field survey.

of these local public goods was incomparably greater than the aforementioned *union* tax (only Tk1,751 per year for the whole village).

However, the above systems had limitations. First, resource mobilization was mostly limited to religion-related projects. In the establishment of a *hat*, which had nothing to do with religion, for example, the village's involvement was limited to site procurement and coordination with neighboring villages and traders, and did not extend to actual development works such as the construction of a roof, a drainage facility, or a hand-tubewell. Second, the resource mobilization rate only reached 50% or so, and it was not an organized enterprise based on the consensus of all villagers. Third, there was no community property in the village other than the farmland donated to the mosque and the *madrasa*. In fact, ponds, which the local *Zamindar* had dug in order to attract settlers (or that farmers dug jointly for themselves), used to be common properties of the village but their ownership was later divided and held by individuals or groups.[34]

In order to examine whether Aira village's resource mobilization system would be able to overcome the above limitations (especially the first limitation) and work effectively in nonreligious development projects, an experiment was undertaken through the JICA project.

A Small-scale Infrastructure Development Experiment

Outline of the Experiment

There was a large pond in the middle of the village's residential zone and an arterial road ran along it (see Figure 7.1). This road was an extension of the rural road (R1) connecting the village with Sherpur city and served as the main route for transporting rice and other farm products by rickshaw or buffalo carts. In recent years, the underground culvert laid at the entrance of a water channel that flowed into the pond on the eastern side was swept away due to sedimentation in the channel, and the road was completely severed by the end of the 1993 wet season. At the same time, severe erosion around the edge of the pond made the adjoining road so narrow that it was only passable on foot. While the water level subsided enough for buffalo carts to drive inside the pond during the dry season, it was obvious that transportation of farm produce would be severely impeded if the road was not repaired by the 1994 wet season. The *matabbor* of the village lodged an application for the proposed repair work (a total cost of about Tk20,000) with the *union* in October 1993. The size of the project would be just right for the TR program but it was not supported by the *union*.

Even when it became clear that the *union* would not grant funds for the project, villagers still believed that public works such as road repairs should be completely financed by the government and never had an inclination to solve the problem by themselves. Under these circumstances, the JICA project made

Table 7.19: Resource mobilization for the provision of local public goods in Aira village II

FARMLAND HOLDING SIZE (ACRES)	NUMBER OF HOUSEHOLDS	CONTRIBUTIONS FOR THE *MADRASA* SPORTS GROUND						MOSQUE ROAD IMPROVEMENT		
		CASH (HOUSEHOLDS)	AMOUNT (*TAKA*)	LAND (HOUSEHOLDS)	SIZE (ACRES)	PARTICIPATION RATE (%)	AVERAGE AMOUNT (*TAKA*/HOUSEHOLD)	POTENTIAL TURNOUT (HOUSEHOLDS)	ACTUAL TURNOUT (HOUSEHOLDS)	TURNOUT RATE (%)
0	96	42	3,675	–	–	43.7	88	65	25	38.5
0.01–0.49	34	12	1,192	–	–	35.3	99	25	11	44.0
0.50–0.99	14	8	2,975	1	0.02	57.1	615	10	1	10.0
1.00–2.49	25	13	4,148	4	0.096	68	793	15	12	80.0
2.50–4.99	17	3	2,167	6	0.20	52.9	2,401	17	11	64.7
5.00–	17	5	7,300	6	0.204	64.7	2,466	15	14	93.3
Total	203	83	33,146	17	0.52	48.8	727	147	74	50.3

Note: Figures for Muslims only.

Source: Prepared by the author based on the 1993 field survey.

a proposal to the village development committee that it would fund part of the project cost under certain conditions. The JICA project would provide a new culvert (approximately one meter in diameter and six meters in length) as long as the village would carry out embankment works. In the end, the JICA project paid Tk8,600 for the purchase and installation of the new culvert, while the village incurred about Tk6,260 (wage equivalent). The village's share of the total project cost was 42%.

Issues Surrounding the Project

The first issue encountered was the procurement of soil for embankment works.[35] Initially, one villager who was planning to convert his field into a fish culture pond agreed to provide the soil but he quit his plan and withdrew his offer when removal of the soil was delayed. The next best plan was considered at the end of January 1994 and involved draining the pond to lower the water level and dig out the soil from the bottom of the pond. However, this plan had to be abandoned because it could not accommodate the need for irrigation water for dry-season *boro* rice production starting in February and the timing of harvesting for the cultured fish in the pond. It was finally decided that the inflow channel (on the government-owned *khas* land) to the pond should be widened and dug down to provide the soil for embankment works.

The village development committee had already decided to carry out embankment works using contributions of gratuitous labor from villagers, but the actual mobilization was extremely difficult. This situation was expected, since the amount of work for this project was far greater than the workload experienced in the past for voluntary projects such as the repair of the mosque road (half a day's work each for a total of seventy-five people). The JICA project had planned to wait until the work had progressed well past the halfway mark before supplying the culvert. The village development committee initially appointed several leaders, each of whom would try to organize a team of ten villagers under his own responsibility and mobilize them to work on set dates, but this arrangement did not work at all. The question of who worked and who didn't work triggered problems such as friction between villagers and discord among the *gusti* so much so that the work was interrupted frequently. In the end, the *matabbor* had to call on villagers individually time and again to work on certain dates in order to advance the project little by little.

An Outcome of the Experiment and Assessment

The work was carried out intermittently for about four months and completed at the end of April 1994. The village development committee decided to plant banana seedlings and deep-rooted vegetation on the road bank beside the pond to stop landslides, and it delegated the responsibility to manage them to a nearby villager in exchange for the right to harvest the bananas. It also put a ban on bathing livestock in the pond in order to prevent landslides.

During the four-month period, the actual number of days worked was eighteen days and the total number of hours of mobilized labor, including some residents from neighboring villages, was 1,250 hours (1,164 hours from Aira residents) or 156 labor-days, which was equivalent to about Tk6,250 in wages.

The work was fraught with difficulties (Table 7.20). On 18 February the work almost reached the halfway point and the culvert was installed, but no further progress was made for more than one month after that day. The work resumed in April, shortly before the arrival of the wet season, and was finished in a short period of time. The number of participants was 121 households, which was 67% of the village's potential participants (households with at least one healthy adult male who could participate in embankment works). The average days worked per participating household was 2.62 days, which amounted to a total of 9.62 hours of work.

Table 7.21 shows turnout rates by religion and *gusti*. It is clear that the participation rate from Kajirai *para* was markedly low among Hindu residents and that the participation rate among Muslims was highest from leading *gusti*, followed by non-leading *gusti*, and lowest from non-*gusti*. The same tendency was observed in the cases of contributions for mosque road improvement and the *madrasa* sports ground in the past.

Table 7.22 shows turnout rates by farmland holding classes. Wealthier classes made greater contributions. This may be a natural result, considering that the project was most beneficial for transportation of farm produce and that the idea of gratuitous labor contribution met some resistance from the poor who earned a living by selling their labor.[36] However, the road improvement work was of great benefit to the poor, as well, since it would enhance the convenience for their daily activities, small businesses, and rickshaw drivers.[37] It might have been out of regard for the JICA project to some extent, but the village leadership worked hard for the benefit of the whole village rather than out of self-interest and took the initiative in contributing a lot of resources (labor, including hired labor).

The experiment achieved a certain measure of success. While both the government and villagers were fixated on the idea that public works should be the sole responsibility of the government, and there was a growing tendency not to make financial contributions even to religious activities as the TR program was expanded to include improvements to religious facilities,[38] this project was able to see the light of day by somehow extracting gratuitous labor from the village. The fact that contribution levels were mostly proportional to the village's income classes indicated the fairness of the village's resource mobilization

Table 7.20: Progression of works in the 'experiment' in Aira village

	MONTH/DAY	NUMBER OF PARTICIPATING HOUSEHOLDS	TOTAL LABOR HOURS	LABOR HOURS PER HOUSEHOLD	% OF COMPLETION
1	12/22	16	16	1.0	1.4
2	1/9	4	4	1.0	1.7
3	1/14	7	31.5	4.5	4.1
4	1/21	22	88	4.0	11.9
5	1/22	5	22.5	4.5	13.8
6	1/25	19	89.5	4.7	21.4
7	1/26	7	31	4.4	24.1
8	1/29	11	39.5	3.6	27.4
9	1/30	8	34	4.3	30.3
10	2/1	5	25	5.0	32.4
11	2/2	4	14.25	3.6	33.7
12	2/16	9	36	4.0	36.7
13	2/18	29	24	4.3	47.3
14	4/3	44	66	3.8	61.4
15	4/8	18	34.5	1.9	64.4
16	4/9	42	88	4.5	80.4
17	4/10	46	72.5	3.8	95.1
18	4/22	18	58	3.2	100.0

Source: Prepared by the author based on field monitoring.

system. The villagers deserve credit for making their own arrangements for the maintenance and management of the repaired road. Yet, a dispassionate analysis of the difficulties encountered by the project inevitably leads to the conclusion that Aira village's resource mobilization system—and the formulation of the structure for provision, maintenance, and management of local public goods based on it—has serious limitations.

Summary

This chapter has addressed the issue of interface between the local administration and the village in relation to small-scale rural infrastructure development in Bangladesh based on the case of Aira village in Bogra district, with the main focus on the examination of a certain aspect of the nature of rural social structure. In the first section, the actual state of infrastructure development projects being implemented through the local administrative structure was considered. It was found that, although the *union parishad* played the central

Table 7.21: Labor input to the 'experiment' in Aira village I

	POTENTIAL PARTICIPANTS (HOUSEHOLDS)	ACTUAL PARTICIPANTS (HOUSEHOLDS)	PARTICIPATION RATE (%)	PER HOUSEHOLD	
				DAYS WORKED	HOURS WORKED
Muslim					
Leading *gusti*	43	36	83.7	4.08	14.93
Non-leading *gusti*	44	33	75.0	2.61	8.86
Non-*gusti*	64	37	57.8	1.73	6.63
Hindu					
Kajirai *para*	8	1	12.5	2.00	9.00
Shatain *para*	23	14	60.1	1.29	5.68
Total	182	121	66.5	2.62	9.62

Source: Prepared by the author based on field monitoring.

Table 7.22: Labor input to the 'experiment' in Aira village II

FARMLAND HOLDING SIZE (ACRES)	POTENTIAL PARTICIPANTS (HOUSEHOLDS)	ACTUAL PARTICIPANTS (HOUSEHOLDS)	PARTICIPATION RATE (%)	PER HOUSEHOLD	
				DAYS WORKED	HOURS WORKED
0	86	49	56.9	1.76	6.89
0.01–0.49	29	18	62.1	2.67	9.72
0.50–0.99	12	7	58.3	1.71	6.96
1.00–2.49	21	16	76.2	2.50	8.20
2.50–4.99	17	15	88.2	4.40	16.42
5.00–	17	16	94.1	4.06	14.05
Total	182	121	66.5	2.62	9.62

Source: Prepared by the author based on field monitoring.

role in the planning of development projects, there was no adequate system for the identification of residents' needs, and that the village depended on the central government (donors, to be more accurate, as a majority of development expenditures were covered by aid money) to provide most project funding, and mobilization of resources such as villagers' gratuitous labor or local taxes was minimal and unreliable.

On the other hand, Aira village carried out a certain level of community activity based on the *samaj* (which primarily operated to maintain social norms and order), had an associated financial (resource mobilization) system, and undertook construction, maintenance, and management of public facilities, mainly religious facilities. Resource mobilization took place in various forms: provision of development sites for the mosque and the *madrasa*, donations of farmland, sharing of building costs, and contributions of gratuitous labor. Separate funds were set up for the mosque and the *madrasa*. The *samaj* had their own funds, which were mainly operated for the purpose of mutual aid for ceremonial events. The following points were worthy of attention: the system centering on the Muslim *samaj* and occasional involvement of the Hindus performed a certain level of public functions through resource mobilization and the scale of such resource mobilization was far greater than that of the *union* tax.

It was also found that these organizational and cooperative relationships had serious limitations. First, resource mobilization was mostly limited to religion-related activities. Even though the experiment to test its applicability to general road improvements achieved a measure of success, there were major limitations.

Second, it was impossible to conduct complex and sophisticated communication or adjustment of various interests among villagers because, except for *bichar* (a forum for conflict resolution), there was no traditional forum (or meeting) where the *executives*, led by the *matabbor*, could gather to discuss important matters for the whole village. Similarly, the leadership, consisting of several *matabbor*, was not supported by an orderly understructure. It was clearly demonstrated by the fact that the ten-member groups that the *matabbor* tried to organize in order to facilitate labor contributions from villagers in the experiment did not work at all.

In the end, it is inevitably concluded that weakness in the functioning of the village as a community was the fundamental reason for the demise of the Village Agricultural and Industrial Development (V-AID)[39] within several years of its inception when it was based on the same concept as this action research and trialed during the 1950s.

Bertocci (1970) once defined Bangladeshi villages as 'elusive villages,' based on his survey in Comilla area. They were elusive because social and political powers were not concentrated at the *gram* (natural village) level but were generally localized in the *reyai*, a smaller unit mainly for ceremonial and dispute mediation purposes, and in powerful kinship groups in the leadership position of the *reyai* (Bertocci 1969: 111). He also found that the *sardar* was officially recognized by constituent members but the status did not always entail coercive power over members (Bertocci 1969: 109). When we substitute the *reyai* with the *samaj* and the *sardar* with the *matabbor*, it becomes obvious that the discussion in this chapter has arrived at almost the same conclusion as Bertocci's.

Bertocci offers the following hypothesis about the historical origin of this village social structure.

> There appears to have been very little interference in local affairs by the *Raja* landlords once rents were paid, nor, until the 1870s, when the British began to intervene more directly in the policing of the rural areas, was there a great deal of direct contact between the inhabitants of the countryside and the ruling colonial power. In this situation, then, it seems likely that the organization of the rural areas evolved in a manner relatively uninfluenced by external, more powerful, authority, and the localization of power seems naturally to have centered around those lineages to which others would concede leadership...The long-term result of such intensive localization of social and political cohesion in initially small scale units seems to have mitigated any process which would have led to the formation of larger, solidary village units with formally centralized authority vested in such a personage as a 'village headman,' as found elsewhere in Bengal and other parts of the Sub-continent. (1969: 111)

I currently do not have the capacity nor latitude to examine and evaluate this hypothesis. However, I would like to offer another hypothesis in the meantime—that the village structure with 'localized powers,' which was not *robust*, was one of the factors that prevented the more powerful and efficient administrative village (*union*) from establishing itself, and this difficulty with the establishment of the *union* reproduced the 'elusive' village structure—and perhaps this vicious cycle has been continuing to date.

According to the Government of Bengal (1915: 92), the *chowkidari panchayat* (the predecessor of the *union*) set up under an act of 1870 during the British colonial period was pressed by serious fiscal problems such as the unpopularity of taxation and mounting debts to finance salaries for the *chowkidar*. Surprisingly, it has been revealed in this chapter that the problem surrounding the *union* taxation from more than a century ago has persisted to this day. Today's *union* has a population of 20,000 to 30,000, which is not so small for an administrative unit. It would be reasonable to think that the fact that an organization of this size has no substance and its administration is being attended by only one secretary stems from an extremely deep-rooted historical factor and that this problem is inextricably linked to the issue of 'elusive villages.'

According to Professor Yūjirō Hayami, 'local public goods can be supplied under the direction of the state' but 'a lot of waste is incurred in the process of collection of required funds through taxation and redistribution to local communities through the political and bureaucratic apparatus by the government' and, further, 'the government generally lacks an ability to identify the need for local public goods at the village level accurately,' hence 'supply of local public goods should be left to local communities' (Hayami 1995: 260).

He also states that 'whether or not it is possible to enhance the provision of local public goods to an optimum level' depends on 'the strength of mutual trust built up within the village and, on [the] reverse side of it, the severity of social sanctions against those who break village rules'; 'a community with inadequate stock of social capital in trust cannot have comparative advantage in provision of local public goods and therefore must rely on the government for supply even if its absolute cost is higher,' and 'it is inevitable that local public goods are undersupplied in such a community.'

Unfortunately, Bangladeshi society appears to be a typical example showing historical evolution where accumulation of such social capital has been stymied. And, where there is a large influx of population from faraway villages in response to growing demands for labor created by the Green Revolution (as we have observed in Aira village), accumulation of social capital becomes increasingly more difficult.

Conclusion

Under the title *Re-thinking Economic Development: The Green Revolution, Agrarian Structure and Transformation in Bangladesh* this book has analyzed and discussed the diffusion of tubewell irrigation, and the structure and transformation of the groundwater market created by it, in Bangladesh and India's West Bengal from the 1980s. Part I had a special focus on income distribution between the wealthy farmer class, which invested in tubewells, and other farmers and agricultural laborers. Next, Part II analyzed Bangladesh's changing agrarian structure, especially from the viewpoint of the *reversing* of interclass flows of rural informal finance, and shed light on how the trickle-down effects of economic progress manifested in changes in finance or economic relations between different rural classes. Part III analyzed the issues of local administration in relation to small-scale rural infrastructure development and village society.

In this final chapter I would like to recapitulate and conclude the entire discussion in connection with Bangladesh's changing agrarian structure and a higher-order organization of rural society. This represents the end point, for the moment, of the body of research on economic development in rural Bengal, especially rural Bangladesh, which I accumulated over the past decade or so using a fieldwork approach.

The Role of Agriculture and Market Mechanism in Economic Development

Both Bangladesh and the Indian state of West Bengal experienced marked acceleration of economic development from the 1980s. To borrow Boyce's (1987) phrase, the region had been in a state of 'agrarian impasse' until the end of the 1970s but its agricultural sector began to record sustained and rapid growth in the 1980s; in particular, substantial increases in the production of the staple crop of rice played a major part.

I have expressed my view in the Introduction that the agricultural sector plays a major role in economic development, especially in its early stages, and that the final demand effect is especially considered very important as rural income growth following agricultural development provides markets for non-agricultural products and services. I have also stated in Chapter 1 that, in my view, agricultural growth during the 1980s prepared the grounds for macroeconomic stabilization and somewhat strong development of the manufacturing sector from the 1990s. I shall not repeat these points here.

In the case of Bangladesh, the acceleration of agricultural growth during the 1980s was triggered by two changes in agricultural policy at the end of the 1970s. One was the deregulation and liberalization of the market for agricultural inputs such as chemical fertilizers and irrigation facilities from 1978. It accelerated the diffusion of small-scale irrigation facilities, especially STWs, which, combined with the increased use of chemical fertilizers, boosted the production of dry-season irrigated *boro* rice markedly. The other change was an expansion of agricultural public finance centering on the Special Agricultural Credit Program of 1977. As mentioned in Chapter 5, this program failed by the mid-1980s due to extremely poor fund recovery rates, but it would be reasonable to say that public finance played an important part in agricultural development to a certain extent in its early stages from the end of the 1970s to the first half of the 1980s. (The situation changed very quickly after that and public finance was no longer needed by the end of the 1980s, but it had been very significant as a pump-priming measure.) Almost at the same time, the diffusion of tubewells was also promoted in India's West Bengal by the availability of credit from the Land Development Bank. It should be recognized that the rural electrification policy from the 1980s also contributed by promoting electrification of tubewells.

Of these two policy measures, the liberalization of agricultural input markets can be considered a typical market mechanism-dependent policy, while the development and strengthening of agricultural public finance may be a slight departure from the mainstream idea of neoclassical economics. I accept a new approach to agricultural and rural finance policy that emphasizes the market's intermediation role in principle (see Izumida and Yurugi (1990), for example), but I have difficulty in supporting any trans-historical argument for it.

Even in the case of irrigation, the liberalization policy measure based on the market mechanism worked largely due to the technological characteristic of STWs. This technological characteristic is, of course, that the scale of irrigation is very small. Where the scale of irrigation is as large as a gravity-flow canal irrigation system over a wide area, or even a groundwater pump irrigation of the size of DTWs, the likelihood of success with deregulation or liberalization policy alone would be very small.

In this sense, agricultural development was made possible in Bangladesh and West Bengal simply by the relaxation of government regulations and the implementation of the liberalization policy because conditions were right for the adoption of STWs as the main means of irrigation. These areas were in a fortunate position in a way. The fact that the real price of diesel engines and electric motors for tubewells decreased substantially, thanks to technological innovations in Korea, China, and India, also worked in their favor.

Having recognized the effectiveness of deregulation and the liberalization policy on the diffusion of STW irrigation, I have pointed out its issues and limitations.

In Chapter 3, for example, I examined in detail why 'overinvestment' continued until a majority of STWs fell into the red in Bangladesh, and concluded that the cause might be found in the lack of coordination among farmers, or the ineffectiveness of community principles in other words. I also pointed out that the market principle alone would be unable to solve not only a similar overinvestment phenomenon but also a certain type of serious environmental problem (a continual decline in groundwater levels threatening the sustainability of irrigated farming) and problems in relation to the management and operation of DTWs that were observed in the state of West Bengal. I was able to learn from these cases that the market mechanism might have to be supplemented by other principles, especially government and community functions, in order to operate effectively, or, in other words, the market economy might be unable to operate effectively on its own.

Trickle-down Effects of Economic Development and Poverty Reduction

It has been empirically demonstrated in this study that the development of the agricultural sector from the 1980s in Bangladesh and West Bengal in India essentially yielded significant benefits and, together with the development of the rural non-agricultural sector accompanying the agricultural development, improved the income and living standards of the rural population, including the lower classes. In other words, there were marked trickle-down effects of agricultural growth, which were clearly observed in the structural transformation of the rural informal finance market in particular.

In view of the fact that tubewell investment was made only by a very small number of wealthy farmers, the existence of these trickle-down effects of rural economic development might look somewhat strange. As I have stated repeatedly, however, the negative aspect of the strong bias in tubewell investment towards the wealthy class hardly came to the fore. Competition was limited and water charges were set at very high levels in the early stages of tubewell diffusion, but these conditions were resolved quite quickly. The ongoing construction of new tubewells increased competition and caused a substantial decline in water charges. The declining interest rates due to the transformation of the informal financial market also resulted in lower water charges. Tubewell investment had an even broader economic effect in that further and more successful investments counteracted to undermine investors.

The above process is none other than the capitalist cycle elucidated by Joseph Schumpeter, a giant in economics, in which the investor initially makes first-mover's profits, which gradually vanish as new entrants come in until the profit rate becomes so low that investment stops. It would be reasonable to say that the same process was applicable to the potato cold storage business, as well as to the tubewell irrigation business.

Agricultural growth led by the diffusion of tubewell irrigation created a virtuous cycle by which it stimulated growth in the non-farm sector through the industry linkage effect and the aforementioned final demand effect and, in turn, was stimulated by growth in the non-agricultural sector. Off-farm employment opportunities increased steadily in rural villages of Bangladesh and West Bengal, and I was often surprised that the role of the non-agricultural sector in terms of days employed or as an income source was more significant in seemingly purely farming villages than I had imagined.

I have no doubt that the flow of finance from the lower class to the upper class in the rural villages discussed in Chapter 5 and Chapter 6 can be interpreted as one of the phenomena that occurred in this context. A particularly noteworthy point is that *bondak* (land mortgage) has been transformed as the main route for small-holding farmers to join the landless into the route for the landless to move upwards by obtaining the usufructuary right. It is clear that the fruit of rural economic development has reached the lower-class people in rural villages, steadily reducing their poverty level.

In Bangladesh the so-called microcredit program ('microfinance' refers to a broader financial services program, including a savings deposit service and others) operated by the Grameen Bank and others spread from the mid-1980s when the collapse of rural public finance became apparent. The popularity of microcredit as a trump card for poverty reduction has not waned even today and still attracts support from many donors.

The fact that it has made a major contribution to poverty reduction by providing poor village women who can barely write their own names with access to credit under the same conditions as in formal finance, and that it maintains incredibly high repayment rates, certainly deserves the highest possible praise. I fully recognize this point.

However, I have raised the question that the poverty reduction mechanism of microcredit might have been seriously misunderstood. If it has been envisioned that poverty is reduced by earnings from a successful investment by the borrower in an income-generating project, I must say that such a view is fundamentally wrong and has the potential to adversely affect the policy and direction for microcredit operation.

What I have emphasized in this study is that microcredit functions as an 'advance for (future) savings', which promotes further thrift and saving among poor households while directing credit into asset investment and asset formation to create stable income flow. The combination of thrift and saving and asset income flow enables the microcredit borrower to gradually escape poverty. My proposition is that this may be the real poverty reduction mechanism. The fundamental concept here is that, for a majority of rural residents to escape from poverty, it may be more important to seize opportunities to earn stable and high wage incomes rather than to start small businesses (such as income-generating projects) of their own. It leads to the notion that it is acceptable to invest microcredit funds in assets such as the acquisition of mortgaged farmland at the initial stage, but they must gradually be directed to human capital investment such as education and health. Investment in human capital is essential in order to acquire opportunities to earn stable and high wage incomes.

On the other hand, as shown in Chapter 5, the reversing of rural informal finance flows does not mean that poverty has markedly decreased or that living standards have substantially improved among the rural poor. Lower-class households are acquiring the usufruct to farmland by lending funds to the wealthy farmer class, but at the same time they do not even have a cooking shed to keep off the rain in the wet season, or they may have a cooking shed but no bed and the whole family has to sleep on the cold dirt floor (it is quite cold in Bangladesh in the winter).

As agriculture achieved rapid growth from the 1980s, Bangladesh's economy underwent a drastic transformation in a matter of a decade or so. As a result of agricultural growth, rice and other food prices fell considerably in real terms and the food problem was resolved to a large extent in the sense that the masses had something to eat. Abundant supply of consumer goods became available in rural villages and standards of living improved accordingly.

However, the employment situation has been very poor in Bangladesh. Wages have remained at very low levels. What kind of economic development in the future will have the power to remove the root causes of such poverty? It is likely to be the introduction of foreign capital and the development of the labor-intensive and export-oriented manufacturing sector by these foreign capital-backed corporations. Also, to allow foreign capital-backed corporations to operate effectively, the broad-based development of the manufacturing sector by domestic capital is essential.

Based on the above outlook, the current structure of the rural informal financial market has a major problem. Currently, financial surplus entities are lending directly to small-scale rural entrepreneurs through the informal financial market. This is due to a deficiency in the formal financial system, including banks, which is their failure to mobilize savings. What is required from now on is the development of a system in which private sector financial institutions can perform their primary function of financial intermediation and issue funds to the manufacturing sector (including foreign capital-backed corporations), which powerfully leads the country's economic development.

From this perspective, Bangladesh's current policy, which is biased towards microcredit, has very serious problems. First, required funds are lent to the poor classes, which are generally not cut out for business, instead of business entrepreneurs. It was shown in Chapter 5 that short-term informal finance was flowing to small business people in rural villages. And the practice of sub-lending of microcredit was discussed in the Addendum. In this sense, sub-lending of microcredit can be regarded as a very sound economic move. Second, the bias towards microcredit may be resulting in misallocation of aid money.

Misallocation means the following. In order to nurture non-agricultural industries centering on the labor-intensive manufacturing sector (which creates stable employment for the poor classes), the development of infrastructure generally has paramount importance. Yet, infrastructure development appears to be misguidedly undervalued as a result of policy bias towards microcredit. Undervaluing of infrastructure and overvaluing of microcredit are, in other words, the undervaluing of public investment and the overvaluing of private investment. However, profitability of private investment is strongly influenced by the level of public investment, including infrastructure. There is a possibility that inadequate public investment will squeeze the profitability of private investment and put restraints on smooth economic development.

One conclusion of this study is that greater priority should be given to infrastructure development, such as rural electrification and rural road improvement, over microcredit in rural development policy for the ultimate purpose of poverty reduction.

Future Economic Development: The Governance Issue

Based on the flow of logic so far, the following two points are clearly important for economic development and poverty alleviation in Bangladesh. The first point is the question of how to nurture business entrepreneurs who will create employment, or how to create an environment that promotes investment by business entrepreneurs. The second point is the question of how to improve education and health conditions and create an environment that promotes human capital formation among future workers. Infrastructure is merely one component of the policy required for the first point.

The Achilles' heel of the first policy is, broadly speaking, the enhancement of governance standards. The most direct example would be Bangladesh's *hartar*, or serious general strike. Since *hartar* inflicts terrible damage on economic activities, political parties during the civil government period in the 1990s agreed repeatedly to abandon the *hartar* tactic but they have never stopped it in reality. Every governing party proposes to eradicate *hartar* but the same party takes advantage of the tactic as soon as it becomes an opposition party.

As I have argued in Note 36 of Chapter 3, there appears to be some commonality between national-level politics that cannot abandon *hartar* and the state of village politics in Bangladeshi village society. The overinvestment in STWs can be interpreted as one of the consequences of this. I have concluded that the overinvestment stemmed from moral hazard behavior on the part of both parties in a water transaction (the 'self-centered' behavior of STW owners in supplying water and the non-payment of water charges by water buyer farmers). Such a problem has to be moderated by nonmarket adjustment through negotiation between the parties, but Bangladeshi rural society is unfortunately not well equipped with the facilities to make such an adjustment, which is why inefficiencies remain unresolved.

For example, a Japanese rural village would probably manage a STW as common property under the land improvement district system, even though the scale of irrigation would be very small. Villagers would agree in advance on matters such as the number and locations of communal STWs, who would operate and when, what water prices to charge, who would collect water charges and when, how to resolve disputes, and so on, and would operate them jointly. Even if STWs were owned by individuals, villagers would discuss who to sell to and what prices to charge at the land improvement district meeting. As discussed in Chapter 7, Bangladeshi villages did not have a land improvement district system nor an informal forum (meeting) of villagers to discuss such matters. STW owners and water buyer farmers had to talk with one another individually to address various problems. To rephrase, extremely high costs of such an adjustment was the root cause of overinvestment in STWs.

Hartar action is taken because disagreements between the government and opposition parties cannot be resolved in the parliament, or there is no adequate forum for resolution. These two phenomena appear to occur by exactly the same mechanism. And, as for the abovementioned second policy, namely, education and health, serious problems stem from the same roots.

The shortest route to discuss this point would be to take a somewhat longer route by mentioning a study on a village called Palanpur in the Indian state of Uttar Pradesh (Lanjouw and Stern (eds.) 1998). The authors point out that, in Palanpur village, surprisingly few improvements have been made in the past fifty years to achieve 'better quality of life' in the fields of elementary education, health care, public hygiene, rural electrification, public distribution, and social security for the aged, despite marked development of the village's economy. However, it was not because the central and state governments did not make an effort to improve these fields. Like other villages in India, access to public services and programs such as government primary schools, financial institutions, the social security system, 'fair price shops,' electricity supply, land consolidation programs, employment promotion programs, vaccination campaigns, and family planning services has become considerably easier for Palanpur villagers. The problem was that these services and programs were functioning only at extremely low levels, or were completely nonfunctional, except for a few cases (Lanjouw and Stern (eds) 1998: 181). The penetration of health care, education, and other public services in Uttar Pradesh state, including Palanpur village, was markedly lower than in South India, especially the state of Kerala, due to the presence of this condition, which was also manifesting at an extremely slow pace in the improvement in literacy rates (in fact, literacy gaps were widening between the castes and sexes).

The authors also provide some specific examples of public services and programs not functioning properly, and I mention the case of a government primary school below.

This government primary school was set up during the 1950s with a principal and five teachers. Due to subsequent staff cuts (as a result of new schools being opened in nearby villages), the school was operated by only one teacher from the time of a 1974–75 survey to 1993. The number of pupils between the ages of six and ten was 158 in 1983–84 and 141 in 1993. The lone teacher was the son of the village headman (as at 1983–84) from the Thakur caste, but he did not even turn up at the school. He only came to the school when he had a dozen or so sons and daughters of his own close relatives with him. Even when the school was 'open as usual,' he merely kept the children quiet or occasionally gave them some exercises to do, but he never gave lessons. In any case, it would have been impossible for him to look after pupils from Grade one to Grade five simultaneously, even if he wanted to. This situation continued until the end of 1992, when the state government adopted a policy to assign teachers from other villages to village primary schools and sent two teachers from nearby villages to Palanpur.

The authors visited Palanpur primary school in 1993 and 1994, after the reform, and reported that there was marginal improvement. Attendance had visibly increased (twenty to thirty pupils were attending daily) and lessons were being given on several occasions during their visits. However, one teacher was never at school when the authors visited and, all in all, the primary school was functioning very poorly (Lanjouw and Stern (eds) 1998: 181–3).

This situation is exactly the same as the one I witnessed in Daskin Chamuria village in Tangail district around 1992–93. Its primary school was often closed, pupils studied by themselves when it was open, and the teacher rarely gave proper lessons. The teacher was also the son of an influential villager and idled about at home most of the time. Some villagers who were keen on their children's education paid a lot of money to send their sons to faraway boarding primary schools. Government field staff in charge of family planning, health care, and agricultural extension were assigned to a few villages but they, too, stayed home whenever they could, instead of going to work.

The most surprising difference between Bangladesh and Japan was that villagers would work harder in their own villages in Japan, whereas the situation was completely opposite in Bangladesh. This grim reality was the reason behind Uttar Pradesh state's decision to send teachers to work outside their own villages. (A similar attempt was made in Bangladesh at the beginning of the 1990s.)

Then, where does this difference between Japan and India or Bangladesh come from? The morality of public servants in general is different in a broad sense. However, I would like to point out here that the village or villagers are lacking the capacity to effectively counteract acts of sabotage or corruption by public servants. I had a strong impression during my extended field survey in Bangladeshi villages that villagers were individually quite frustrated and alarmed by acts of sabotage or corruption by public servants, but these feelings did not prompt them to take joint action. Or, to go one step further, they were envious of these public servants and only wished they or their families were in such positions. Put simply, local administration and village society were not what they were supposed to be.

The organizational and institutional problems of local administration and village society concerning small-scale rural infrastructure development (discussed in Chapter 7) constituted merely a small portion of this larger, more expansive problem. The same problem was found in every other administrative service and this was the grim reality that existed in Bangladesh. If Bangladesh's failure to attract direct foreign investment sufficiently is the main reason for its failure to take full advantage of the chance for economic development during the 1990s (as mentioned in Chapter 1), it is possible to trace its origin to problems such as underdeveloped infrastructure, human capital shortage, and political instability epitomized by frequent *hartar*, all of which had the same root cause.

At this point, issues representing the truly sorry state of the administrative system manifest themselves with great importance; for example, the *union* at the lowest level of Bangladesh's administration only had one chairperson, several members, one secretary, and several night watchmen, despite its relatively large size with a population of 20,000 to 30,000 people; or a large *gram* (natural village) with more than 500 households had no administrative structure and simply ran under the informal guidance of the *matabbor* (the *samaj* leadership). Making improvements to this situation is an enormous challenge, as well as a pressing need. What I regard as the biggest problem with policy attaching too much importance to microcredit is that microcredit completely ignores these fundamental and important matters that are vital to long-term economic development.

In this sense, the Participatory Rural Development Project in Bangladesh, the third phase of a series of Bangladesh research projects since 1986 led by Professor Yoshihiro Kaida of the then Center for Southeast Asian Studies, Kyoto University, deserves recognition for its effort to grapple squarely with the above problems with the rural development administration. Although it would be very difficult for a single project to solve such enormous and deep-rooted problems within a short period of several years, making a breakthrough would greatly benefit the society.

Finally, this is somewhat superfluous but I would like to make a point about implications of this study for economic theory. Professor Masahiko Aoki sharply criticizes agency theory, which has become an important analytical tool in today's economics, in his recent tome, *Hikaku seido bunseki ni mukete* (Toward a comparative institutional analysis) (2001). He states that agency theory 'provides a powerful partial equilibrium analysis of an institution in a particular domain of interaction between the principal and the agent(s), with institutional arrangements in other domains taken as given environments' but that it cannot explain 'why a particular institution emerges in a domain of one economy but not in a similar domain of another economy' (Aoki 2001: 23–4). It should be clear from discussions in this study that this is a very pertinent criticism.

I used the example of Japan's land improvement district system earlier to consider briefly the problems with irrigation arrangements in rural Bangladesh. While STW owners and water buyer farmers transacted with one another individually without intermediation by any organizations in Bangladesh, if STW irrigation was developed in Japan, Japanese farmers would almost certainly operate STWs in a communal framework through an organization such as the land improvement district cooperative, even if STWs were owned by individual farmers.

Now, economic transactions and associated problems that would arise between STW owners and water buyer farmers would be essentially the same whether they were in rural Japan or in rural Bangladesh. In this sense, economic actions of farmers in both regions could be considered in the same agency theory framework. In that case, it should be safe to assume that both STW owners and water buyer farmers would be rational economic entities.

I believe, however, that these transactions would likely produce totally different economic outcomes if there was a 'meeting' in a domain such as the land improvement district (supported by higher organizations/institutions such as hamlets, villages, or local government), or if there was no meeting, of even if a meeting took place within the same agency theory framework. For example, a decline in the water charge might be smaller in Japanese villages but situations such as overinvestment in tubewells would likely be avoided.

If that is the case, what Aoki calls 'institutional arrangements in other domains' becomes important. To repeat my argument in Chapter 7, it appears that lack of coordination within a village community (where there is not even a meeting of villagers) and the weakness of Bangladesh's local administration system are two sides of the same coin and share the same historical background. In this sense, the analyses in Parts I and II are by themselves incomplete and make better sense only when the perspectives presented in Part III are incorporated.

In the small-scale irrigation sector in rural West Bengal, India, where irrigation facilities are not limited to STWs, where mini-deeps have been introduced to address the problem of falling groundwater levels, and where privatization of state-operated DTWs is imminent, the importance of these 'institutional arrangements in other domains' is likely to increase in the future.

While agency theory is useful because it can be applied to any economic entity in any parts of the world, I believe that very rudimentary and fundamental errors can be made unless differences in 'institutional arrangements in other domains' are taken into account.

Notes

Introduction

1 Kikuchi (2002) is an excellent study emphasizing this point.
2 See Chapter 4 for details.
3 The Bangladesh research project led by Professor Kaida began in 1986 and accumulated an enormous amount of research and results in relation to rural development through the Joint Study on Agricultural and Rural Development in Bangladesh (Phase 1), the Joint Study on Rural Development Experiment in Bangladesh (Phase 2), and the Participatory Rural Development Project in Bangladesh (Phase 3). The recent publication of Kaida (ed.) (2003) is one such result. (The Japanese leader was Professor Yoshihiro Kaida of the Center for Southeast Asian Studies, Kyoto University, at the time.)
4 Rice crops that are grown in Bangladesh and the state of West Bengal in India include *aus*, transplanted *aman*, broadcast *aman*, and *boro*. These are sub-varieties of *Indica* rice. *Aus* is originally non-photosensitive and is mainly grown in highlands by direct sowing in the light rain months of March and April and harvested at the height of the wet season. Transplanted *aman* is the traditional main crop grown in medium altitude lands. Transplantation starts in early July, when floodwaters rise and begin to fill paddy fields, and ends by early September at the latest. Rice is harvested around December when floodwaters recede. Broadcast *aman* is grown in lowlands where floodwaters exceed a certain depth and prevent cultivation of transplanted *aman*. It is a so-called deepwater or floating rice type. It is directly sowed in the light rain period from March to April but, as with transplanted *aman*, it is not harvested until around December, as the plant is highly photosensitive. Finally, *boro* has been cultivated during the dry season in very low-lying areas where floodwaters in the wet season are so deep that even floating rice varieties cannot grow. In recent years, cultivation of *boro* has gradually been spreading to lowlands, medium altitude lands, and highlands, thanks to the development of dry-season irrigation. See Chapter 2 in Fujita (1993a) for more details.

Chapter 1

1 See Osada (1980) for more details.
2 See Chapter 5 for more details.
3 See Fujita (1986 and 1993a).

4 The development of irrigation systems in Bangladesh initially took place in the southeastern region, then in the northwestern region a little later. See Fujita (1990b) for regional characteristics of irrigation development.

5 Very simply stated, the Ricardian Trap refers to the situation in which a slump in the food production sector holds down the development of the economy as a whole. See Ishikawa (1990), Hayami (1995), and Ōno (1991).

6 One symbolic result of this was the slow pace of industrial structural change. In terms of the share of GDP, the agriculture/forestry/fishery sector's representation continued to fall from 65.2% in 1950 to 31.9% in 2000 but the manufacturing sector only grew from 3.9% to 11.1%, and only the tertiary sector, including the service industry, expanded rapidly. Manufacturing's stagnation is clear from the fact that it had already represented 10.5% of GDP in 1975. The other result was a difficult labor/employment situation. Based on the 1996 labor force survey, the unemployment rate was only 2.5% but the sum total of the *effective* unemployment rate (fourteen working hours or less in the week prior to the survey) and the *underemployment* rate (from fifteen to thirty-four working hours) reached 38.6%. In particular, the rate was 13.7% for men but 78.9% for women, indicating that a majority of female workers were in a state of semi-unemployment. In terms of employment structure, 4.2% of the labor force was absorbed by the public sector, 8.8% by the organized private sector, and 87.0% by the non-organized private sector. The figures were 10.5%, 21.3%, and 68.2% respectively after the primary sector was omitted. The largest was the non-organized private sector, or the so-called informal sector, which generally offered poor working conditions.

7 Based on slightly old data from the World Bank, the ratio of direct foreign investment to GDP in 1993 for Bangladesh was only 0.07% (although it was a rapid rise from 0.01% in 1990), incomparably lower than 6.75% for Malaysia, 5.43% for China, and even 1.79% for Sri Lanka, 1.64% for India, 1.41% for the Philippines, 1.38% for Indonesia, 1.20% for Thailand, and 0.60% for Pakistan. Major obstacles include its political instability, underdeveloped infrastructure, frequent labor-management disputes, and low labor *quality* typified by a low literacy rate (male 49%, female 26% in 1995).

8 This argument was discussed in more detail in Fujita (2000b).

Chapter 2

1 See Chapter 2 in Fujita (1993a).

2 For example, Bardhan (1984: 216–17) argues that 'Land fragmentation is excessive in India, particularly in the eastern regions, and the progress of consolidation, in spite of copious legislation, has been very poor (except in northwest India)', and 'Land-size and fragmentation disabilities afflict investment in private investment in electric and diesel tubewells.'

3 One recent study that clearly presents this hypothesis is the analysis by Dubash (2002) of tubewell irrigation in the Indian state of Gujarat. Dubash emphasizes the importance of the elimination of usury capital by the government—that is, a series of policy measures for the regulation of usurers and the provision of policy-oriented finance—as a factor for the dissemination of tubewells.

4 Boyce (1987) is most notable.

5 Bhaduri's semi-feudal mode of production model (Bhaduri 1973), based on rural eastern India, is widely known.

6 See Chapter 3 in Fujita (1993a) for further details about the discussion below.

7 There are several studies on the groundwater market, such as Bangladesh Agricultural University (1985, 1986), Quasem (1990) of Bangladesh, and Pant (1992), Janakarajan (1992), Kahnert and Levine (eds) (1993), and Shah (1987, 1993) of India, but they either do not carry out full economic analysis or stop at the estimation of *w/c* (the ratio of water charge to variable irrigation cost, to be discussed later) or the internal rate of return on tubewell investment without going further into the estimation of factor shares of irrigated rice production as a whole. Certainly, in my view, the most important characteristic of tubewell irrigation is the formation of capital that does not merge with land and therefore a conflict between land rent and profit must be a focal point of analysis.

8 If the water charge is exorbitantly high, one option available to a water buyer farmer is to buy water from an adjoining tubewell; however, this is technologically difficult unless his land is near the boundary between two tubewell coverage areas. Conversely, competition between tubewells arises through selective behavior of landowners in the boundary zone and limits monopoly power to that extent. In the long run, farmers are able to set up their own tubewells and promote competition further. As a result of this competition, water charges within a village usually converge at a certain level (some variations may remain, reflecting differences in farmland quality) but substantial price variations remain between larger areas across village boundaries. The degree of competition is considered to be determined by factors such as topographic condition, unequal distribution

of capital required for tubewell installation, and the maturity of the financial market.

9 The total irrigation coverage by the thirty tubewells was approximately 307 acres, which is much less than the village's irrigated area shown in Table 2.2 (379 acres, assuming all *boro* rice cropping lands were irrigated). This is a reflection of the presence of substantial areas within the village cultivated by non-residents and irrigated by STWs owned by non-residents.

10 According to Shah (1993), the lowest *w/c* in the Indian groundwater market was 1.2 to 1.3 for West Godavari and the highest was 2.7 to 3.5 for Madurai district in the state of Tamil Nadu and Karimnagar district in the state of Andhra Pradesh.

11 Allocation of risks due to crop failure or price fluctuations varies depending on the mode of water transaction. All risks are shouldered by the tubewell owner in the *chaunia* arrangement and by the water buyer farmer in the fixed rate cash payment arrangement. The crop-sharing arrangement lies between the two, with risks being shared according to the crop share ratio. Consequently, it is also possible to consider the surplus in the hands of the water buyer farmer after deduction of land rent as a risk premium. However, it is treated as capital interest in this chapter.

12 Interest rate on short-term finance in the village was 8.3% per month in many cases, which is 100% per annum. It was assumed that it would take two months on average to recover working capital, since it was three to four months from the preparation of farmland to the harvesting of *boro* rice.

13 The considerable disparities in the rate of return on investment are considered to reflect differences in management skill and farmland quality rather than monopoly power of individual STW owners. In other words, it is possible to say that the large differences in investment returns arose because water charges were determined at a mostly uniform level (due to reasons such as high transaction costs) without fully reflecting differences in quality of individual farmlands.

14 If capital interest on working capital was not taken into account, the average rate of return on STW investment would be 103%.

15 Observant readers would notice that the water charge in the fixed cash rate payment mode would be Tk2,915 per acre, the sum total of irrigation cost and profit in Table 2.2, and there would be a significant gap between that and the actual rate of Tk2,100–Tk2,400 per acre. However, this is an averaging error. Since farms under the fixed cash rate arrangement may have low yield or more than average cultivation cost, there is no case of the water buyer farmer's share eating into the tubewell owner's profit in reality. This point

is supported by the fact that the water buyer farmer's surplus amounts for No. 4, No. 9, No. 17, No. 22, and No. 25 tubewells in Table 2.8 are close to zero (No. 22 is the exception).

16 The estimation from Rashid (1994) was used here.

17 A dramatic reduction in the share of land appears to have been occurring widely, not only in this village. In another study village, Daskin Chamuria village in Tangail district, where the groundwater market has developed based on the crop-sharing system (with the tubewell owner's share of 25%), land share of irrigated *boro* production was 21%, which was markedly lower than the wet season land share of 50%. Bangladesh adopted a measure to protect sharecroppers for the first time under the Tenancy Act of 1984, which stipulated (setting aside its practical effect) that the sharecropper cultivating HYVs should either shoulder all the costs and receive two-thirds of gross production or go halves on both the cost and the gross production with the landlord. The share of land in this case is about 33%. The analysis in this chapter suggests the need for a clear distinction between transplanted *aman* rice and *boro* rice for the purpose of land rent control. The traditional crop-sharing tenancy contract (no cost sharing and 50% of gross production to the landlord) matched the actual share of land in the case of transplanted *aman* rice cultivation, whereas returns to the landlord would be excessive even under the provisions of the new law and no protection would be provided to sharecroppers in the case of *boro* rice cultivation.

18 This is exactly what was taking place on a large scale in Daskin Chamuria village (see Chapter 5).

19 According to Rahman (1986: 166), for example, 'Money-lenders interviewed by us came from various land-owning groups but most of them obviously came from the land-rich groups...We found that usufructuary mortgage coupled with money-lending which forced people into distress sales did, in fact, still play an important role in the process of increasing landlessness in Bangladesh.'

20 In Daskin Chamuria village, *bondak* (which is different from *khaikhalashi* in that the usufructuary right is not returned to the borrower unless he repays the principal) was more common and *khaikhalashi* was hardly used. Yet, the flow of credit from the poor to the wealthy, and the flow of land in the opposite direction, was clearly observed, just as in Aira village (see Chapter 5).

21 In fact, the rice price began to decline from the autumn of 1992 and continued to be about 30% lower for nearly one year. As a result, many STW owners in Aira village suffered a loss for the 1993 *boro* season, which led to concern that the planting area for *boro* rice for 1994 would be curtailed

dramatically. A rapid recovery in the rice price from the end of 1993 kept the damage to a minimum. Nevertheless, the excessive price sensitivity of irrigated *boro* rice cultivation means that it has become difficult for the Bangladeshi government to manage adjustment of supply and demand for rice.

Chapter 3

1 Table 21 in Meinzen-Dick (1996: 52) suggests a crop yield differential between the water buyer farmer and the tubewell owner, but it does not test for significance and the large standard error means that the difference is unlikely to be statistically significant. Table 22 (p. 55) shows considerable differentials in income per acre, which are likely to be statistically significant. On these points, the findings are likely to be consistent with Kurosaki's conclusion. (Based on advice given by Dr. Takashi Kurosaki of the Institute of Economic Research, Hitotsubashi University.)

2 Bangladesh Agricultural University (1985, 1986) also evaluates efficiency, mainly from the viewpoint of the capacity utilization rate of irrigation facilities.

3 See Chapter 3 in Fujita (1993a) for details in relation to this statement. For assessments of the irrigation facilities' privatization/liberalization policy, see Ministry of Agriculture (Bangladesh) and Asian Development Bank (1992).

4 The national average price of coarse rice according to the Food Planning and Monitoring Unit (1994).

5 According to Abudullah et al. (1995), the domestic purchase (procurement) of rice by the government decreased sharply from 960,000 tons in 1992 to 230,000 tons in 1993 and 150,000 tons in 1994. While some argue that these reductions in the government procurement of rice contributed to the slump in rice prices, I hold a negative view about this argument, taking into account that the domestic release of rice by the government also decreased sharply at the same time.

6 See Abdullah and Shahabuddin (1997) for details about the 'fertilizer crisis.'

7 The *aman* rice failure because of major flooding in 1998 was followed by a bumper *boro* rice harvest, which boosted the total rice and wheat production for 1998–99 to 21.13 million tons, an increase of 2.2% from the previous year. It achieved a record-breaking increase of 16.1% by rising to 24.54 million tons in 1999–2000 (Food Planning and Monitoring Unit 2000).

8 Although this cannot be fully substantiated due to unavailability of data after 1998–99 when the yield of *boro* rice jumped, the three-year moving averages for 1985–86, 1990–91, and 1996–97 are a planting area of 1,057,000 hectares and a yield of 3.66 tons per hectare, 1,718,000 hectares and 3.75 tons per hectare, and 1,883,000 hectares and 4.04 tons per hectare respectively.

9 The NMIC data were gathered by block supervisors (agricultural extension workers) who were operating in 12,091 blocks all over the country. The BBS estimates were less reliable as they were gathered by statistics officers in *thana* (496 nationwide), with the help of clerks and secretaries of the *unions* (4,451 nationwide).

10 See Ministry of Agriculture (Bangladesh) (1998). Although not noted in the report, Figure 3.2 suggests that the NMIC series prior to 1992–93 was prepared based on the BBS series. The numbers of STWs estimated by the BBS are also highly questionable, and this is perhaps why the STW irrigation area does not increase very much in response to a rapid increase in the *boro* rice planting area at the end of the 1980s shown in Figure 3.2. In other words, it is highly likely that the STW irrigation areas from 1988–89 to 1992–93 have been underestimated.

11 According to the 1996–97 NMIC report by the Ministry of Agriculture (Bangladesh) (1998), the average dry-season irrigation area per STW was 8.47 acres. However, this figure is a slight overestimation, considering that these STWs included electric STWs with a greater irrigation capacity and that dry-season crops included potato and mustard, which were grown at slightly different times from the cropping seasons for *boro* rice and wheat. When the estimate is adjusted to take these factors into account, the average irrigation area per diesel STW (for *boro* rice and wheat) is 7.47 acres, which clearly indicates a decrease in the capacity utilization rate. Note that the report states that the potential irrigation capacity of a STW is eighteen acres.

12 Ajia Keizai Kenkyūjo (Institute of Developing Economies) (1991: 298–308) gives a vivid description of the thriving business activity in Bogra city's retail area shortly after the liberalization of STW engine importation in 1988.

13 See Andō, Rashid, and Kaida (1991) for the study of Tetulia village and Chapter 2 of this book for the study of Aira village.

14 All groundwater transactions other than irrigation of self-cultivated land of the tubewell owner. Some readers may object to the inclusion of farmland tenancy by the tubewell owner but it has been included here for reasons of convenience.

15 A question arises about why the land rent in kind at a fixed quantity per acre was not adjusted under the *chaunia* system. This question has to be addressed in the future.

16 Similarly (to note 15 above), one must wonder why the crop-sharing system was not retained by simply adjusting the crop share ratio. This is also a question to be addressed in the future.

17 Possible reasons for the disappearance of the crop-sharing system include decreasing interest rates and decreasing risks. Interest burden is different between the fixed-rate cash payment contract and the crop-sharing contract since the water charge is paid in advance under the former and at the end under the latter. Needless to say, risk burden also changes when the payment arrangement is changed from crop sharing to fixed rate. This issue needs to be explored more deeply in the future.

18 Another example of a favorably located village is Sikar village (Figure 3.3). The water charge for the electric STW in the village at the time of the December 1999 survey was Tk1,500 per acre, which was the same as in Titkle village.

19 However, the December 1999 survey found that the number of tubewells did not increase at all during the 1990s in the other study village in Kalihati *thana*, Tangail district (Daskin Chamuria village in Chapter 5). Accordingly, it would be a little premature to think that this was a nationwide phenomenon.

20 The number of households had increased to 216 by the time of the December 1999 survey.

21 The purpose of this study was to compare and evaluate the impacts of the Grameen Bank between the base year (August 1996) and a comparative year (several years later). It was conducted by Shapla Neer (a citizens' association for overseas cooperation) in three study villages, including Titkle village, a village in Comilla district, and a village in Barisal district.

22 Accumulation of farmland by tubewell owners through *chaunia* seasonal tenancy was not necessarily a common phenomenon, even in Bogra district, and it was rather uncommon at the national level. One study of *chaunia* in Bangladesh is Glaser (1989), a case study of Samitigram village in Singra *thana*, Natore district, which is further south from Titkle village along the highway connecting Bogra city and Natore city.

23 It is based on somewhat incomplete information gathered by interviews with current STW owners (a small number of owners declined to be interviewed) and hence did not include information about past owners who no longer owned STWs (the proportion of which would not be negligible since STWs were being bought and sold more actively than expected).

24 A usufructuary right to one acre of farmland for a period of seven years could be bought for Tk7,000–Tk11,000. In a way, it was a long-term tenancy contract with advance rent payment. It is classified as mortgaged land here in order to distinguish it from short-term tenancy for a single crop season or a year.

25 It is somewhat arbitrary, but a slightly lower interest rate of 5% per month is used here because the village is on a major highway. It is possible to calculate the going long-term interest rate in Titkle village based on the relationship between rents for *khaikhalashi*, mentioned below, and year-round lease. A farmer who acquired the use of a field for seven years for a price of Tk7,000–Tk11,000, then let it to others for year-round lease, would earn Tk3,000 per year for the period (the lowest figure in the range is used here as the *khaikhalashi* rate is slightly older). Its present value (discounted at the going interest rate) is supposed to be Tk7,000–Tk11,000. This calculation produces a long-term interest rate of 30% to 72% per annum. The average rate is 51%. Assuming that a short-term interest rate is higher than this, a monthly interest rate of 5%, which is equivalent to 60% per annum, has a certain degree of validity.

26 The hand-operated pump is an auxiliary pump used to lift groundwater to the surface manually at the beginning of STW operation.

27 SE1 was the only tubewell other than diesel STWs that was operating at a loss. The main reason for this was likely to be low power efficiency. If it had achieved the level of power efficiency of SE2, it would have made a net profit of Tk1,184 instead of a loss of negative Tk3,092. Unlike in India (see the West Bengal case in Chapter 4 for example), a meter system was used for electricity supply to tubewells and the electricity charge was levied in proportion to the utilization volume of each tubewell.

28 The irrigation coverage was not something that could freely be determined by the tubewell owner's profit-maximizing behavior. It was more of a predetermined variable to the tubewell owner in the sense that he could not increase the coverage even though he wanted to. Accordingly, the profit and the irrigation coverage were not determined simultaneously, and therefore the regression formula did not have an endogenicity problem.

29 Another notable comment by DTW owners in relation to externalities of irrigation was about the fact that the owner of an island-like non-irrigated field within a DTW command area could enjoy the benefit of irrigation water trickling in from the surrounding irrigated fields and therefore only needed small amounts of water from his own STW. However, if such a benefit really existed, STWs within a DTW command area should have improved fuel efficiency. As mentioned above, this was not the case in reality.

30 This type of vicious cycle is frequently observed with public irrigation systems (Kikuchi 1992). However, I do not know of any other example of this phenomenon being observed among farmers as in Titkle village. Andō, Rashid, and Kaida (1991: 73) also point out the presence of this tendency for non-payment of water charges in private tubewell irrigation in Bangladesh.

31 It was found from group discussions that the average yield of *boro* rice for tubewell owners was sixteen *maund* per *bigha*, whereas water buyer farmers tended to produce ten to fifteen *seer* (one *maund* = forty *seer*) less due to unstable irrigation water supply. This difference amounts to 1.6% to 2.3%.

32 Based on the average *boro* rice irrigated area for the unprofitable STW owner of 2.95 acres and the gross income per acre from *boro* rice production of Tk12,916 (Table 3.7), a 2% drop in yield amounts to an income drop of Tk762.

33 In the social environment of Bangladesh, it was likely that water buyer farmers paid a very high transaction cost (for example, tough negotiations with the tubewell owner) in order to keep the *boro* yield differential to as low as 2%. It is practically impossible to calculate such transaction costs and therefore an attempt to demonstrate economic rationality at the individual level entirely in monetary terms has its limits.

34 One may ask why they did not install more DTWs and electric STWs to drive out high-cost diesel STWs in the first place. DTWs were previously owned by BADC and were sold to the private sector with favorable subsidies. Electric STWs needed a large amount of initial investment, and electricity connection required time and cost, slowing the pace of additional investment.

35 Another noteworthy point is the significance of the water charge collection system by fixed-rate cash payment per acre from the perspective of the enforceability of the irrigation supply contract. It can be said that its contractual enforceability is higher than the fixed-rate cash payment per use system, which is commonly found in India and Pakistan. A contract by fixed-rate cash payment per use is basically a spot transaction and the water buyer may receive proper water supply once but he has no effective recourse if the tubewell owner refuses the next supply. The groundwater market in Pakistan appears to be less efficient than in Bangladesh, since the cropping area for wet-season rice, which is the main crop, is quite small in the case of water buyer farmers (Kurosaki 1998; Meinzen-Dick 1996). One reason for this is that Pakistan's groundwater market is less developed than Bangladesh's. Another hypothetical reason is found in this drawback of the water charge system by fixed-rate cash payment per use.

On the other hand, the fixed-rate cash payment per acre system is a single-season contract, which, at least, imposes an obligation on the tubewell owner to supply water; therefore, its contractual enforceability is relatively strong. However, since the contract amount is fixed, the tubewell owner's income does not change, even if he supplies water improperly. This provides less incentive for the tubewell owner to honor the contract than the fixed-rate payment in-kind system (crop sharing) under which his income increases by the amount of his share of the crop. However, if non-performance of contract on the part of the tubewell owner and the resultant inefficiency were serious, the number of water transactions would decrease and leasing of farmland to tubewell owners would become the predominant form of transaction. What was happening in villages around Bogra city was the opposite of this, and water sale was the predominant form of transaction also in Titkle village. The reason for this is not entirely clear and requires future study.

36 Generally speaking, Muslims in Bangladesh have a strong tendency to enter disputes with each other over trivial matters and refuse to compromise with a stubbornness that irks outside observers. (There is no room to provide a full account here but, to give one example, estrangement between siblings who even refuse to attend each other's weddings is an everyday occurrence. In a survey village in Tangail district (Daskin Chamuria village), there is no stopping fragmentation of the ceremonial community unit called *samaj* over minor disputes such as distribution of meat for the Eid festival.) It is conceivable that this culture of uncooperative interpersonal relations was manifest in the groundwater market.

Maloney (1984) sought to identify the real cause of Bangladesh's poverty and came to the conclusion that it was the behavioral pattern of Bangladeshi Muslims (which, with a touch of diplomatic euphemism, he called *pragmatic individualism*). A clear example is the frequent occurrence of hard-line general strikes (*hartar*), which are an obvious impediment to Bangladesh's economic development. They stem from the fact that there is no platform for last-minute adjustments of conflicting interests between the ruling and opposition parties, or the employer and the employee, and therefore they never attempt to reconcile by making a compromise. According to Takada (1998: 262–4), 'social and economic activities become paralyzed by *hartar*' and 'the most significant feature of the current Bangladesh politics is found in "*hartar* politics".' He quotes the case of the previous ruling party, the BNP, which condemned *hartar* severely while in office, then began to use it actively as soon as it came to opposition, and argues how serious and ingrained a problem it is. *Atomism* (unlike the Western concept of individualism, this is more a *me-ism* tendency to put one's self-interest before everything else) referred to by Khan et al. and quoted by Takada is considered to mean mostly the same cultural tendency as Maloney's pragmatic individualism (Khan, Islam, and Haque 1996).

The fact that inefficiency is caused by the lack of adjustment of conflicting interests between farmers (or their inability to do so) with regard to tubewell water distribution points to the possibility that a culture engendering *hartar* is entrenched not only at the level of national politics but also among the general public. In that case, it also points to the fact that the market mechanism would have to be complemented by cooperative behavior among residents, a type of community principle, for it to be able to function properly.

37 Consequently, the gathered data are doubly biased. One bias stems from the fact that STW ownership was weighted towards wealthier farmers and the other bias stems from a high degree of freedom associated with water supply enjoyed by tubewell owners. However, these sample biases are not considered significant enough to influence the conclusion.

38 It does not include tasks that take up only small proportions of labor hours such as compost management and supervision of employees. This is why family labor cost is zero for *boro* rice and transplanted *aman* rice (Table 3.7).

39 There were some cases of seasonal leasing for *boro* rice cropping by payment in kind at a fixed amount. The going rent was twelve *maund* of paddy per acre, which was about Tk3,000 at the rice price of that time. It was substantially lower than the rent under the fixed-rate cash payment system, especially considering it was paid at the end. The existence of the fixed-amount in-kind payment system and its significance are still unclear.

40 This is likely to have been because double transplanting technology for transplanted *aman* rice cultivation began to spread in around 1995, but its dissemination was limited in size. According to a survey conducted in the rural area of Bogra district on 21 April 2000 by Dr. Kazuo Andō (Center for Southeast Asian Studies, Kyoto University), the double transplanting method works as follows. Rice seedlings are grown in the first seedling bed for twenty to twenty-five days, then transplanted into the second seedling bed (*gushi bisun*), which is set up in one section of the main paddy field (about one-third of the main paddy field), and grown again for twenty to twenty-five days, when it is then transplanted to the main paddy field. Compared with the normal single transplanting method, it requires more labor but only uses about one-third of the amount of seeds and increases yield by 30% to 50%, even though the amount of fertilizer used is the same. However, due to factors

associated with employment costs and preparation of the main paddy field, this method is only used for a small area of *gushi bisun* that can be set up in one day, which is about 10% of the total transplanted *aman* rice planting area.

41 It goes without saying that a single-year production cost survey requires very careful analysis since it is easily influenced by fluctuations in yields and prices. A supplementary survey in September 2000 confirmed that yields of transplanted *aman*, *boro*, and *rabi* crops in the survey year were mostly normal. While some increases in the yield of *boro* rice were observed at the macro level and also in two villages in Bogra district (Table 3.1) in the second half of the 1990s, interviews confirmed that there was no marked upward or downward trend in the yield of *boro* rice in Titkle village. In addition, it was confirmed by data in a report by the Food Planning and Monitoring Unit (2000) that farm product prices in the survey year were normal.

42 There were some cases of year-round leasing by payment in kind at a fixed amount. The going rent was thirty to thirty-six *maund* of paddy per acre, which was about Tk8,700–Tk9,300 at the rice price of that time. Again, it was substantially lower than the rent under the fixed-rate cash payment system, especially considering it was paid at the end. As per Note 39, the existence of the fixed-amount in-kind payment system and its significance are still unclear.

43 A year-round lease begins after the harvesting of transplanted *aman* rice and ends with the harvesting of transplanted *aman* rice, which means crops are cultivated in the order of *rabi*, *boro* rice, and transplanted *aman* rice. Since the rent for year-round leasing is collected in installments from the *rabi* harvest, the *boro* rice harvest, and the transplanted *aman* rice harvest, the calculation of the advance payment period is slightly more complicated. If only *boro* rice and transplanted *aman* rice are cultivated, the lease period for the former is six months and twelve months for the latter, which results in an average lease period of nine months. In view of the 14% average for fields that were capable of *rabi* cropping, an overall average of eight months was used in this estimation.

44 Considering that a greater proportion of farmland would be used for *rabi* cropping in the case of year-round leased land than general farmland and that farmers could, with reasonable certainty, expect a substantial amount of additional income from potatoes if they sold them after seven to eight months in cold storage despite the storage cost and interest, the net profit would be slightly higher. For example, potatoes stored in a refrigerated warehouse in town for seven months from April to November incur a storage charge of Tk85 per *maund* (a fixed charge regardless of the storage period) and a freight

charge of about Tk7. After adding interest at 5% per month, the production cost would almost double. However, the price of potato would almost always be at least two to three times higher (confirmed by BBS statistical data), earning the farmers additional income from cold storage.

45 The same year-round leasing system was found in Tetulia village and Sikar village, where rent was Tk6,000 per acre, which was 30% to 40% lower than Titkle's Tk9,000–Tk9,900. The cropping system in Tetulia village consisted of 90% double cropping of rice (transplanted *aman–boro*) and 10% triple cropping (transplanted *aman–rabi–boro*), which was very similar to the system in Titkle village. The cropping system in Sikar village was 80% triple cropping (transplanted *aman–rabi–boro*) and 20% double cropping of rice (transplanted *aman–boro*), which was more intensive than the farming method in Titkle village. The exploration of this issue has to be left to future studies.

46 See Fujita (1999).

Chapter 4

1 The Green Revolution in India can be roughly divided into the pre-1980 and post-1980 phases. While the first phase saw the resolution of the country's food problem (in the sense that it no longer needed to import food) but failed to achieve an improvement in the nutrition standards of the general public (that is, poverty reduction), the second phase, combined with accelerating economic growth, brought about a nationwide improvement in the rural income level and achieved freedom from hunger in the true sense (see Fujita 2000a for details). According to the Food and Agriculture Organization, the food supply per capita in South Asia, which is almost interchangeable with India based on its share of population in the region, was sluggish at 1,900 to 2,100 calories up to the end of the 1970s; it improved markedly during the 1980s and reached 2,300 calories at the beginning of the 1990s. It opened a definitive lead on sub-Saharan Africa, which remained stagnated throughout the period (Food and Agriculture Organization of the United Nations 1996: 62). Since the definition of poverty line in India was below 2,400 calories for the rural population and below 2,100 calories for the urban population, it is clear that the aforementioned improvement in the nutrition standards was accompanied by a marked poverty reduction.

I would like to present some statistics to verify these two phases of India's Green Revolution (Fujita 1995). Looking at different crops first, the average annual growth rate (three-year moving average) for the 1980s was favorable at 4.3% for wheat, 4.1% for rice, 3.9% for maize, 2.4% for pulses, 6.1% for oilseeds, 4.4% for sugar cane, and 3.2% for cotton. It contrasted starkly with the 1970s when growth was generally slow at 1.7% for rice, 0.0% for maize, negative 1.2% for pulses, 0.4% for oilseeds, 2.3% for sugar cane, and 2.7% for cotton, with the exception of 4.1% for wheat. Coarse grains other than maize continued to slump even after 1980 because they were inferior goods, demand for which had a negative income elasticity. In the coarse grain production zone, these crops were progressively replaced by oilseeds.

Looking at different areas next, the average annual growth rate for food grains (grains plus pulses) over ten years from 1981/82 to 1991/92 was notable in the eastern states (such as 3.8% in Bihar, 6.5% in West Bengal, 2.7% in Assam, and 4.1% in Orissa), as well as in the northwestern states (such as 4.0% in Punjab, 4.3% in Haryana, 3.8% in Himachal Pradesh, and 3.5% in Uttar Pradesh). Although growth was generally sluggish in the southern and western states (such as 0.9% in Andhra Pradesh, 0.5% in Karnataka, 2.9% in Tamil Nadu, negative 2.1% in Kerala, 1.2% in Maharashtra, negative 1.9% in Gujarat, and 0.9% in Rajasthan), the coarse grain zone that represented a large portion of these areas achieved its agricultural growth from the increased production of oilseeds, which were not classified as food grains, as mentioned above.

2 Tubewell development initially took the form of direct control by the state government but the number of privately owned tubewells increased rapidly and far exceeded the number of state-run tubewells. This data is slightly old but Shah (1993) estimated that the number of privately owned tubewells had reached eight million, while the number of state-operated tubewells was approximately 40,000 (mostly in the basin of the Ganges). Kahnert and Levine (eds) (1993) is the most comprehensive study on tubewell development in the Ganges River areas, including Nepal, India, and Bangladesh, with well-organized literature reviews by country and theme at the end.

3 Statistical information about the number of privately owned tubewells and their irrigation coverage in West Bengal, especially their geographical distribution and chronological changes, is extremely deficient; not only is it unusable for economic analysis but it is also incapable of providing even a rough picture. This problem of statistical deficiency is the background factor for the persistence of the argument that simply attributes the state's agricultural growth to agrarian land reform and local government reform, as discussed below.

4 For example, according to the state's equivalent of an economic white paper, *Economic Review 1994–95*, 'This breakthrough is related to the development

strategy followed in the rural areas of the State' and the core of this strategy is 'the successful implementation of land reform measures which involves distribution of ceiling-surplus land to the landless and providing security of tenure to the sharecroppers'; further, it 'ensures the availability of crucial non-land inputs like seeds, fertilizers, credit, irrigation facilities etc. to the beneficiaries of land reform measures as well as to the small and marginal farmers.' And this basic strategy was effectively implemented through 'the introduction of decentralized district level planning in the State by which the rural poor through the elected Panchayats get an opportunity for participating directly in the development process.' With regard to the productivity effect of land reform, it resorts to the well-known argument that poorer and smaller farms tend to achieve higher labor absorption and production per acre (Government of West Bengal 1995: 18–19). I would like to add that these views and statements remain unchanged up to the latest available issue of *Economic Review 1999–2000.*

5 For instance, the world's leading researchers of the Bengal economy gathered in Kolkata for a workshop in January 1995 and its report (Rogaly, Harris-White, and Bose (eds.) 1999) unmistakably reflected this tendency.

6 One example is a paper by Webster (1999) in Rogaly, Harris-White, and Bose (eds.) (1999), which points out the fact that STWs are exclusively owned by wealthy farmers and certain high castes and which makes a rather simplistic accusation about the monopoly of agricultural profits by these waterlords. It definitely lacks a close examination of water charges or an analysis of farming operation by water buying farmers. Rao (1994) is another example of the widespread dominance of the waterlord argument in India.

7 See the review in Fujita (1988).

8 See Fujita (1996). Rice production growth was more rapid in West Bengal than in Bangladesh, where the average annual production increase for the same period was about 3.3%.

9 On the back of the expansion of *boro* rice cropping, there was an acreage reduction for pulses and coarse grains, which were replaced by *boro* rice. A notable change outside of rice cropping was a rapid increase in the cultivation of oilseeds. See Suda (1999: 31–6) for details.

10 An argument by Gazdar and Sengupta (1999) in Rogaly, Harris-White, and Bose (eds.) (1999) is worthy of attention and is summarized below.

First, there are well-known arguments about the relationship between agrarian structure and productivity (the negative correlation between farm size and land productivity, the relationship between the tenancy system and productivity, and so on) but these arguments, especially the former, are invalid. A powerful alternative hypothesis is irrigation development. I accept the fact that private irrigation investment in tubewells was more important than the land capital-forming public irrigation investment suggested by Boyce and that it played a leading role in agricultural development. However, agricultural development in West Bengal cannot be fully explained by this fact alone. A certain multiple regression analysis shows that agrarian land reform indicators also had significant effects on agricultural growth. Among agrarian land reform programs, the strengthening of the sharecroppers' rights, rather than land redistribution, is expected to have contributed to agricultural growth. The raising of the sharecropper's share of crops and the establishment of tenancy rights protection measures motivated tenant farmers; in addition, policy support for nonmarket input supply (author's note: I am unsure what this refers to), in combination with the strengthening of the sharecropper's rights, is considered to have been effective (Rogaly, Harris-White, and Bose (eds.) 1999: 65–8).

My view on this argument is as follows. The acknowledgement of the importance of tubewell irrigation investment as a growth factor is estimable. And I have no objection about the argument that other factors besides tubewell investment were involved. However, there is a gap in the argument that immediately links these other factors with agrarian land reform.

Gazdar and Sengupta (1999) also present the following interesting argument as an issue for future consideration. Agrarian land reform had been implemented only halfheartedly prior to the establishment of the Communist Party government. There had been uncertainties about land rights, which discouraged land-related investment (tubewell construction). The Communist Party government might have reduced these uncertainties and helped accelerate tubewell construction by carrying out the reform more thoroughly (Rogaly, Harris-White, and Bose (eds.) 1999: 68–70). It still feels like an abstract argument and I believe it is important to substantiate it through empirical research.

11 The total redistributed land area (cumulative) through agrarian land reform up to the end of September 1999 was just over a million acres (7.5% of the total farmland) in the state of West Bengal but it was only approximately 19,000 acres (0.03%) in Nadia district, where the study village was located, which meant that agrarian land reform virtually did not happen in this district (Government of West Bengal 2000: 73, 107). This is the likely reason why no one talked about agrarian land reform, including Operation Barga, or raised it as an issue during our survey of the village.

12 See Chatterjee (1995) for the time being.

13 Dr. Toshihiko Suda, associate professor at Daito Bunka University, began a

survey of Gontra village mainly on the subject of agricultural cooperatives and finance in March 1998, since the village had an excellent agricultural cooperative. Through his introduction and guidance, the survey discussed in this chapter was conducted in this village.

14 A breakdown of farmland use in the whole of Chakda block (a total net planting area of 298,000 hectares) is as follows: *aus* rice, 67,000 hectares; *aman* rice, 126,000 hectares; *boro* rice, 107,000 hectares; wheat, 65,000 hectares; pulses, 46,000 hectares; oilseeds, 93,000 hectares; and jute, 114,000 hectares (Bureau of Applied Economics and Statistics 1998: 63, 69). The near 100% dominance of double rice cropping of transplanted *aman* and *boro* in Gontra village was rather unique in the area, but it goes without saying that this situation was a result of tubewell irrigation development.

15 The cooperative had 714 members and seven full-time staff as of September 1998 and energetically carried out various activities such as finance (saving and loan), chemical fertilizer co-purchasing, high-quality seed production (by contract farmers) and sale, general goods co-purchasing, and irrigation.

16 Many state-operated DTWs were constructed in neighboring villages at around the same time. The excavation of DTWs in West Bengal started far back in the early 1950s. See Chowdhury, B. K. (1971) for its progression and the state of irrigated farming at the time.

17 The seasonal tenancy system called *chaunia* was the predominant mode of transaction in the groundwater market in Bogra district, Bangladesh, during the initial phase of the tubewell irrigation development. The rent was also three *maund* of paddy per *bigha*. They were identical in form and standard (Chapter 2).

18 Dubash (2002) considers that the expansion of policy-oriented agricultural finance and the policy of restraint on usurious money lending played an important role in the diffusion of tubewells in the state of Gujarat, India.

19 Improved management of the Gontra village agricultural cooperative after the end of the 1980s is cited as supporting evidence. Its success in savings mobilization during the period was most symbolic of such improvement. See Suda (2002).

20 Since the farmland size distribution of all farmers in Gontra village is unknown, I cite the farmland size distribution in Chakda block for 1990–91 as a reference. Of 471,000 farm households, 326,000 households (69.2%) owned less than an acre, 100,000 households (21.2%) owned one to two acres, 38,000 households (8.1%) owned two to four acres, 7,000 households (1.5%) owned four to ten acres, and 106 households (0.02%) owned more

than ten acres (Bureau of Applied Economics and Statistics 1998: 64–5). It is easy to imagine how heavily tubewell ownership was concentrated among upper-class farmers in Gontra village.

21 The reason for excluding the depreciation cost from the calculation is that the use of purchase prices would cause a serious problem because the tubewells (other than SMs) were purchased a long time ago. The depreciation cost of the SM was estimated at approximately Rs3,000 per annum, as mentioned below. The reason for excluding the interest on working capital for tubewell operation is that the working capital comprised mostly family labor costs, with no cash outlay, and electricity charges for which late payment was permitted to a certain extent. Also, the effective interest rate would not be so high in Gontra village, since, compared with Bangladesh, it had well-developed institutional lending practices by the agricultural cooperative and other lenders.

22 A certain level of sample bias exists, since tubewell ownership is skewed towards wealthy farmers.

23 The figure for 'seedlings' in the production cost was constructively calculated in view of the trading of seedlings that often took place around Gontra village.

24 A separate rough calculation based on the interviews estimates that the irrigation cost was about 25% of gross *boro* rice production value in the early 1980s (when diesel STWs were predominant) and fell to about 15% at the end of the 1980s; it fell further to about 10% by the time of our survey.

25 In the case of Titkle village in Bangladesh, the interest on working capital and the interest on advance payment of rent were included in the calculation of the production cost for comparison. In the case of Gontra village, the interest on working capital was not included in the calculation of production cost and therefore the interest on land rent (paid in advance) for comparison was not included either. However, the interest on working capital, in the absolute amount and as a percentage of the total cost, is considered to be small enough not to influence the conclusion here, as shown in Table 3.7.

26 Capital interest included in labor cost in Table 3.7 (Chapter 3) comprised mainly plowing and land preparation by draft cattle and threshing work and also included power tillers used by some farmers. These items were included in the works listed under labor costs in Table 4.5 and therefore these two cases are comparable.

27 Inconsistency in the labor cost estimate for the two areas may be partially responsible for this. For example, in the case of Bangladesh, the family labor cost of zero mostly reflected the actual situation but it excluded items such as fertilizing and therefore resulted in a slightly underestimated figure.

In the case of Gontra village, Table 4.5 shows data based on labor hours by works without distinction between family labor and employed labor. A comparison of labor costs between the two areas using a uniform method is a task for future studies.

28 Dasgupta (1998) claims that the benefits of the Green Revolution did not reach the poor in Bangladesh as much as they did in West Bengal, and argues the reasons from the viewpoint of differences in government intervention and rural power structure. I believe that discussion must begin from the most fundamental fact, which is the disparity in the factor shares in irrigated agriculture as demonstrated in this chapter.

29 Government of West Bengal (2000: 170).

30 The issue of arsenic contamination is extremely important but details are not discussed further due to limitations of space. See Suda (1999: 36–9) for the arsenic poisoning problem in Gontra village.

Chapter 5

1 There are two broad groups of cooperatives in Bangladesh. One is the Comilla-type cooperative and the other is the type of cooperative that originated in the early twentieth century and became affiliated with the Bangladesh *Samabaya* (cooperative) Bank following the partition of British India in 1947. The total membership of the latter cooperatives at the time of the partition was 4.1 million, 1.22 million of which were members of the Union Central Cooperatives and the Union Multipurpose Cooperatives, 1.19 million were farmers, 0.49 million were hand weavers, and 0.12 million were sugarcane growers (Maloney and Ahmed 1988: 116). A majority of them are now largely inactive *paper* cooperatives.

2 See Saitō (1992) for the historical development process of the activity of cooperative societies and *samity* (NGO-led cooperatives) and their current problems.

3 This problem was universal in nature in Bangladesh and was serious in the manufacturing sector, as well (Sobhan 1991).

4 As a starting point, see Hossain, M. (1988) and Fujita (1990a) regarding the Grameen Bank.

5 The Grameen Bank underwent a remarkable expansion in rural Bangladesh during the 1990s and wielded considerable influence over rural finance. Its total national lending increased from less than Tk900 million in 1987 to Tk1.8 billion in 1989, Tk2.6 billion in 1991, and to more than Tk5 billion in 1992 (Grameen Bank 1995).

6 A total of 176,759 households were selected for the survey through two-stage random sampling in which 5,992 of the 170,209 rural enumeration areas (3.52%) in 61 *zila* (districts) (except Chittagong Hill Tracts) were selected first and one-third of households were selected from these areas next. The survey included questions about the landholdings, financial transactions for the previous twelve months, loan terms, loan purposes, repayment progress, loan balance, financial transactions in the previous period, annual household income, and saving, as well as basic information about the survey household. See BBS (1989) for more detail.

7 The practice of sub-lending funds borrowed from financial institutions to others is considered to have been common mainly in the agricultural product processing and marketing sectors (Lewis 1991, for example) but it is not easy to quantify its scale. One study estimates the percentage of sub-lending amounts in each bank's lending balance as 56.5% for the BKB, 57.0% for the Sonari Bank, and 38.0% for the Rupali Bank, with the value-weighted average reaching 50.5% (Khurshed 1988: 27).

8 In relation to the share of informal finance, Murshid and Rahman (1990: 1) conclude that 'although there is no definitive estimate, fragmentary evidence based on various micro-studies undertaken in the last twenty years or so suggests that Bangladesh's informal finance fills about two thirds of rural demand for funds.'

9 According to a survey by the Reserve Bank of India, informal finance lenders were classified into relatives and friends, landlords, agriculturalist moneylenders, professional moneylenders, traders and commission agents, and other, and the share of each lender type fluctuated considerably and irregularly from survey to survey. This suggests the existence of possible problems such as arbitrariness of responses by survey respondents due to ambiguity of the classification and false responses motivated by changes in the policy conditions, such as tightening of professional moneylender regulations (Bell 1990).

Similar problems are found with the classification of informal finance lenders in BBS statistics. As discussed later, financial transactions between ordinary villagers, who are not moneylenders nor friends/relatives, account for a large share of informal finance in today's rural Bangladesh and therefore the percentage figures for moneylenders, friends/relatives, and others in Table 5.1 must not be taken at face value.

10 The two villages practiced very different types of farming before the introduction of tubewells. In Daskin Chamuria village, in the deepwater area, the cropping system centered on wet-season broadcast *aman* rice or a mixture of broadcast *aman* rice and *aus* rice, with dry-season field

crops (*rabi*) such as pulses, oilseeds, and coarse grains being an important component, as well. Farming was very simple in Aira village, where mostly single cropping of transplanted *aman* rice was practiced. See Andō and Uchida (1994) and Rashid (1994) for details about each village.

11 HYVs developed by the Bangladesh Rice Research Institute.

12 An ongoing series of surveys has been conducted in Daskin Chamuria village and the 1986 census survey of all households recorded 386 households and a population of 2,218 people. The number of households and the population expanded to 538 and 2,665 respectively by 1992, which means the rate of population increase of 3.1% per annum over the six-year period was very high. This high population growth rate, combined with the Islamic system of equalized inheritance (although a daughter's inheritance is only half of a son's), accelerated the pace of farmland fragmentation. As a rather superfluous but noteworthy point, a dramatic decrease in the household size (5.75 people in 1986 down to 4.95 people in 1992) appears to suggest that rapidly increasing numbers of young couples were separating from their parents' households earlier than before (increasing nuclear families).

13 Specific farmland transfer rates are shown below. ('Mortgage' means *bhograhani* (discussed later) in Daskin Chamuria village and *khaikhalashi* in Aira village.) They are especially low in Aira village. Even in Daskin Chamuria village, they would be considerably lower if transfer through tenancy alone was taken into account. The agrarian structure with such characteristics as the small scale of land lease markets and the landless class staying as mere laborers is something that I once termed the *South Asian-type* (Fujita 1993). The existence of such characteristics was observed also in these study villages.

	Tenancy	Mortgage	Total (acres)	Ratio to owned land	Ratio to operated land
Daskin Chamuria village					
Lending	62.9	69.9	132.8	35.9%	
Borrowing	56.7	37.9	64.6		19.4%
Aira village					
Lending	21.1	13.3	34.4	14.9%	
Borrowing	57.2	10.6	67.8		23.5%

14 The number of people who work away from home (migration) was very small, however. Of Daskin Chamuria's working population of 920, only twenty-five people (2.7%) worked away from home: thirteen in Dhaka (one lawyer, one military officer, one police officer, one government worker, one Red Cross worker, four private company workers, two sewing factory

workers, and two others), one in Chittagong, one in Jessor, one in Pabna, one in Mymensingh, one in Rajshahi, one in Narayanganj, and six in other cities in the country. Those who worked overseas included one in the United States of America, four in Saudi Arabia, one in Qatar, and one in Malaysia. The number was even smaller in Aira village.

15 The survey was a baseline survey for a rural development action research project of the Japan International Cooperation Agency (JICA), which was conducted to gather basic data for assessment of the outcome of an action. Accordingly, the study villages were not selected specifically for the purpose of a finance survey and financial details were not the focus of the survey.

16 In Daskin Chamuria village, where both the borrowing and lending sides of informal finance were surveyed, there were cases in which, for example, villager A mentioned an outstanding loan to villager B but villager B did not mention an outstanding loan from villager A. Such cases were resurveyed and inconsistencies were corrected as much as possible, but there was not enough time to resurvey all such cases. The remaining inconsistent cases were included in the estimate on the assumption that, in the above example, villager B failed to declare it. On the other hand, only borrowings were surveyed in Aira village and therefore the estimate was made on the assumption that there were corresponding amounts of lending without exception. As a result of this treatment, the intra-village balances between lending and borrowing in Table 5.12 and Table 5.13 are zero.

17 The *shonchoi samity* (informal savings association), which is listed as a lending entity in Daskin Chamuria village (Table 5.7), requires some explanation. There had been very few mutual financing associations in rural Bangladesh in the past but, as reported by Maloney and Ahmed (1988: 64–113), savings associations have been spreading to both the urban and rural areas in recent years, and Daskin Chamuria village was no exception. A savings association was formed typically by fifteen to twenty villagers, each of whom saved Tk5 or so per week (or 1.25 kilograms of rice (about Tk3) at some women's savings associations). Once the amount of savings reached a certain level, typically several thousand *taka*, the money was spent on 'investment' as agreed by all members and profits were distributed to them according to their respective amounts of investment. The investment, here, was interest-yielding lending (generally to non-members), not a joint enterprise. Typically, they acquired a usufructuary right to farmland (through *bhograhani*, and leased it to a tenant farmer to earn rent) or extended short-term loans for interest receipts in paddy.

An interesting point is that many savings associations appeared in Daskin Chamuria village at the beginning of the 1980s and after 1988, which were periods immediately after the formation of the Comilla-type cooperatives in the village. According to Dr. Kazuo Andō (Center for Southeast Asian Studies, Kyoto University), who interviewed the villagers, the village's youths and women who were not members of the cooperatives took a hint from the cooperative savings system and started many of these savings associations. However, savings associations were organizationally unstable and formed and dissolved quickly. They were dissolved when, for example, many of the members wished to withdraw their money or payments from their investment fell into arrears.

18 Roughly speaking, proceeds from the sale of land were about three times the amount of a *bhograhani* loan and therefore the debtor would keep about two-thirds of the proceeds after repayment of the debt.

19 The *boro* rice production cost structure in Aira village (Table 2.10) was worked out as a final product of an economic analysis in relation to the groundwater market. Its feature was that an annual interest rate of 100% was applied to the working capital required for irrigation and crop cultivation and included as an expense in the estimate. Factor shares in *boro* rice production were explained coherently for the most part with this (see Chapter 2 for details). Production costs of *aman* rice in Aira village and various crops in Daskin Chamuria village were estimated in the same manner, including capital interest.

Another point to note is that, in estimating the *boro* rice production cost structure, the imputed tubewell investment profit to the tubewell owner was treated as the residual in the case of Aira village, whereas the land rent was treated as the residual in the case of Daskin Chamuria village. This was because it was possible to predetermine the land rent in Aira village based on the *chaunia* system, whereas it was not possible to estimate the land rent directly in Daskin Chamuria village, since *chaunia* did not exist there.

20 Looking at the relationship between land price and land rent in Daskin Chamuria village, the land price per acre was Tk45,000–Tk75,000, which was about three times the loan amount through *bhograhani*, and the land rent was Tk3,690–Tk5,570. Based on this land rent and assuming an interest rate of 16%, which was the going rate in formal finance, the capitalized value of land would be Tk23,100–Tk34,800 and therefore the actual land price was about twice the capitalized value. It is needless to say that the gap between the two values would be even wider if the going rate in informal finance was to be used. In Daskin Chamuria village, there was no upward path through purchase of land using a formal loan and repayment from agricultural income.

21 Where a person who obtained a usufruct to farmland through lending self-

cultivates the farmland and the family labor wage was valued lower than the market wage (that is, the labor market was imperfect for some reason), the calculation would arrive at a slightly higher rate of return on lending.

22 The inflation rate hovered around 10% consistently (9.9% in 1985 (from July 1985 to June 1986), 10.4% in 1986, 11.4% in 1987, 8.0% in 1988, 9.3% in 1989, and 9.0% in 1990) but it dropped to 5.1% in 1991 (World Bank 1993) and dropped further in 1992. This was the effect of the rice price slump (a 30% fall), which lasted for about a year from the autumn of 1992 (see Chapter 3).

23 Chapter 6 ('Problems in Bank Credit') in Maloney and Ahmed (1988) provides a specific and easy-to-understand description of how high the transaction costs are for rural Bangladesh residents to borrow a formal loan. And according to one study, the effective interest rates for loans from the BKB, including transaction costs, were 146% for a borrowing under Tk500, 169% for Tk501–Tk1,000, 59% for Tk1,001–Tk3,000, and 16% for over Tk3,000 (Ahmed 1989). However, the estimation only included a transport cost and an opportunity cost for labor, and did not take into account items such as a cost for 'wining and dining bank' officers and a psychological barrier.

24 Professor Hiroyoshi Kanō and others, in examining 'the relevance of the landholding size to the level of material wealth of the rural household,' chose to 'use the level of "stateliness" of the dwelling building of each household as an expedient barometer' of material wealth in their study of rural Central Java (Kanō (ed.) 1994). More specifically, they used two indicators: the house value and the 'house index' based on the floor space and the materials used for the roof, floor, and walls. They calculated the correlation coefficient between the landholding size and these indicators for each village and then examined the relationship between these correlation coefficients and the off-farm employment rates. They found that the correlation coefficient with the house index ranged widely from 0.262 to 0.802, depending on the village, and that the correlation coefficients were lower in villages with larger off-farm employment opportunities. The findings suggest that the landholding size becomes less relevant as a decisive factor for material wealth of a farm household as off-farm employment opportunities increase.

I had also considered the use of the stateliness of house as a barometer but it was not possible because the survey only included the house value, which was an acquisition value, not a replacement value, and the time of building varied considerably. In the case of rural Central Java, the correlation between landholding and wealth generally disappeared when the off-farm employment rate exceeded 60%. (Kanō and others calculated the off-farm employment rate for all people employed, whereas it was calculated on the number of household heads employed in this chapter. However, a recalculation on a household head basis produced the same result.) According to Table 5.6 and Table 2.3, the off-farm employment rate was 44% in Daskin Chamuria village and 20% in Aira village. If the benchmark from rural Java is applied to these villages, it is possible to say that they were at the stage where landholding was still a significant factor in determining material wealth.

25 Its English name is wild sugarcane and its botanical name is *Saccharum spontaneuml.*

26 The details are as follows. (Member numbers in brackets are numbers of Daskin Chamuria villagers among members.)

COOPERATIVE	MONTH/ YEAR FOUNDED	MEMBERS	YEAR BORROWED	TOTAL AMOUNT (*TAKA*)	RECIPIENTS	SHARE (*TAKA*)	SAVINGS (*TAKA*)
BSS	10/1980	45 (40)	1985/86	10,000	14	500	1,278
BSS	06/1981	46 (41)	1985/86	10,000	5	630	1,078
MSS	02/1987	40 (32)	1991/92	14,000	10	4,200	11,396
KSS	07/1987	25 (25)	–	–	–	600	12,238

27 The general loan ranged from Tk1,500 to a maximum of Tk10,000 for unspecified uses (productive activities only); 2% of the principal was repaid weekly and the interest at 16% per annum was paid during the final two weeks of the loan period. Full repayment would ensure an increased loan amount in the following year. The housing loan ranged from Tk10,000–Tk18,000 for residential construction and it was a long-term loan of ten to eighteen years, depending on the loan amount, at an annual interest rate of 5% with weekly repayments. The hand-tubewell loan (or the toilet loan) was a two-year loan of about Tk2,500 (Tk500) for the purchase and installation of a hand-pump for drinking water (or a toilet) and was charged at a lower rate than the general loan rate, with weekly repayment. The seasonal loan of up to Tk3,000 was extended in the sowing season for agricultural purposes such as the purchase of fertilizers, with weekly repayment of 1% to 2% of the principal and a lump sum payment of the remaining principal and the interest after harvesting (a maximum period of six months). This type of loan was usually available twice a year to cater for *aman* rice cropping and *boro* rice cropping. See Fuglesang and Chandler (1993: 103–18) for details.

28 A KSS was organized in Aira village a long time ago but it effectively ceased to operate without receiving a loan and became a *paper* cooperative.

29 In Aira village, eighteen (50%) of the total thirty-six members of the Grameen Bank were surveyed. The average borrowing per person is based on this sample survey.

30 The numbers of handlooms owned by the ten factory owners were as follows. There was one owner with sixteen looms, one owner with nine looms, three owners with eight looms, one owner with six looms, one owner with five looms, two owners with four looms, and one owner with three looms.

31 The criteria for the target household for assistance activities of Shapla Neer are as follows (Shapla Neer 1995: 6).

(1) A low-income household that relies on income from agricultural labor and other low-wage labor (rickshaw pulling, maid, and so on).

(2) If the household owns farmland, the landholding must be less than one acre.

(3) Members of the household who may join the Shapla Neer *samity* must be between the ages of eighteen and forty-five.

(4) Members of the household who may join the Shapla Neer *samity* have not had a high education.

(5) Members of the household who may join the Shapla Neer *samity* must not be absent for a long period for reasons such as work away from home.

(6) No members of the household and its lineal relatives have a high income, a high education, or a high position in the village.

32 Moazzem (2003) empirically demonstrated the fact that the funds borrowed from the lower class at 'usurious' rates were spent on high-profit investment by the upper class.

33 See Egaitsu (1988), Izumida and Yurugi (1990), and others regarding the debate on rural finance in developing countries.

34 Some may say that a low interest rate deposit at financial institutions will mean a loss to the lower class, which turns over surplus funds at high interest rates in the informal financial market. And there is some doubt whether Bangladesh's financial institutions are capable of managing the mobilized funds in a manner that is optimal for the national economy. I must therefore agree with the argument that the mobilization of savings of the rural poor by the modern sectors would not necessarily produce a good result in the short term. However, I do not anticipate strong counterarguments to the notion that the mobilization of domestic savings and the development of an efficient financial market are essential for the development of Bangladesh's economy in the long term. Stable employment opportunities that are also favorable to the rural lower class should expand through such development in the long term.

Chapter 5 Addendum

1 Hossain, M. (1988) is a notable example.
2 The word *purdah* originally means curtain or screen in Persian and it is used to mean rules or customs to segregate women in South Asia.
3 See Goetz and Gupta (1996) for the fact that much of the funds borrowed by female GB members are actually used by men.
4 It should be noted, however, that family labor cost is valued at the market wage rates (different rates for men and women) in the process of estimating the costs to be deducted from the gross income in the calculation of the rate of return in Table 5A.2. The rate of return is highly sensitive to the valuation of family labor cost. The survey found that the unemployment rate prior to joining GB was 2.5% among men and 65.3% among women. It is highly likely that the valuation of family labor cost was much lower than the market wage rate, especially in the case of women. By simply setting the shadow price of female labor at 80% of the market wage rate, the average rate of return for female members changes from negative 87% to 27% (Hossain, M. 1985b: 89). It is therefore likely that women's traditional jobs become profitable when *exploitation* of family labor is taken into account.
5 Momen (1983) also presented the empirical finding of low profitability based on an analysis of fifty projects.
6 This is the result of a calculation where the family labor cost was valued at the market wage rate (for daily labor) in agriculture. The rate of return for *bhograhani* will be higher if the valuation of the family labor cost is lower.
7 We must not overlook the fact that the dropout rate exceeded 30% at some branches (Karim and Osada 1998).
8 One detailed study of GB members based on the length of membership reports that they can escape from poverty in five years and 'graduate' (no longer require a loan) in seven to eight years (Khandler et al. 1995).
9 See Sanyal (1991) regarding how skeptical the Bangladeshi government and donors were about the profitability and sustainability of IG projects in 1985 prior to GB's rapid expansion.

Chapter 6

1 According to the Food Balance Sheet 1992–94 Average by the Food and Agriculture Organization, Bangladesh's per capita food supply includes rice (175.3 kilograms), wheat (19.9 kilograms), potato (9.8 kilograms), sweet

potato (3.5 kilograms), pulses (4.4 kilograms), and vegetables (8.6 kilograms, except tomato and onion). Potato is the third most important food after rice and wheat (FAO 1996). According to the BBS, potato consumption per person per day increased from 39.5 grams in 1988/89 to 43.7 grams in 1991/92 and 49.5 grams in 1995/96 (BBS 1995, 1998).

2 Although the graph shows a further price rise in December, shipment from the main producing region is over by then. The price in December is for fresh potatoes, not cold-stored potatoes, coming from another production region in northern Bangladesh (Dinajpur, Rangpur, Bogra, Rajshahi, Mymensingh, and so on). These northern areas take advantage of different climatic conditions to produce potatoes for the between-cop season but the production quantity is not large. Historically, however, the northern region is the traditional potato-growing region. Dhaka (especially Munshiganj district) and Comilla increased their potato production rapidly from the mid-1960s (especially after the 1980s) to claim the position of the main potato-growing region today.

3 A small number of households in these two hamlets were omitted from the census survey for reasons such as the absence of the household head. In order to include as many potato traders as possible in the survey, one household from the west *para* and five households from three neighboring villages were also surveyed. The total of 106 survey households consisted of seventy-one in the east *para*, twenty-nine in the middle *para*, one in the west *para*, and five in other villages.

4 There were quite a few landless households engaged in farming due to a high level of farmland transfer through *bondak* and tenancy. In addition to year-round tenancy, single-season tenancy was also fairly common.

5 The situation concerning overseas employment in the Middle East changed greatly after the Gulf War. While wages in host countries were high before the war, risks were also high, with frequent problems in relation to emigration agents (operating in Dhaka and other cities). After the war, it became easier and safer to find work in the Middle East through relatives and acquaintances already working in the area but wage rates dropped considerably. The fall in wage rates in the Middle East was the biggest reason for members of medium and large farm households in Ashora village heading to Singapore and Malaysia where wages were higher (Moazzem 2003, 2004).

6 According to one estimate, BADC-certified seeds satisfied only 5% to 7% of the total demand for seeds (Modern Industries Ltd and Agricultural Marketing Department 1998).

7 Strictly speaking, potatoes may be sold literally immediately after

harvesting or after drying for a couple of weeks. Drying for two weeks or so makes potato skin thicker and more suitable for cold storage.

8 The high price of potatoes at the start of 2000/01 was reportedly brought about by the following two factors that had originated in 1999/2000. One was a low supply of off-season potatoes due to a poor harvest in northern Bangladesh; the other was a failure of the vegetable crops that were potato substitutes for consumers at the same time.

9 In 2000/01, production of HYV potatoes was strong in northern Bangladesh and they reached the market with a one- to two-month time lag, keeping the potato price low after June.

10 Under a system called the C. C. loan (cash in credit loan), cold storages were able to draw funds within their credit limits and make repayment any time within one year.

11 The example of BRAC, a major NGO, which used a useful life of fifty years in calculating the depreciation cost of its cold storage, was followed.

12 One cold storage not included in the survey even paid the cost of transporting potatoes to the warehouse.

13 The net margin rate of 2% to 3% is a sufficiently low margin in a general sense and often seen as evidence of a competitive market (Hayami and Kawagoe 1993, for example). However, there is no economic basis for judging market competitiveness by the net margin rate alone. To use it in an economic argument, it must be multiplied by the capital turnover rate to estimate the rate of return on capital.

14 Figure 6.1 shows that the potato price recovered slightly in October and November after a further fall in September but, in any case, 2000/01 was a difficult year for those economic entities that cold-stored their potatoes (this point was confirmed by a supplementary survey).

15 The price was the wholesale price in the urban areas and therefore included the urban wholesaler's margin, as well. Assuming that both the March and November prices included the wholesaler's margin, which stayed at the same level throughout the season, however, the seasonal wholesale price difference derived here would be applicable only to the rural local traders.

16 The following regression equation is found between the net margin rate (y) and the year (t):

$$\underset{(2.77)}{y = 10.33} - \underset{(-1.40)}{0.83t}$$

The figures in brackets are t-statistic values. The p-value for the parameter of the variable t, –0.83, is 0.1727, which indicates that the probability of the parameter being not significantly different from zero is 17%. Therefore, although it is not sufficiently significant in statistical terms, the net margin rate has been showing a downward trend.

17 The possible reasons for the downward trending of the net margin rate include the following. First, the supply of cold-stored potatoes increased as the number of cold warehouses increased. Second, the production and market supply of HYV potatoes from northern Bangladesh increased, especially after the completion of the Jamuna Bridge (1997). Third, the production of vegetables that were substitutes for potato at the consumer level increased in recent years. It is likely that these three factors depressed the potato price in the second half of the season and reduced seasonal price variations, thus reducing the gross margin rate.

18 The rent for tenancy in the village was Tk13,300 per acre (paid in advance) at the time of the survey. The relationship here can be expressed as 100,000 = 13,300 (1 + r), where r is the effective interest rate of *bondak*. The r value in this case is 0.153.

19 Short-term informal finance included borrowings from the *samity* (informal savings association). There were two *samity* groups (Ashora *Samity* and Jubaka *Samity*) in the east and middle *para*. Ashora *Samity*, formed in April 2002, collected a weekly saving of Tk10 from each of its seventy-seven members and, once the total amount of funds reached a certain level, issued loans at an interest rate of 16% per annum. In some cases, it used its funds to acquire farmland through *bondak* and leased it to tenant farmers to receive rent income.

20 Dreze, Lanjouw, and Sharma (1998) reported that a majority of interest-free loans in their survey village in the state of Uttar Pradesh, India, were borrowed from the wife's family and relatives residing in other villages, and argued that this phenomenon had a special social meaning in the context of the custom of village exogamy and the patrilineal norms. The survey in this chapter found that loans of a similar nature had a considerable share of interest-free loans in this Bangladeshi village, as well.

Chapter 7

1 There is no definitive definition of infrastructure. Infrastructure is a collective term for what was called social overhead capital by early development economists such as Rosenstein-Rodan, Nurkse, and Hirschman, and which possessed certain technological attributes (for example, economies of scale) and economic attributes (for example, spillovers from the user to the nonuser) together (World Bank 1994).

2 It was a JICA research cooperation project called the Joint Study on Rural Development Experiment (January 1992–December 1995). Its main aim was

to identify and propose a rural development model that was more suitable for the Bangladeshi society, based on observations and analysis of responses from villages, villagers, and administrative bodies to action programs conducted in five experimental villages.

3 Studies focusing on the *upazila* and the *union* include Ahmad and Satō (1985), Satō (1986), and Mondal and Asaduzzaman (1993). Arn (1989) approached the issue of infrastructure development from the viewpoint of the relationship between the *union* and its residents, but he stopped short of analyzing the inner workings of the village community.

4 The Planning Commission's guidelines on expenditures of *upazila* development subsidies are set out as follows: 30% to 40% for agriculture/irrigation/industry, 25% to 30% for physical infrastructure such as roads, 17.5% to 27.5% for social and economic infrastructure such as schools, 5% to 10% for sport and cultural activities, and 2.5% to 7.5% for other (Satō 1986: 14). However, the interview survey in Sherpur *thana* (1993) found a higher proportion of infrastructure spending, with 15% to 30% for agriculture/irrigation, 25% to 60% for roads, 10% to 15% for public health engineering/drinking water, and 10% to 15% for education. In fact, however, the whole amount was used for road and school renovation projects, as discussed below.

5 Following the abolishment of the *upazila parishad*, the Commission for Reviewing the Local Government Structure was set up and its report was released in July 1992, but there has been no concrete action for local government reform on the part of the government since then (Westergaard and Alam 1995).

6 GCCR was one of the key LGED programs and entailed a plan to improve feeder roads 'B' in Table 7.2 connecting about 1,600 market locations nationwide. RDP was an integrated regional development program with two key projects: a microcredit project through cooperative societies and an infrastructure development project, which divided the country into several divisions and was supported by donors. RD7 was under way in the study area.

7 In Bangladesh, which is located on the vast Bengal Delta, roads are constructed on top of two- to three-meter high embankments and block floodwater flows in the wet season. For this reason, roads have to be cut in places to create passages for water and bridges have to be built over these gaps. For smaller streams, culverts (drainage pipes) are buried to provide passageways for floodwater.

8 CARE delegated project selection and implementation to the *thana* and only carried out project feasibility studies and implementation and monitoring by itself.

9 A day's wage was seven kilograms of wheat (which was about Tk42 in monetary terms, since the price of wheat as of 1991 was about Tk6 per kilogram).

10 The main role of the *matabbor*, the informal leader of the village, was conflict mediation, as discussed below. Desirable qualifications of the *matabbor* included 'generally being "well informed", "eloquent" and "a good mediator",' and they were usually people with 'wealth, land and education' but there were many exceptions (Andō et al. 1995: 43).

11 Educated youths who were destined for future *matabbor* positions and worked as assistants to the *matabbor*. In a village with a youth club, they tended to be in the leadership group.

12 See Yajima (1994) regarding the fragile state of the *union* as an administrative body. Also see Ahmed (1988) about the actual state of Mirzapur *union*.

13 At the time of the survey, an institutional reform proposal to centralize infrastructure programs under LGED control was under consideration following a joint taskforce report (Ministry of Planning 1989).

14 To be exact, the *union* was entitled to collect two local taxes from residents: the property tax based on the house value and the *chowkidari* tax for the operation of the village security. In reality, they were combined into one tax, with the farmland size and the occupation being taken into account, as well.

15 Allowances for the *union* chairman and members (shared equally by the central government and the *union*) had been unpaid since July 1993 according to the financial audit report of Mirzapur *union* dated 30 November 1993, and it was recommended that they should be paid as soon as *union* taxes were collected. There were similar problems with salary payment for the *union* secretary and security forces.

16 The right to collect tax from the distinctly large Sherpur Market was awarded to Sherpur Municipality (*pourashava*). The Mirzapur Market was the largest of the nine periodical markets on which Sherpur *thana* had the right of taxation and accounted for 75% to 85% of the total tax collection.

17 See Hossain, Rahman, and Akash (1985) for details.

18 It was successfully enticed to Aira village with the help of a high-ranking officer in Dhaka who was a former resident of the village. As discussed below, this was the person who contributed a large portion of the mosque construction cost and played a major part in the development of the village as a patron.

19 The number of landless households included some households, though not many, who became independent while their parents were still alive and would inherit some farmland in the future.

20 It is likely that the obscurity of *bari* groupings in Aira village was due to their peculiar conditions, such as upland locations and fewer flood disasters. In house construction, the foundations are elevated by fifteen centimeters or so, but the grounds were not raised in this area. On the other hand, the whole ground in the regular flooding area was highly elevated, creating distinct geographical boundaries for a *bari* (or a cluster of several *bari*), which looked like a floating island during a flood.

21 While there was no Hindu *gusti* in Kajirai *para*, fourteen of thirty-one households in Shatain *para* formed a total of five *gusti*.

22 Some *gusti* contained households with no blood relationship. Such pseudo kinship relationships were often found in cases in which families who had settled around the same time continued mutual aid relationships, or in which the son of a migrant family had boarded with another household under a student houseboy system called *jagir*, or in which households used to belong to *gusti* of the same name prior to settlement. As far as I understand, N1 and M7 included one household each of such pseudo kinship relationships.

23 When the *gusti* had to sell land, it was customary to give the first right of purchase at the same selling price in the following order: (1) people with inheritance rights according to the order of inheritance under the law, (2) a person with a vital interest in the land, (3) a neighbor, and (4) a non-related person (Hara 1979: 10). This custom had the effect of preventing loss of land to outsiders of the *gusti*.

24 Settlers came from various places but a high proportion of them came from faraway districts such as Shirajganj and Kurigram after losing their lands by erosion of the Jamuna riverbanks. A typical migration pattern was as follows. They initially started as seasonal agricultural laborers, gradually settled in the village after several visits, ended up marrying local women, set up homes on granted home sites, and became independent households. Their relatives might follow, seeking their help.

25 See Chowdhury, A. (1982: 46).

26 According to Jansen, 'a *samaj* is an institution which is vested primarily with the task of ensuring that people conform to a morally proper mode of conduct' and 'for religious purposes *samaj* is also an important unit' (Jansen 1987: 86–9). Chowdhury, A. (1982: 45) considered that 'social control of individuals who are involved in activities against the social and religious tradition of the society' was the most important function of the *samaj*. The word *samaj* stems from the notion of 'co-existence' (Chowdhury, A. 1982: 45) and it is used to mean 'society' or 'the world' in general in everyday conversation.

27 See Satō (1985) for the judicial function of the *union*.

28 Andō (1995: 42–3).

29 Discord among the *matabbor* is not the only cause of disintegration of the *samaj*. In Aira village, one split was caused by factional infighting between the *matabbor*, but the other split occurred when the *samaj* grew larger than the optimal size and financial burden on each member household for ceremonial occasions became too heavy.

30 Mosques in rural Bangladesh generally do not manage their own finances but some cases of independent finances have been reported. For example, a mosque in one village in Kishoreganj district had its own farmland and fund, with the imam and the *moazzam* (prayer) having the right to cultivate part of the farmland, and revenue from the village's *hat* was put in the fund as well (Ali 1988: 109–11).

31 Expenditure figures for the *jarimana* fund were Tk15 in 1980, Tk2,306 in 1985, Tk220 in 1986, Tk46 in 1987, Tk3,345 in 1989, Tk600 in 1991, and Tk2,500 in 1993, with the balance at the end of the period being Tk930. Based on these, the size of the *jarimana* fund was just over Tk700 per year on average, which was only one-thirteenth of the mosque fund.

32 According to slightly old information from India, disputes that could not be resolved by the caste *panchayat* were referred to the headman of the village and 'settlement of such disputes could involve penalties. It was common for the owner of domestic animals which damaged fields to pay a penalty. It was not uncommon that part of the penalty was vested in the village and it was the headman's responsibility to keep and use the money. It is likely that most of such monies were used for religious rites in the village' (Fukutake 1964: 245–6).

33 In some neighboring villages, the same decision-making process was used for appropriation of funds but penalties were expended as soon as they were received. In one case, the *jarimana* fund was used to cover the cost to marry off a daughter of a poor household in the *samaj*.

34 Records show that division of ownership occurred for three ponds in 1935, for one in 1937, for one in 1942, and for six in 1967. The largest pond at the center of the village has been under joint ownership by twenty-one people since 1967.

35 Soil for embankment is often obtained from the land adjoining the road in Bangladesh. However, it would be difficult to elicit agreement from the landowner if it is a crop field because he would not like to lose fertile top-soil. The government does not provide compensation for land requisition in the case of non-arterial roads below a certain level, let alone compensation for supply of soil. This is one of the major obstacles to rural infrastructure

development as land became increasingly scarce in Bangladesh due to population growth and equalized inheritance.

36 There were some attempts for infrastructure improvements using gratuitous labor contributions from rural residents in the past but only a few studies conducted an analysis of burdens and benefits by economic classes. One of them is a study by Hossain, M. et al. (1982) about the *Swanirvar* Movement, which reports that the wealthy farmer class was the only beneficiary, while the poor farmer class bore a greater share of burdens—the opposite of the outcome of this experiment.

37 For example, it was the wealthy farmer class (the village leadership) that made various arrangements for the establishment of a *hat* in the village, but among those who started businesses at the *hat* were many villagers from the poor class. The *hat* opened a total of forty-one times from 6 June to 31 October 1994. A breakdown of fourteen villagers who participated as traders for more than a quarter of the times shows that three were from the landless class, three had a landholding of less than 0.5 acres, one had 0.5–1.0 acre, three had 1.0–2.5 acres, two had 2.5–5.0 acres, and two had 5.0 acres or more.

38 TR was used for repairs or improvements of religious facilities in a broad sense in Mirzapur *union* in the following cases: three out of fourteen cases in 1987 (one mosque work and two mosque road works), four out of twelve cases in 1988 (one mosque work, one mosque site work, one *madrasa* site work, and one *pujamondir* (a Hindu rite) site work), four out of thirteen cases in 1989 (two *madrasa* works, one Eid festival site work, and one *pujamondir* site work), twenty-two out of forty-six cases in 1990 (six mosque works and four mosque site works, one mosque road work, two Eid festival site works, three *madrasa* site works, and six *pujamondir* site works), one out of seven cases in 1991 (mosque work), one out of seven cases in 1992 (*madrasa* work), and one out of fourteen cases in 1993 (*madrasa* work). They amounted to about one-third of TR works on average.

39 See Andō (1995) and Hossain, Z. (1993) regarding V-AID, which was promoted in Bangladesh (Pakistan at the time) at around the same time as the promotion of the community development program in India, which was based on the same idea.

References

Japanese publications

Note: Books in this part of the bibliography were published in Tokyo unless specified otherwise.

Ajia Keizai Kenkyūjo (Institute of Developing Economies) (1991), *Kunibetsu keizai kyōryoku kenkyū hōkokusho Myanmā Banguradeshu* (Study report on economic cooperation by country: Myanmar and Bangladesh).

Andō, Kazuo (1995), 'Banguradeshu no nōson kaihatsu no genjō to kadai (The current state and issues of rural development in Bangladesh)' in Akinobu Kawai (ed.), *Hattentojōkoku sangyō kaihatsu-ron* (Industrial development in developing countries): Hōsō Daigaku Kyōiku Shinkōkai, pp. 172–86.

Andō, Kazuo and Haruo Uchida (1994), 'Dentō inasaku nōgyō no tokushoku (The characteristics of traditional rice farming)' in Masayuki Usuda, Hiroshi Satō, and Shinkichi Taniguchi (eds.), *Motto shiritai Banguradeshu* (Know more about Bangladesh): Kōbundō, pp. 20–36.

Andō, Kazuo, H. Uchida, H. Rahman, and A. Hossain (1995), 'Matabōru tachi to zaichi no nōson kaihatsu—Banguradeshu, Dokkinchamuria-mura ni okeru akushon risāchi no kiroku—(Matabbors and village development: An account of action research in Dakhsin Chamuria village, Bangladesh),' *Bangladesh Rural Development Studies*, 33 (1), June 1995, pp. 39–65.

Aoki, Masahiko (2001), *Hikaku seido bunseki ni mukete* (Towards a comparative institutional analysis): NTT Shuppan.

Egaitsu, Fumio (1988), 'Ajia shokoku no nōson kinyū shijō—Futatsu no mikata—(Rural financial markets in Asian countries: Two viewpoints),' *Kinyū kōzō kenkyū* (Studies on financial structure), No. 10, pp. 33–9.

Esho, Hideki (1987), *Gendai Indo keizai kenkyū* (A study of the contemporary Indian economy): Hosei University Press.

Food and Agriculture Organization (FAO) of the United Nations (ed.) (1996), *FAO 2010-nen no sekai nōgyō* (World agriculture: Towards 2010).

Fujita, Kōichi (1986), 'Banguradeshu ni okeru nōgyō hatten—Nōgyō kōzō to gijutsu henka no kanren wo chūshin ni (Agricultural development in Bangladesh: Centering on the relationship between agrarian structure and technological change),' *Ajia keizai* (Bi-monthly journal of the Institute of Developing Economies), 27 (12), December 1986, pp. 2–23.

Fujita, Kōichi (1990a), 'Banguradeshu ni okeru tochinashi hinkonsō heno kinyū—Guramin Ginkō wo megutte—(Finance for the landless poor class in Bangladesh: On the Grameen Bank),' *Ajia keizai* (Bi-monthly journal of the Institute of Developing Economies), 31 (6 & 7), July 1990, pp. 143–60.

Fujita, Kōichi (1990b), 'Kangai kaihatsu no seidoteki shomondai (Institutional problems of irrigation development)' in Hiroshi Satō (ed.), *Banguradeshu: Teikaihatsu no seiji kozō* (Bangladesh: The political structure of underdevelopment): Ajia Keizai Kenkyūjo, pp. 209–57.

Fujita, Kōichi (1993a), *Banguradeshu nōgyō hatten-ron josetsu* (An introductory study of agricultural development in Bangladesh), Kenkyū sōsho (Research series) No. 114: Nōgyō Sōgō Kenkyūjo.

Fujita, Kōichi (1993b), 'Nōson no atarashii henka (New changes in the rural area)' in Masayuki Usuda, Hiroshi Satō, and Shinkichi Taniguchi (eds.), *Motto shiritai Banguradeshu* (Know more about Bangladesh): Kōbundō, pp. 215–27.

Fujita, Kōichi (1995), 'Nōgyō kaihatsu (Agricultural development)' in Kokusai Kaihatsu Sentā, *Keizai kyōryoku keikaku sakutei no tameno kiso chōsa—Kunibetsu keizai kyōryoku keikaku (Indo)*—(Baseline survey for planning of economic cooperation programs: Economic cooperation program by country (India)),' pp. 155–207.

Fujita, Kōichi (1996), '1980-nendai no Bengaru nōgyō hatten ni kansuru nōto (Notes on Bengal's agricultural development in the 1980s)' in Hiromi Yamamoto (ed.), *Ajia nōgyō no jizokuteki hatten—Shijōka to seido soshiki no shinka*—(Sustainable agricultural development in Asia: Marketization and institutional and organizational evolution): Ajia Keizai Kenkyūjo, pp. 166–91.

Fujita, Kōichi (1999), 'Banguradeshu—"Ōgon no Bengaru" fukkō he mietekita ichijō no hikari—(Bangladesh: A ray of hope for the revival of "Golden Bengal")' in Yōnosuke Hara (ed.), *Ajia keizai-ron* (Asian economies): NTT Shuppan, pp. 422–99.

Fujita, Kōichi (2000a), 'Indo no shokuryō jukyū to nōgyō wo doumiruka (A perspective on India's demand and supply for food and agriculture),' *Shokuryō seisaku kenkyū* (Food policy research journal), No. 104, pp. 45–93.

Fujita, Kōichi (2000b), 'Banguradeshu no keizai jiyūka to shijō no henyō (Economic liberalization and market transformation in Bangladesh)' in Hideki Esho (ed.), *Minami Ajia keizai no kōzō to hendō—Dai 1-pan (keizai han) chūkan seika hōkokusho* (The structure of the South Asian economy and change: Interim report by Team 1 (economics team), pp. 161–77.

Fukutake, Tadashi (1964), *Indo nōson no shakai kōzō* (The socio-economic structure of the Indian village): Ajia Keizai Kenkyūjo.

Hara, Tadahiko (1979), 'Banguradeshu nōgyō kaihatsu no shakaiteki kiban

(Social infrastructure for agricultural development in Bangladesh),' *Shakai jinruigaku nenpō* (Bulletin of social anthropology), Vol. 5, pp. 1–36.

Hayami, Yūjirō (1995), *Kaihatsu keizaigaku—Shokokumin no tomi to hinkon—* (Development economics: From the poverty to the wealth of nations): Sōbunsha.

Ishikawa, Shigeru (1966), 'Nōgyō kaihatsu ni okeru sendōteki tōnyū no bunseki (jō) (An analysis of leading input in agricultural development, Part I),' *Ajia kenkyū* (Journal of Asian Studies), 12 (4), pp. 1–32.

Ishii, Shigeru (1990), *Kaihatsu keizaigaku no kihon mondai* (Fundamental problems of developmental economics): Iwanami Shoten.

Ishii, Yoneo (1975), 'Rekishi to inasaku (History and rice farming)' in Yoneo Ishii (ed.), *Taikoku—Hitotsu no inasaku shakai*—(Thailand: A rice farming society): Sōbunsha, pp. 16–45.

Izumida, Yōichi and Takao Yurugi (1990), 'Ajia no nōson kinyū to nōson kinyū shijō riron no kentō (Rural financial market theory: Its relevance to rural finance in Asia),' *Ajia keizai* (Bi-monthly journal of the Institute of Developing Economies), 31 (6 & 7), June/July, pp. 6–21.

Kaida, Yoshihiro (ed.) (2003), *Banguradeshu nōson kaihatsu jissen kenkyū—Atarashii kyōryoku kankei wo motomete*—(An action research for the Bangladesh rural development: Searching for new cooperative relationships): Commons.

Kanō, Hiroyoshi (ed.) (1994), *Chūbu Jawa nōson no keizai henyō—Chomarugun no 85-nen*—(Economic change in rural Central Java: Eighty-five years of Chomal district): The University of Tokyo Press.

Kikuchi, Masao (1992), 'Ajia kaihatsu tojōkoku kangai shisutemu tekisei kanri no tameno senryaku (Strategies for optimum control of the irrigation systems in developing Asian countries),' *Nōgyō sōgō kenkyū* (Quarterly journal of agricultural economics), 46 (1), January 1992, pp. 1–7.

Kikuchi, Masao (2002), 'Nettai monsūn, Ajia inasaku nōgyō no 50-nen—Suriranka to Firipin no keiken wo chūshin toshite—(Phases of irrigation development in Asian tropics: A case study of the Philippines and Sri Lanka),' presented as a background paper for the symposium commemorating the 50th year of Theoretical Economics and Agriculture in 2002, downloadable from *http://muses.muses.tottori-u.ac.jp/dept/E/wfarm/matsudat/TEA.html.*

Kurosaki, Takashi (1996), 'Pākisutān—Yōsuiro, chikasui kangai no keizai bunseki—(Pakistan: An economic analysis of channel and groundwater irrigation)' in K. Horii, H. Shinoda, and T. Tada (eds.), *Ajia no kangai seido—Mizu riyō no kōritsusei ni mukete*—(Irrigation systems in Asia: Towards efficiency in water use): Shinhyōron, pp. 357–88.

Kurosaki, Takashi (1997), 'Kangaisui shijō no kōritsusei—Fujita Kōichi ronbun no bunseki moderu heno daitaiteki teian—(Irrigation water market efficiency: An alternative to the analytical model proposed in Kōichi Fujita's study),' *Nōgyō keizai kenkyū* (Journal of rural economics), 68 (4), March, pp. 207–14.

Ōno, Akihiko (1991), 'Indo no taigai jiyūka to sono makuroteki kisei yōin—Rikādo no seichō no wana no shiten kara (India's trade liberalization and its macro control factors: From the viewpoint of the Ricardian Trap)' in Sueo Sekiguchi and Akihiko Ōno (eds), *Ajia keizai kenkyū: Bōeki, tōshi, gijutsu seisaku no tenkai: Chūōkeizaisha* (A study of the Asian economy: Policies in trade, investment and technology transfer), pp. 223–66.

Osada, Mitsue (1980), 'Kokumin keizai to nōgyō (The national economy and agriculture)' in Kokusai Nōringyō Kyōryoku Kyōkai, *Banguradeshu of nōgyō—Genjō to kaihatsu no kadai*—(Agriculture in Bangladesh: The current status and development issues), pp. 1–40.

Saitō, Chihiro (1992), 'Banguradeshu ni okeru kyōdō kumiai no rekishiteki hensen to ruikei—Hinkonsō no sanka no shiten kara—(Historical changes and patterns of cooperative societies in Bangladesh: From the viewpoint of participation by the poor),' *Ryukoku Daigaku keizai keiei ronshū* (Ryukoku journal of economic and business studies), 31 (1), June 1992, pp. 36–49.

Satō, Hiroshi (1986), 'Banguradeshu chihō gyōsei kaikaku no seiji-keizaiteki haikei (Politico-economic background of local government reform in Bangladesh),' *Ajia keizai* (Bi-monthly journal of the Institute of Developing Economies), 27 (3), March, pp. 2–27.

Shapla Neer (1995), *Banguradeshu Ishorugonji-gun ni okeru nōson seikatsu jittai chōsa—Shapla Neer no purojekuto hyōka no kokoromi*—(A field study of rural life in Ishwarganj *thana*, Bangladesh: For an evaluation of the Shapla Neer project), a baseline survey of rural Bangladesh and working paper for debriefing on 7 July, 1995.

Suda, Toshihiko (1991), *Banguradesh nōson ni okeru keizai kaisō no henka to kaisōsei—Jinkō zōka tono kanren wo chūshin ni*—(Changing economic strata and stratification in rural Bangladesh: Centering on its relationships with population growth): Kokusai Kyōryoku Jigyōdan Kaigai Seinen Kyōryokutai Jimusho.

Suda, Toshihiko (1999), *Indo ni okeru kokumotsu zōsan no tenbō—Kangai fukyū no yakuwari to kankyō heno eikyō no bunseki wo chūshin ni*—(Outlook for growth in grain production in India: Centering on an analysis of the role of irrigation development and its environmental impact): Nourinchukin Research Institute.

Suda, Toshihiko (2002), 'Indo no shinyō nōkyō kaikaku—Nishi Bengaru-shū yūryō nōkyō no jirei karano kōsatsu (Reforms of agricultural credit cooperatives in India—A case study of a primary agricultural credit society in West Bengal),' *Ajia keizai* (Bi-monthly journal of the Institute of Developing Economies), 43 (12), December, pp. 2–29.

Takada, Mineo (1998), 'Banguradeshu—Minshuka wa teichakusurunoka (Bangladesh: Is democratization here to stay?)' in H. Satō and I. Iwasaki (eds), *Ajia seiji dokuhon* (Readings in Asian politics): Tōyōkeizaishimpōsha, pp. 255–68.

Watanabe, Toshio (1982), 'Zettaiteki hinkon no kōzō (The structure of absolute poverty),' *Ajia keizai* (Bi-monthly journal of the Institute of Developing Economies), 23 (5), May, pp. 2–25.

Watanabe, Toshio (1985), *Seichō no Ajia teitai no Ajia* (Growth and stagnation in Asia): Toyōkeizaishimpōsha.

Yajima, Kichiji (1994), 'Banguradeshu ichi nōson ni okeru yunion hyōgikai no kinō to shigotoburi (Function and performance of *union parishad* in one Bangladesh village),' *Ajia keizai* (Bi-monthly journal of the Institute of Developing Economies), 35 (12), December, pp. 37–54.

Non-Japanese publications

Abudullah, A., M. Hassanullah, and Q. Shahabuddin (1995), 'Bangladesh agriculture in the nineties: Some selected issues,' in *Experiences with Economic Growth: A Review of Bangladesh's Development 1995*, Centre for Policy Dialogue, Dhaka: University Press Limited, pp. 127–79.

Abdullah, A. and Q. Shahabuddin (1997), 'Recent developments in Bangladesh agriculture: Crop sector,' in *Growth or Stagnation?: A Review of Bangladesh's Development 1996*, Centre for Policy Dialogue, University Press Limited, pp. 221–52.

Ahmad, Q.K. and H. Sato (1985), *Aid and Development Administration in Bangladesh*, Tokyo: Institute of Developing Economies, JRP Series No.51.

Ahmed, A.J.M. (1988), *Local Government in Action (A Case Study of Mirzapur Union Parishad)*, Bogra: Rural Development Academy.

Ahmed, A. and M. Hossain (1990), *Developmental Impact of Rural Infrastructure in Bangladesh*, Washington, D.C.: International Food Policy Research Institute, Research Report No. 83.

Ahmed, Z.U. (1989), 'Effective costs of rural loans in Bangladesh,' *World Development*, 17 (3), pp. 357–63.

Alamgir, M. and L.J.J.B. Berlage (1974), *Bangladesh: National Income and*

Expenditure 1949/50–1969/70, Dhaka: Bangladesh Institute of Development Studies.

Ali, M.H. (1988), 'Administration, leadership and institutions,' in H. Uchida (ed.), *Jawar Village in Kishoreganj*, Dhaka: Japan International Cooperation Agency.

Ando, K., A. Rashid and Y. Kaida (1991), 'Rice cultivation and land tenancy system under shallow tubewell irrigation in Barind Tract, Bangladesh: A case study in Tetulia village, Bogra district', *Journal of the Japanese Association for South Asian Studies*, pp. 62–81.

Arn, A. (1989), *The Making of Institutions and Leaders at Rice Root Level: Inside the Rural Works Programme in Bangladesh*, Copenhagen: Center for Development Research.

Bangladesh Agricultural University (Department of Irrigation and Water Management) (1985), *Evaluating the Role of Institutions in Irrigation Programme.*

Bangladesh Agricultural University (Department of Irrigation and Water Management) (1986), *Water Market in Bangladesh: Inefficient and Inequitable?*

Bangladesh Bank (2003), *Annual Report 2002–2003*, Dhaka.

Bardhan, P.K. (1984), *Land, Labor, and Rural Poverty: Essays in Development Economics*, Oxford University Press.

Bardhan, P.K. and A. Rudra (1978), 'Interlinkage of land, labor and credit relations: An analysis of village survey data in East India,' *Economic and Political Weekly*, Annual Number (February), pp. 367– 84.

BBS (Bangladesh Bureau of Statistics) (1988), *Small Areas Atlas of Bangladesh: Mallahs of Bogra District.*

BBS (1989), *Rural Credit Survey in Bangladesh 1987*, Dhaka.

BBS (1993a), *Twenty Years of National Accounting of Bangladesh 1972/73 to 1991/92*, Dhaka.

BBS (1993b), *Bangladesh Population Census 1991, Vol. 2 Union Statistics*, Dhaka.

BBS (1995), *Report on the Household Expenditure Survey 1991–92*, Dhaka.

BBS (1996), *Report on the Labour Force Survey in Bangladesh 1995–96*, Dhaka.

BBS (1997), *Statistical Pocket Book of Bangladesh 96*, Dhaka.

BBS (1998), *Household Expenditure Survey 1995–96*, Dhaka.

Bell, C. (1990), 'Interaction between institutional and informal credit agencies in rural India,' *The World Bank Economic Review*, 4 (3), September 1990, pp. 297–327.

Bertocci, P.J. (1969), 'Patterns of social organization in rural East Bengal,' in L. Alexander (ed.), *Bengal East and West*, Michigan: Asian Studies Centre, Michigan State University.

Bertocci, P.J. (1970), *Elusive Villages: Social Structure and Community Organization in Rural East Pakistan*, unpublished Ph.D. dissertation thesis, Michigan State University.

Bhaduri, A. (1973), 'A study of agricultural backwardness under semi-feudalism,' *Economic Journal*, 88, March 1973, pp. 120–37.

Boyce, J.K. (1987), *Agrarian Impasse in Bengal: Institutional Constraints to Technological Change*, Oxford University Press.

BRDB (Bangladesh Rural Development Board) (1992), *Annual Report 1991–92*, Dhaka.

Bureau of Applied Economics and Statistics (Government of West Bengal) (1995), *Statistical Abstract West Bengal 1994–95*, Calcutta.

Bureau of Applied Economics and Statistics (Government of West Bengal) (1998), *District Statistical Handbook Nadia 1996 and 1997 (combined)*, Calcutta.

Centre for Policy Dialogue (1997), *Growth or Stagnation?: A Review of Bangladesh's Development 1996*, University Press Limited.

Chatterjee, N. (1995), *Irrigated Agriculture: A Case Study of West Bengal*, Jaipur and New Delhi: Rawat Publications.

Chowdhury, A. (1982), *Agrarian Social Relations and Development in Bangladesh*, New Delhi: Oxford and IBH Publishing Co.

Chowdhury, B.K. (1971), *Economics of Tubewell Irrigation in West Bengal*, Santiniketan: Agro-Economic Research Center.

Crow, B. (1989), 'Plain tales from the rice trade: Indications of vertical integration in foodgrain markets in Bangladesh,' *The Journal of Peasant Studies*, 16 (2), pp. 198– 229.

Crow, B. and K.A.S. Murshid (1994), 'Economic returns to social power: Merchants' finance and interlinkage in the grain markets of Bangladesh,' *World Development* 22 (7), pp. 1011–30.

Dasgupta, A. (1998), *Growth with Equity: The New Technology and Agrarian Change in Bengal*, New Delhi: Manohar.

Dreze, J., P. Lanjouw, and N. Sharma (1998), 'Credit,' in P. Lanjouw and N. Stern (eds), *Economic Development in Palanpur over five Decades*, Oxford University Press, pp. 506–83.

Dubash, N.K. (2002), *Tubewell Capitalism: Groundwater Development and Agrarian Change in Gujarat*, Oxford University Press.

FAO (Food and Agriculture Organization of the United Nations) (ed.) (1996), *Food Balance Sheet 1992–94 Average*, Rome: FAOSTAT.

Food Planning and Monitoring Unit (Ministry of Food, Bangladesh) (1994), *Food Situation Report for the Month of February.*

Food Planning and Monitoring Unit (Ministry of Food, Bangladesh) (2000), *Bangladesh Food Situation Report,* Vol. 45, July.

Fuglesang, A. and D. Chandler (1993), *Participation as Process—Progress as Growth: What we Can Learn from Grameen Bank Bangladesh*, Dhaka: Grameen Trust.

Fujita, K. (1988), Book Review, 'Agrarian Impasse in Bengal: Institutional Constraints to Technological Change' by J. K. Boyce, *The Developing Economies*, 26 (3), pp. 292–5.

Gazdar and Sengupta (1999), 'Agricultural growth and recent trends in well-being in rural West Bengal,' in Rogaly et al. (eds), *Sonar Bangla?: Agricultural Growth and Agrarian Change in West Bengal and Bangladesh*, Dhaka University Press Limited, pp. 60–91.

Geertz, C. (1963), *Agricultural Involution: The Process of Ecological Change in Indonesia*, Berkeley: University of California Press.

Glaser, M. (1989), *Water to the Swamp: Irrigation and Patterns of Accumulation and Agrarian Change in Bangladesh*, unpublished Ph.D. thesis, University of Bath.

Goetz, A.M. and R.S. Gupta (1996), 'Who takes the credit? Gender, power, and control over loan use in rural credit programs in Bangladesh,' *World Development*, 24 (1), pp. 45–63.

Government of Bengal (1915), *Bengal District Administration Committee 1913–1914 Report*, Calcutta: Bengal Secretariat Press (reprinted by National Institute of Public Administration, 1966).

Government of West Bengal (1995), *Economic Review 1994–95.*

Government of West Bengal (2000), *Economic Review 1999–2000 Statistical Appendix.*

Grameen Bank (1995), *Annual Report 1994*, Dhaka.

Hayami, Y. and T. Kawagoe (1993), *The Agrarian Origins of Commerce and Industry—A Study of Peasant Marketing in Indonesia*, New York: St. Martin's Press.

Hossain, A. (1996), *Macroeconomic Issues and Policies: The Case of Bangladesh*, New Delhi: Sage Publications.

Hossain, M. et al. (1982), '"Participatory" development efforts in rural Bangladesh: A case study of experiences in three areas,' in A. Bhaduri et al. (eds), *Studies in Rural Participation*, New Delhi: Oxford and IBH Publishing Co.

Hossain, M. (1985a), 'Institutional credit for rural development: An overview of the Bangladesh case,' *Bangladesh Journal of Agricultural Economics*, 8 (1) , June, pp. 2–16.

Hossain, M. (1985b), *Credit for the Poor: The Grameen Bank in Bangladesh*, Dhaka: Bangladesh Institute of Development Studies.

Hossain, M. (1988) *Credit for Alleviation of Rural Poverty: The Grameen Bank in Bangladesh*, Research Report No. 65, Washington D.C.: International Food Policy Research Institute.

Hossain, M., A. Rahman, and M.M. Akash (1985), *Agricultural Taxation in Bangladesh: Potential and Policies*, BIDS Research Report No. 42.

Hossain, Z. (1993), 'Village agricultural and industrial development (V-AID) Programme,' in A. Quddus (ed.), *Rural Development in Bangladesh: Strategies and Experiences*, Comilla: Bangladesh Academy for Rural Development.

Ito, S. (1999), *The Grameen Bank: Rhetoric and Reality*, unpublished Ph.D. dissertation thesis, University of Sussex.

Janakarajan, S. (1992), 'Interlinked transactions and the market for water in the agrarian economy of a Tamilnadu village,' in S. Subramanian (ed.), *Themes in Development Economics: Essays in Honour of Malcolm Adiseshiah*, Oxford University Press, pp. 151–201.

Jansen, E.G. (1987), *Rural Bangladesh: Competition for Scarce Resources*, Dhaka: University Press Limited.

Kahnert, F. and G. Levine (eds) (1993), *Groundwater Irrigation and the Rural Poor: Options for Development in the Gangetic Basin*, Washington D.C.: World Bank.

Karim, M.R. and M. Osada (1998), 'Dropping out: An empirical factor in the success of microcredit-based poverty alleviation programs,' *The Developing Economies*, 36 (3), September, pp. 257–88.

Khan, A.R. (1984), 'Real wages of agricultural workers in Bangladesh,' in A.R. Khan and E. Lee (eds), *Poverty in Rural Asia*, ILO (ARTEP).

Khan, S.I., S.A. Islam and M.I. Haque (1996), *Political Culture, Political Parties and the Democratic Transition in Bangladesh*, Dhaka: Academic Publishers.

Khandler, S.R. et al. (1995), *Targeted Credit Programs and Rural Poverty in Bangladesh*, World Bank and Bangladesh Institute of Development Studies.

Khurshed, A. (1988), *A Study on On-lending in Informal Financial Market in Bangladesh*, Dhaka: BIDS IFM Working Paper No. 13.

Kurosaki, T. (1998), *Risk and Household Behavior in Pakistan's Agriculture*, Institute of Development Studies.

Lanjouw, P. and N. Stern (eds) (1998), *Economic Development in Palanpur over Five Decades*, Oxford: Oxford University Press.

Lewis, D.J. (1991), *Technologies and Transactions: A Study of the Interaction between New Technology and Agrarian Structure in Bangladesh*, Dhaka: Centre for Social Studies.

Local Government Engineering Bureau (1992), *Report on Maintenance of Rural Infrastructure: Compiled for Consideration in the Workshop held in Dhaka during 17–18 February 1992*, Dhaka.

Maloney, C. (1984), *Behavior and Poverty in Bangladesh*, Dhaka: University Press Limited.

Maloney, C. and A.B.S. Ahmed (1988), *Rural Savings and Credit in Bangladesh*, Dhaka: University Press Limited.

Meinzen-Dick, R. (1996), *Groundwater Markets in Pakistan: Participation and Productivity*, Research Report No. 105, Washington D.C.: International Food Policy Research Institute.

Mellor, J.W. (1966), *The Economics of Agricultural Development*, Ithaca, N.Y.: Cornell University Press.

Ministry of Agriculture (Bangladesh) and Asian Development Bank (1992), *Study on Privatization of Minor Irrigation in Bangladesh: Final Report.*

Ministry of Agriculture (Bangladesh) (1998), *National Minor Irrigation Census 1996/97.*

Ministry of Finance (Bangladesh) (1999), *Bangladesh Economic Review 1999* (in Bengali).

Ministry of Planning (Bangladesh) (1989), *Joint Government of Bangladesh/ Donor Task Force on Strengthening the Institutions for Food Assisted Development: Final Report* (*Volume I*).

Moazzem, K.G. (2003), 'Structure of income, savings and investment in rural Bangladesh: Case study of increasing money flow in a village of Comilla district,' *Journal of Rural Economics*, Special Issue, pp. 437–42.

Moazzem, K.G. (2004), *Transformation of Economic Relations of the Poor and Rich in Rural Bangladesh: Focusing on Credit Market in a Potato-Growing Village*, doctoral thesis submitted to Graduate School of Asian and African Studies, Kyoto University.

Modern Industries Ltd and Agricultural Marketing Department (1998), *Production of Potato by Sustainable Technology* (in Bengali).

Momen, M.A. (1983), *A Study of the Impact of Income Generating Activities Among Poor Rural Women in Bangladesh*, Report No. RAS/79/21, Dhaka: The Institute of Social Welfare and Research.

Mondal, A.H. and M. Asaduzzaman (1993), *Maintenance of Rural Infrastructure at the Local Level: Experiences with the Defunct Upazila System in*

Bangladesh, Research Report No. 134, Dhaka: Bangladesh Institute of Development Studies.

Murshid, K.A.S. and A. Rahman (1990), *Rural Informal Financial Markets in Bangladesh: An Overview*, Dhaka: BIDS Research Paper No.126.

Pant, N. (1992), *New Trend in Indian Irrigation: Commercialization of Ground Water*, New Delhi: Ashish Publishing House.

Quasem, M.A. (1990), 'Financial return of irrigation equipment to owners and users: The case of shallow tubewells in Bangladesh,' in O.D.K. Norbye, (ed.), *Bangladesh Faces the Future*, Dhaka: University Press Limited.

Rahman, A. (1986), *Peasants and Classes: A Study in Differentiation in Bangladesh*, University Press Limited.

Rao, C.H. Hanumanta (1994), 'Policy issues relating to irrigation and rural credit in India,' in G.S. Bhalla (ed.), *Economic Liberalization and Indian Agriculture*, New Delhi: Institute for Studies in Industrial Development.

Rashid, A. (1994), *Development of Rice-Based Traditional Cropping Systems and Performance of Boro Rice Cultivation under STW Irrigation in Two Different Agro-Ecological Setting of North-West Bangladesh*, Master's thesis, Kyoto University.

Rogaly, B., B. Harris-White, and S. Bose (eds) (1999), *Sonar Bangla?: Agricultural Growth and Agrarian Change in West Bengal and Bangladesh*, Dhaka: University Press Limited.

Rutherford, S. (1998), 'The savings of the poor: Improving financial services in Bangladesh,' *Journal of International Development*, 10 (1), pp. 1–15.

Sanyal, B. (1991), 'Antagonistic cooperation: A case study of nongovernmental organizations, government and donors' relationship in income-generating projects in Bangladesh,' *World Development*, 19 (10), pp. 1367–79.

Sato, H. (1985), 'Case studies on local administration at *upazila* and union levels,' in Q.K. Ahmad and H. Sato (eds), *Aid and Development Administration in Bangladesh*, Tokyo: Institute of Developing Economies, JRP Series No. 51.

Schendel, William van and A.H. Faraizi (1984), *Rural Laborers in Bengal, 1880 to 1980*, Rotterdam: CASP, Faculty of Social Sciences, Erasmus University Rotterdam.

Sen, B. (1997), 'Poverty and policy,' in Center for Policy Dialogue, pp. 115–60.

Shah, T. (1987), *Externality and Equity Implications of Private Exploitation of Groundwater Resources*, Anand, Gujarat: Institute of Rural Management.

Shah, T. (1993), *Groundwater Markets and Irrigation Development: Political Economy and Practical Policy*, Oxford University Press.

Sobhan, R. (1991), *Debt Default to the Development Finance Institutions:*

The Crisis of State Sponsored Entrepreneurship in Bangladesh, Dhaka: University Press Limited.

Takaya, Y. (1987), *Agricultural Development in Tropical Delta: A Study of the Chao Phraya Delta*, Honolula: University of Hawaii Press.

Todd, H. (1996), *Women at the Center: Grameen Bank Borrowers Ten Years On*, Dhaka: University Press Limited.

Webster, N. (1999), 'Institutions, actors and strategies in West Bengal's rural development—A study on irrigation,' in Rogaly el al. (eds), pp. 329–56.

Westergaard, K. and M.M. Alam (1995), 'Local government in Bangladesh: Past experiences and yet another try,' *World Development*, 23 (4), pp. 679– 90.

World Bank (1990), *Bangladesh: Managing the Adjustment Process—An Appraisal*, Dhaka.

World Bank (1993), *Bangladesh: Implementing Structural Reform*, Dhaka.

World Bank (1994), *World Development Report 1994: Infrastructure for Development*, Washington D.C.

World Bank (1996), *Bangladesh: Public Expenditure Review*, Dhaka.

Subject Index

absolute poverty/poor (ratio) 17, 32–34; see also 'poverty'
action research 228, 264
  action research project 155
administrative village; see *union*
advance for (future) saving 11, 162, 235
agency theory 240
agrarian impasse 33, 231
agrarian land reform 89, 92, 258
agrarian structure 33, 40, 91, 257
agricultural credit 113; see also 'credit'
agricultural involution 39
agricultural laborer 32, 44, 145, 124
seasonal agricultural laborer 275
agronomic adaptation 39
aman rice 7, 20, 44, 91, 169, 242; see also '*boro* rice'
  broadcast *aman* 242
  transplanted *aman* 242
Annual Development Program (ADP) 197
aratdar (commission agent) 175
arsenic contamination 108
Association for Social Advancement (ASA) 155
arterial road 208
atomism 252
aus rice 91, 169, 242
Awami League 16, 31

Bangladesh Academy for Rural Development (BARD) 15, 113
Bangladesh Agricultural Development Corporation (BADC) 16, 63, 169
  BADC-certified seed 171, 270
Bangladesh Bureau of Statistics (BBS) 65, 115
Bangladesh *Krishi* (Agricultural) Bank (BKB) 113, 137, 140
Bangladesh Nationalist Party (BNP) 22, 31
Bangladesh Rice Research Institute 263
Bangladesh Rural Advancement Committee (BRAC) 70, 155
Bangladesh Rural Development Board (BRDB) 15–16, 113, 155, 195
Bangladesh *Samabaya* (cooperative) Bank 261
bari 210, 275
baseline survey 122, 143, 264
beneficiary committee 95
bepari (local trader) 174
bhograhani 10, 127, 130, 145
bias of technological change 57
bichar (a forum for conflict resolution) 203, 211, 228
bidhi (popular tobacco) 27, 122
bigha 47, 71, 96
Bittohin Samabaya Samity (BSS) 113, 137
BKB, see 'Bangladesh *Krishi* (Agricultural) Bank'
BNP, see 'Bangladesh Nationalist Party

bondak 10–11, 59, 130, 150, 171, 188
boro rice 7, 20, 40, 44, 63, 91, 169, 210, 242
BR-line 119
breaking even 105
broadcast *aman* 242; see also '*aman*'
BSS, see '*Bittobin Samabaya Samity*'

canal irrigation 4, 40; see also 'irrigation'
capacity utilization (rate) 62, 66, 78, 101, 176, 183, 191, 247
capital
  capital constraint 19, 40
  capital depreciation 49
  capital turnover (rate) 183, 271
  fixed capital 49
  foreign capital 18
  human capital 152, 235, 237
  interest on working capital 53
  land-saving and capital-using bias 57
  land-saving and capital-using technology 85
  rate of return on capital 271
  working capital 11, 55, 97, 118, 143, 147, 180, 187
capitalized value 265
caste *panchayat* 276
center (Grameen Bank's customer management unit comprised up to eight five-member group) 139, 155
Centre for Policy Dialogue 8
channel excavation 77
chaunia (seasonal tenancy) 47, 61, 68, 73, 147, 249
chouka (portable stove) 134
chowkidar 202, 229
chowkidari panchayat 229
chowkidari tax 274
chronic indebtedness 117
chula (cooking stove) 134, 210
civilian government 22
classical monopoly model 61
cluster system 96
cold storage 11, 166, 171, 176, 180
collateral 11, 131
Comilla Model 15, 113, 195; see also location name index 'Comilla district'
Comilla-type cooperative 114, 136, 261
command area 84, 108
commercial bank 57
Communist Party (government) 89, 108, 258
community
  community principle 233
  community property 222
  mobilization of local community resources 206
  village community 5, 11, 196, 241
consumer loan 117; see also 'loan'
contractual enforceability 251
cooking shed 134
Cooperatives for American Relief Everywhere (CARE) 198
coordination (mechanism) 88, 108, 241
corruption 239
cottage industry 13
credit
  credit entity 118, 127, 150
  agricultural credit 113; see also credit
crop loan 113; see also 'loan'
crop sharing 47, 69
  crop-sharing arrangement 61
  crop-sharing system 145

cost
current input cost 178
depreciation cost 49, 77, 85, 98
fixed cost 77
marginal cost
marginal irrigation cost 61; see also 'irrigation'
transaction cost 133
valuation of family labor cost 269
culvert 201, 224, 273
current expenditure 77
current input cost 178; see also 'cost'

dadan (advance payment) 11, 167, 192
dafadar 202
debt recovery rate 153; see also 'recovery rate'
deep tubewell, see DTW
deferred payment 167
deficit entity 118, 127, 150
deflator 33
dekhi project 136
democratization movement 22
dependency capitalism 167, 191
depreciation cost 49, 77, 85, 98; see also 'cost'
deregulation 63
differentiation of peasantry 116
diluvial plateau 43
discount rate 130
disintegration of the peasantry 59
disintegration of the *samaj* 276
domestic savings rate 17
double rice cropping 142
double transplanting technology 253
dropout 164
DTW (deep tubewell) 4, 40, 63, 169
rehabilitated DTW 106
state-operated DTW 90, 105–106, 241

East Pakistan Industrial Development Corporation 15
economic disparity 14
economies of scale 40
effective interest rate 53, 176, 181, 260; see also 'interest rate'
Eid festival 211, 214, 252, 277
electricity charge 107
electrification of rural area 96, 236
electrification of tubewells 232
elusive village 228–229
embankment construction 200
embankment work 224
employment opportunity
non-farm employment opportunity 60
off-farm employment opportunity 122, 152, 168
Engel coefficient 34
engineering adaptation 40
export processing 19
export processing zone 27
export-oriented (manufacturing) industry 18, 32
externality 42, 102, 196

factor share 5, 57, 265
factors of production 52
faria (petty trader) 176
farmer class 44
farmland fragmentation 41, 134, 263
federation of cooperatives 113
fiscal deficit 17
fieldwork 6
final demand effect 3, 59, 142
finance
informal finance 124, 136, 143, 150, 188, 262
inter-class flow of informal finance 118

microfinance 234; see also 'finance'
rural informal finance 115, 235; see also 'finance'
financial contribution 225
financial recovery 114
fixed capital 49; see also 'capital'
fixed cost 77; see also 'cost'
flat-rate (charge system) 106–107
'flood of 1988' 41
floodplain 119
Food and Agriculture Organization 255
food expenditure 17
Food for Works Program (FFW) 198
food self-sufficiency 4, 32
foreign capital 18; see also 'capital'
foreign currency reserves 27
forward and backward linkage (effects) 3, 59
fragmentation of farmland 40
free-rider problem 82, 196
fuel efficiency 78
functional distribution 52
functionally landless 70; see also 'landless/landlessness'

garment 27
general loan 139; see also 'loan'
gram (natural village) 155, 197, 228
gram panchayat (administrative villages) 95
Grameen Bank 2, 8, 11, 70, 113, 115, 136–137, 140, 153, 155, 188, 249, 261
gratuitous labor 224; see also '*seccha sram*'
Green Revolution 2, 20, 22, 35, 40, 57, 89, 97, 255
gross domestic product (GDP) 13
gross domestic saving rate 23
groundwater
groundwater depletion 10
groundwater irrigation 20; see also 'irrigation'
groundwater level 108
over-extraction of groundwater 107
transformation of the groundwater market 85
groundwater market 5, 9–10, 39, 42, 53, 59, 61, 67, 89, 105, 145, 150, 244, 251, 259; see also 'market'
groundwater market transformation 62, 68, 85
Growth Center Connecting Roads (GCCR) 198
Gulf War 64, 71, 171, 270
gusti (patrilineal kinship group) 208–210, 275

hand-tubewell loan 139; see also 'loan'
hand-weaving industry 142, 156
handloom 122
handloom weaver 145
hartar (general strike) 32, 237, 252
hartar politics 252
hat (periodical market) 135, 169, 208, 277; see also 'market'
haulat (interest-free loan) 188, 272; see also 'loan'
high-yielding variety, see 'HYV'
Hindu 70, 207
historical price 102
house index 266
human capital 152, 235, 237; see also 'capital'
HYV (high-yielding varieties) 40, 57, 119, 246
HYV potato 271

IG project, see 'income generating (IG) project'
imam 202, 211
import liberalization policy 41
income distribution 59
income generating project (IG project) 155, 269
India's Integrated Rural Development Program 164
Industrial Bank 19
Industry Financial Corporation 19
inefficient from a social point of view 84
inequality of access 153
inflation 17–18, 27, 68, 107, 114, 266
informal education program 220
informal finance 124, 136, 143, 150, 188, 262; see also 'finance'
  informal financial market 10, 234; see also 'market'
informal sector 243
infrastructure 2
  infrastructure development 6, 206, 226, 236
institutionalized forum 84
Integrated Rural Development Program 15
inter-class flow of informal finance 118; see also 'finance'
inter-class 'reverse flow' 171
inter-industrial linkage effect 142
interest on working capital 53; see also 'capital'
interest rate 57
  effective interest rate 53, 176, 181, 260
  long-term interest rate 60, 134
  real interest rate 17
  short-term interest rate 53, 133–134
interest-free loan; see '*haulat*'
International Monetary Fund 1, 23
investment behavior 62
irrational 82, 84
irrigation
  irrigation capacity 40
  irrigation channel excavation 49
  irrigation coverage 67, 87, 99
  irrigation efficiency 61
  irrigation privatization policy 20
  irrigation technology 4
  canal irrigation 4, 40
  marginal irrigation cost 61
  groundwater irrigation 20
  net irrigation surplus (NIS) 42–43
  privatization of irrigation facility 19
  subsidy for minor irrigation 106
  supplementary irrigation 57
  surface water irrigation 20
  tubewell irrigation 9

jagir 275
Japan Bank for International Cooperation 8, 70
Japan International Cooperation Agency (JICA) 6, 196
  JICA project 214, 222
jarimana (penalties) 219
  jarimana fund 219, 276
Joint Study on Rural Development Experiment in Bangladesh 6
jute product 23
jute-processing mill 13

Kangsabati project 92
Keynesian economics 195
khaikhalashi (long-term tenancy system with advance rent payment) 53, 59, 73, 130, 147, 217
khana (household) 210
khas land 224

khuchra bikreta (retailer) 174
knit 27
Krishi Samabaya Samity (KSS) 113, 137

labor contribution 203
labor-intensive manufacturing sector 236
laissez-faire policy 196
land 43
land collateral 113
land consolidation 40–41
land fragmentation 244
land lease market 104; see also 'market'
land mortgages 160
land rent 52, 85, 88
land-saving and capital; see also 'capital'
-using bias 57
-using technology 85
landless/landlessness 70, 121, 246, 257
landless laborer 116, 150
functionally landless 70
rural landless poor 155; see also 'poverty/poor'
leading input 4
liberalization 63
liberalization of agricultural input market 232; see also 'market'
linkages between the agricultural and non-agricultural sectors 3
literacy rate 207
loan
loan repayment 156, 163
consumer loan 117
crop loan 113
general loan 139
hand-tubewell loan 139
haulat (interest-free loan) 188
low-interest rate loan program 41; see also 'interest rate'
nonperforming bank loan 63
seasonal loan 139
local administration 11, 196, 239
Local Government Engineering Department (LGED) 198
local government 5; see also '*panchayat*'
local government reform 92, 197
local public goods 195, 220, 226, 230
long-term interest rate 60, 134; see also 'interest rate'
long-term tenancy (system) 53, 130; see also '*khaikhalashi*'
low lift pump (LLP) 15, 17, 20, 63
low-interest rate loan program 41; see also 'interest rate' and 'loan'
low-level equilibrium 32

macroeconomic indicator 23
macroeconomic stabilization 32
madrasa 70, 81, 198, 202, 217, 277
Malthusian world 32
marginal cost 107; see also 'cost'
marginal irrigation cost 61; see also 'cost' and 'irrigation'
market
market mechanism 102, 196
market principle 233
groundwater market 5, 9–10, 39, 42, 53, 59, 61–62, 67–68, 85, 89, 105, 145, 150, 244, 251, 259
hat (periodical market) 135, 169, 208, 277
informal financial market 10, 234
land lease market 104
liberalization of agricultural input market 232

monopoly in the groundwater market 60
non-market adjustment 102
potato-marketing system (potato-marketing business) 11, 166, 191
rural financial market 153
rural informal financial market 5, 9
secondhand market 77
matabbor 202, 207, 217, 222, 240, 274
maund 47, 95, 119, 166, 251
mauza (revenue villages) 93, 114
Mayurakshi project 92
micro-topographic undulation 39
microcredit program 2, 10, 70, 195, 234
microfinance 234; see also 'finance'
middlemen 175
Ministry of Relief and Rehabilitation 198
Minor Irrigation Department 94
misappropriation of wheat 203
moazzam (prayer) 276
mobilization of local community resources 206; see also 'community'
mobilization of resources 227
mode of water charge payment 47
mode of water transaction 47
Mohila Samabaya Samity (MSS) 113, 137
moneylender 57, 131, 262
monopolistic 49
monopoly 43, 53
monopoly in the groundwater market 60; see also 'market'
mortgage 121
mortgaged land 73
mosque 198, 217, 276
MSS, see '*Mohila Samabaya Samity*'
munshi (religious leader) 211
Muslim 70, 207
musolmani (male circumcision) 211

National Minor Irrigation Census (NMIC) 65
nationalized commercial bank 114
neoliberalism 42
net irrigation surplus (NIS) 42–43; see also 'irrigation'
net margin rate 187, 190, 271
'New Industrial Policy of 1982' 18
NGO 2, 17, 113, 115
non-farm employment opportunity 60; see also, 'employment opportunity'
non-food expenditure 17
non-land asset 134
non-market adjustment 102, 237; see also 'market'
non-performing bank loan 63; see also 'loan'

off-farm employment opportunity 122, 152, 168; see also, 'employment opportunity'
official judicial system 214
on-lending 161
Operation Barga 89
operator's surplus 85, 104
opportunistic behavior 108
optimum level of investment 196
over-extraction of groundwater 107; see also 'groundwater'
overinvestment 10, 62, 87, 237
Overseas Economic Cooperation Fund 8, 70
overseas work 171

paikar (wholesaler) 174, 184
Pakistan Industrial Development Corporation 14
Palli Karma-Sahayak Foundation (PKSF) 155
panchayat (local government) 89
para (hamlet) 7, 70, 169, 207
parboiling 156
Partition 13
patrilineal norm 272
patron-client relationship 127
permanent income 11
personal distribution 52
pessimism 33
polarization 60
population explosion 33
population pressure 32
postal savings system 152
potato-marketing system (potato-marketing business) 11, 166, 191; see also 'market'
potton (seasonal leasing) 73
poverty/poor
  poverty alleviation 161
    poverty alleviation mechanism of Grameen Bank 163
  poverty reduction mechanism 235
  'Poverty Reduction Strategy Papers' 1
  absolute poverty/poor (ratio) 17, 32–34
  rural landless poor 155; see also 'landless/landlessness'
  rural poverty/poor 155, 161
power efficiency 81
power subsidy 106–107
pragmatic individualism 252–253
primary cooperatives 113
private investment 23
private sector investment 18
privatization of fertilizer distribution 19
privatization of irrigation facility 19; see also 'irrigation'
privatization policy 169
professional moneylender 115
profit 43, 53
profit-maximizing behavior 250
Project Implementation Committee (PIC) 201
project implementation officer 201
Project Selection Committee 200
pseudo kinship relationship 275
public sector investment 23
public servant 239
public tender 206
pujamondir (a Hindu rite) 277
purdah 157

quasi-rent 83

rabi 70, 82, 86, 119
rate of return on capital 271; see also 'capital'
rational behavior 87
real interest rate 17; see also 'interest rate'
real wage (rate) 17–18, 32, 34, 88
real water charge 68, 86, 104
reclamation 39
recovery rate 153
  debt recovery rate 153
redistribution of farmland 89
regular income source 162
rehabilitated DTW 106; see also 'DTW'
rehabilitation work 106
religious facility 277

repayment rate 19
Reserve Bank of India 262
resource allocation efficiency 61
resource mobilization (system) 11, 220, 222
reverse flow of credit 11
reverse flow of fund 152
'Revised Industrial Policy of 1986' 18
Ricardian Trap 31
rice business 156
rice double-cropping 210
rice self-sufficiency 30
rickshaw pulling 70
river lift pump 107
rural development 195
Rural Development Program (RDP) 198
rural electrification, see 'electrification of rural area'
rural financial market 153; see also 'market'
rural informal finance 115, 235; see also 'finance'
rural informal financial market 5, 9; see also 'market'
rural infrastructure (development) 5, 195
small-scale rural infrastructure (development) 196, 239
rural landless poor 155; see also 'landless/landlessness' and 'poverty'
Rural Maintenance Program (RMP) 198
rural non-farm sector 58
rural non-farming activity 34
rural poverty/poor 155, 161; see also 'poverty/poor'
rural power structure 261
rural road improvement 236
rural social structure 226
Rural Works Program 15, 195

sabotage 239
salish 211
sam 211
samaj 211, 240, 252
samaj sebak 202
samity (informal savings association) 261, 272; see also '*shonchoi samity*'
sample bias 260
sardar 228
seasonal agricultural laborer 275; see also 'agricultural laborer'
seasonal fluctuation 39
seasonal leasing 85; see also '*potton*'
seasonal loan 139; see also 'loan'
seasonal migrant laborer 169
seasonal price variation 166
seasonal tenancy (*chaunia*) 61, 87, 96; see also '*chaunia*'
seccha sram (gratuitous labor) 217
secondhand market 77; see also 'market'
sedimentation 222
seed potato 171
seer 32, 251
self-employment 155
self-sufficiency in rice 20
semi-feudal 89
semi-feudal mode of production 40, 244
semi-feudal model 117
shallow tubewell, see STW
Shapla Neer 150, 249, 268
share-cropping arrangement 53
sharecropper 246, 257

shonchoi samity (informal savings association) 264
short-term interest rate 53, 133–134; see also 'interest rate'
single-cropping 44
small business operator 143, 147
small-scale rural infrastructure (development) 196, 239; see also 'rural infrastructure'
social inefficiency 87
social investment 164
social sanction 230
social stratification 44
socialist economic policy 16
sompotton (year-round leasing) 73, 86
Sonari Bank 114, 137
Special Agricultural Credit Program 113, 232
speculation 192
spot transaction 251
state enterprise 16–17
state-operated DTW 90, 105–106, 241; see also 'DTW'
state-run corporation 16
stockist 177
structural adjustment 1, 23
STW (shallow tubewell) 4, 10, 41, 44, 62–63, 169, 174, 241
  STW diffusion 30
  STW owner 30
  submergible STW 90, 94
sub-lending 114, 156, 160–161, 163, 236, 262
subdistrict 197; see also '*thana*' and '*upazila*'
submergible STW 90, 94; see also 'STW'
subsidy for minor irrigation 106; see also 'irrigation'
supplementary irrigation 57; see also 'irrigation'
surface water irrigation 20; see also 'irrigation'
Swanirvar Movement 277

technological bias 60
technological change 92
technological innovation 33
tenancy 121
terms and conditions 118
terms of trade 69
Test Relief (TR) 198
thana (subdistrict) 196
  thana engineer 198
  thana nirbahi officer 201
  Thana Irrigation Program 15–16
  Thana Training and Development Center 15
Thengamala Mohila Shabuj Sangha (TMSS) 70
thrift and saving 162, 235
trade deficit 17
traditional export item 23
transaction cost 133; see also 'cost'
transformation of the groundwater market 85; see also 'market' and 'groundwater'
transplanted *aman* 242; see also '*aman*'
trickle-down effect 142, 168, 192, 196, 233
tropical delta 39
tubewell 4, 20, 43; see also 'DTW' and 'STW'
  tubewell installations 79
  tubewell investment 40, 61
  tubewell irrigation 9; see also 'irrigation'
  tubewell owner 43

tubewell spacing regulation 64
two-tiered agricultural cooperative 15

uncooperative behavior 88
underground pipe system 95
union (administrative village) 139, 196–197
union chairmen 201
union parishad 202
union tax 205
Union Central Cooperatives 261
Union Multipurpose Cooperatives 261
upazila (subdistrict) 169, 197, see also 'subdistrict'
upazila development subsidy 197, 273
upazila parishad 197, 273
urban entrepreneur 11, 168, 176, 191
usufructuary mortgage 130, 132–133, 143, 246
usufructuary right 124, 130, 160, 188, 250
usury 117

V-AID, see 'Village Agricultural and Industrial Development'
valuation of family labor cost 269; see also 'cost'
vicious cycle 62
Village Agricultural and Industrial Development (V-AID) 228, 277
village community 5, 11, 196, 241; see also 'community'
village development committee 214, 224
village exogamy 272
village society 196, 239

ward 200
water charge 9, 43, 68, 88
water control 39
waterlord 9, 42, 90, 99, 109, 257
wheat import 30
wholesale price index 107
working capital 11, 55, 97, 118, 143, 147, 180, 187; see also 'capital'
World Bank 1, 23, 243
World Food Program 198

Zamindar 222
zila (district) 197

Name Index

Adams, D. W. 153
Ando, K. 253, 265
Aoki, M. 240
Bertocci, P. J. 228
Bhaduri, A. 117
Ershad, H. M. 18, 197
Esho, H. 116
Hayami, Y. 229
Hasina, S. 30
Hirschman, A. O. 272
Kaida, Y. 240, 242
Kano, H. 266
Kurosaki, T. 247
Lewis, D. J. 166
Maloney, C. 253
Moazzem, K. G. 8
Nurkse, R. 272
Rahman, Mujibur 16, 30
Rahman, Ziaur 17–18
Rosenstein-Rodan, P. 272
Schumpeter, J. 234
Suda, T. 9, 258
Yunus, M. 115, 155
Zia, Khaleda, 22, 30, 197–198

Location Index

Ayeyarwaddy Delta 39
Barind Tract 8, 43, 119, 207, 210
Bengal Delta 39, 273
Bogra district 7, 43, 118, 195
British India 13
Chao Phraya Delta 39
Chittagong 19, 169, 191
Comilla district 8, 166, 168
Dhaka 6, 118, 168
East Pakistan 13
Ganges River 256
Gujarat 244
Jamuna Bridge 8, 118, 272
Jamuna River 119
Kalyani town 9, 93
Kerala 238
Kolkata 9, 13, 93, 107
Mekong Delta 39
Middle East 270
Munshiganj district 168
Mymensingh district 150
Nadia district 8, 92
Palanpur 238
Punjab 3, 40, 89, 108
Sherpur city 57, 207
Tangail district 6, 118
West Bengal 8, 42, 89
West Pakistan 13